Hist 959.5 C649c
Clutterbuck, Richard L.
Conflict & violence in Singapore and Malaysia $28.00

DISCARD

MAIN LIBRARY
Memphis and Shelby
County Public Library and
Information Center

For the Residents
of
Memphis and Shelby County

Conflict and Violence
In Singapore and Malaysia
1945-1983

By the same author:

ACROSS THE RIVER (as Richard Jocelyn)
THE LONG LONG WAR
PROTEST AND THE URBAN GUERRILLA
RIOT & REVOLUTION IN SINGAPORE & MALAYA 1945-1963
LIVING WITH TERRORISM
GUERRILLAS AND TERRORISTS
KIDNAP AND RANSOM
BRITAIN IN AGONY
THE MEDIA AND POLITICAL VIOLENCE
INDUSTRIAL CONFLICT AND DEMOCRACY

Conflict and Violence in Singapore and Malaysia 1945-1983

RICHARD CLUTTERBUCK

Westview Press/Boulder, Colorado

All rights reserved. No part of this publication may be reproduced or transmitted in any form or any means, electronic or mechanical, including photocopy, recording, or any information storage and retrieval system, without permission in writing from the publisher.

Published in the United States of America in 1985 by
Westview Press, Inc.
5500 Central Avenue
Boulder, Colorado 80301
Frederick A. Praeger, Publisher

Copyright © 1985 by Richard Clutterbuck

Library of Congress Catalog Card Number: 84-52200

ISBN (Westview) 0-8133-0168-8

Printed by Singapore National Printers (Pte) Ltd

Contents

		page	
Abbreviations			11
Preface			15
1. INTRODUCTION			17
The Aim of this Book			17
Urban and Rural Revolution			18
How a Revolution Ends			19
The Developing Pattern of Urban Revolution			20
Revolutionary Errors Between the World Wars			23
The Reaction Against Leninism			24
The Pattern of Guerrilla Revolution			28
Popular Support			29
Escalation			31
Malaya and Singapore – The Background			32
The Malayan Communist Party and the Japanese Occupation			37
Reoccupation by the British			39

Part I – Urban Revolution – Singapore

2. THE FIRST ATTEMPT AT AN URBAN REVOLUTION – 1945–8 — 45

The Decision to Adopt an Urban Strategy in 1945 — 45
The Difficulties of the MCP as an Open Political Party — 47
The British Military Administration — 49
'Peaceful Agitation' — 51
A Change of Leader — 53
The Government Reacts — 56

3. THE COMMUNIST PARTY STRUCTURE IN SINGAPORE – 1946–50 — 58

The Open and Secret Organizations of the Party — 58
Recruitment and Advancement — 63
The Student Organization — 65
1948 – A Drastic Reorganization — 66
A Tightening of Security in the MCP in Singapore — 66
The Arrest of the Town Committee — 71
The Hertogh Riots — 72
Reorganization of the Police — 73

CONTENTS

4. THE SURVIVAL OF THE STUDENT ORGANIZATION –
   1950–4   *page* 75
   - Resilience   75
   - Security – Strengths and Weaknesses   77
   - The Schools as a Training Ground for Party Workers for the Jungle War   79
   - The Revival of the Urban Campaign in Singapore   81

5. SUBVERSION IN THE CHINESE MIDDLE SCHOOLS 1954–6   84
   - Formation of the SCMSSU   84
   - Party and Open Front Structure in the Schools   86
   - The Secret Organization   91
   - Study and Tuition Cells   93
   - Self-criticism and Intimidation   94
   - The Position of the Teachers   96
   - The Baling Truce Talks and the Razak Report   98

6. SELF-GOVERNMENT   99
   - The 'Middle Road' Group of Trade Unions   99
   - Self-Government   101
   - The People's Action Party   103
   - The Emergency Regulations   106
   - The Hock Lee Bus Strike   108
   - David Marshall Faces the Communists   111
   - The London Talks of April/May 1956   112
   - The PAP Central Executive Committee Election   115
   - A New Plan for Internal Security   116
   - The Government's Ultimatum   117

7. THE RIOTS OF OCTOBER 1956   121
   - Clearing the Schools   121
   - Keeping the Crowds down to Manageable Size   123
   - The Special Branch Swoop   130
   - The Riots Subside   131
   - Summary of Events   132
   - The Performance of the Government Forces   133
   - The Performance of the Revolutionaries   136
   - A Comparison with the Hong Kong Riots of 1967   138

8. THE STRUGGLE FOR POLITICAL CONTROL   142
   - Constitutional Conference in London 1957   142
   - Responsibility for Internal Security   144
   - The PAP Executive Committee Changes Hands   145
   - The Communists Send a Plenipotentiary   148
   - The 1959 Elections   150
   - Lim Chin Siong Released   151

CONTENTS

The Hong Lim By-Election	*page* 152
The Plenipotentiary Identified	153
The Formation of the Barisan Sosialis	154
'The British Plot'	154
The Proposal for Merger	155
The Referendum on Merger	157
Indonesian Confrontation and the Renewed Detention of Lim Chin Siong	158
Independence and the 1963 Elections	160
The End of the Merger, and Lee Kuan Yew's Consolidation	161

Part II – **Rural Guerrilla Revolution – The Emergency in Malaya**

9. THE FIRST YEARS OF THE EMERGENCY	167
Launching the Armed Struggle	167
A State of Emergency	168
Guerrilla Strategy and Tactics 1948	169
Controversy in the MCP	172
Sir Harold Briggs	174
Resettlement	175
Special Branch	178
Rewards	180
Surrendered Enemy Personnel (SEPs)	181
Another New Communist Directive – October 1951	183
Sir Gerald Templer	186
Village Government	189
Psychological Warfare and the Information Services	190
White Areas	194
10. ORGANIZATION FOR SURVIVAL	195
The MCP Reorganization, 1952–3	195
The Parallel Hierarchy	199
MCP Security	202
Target for 1954–6 – A Typical MCP District (Yong Peng)	206
11. THE DEVELOPMENT OF A SUCCESSFUL TECHNIQUE	211
A Difficult Target	211
Food Denial Operations – Early Attempts	212
The Latimer Report	217
Improving the Pattern	218
12. THE FINAL PATTERN	220
Selection of the Target	220
Outline of Phases	221

CONTENTS

Phase I – Acquiring Agents .... page 221
D Day 223
Phase II 225
Phase III 226
A Strategy to Finish the War 226

13. OPERATION COBBLE – 1956–7 – AN EXAMPLE OF A FEDERAL
    PRIORITY OPERATION BASED ON FOOD DENIAL 230
    Operation COBBLE – The Setting 230
    The Selumpur Branch 231
    The Bukit Siput and Tenang Branches 237
    Operation COBBLE Phase I – Intelligence Activity ... 240
    Phase I – Operations in Support of Special Branch ... 241
    Operation COBBLE Phase II 244
    Operation COBBLE – The End of Phase II 249

14. THE CRUMBLE AND THE HARDCORE 251
    A Successful Framework Operation 251
    Hor Lung and the Collapse in Johore 252
    Perak 255
    Kedah – A Different Approach 257
    The Aborigines 258
    The Thai Border 259

Part III – The Aftermath and The Prospects for Malaysia and Singapore

15. THE BALANCE SHEET IN 1963 263
    A Year of Decision 263
    Urban and Rural Revolution 264
    The MCP Organization in Singapore 266
    Achievements and Failures of the MCP in Singapore ... 268
    The Singapore Government's Handling of Violence
      and Coercion 270
    Lee Kuan Yew 271
    The Communists' Balance Sheet in the Village War in Malaya ... 271
    The Government's Response 273
    Leninism or The New Left? 276

16. MALAYSIA AND HER NEIGHBOURS 278
    Confrontation 278
    The End of the Merger 282
    ASEAN 284
    The Resurgence of Guerrilla Warfare in Malaysia 284

CONTENTS

17. THE 1969 RIOTS IN KUALA LUMPUR	289
Race and Politics in Peninsular Malaysia	289
The Alliance	291
The 1969 Elections	292
The Riots of 13 May 1969	297
Parliamentary Government Suspended	301
18. MALAYSIA'S NEW ECONOMIC POLICY AND FUTURE PROSPECTS	303
The Creation of a National Front	303
The New Economic Policy	305
Dr. Mahathir	309
Economic and Political Prospects for Malaysia	312
19. SINGAPORE: THE SOCIAL AND ECONOMIC MIRACLE	319
The Race Riots of 1964	319
The Foundation of PAP Dominance	322
Housing, Health and Population Growth	325
Education	327
Savings and Incomes	330
Singapore's Economic Performance	334
20. THE PRICE OF SUCCESS	337
Is the Price too High?	337
Detention and Dissent	338
The Trade Unions	340
Freedom of Speech and Freedom of the Press	341
The Law in an Orderly Society	343
A Parliamentary Democracy or a One-Party State?	344
Does it Work?	348
Prospects for Singapore	351
Notes	354
Bibliography Parts I and II	382
Part III	395
Index	399

Maps and Diagrams

1. Federation of Malaya, showing States	*page* 34
2. Federation of Malaya, showing Main Rubber, Tin and Rice Growing Areas	36
3. Singapore Communist Party Organization 1947	60
4. MCP Cell Organization in Singapore, 1947–50	61

MAPS AND DIAGRAMS

5. MCP Organization in Singapore, August 1948–50	67
6. MCP Communication System from the Jungle to Singapore, 1948–50	68
7. Security Procedure if MCP Cell Member Compromised	70
8. MCP Student Organization up to 1953	76
9. Parallel Open and Secret Party Organizations in the Chinese Middle Schools, 1954–6	87
10. Singapore, General Map	125
11. Singapore, Main Roads into the City	127
12. Malayan Communist Party Organization, before 1949 and 1949–51	171
13. Resettlement and Regroupment	177
14. Monthly Statistics	185
15. Casualties in the Emergency, 1948–60	188
16. MCP Political and Logistic Organization and Fighting Units 1951–7	196
17. Malayan Communist Party Organization 1952–8	197
18. The Parallel Hierarchy	200
19. MCP Branch Organization	201
20. Branch Organization, Yong Peng MCP District	207
21. Map of Yong Peng	208
22. Federal Priority Operations, 1957–8	228
23. Operation COBBLE, Villages and Police Posts	232
24. Selumpur Area, Chinese Smallholdings	234
25. Selumpur Branch	236
26. Bukit Siput and Tenang Branches	239
27. Charted Strength of CPM Guerrillas in 1982	287
28. General Elections, Peninsular Malaysia, 1964 and 1969	294
29. Election Results in Three States, 1964 and 1969	296
30. Kuala Lumpur Riots, 13 May 1969	299
31. General Elections, Peninsular Malaysia, 1969 and 1974	304
32. Economic Performance: Malaysia and Neighbours	313
33. Voting in Singapore General Elections	324
34. Population Growth in Singapore	325
35. Highest Qualification Achieved, Age 5 and over (Singapore)	329
36. Performance in English Stream Education 1973–81 (Singapore)	331
37. Examples of Incomes, Singapore, 1983	332

Abbreviations

ABIM	Angkatan Belia Islam Malaysia (Islamic Youth Movement)
ABL	Anti-British League
ARO	Assistant Resettlement Officer
ASEAN	Association of South East Asian Nations
ASP	Assistant Superintendent of Police
AWC	Armed Work Cell
AWF	Armed Work Force
BBC	British Broadcasting Corporation
BCM	Branch Committee Member
BCS	Branch Committee Secretary
BERI	Business Environment Risk Information
BMA	British Military Administration
BN	Barisan Nasional (National Front)
BS	Barisan Sosialis (Socialist Front)
CCC	Citizens' Consultative Committee
CCO	Clandestine Communist Organization (Sarawak)
CEP	Captured Enemy Personnel
Com	Person interviewed who was involved with the Communists
CP	Commissioner of Police
CPF	Central Provident Fund
CPM	Communist Party of Malaya (after 1963)
CPO	Chief Police Officer
CSBO	Circle Special Branch Officer
DAP	Democratic Action Party
DCM	District Committee Member
DCS	District Committee Secretary

ABBREVIATIONS

DLP	Dutch Labour Party
DO	District Officer
DSP	Deputy Superintendent of Police
DWEC	District War Executive Committee
ER	Emergency Regulations
ESI	English-Speaking Intelligentsia
FTU	Federation of Trade Unions
GDP	Gross Domestic Product
GLU	General Labour Union
GNP	Gross National Product
GOC	General Officer Commanding
Gov	Person interviewed who was in Government service
HDB	Housing and Development Board
HE	His Excellency (The British High Commissioner)
HQ	Headquarters
HSB	Head, Special Branch
IS	Internal Security
ISA	Internal Security Act
ISC	Internal Security Council
LPM	Labour Party of Malaya
MARA	Majlis Amanak Ra'ayat (successor to Rural and Industrial Development Agency)
MCP	Malayan Communist Party (until 1963)
MDU	Malayan Democratic Union
ME	Masses Executive
MHB	Multipurpose Holdings Berhad
MIC	Malaysian Indian Congress
MIO	Military Intelligence Officer
MPABA	Malayan People's Anti-British Army
MPAJA	Malayan People's Anti-Japanese Army
MPAJU	Malayan People's Anti-Japanese Union
MRLA	Malayan Races' Liberation Army

ABBREVIATIONS

NDYL	New Democratic Youth League
NEP	New Economic Policy
NOC	National Operations Council
NRIC	National Registration and Identity Card
NTUC	National Trade Union Congress
NV	New Village
NWC	National Wages Council
OSPC	Officer Superintending Police Circle
PAP	People's Action Party
PAS	Partai Islam Se Malaysia
PERNAS	Perbadanan Nasional
PKI	Indonesian Communist Party
PLEN	Plenipotentiary of the Malayan Communist Party
PMFTU	Pan-Malayan Federation of Trade Unions
PPP	People's Progressive Party
PPSO	Preservation of Public Security Ordinance
PR	Partai Ra'ayat *or* Proportional Representation *or* Public Relations
RCM	Regional Committee Member
RCS	Regional Committee Secretary
SATU	Singapore Association of Trade Unions
SB	Special Branch
SCMSSU	Singapore Chinese Middle School Students' Union
SCM	State Committee Member
SCS	State Committee Secretary
SEAC	South East Asia Command
SEP	Surrendered Enemy Personnel
SF	Security Forces *or* Socialist Front
SFSWU	Singapore Factory and Shop Workers' Union
SFTU	Singapore Federation of Trade Unions
SHBEU	Singapore Harbour Board Employees' Union
SHLU	Singapore Harbour Labourers' Union
SLA	Singapore Legislative Assembly
SMAA	Students Mutual Assistance Association
SMB	South Malaya Bureau
SPA	Singapore People's Alliance

ABBREVIATIONS

SPC	Self-Protection Corps
SWA	Singapore Women's Association
SWB	South Wales Borderers
SWEC	State War Executive Committee
TUC	Trade Union Congress
UDP	United Democratic Party
UMNO	United Malay National Organization
UPP	United People's Party

Malay and Chinese Words Used in Text

Attap	Platted palm leaves for roofing
Barisan Sosialis	Socialist Front
Blukar	Secondary jungle or undergrowth
Bumiputra	Son of the Soil (i.e. person of indigenous race)
Dato (Datuk)	Honorific Malaysian title ('Sir')
Gerakan	A Malaysian political party
Kampong	Malay village
Kattie	Measure of weight ($1\frac{1}{3}$ lb)
Merdeka	Freedom (also Malaysian Independence Day 31st August 1957)
Min Yuen	People's Organization
Parang	Machette used for reaping or as a weapon
Pekamas	Breakaway party from Gerakan
Rukunegara	Malaysian national philosophy of Racial Unity
Tun	Honorific Malaysian title ('Lord')
Tunku	Honorific Malaysian title ('Prince')

Preface

Four years of my life since 1956 have been spent in Singapore and Malaysia and the main research for this book was done in two periods, 1966–72 and 1981–83. Parts I and II were originally published in 1973 as *Riot and Revolution in Singapore and Malaysia 1945–1963* – the period of turmoil from which both countries emerged with strong and stable democratic governments and economies set on a course of growth.

In 1981, Mrs Choo Campbell of Graham Brash invited me to update that book and add a part III about how things worked out after the years of crisis: about the 1964 and 1969 riots, Confrontation and, above all, the remarkable political, social and economic development of the two countries, which has exceeded anything which they or their greatest friends could have hoped when they looked at the prospects in the 1960s.

Graham Brash invited me to visit both countries again in 1982 to refresh my own memory and to see and talk to people in Singapore and Malaysia. I had some 40 interviews as such and talked to countless other people, giving me a vivid basis of reality on which to interpret the mass of documentary evidence I have consulted. (Can there be any country better documented than Singapore?).

In Singapore I had long interviews with President Devan Nair, the Prime Minister Mr. Lee Kuan Yew and his two deputies, Dr. Goh Keng Swee and Mr. S. Rajaratnam, plus a large number of others in Government service, business and industry. I also had tremendous help from the University of Singapore, especially from Professor Lau Teik Soon, MP and Professor Chan Heng Chee, whose book I have quoted freely in the closing chapters. I was particularly lucky in having a point of contact with the younger generation through Lim Lee Im, in the airport security police, whom I had known for some years. She and her family and friends brought me into the mainstream of Singapore life in the 1980s, viewed from

PREFACE

the high rise HDB flats in which they all lived. They gave me a feel for its vitality and a perspective which nothing else could have given me.

In Malaysia I again began with two friends of long standing, Dr. Goh Cheng Teik, Deputy Minister in the Prime Minister's Department and Mr. C.C. Too with whom I had worked closely during the Malayan Emergency and had kept touch ever since. I also spent many valuable hours at Police Headquarters where I had worked in the 1950s and where I was made to feel I was a trusted friend. Datuk Harun Bin Idris, (I have used the form 'Dato' in the book as this was current during the events described), Enchik Nordin Sofee and Anwar Ibrahim (now a Minister) were also very generous with their time, as were many others in the academic and business world.

All of these people in both countries were extremely frank with me. Except on matters of uncontroversial fact I have *not* attributed anything they told me. I asked for the interviews on that basis because I have always found that discussions with people carrying heavy responsibilities are more productive if non-attributable. Obviously their views varied widely, so the interpretation must be my own, aided by my documentary sources.

As the two periods 1945–63 and 1964–83 are quite different, with different problems, and different sources, the publishers and I decided that it would be more convenient for the reader if we kept the bibliographies separate as well.

Parts I and II are history and I have struck a balance as at 1963 in Chapter 15. Part III is more controversial. The current success and stability of the two societies is not in doubt, but I have faced two questions about the future. Is there a risk that Malaysia's racial mixture and its weighted political and economic structures could again explode into the kind of violence which, in 1969, was only just prevented from setting the whole country on fire? And has Singapore's success been bought at a price in civil liberties too high for its health in the future?

July 1984   RICHARD CLUTTERBUCK

Chapter 1 Introduction

The Aim of this Book

Robert Macnamara once observed that 90 per cent of the world's conflicts were internal and not between states; that the exploitation of such conflicts had become a prime technique of foreign policy; and that their incidence had been highest in the poorest countries and lowest in the richest.[1] Professor J. K. Zawodny calculated that in 1958-70 there were over 500 such outbreaks, involving 93 extra legal movements in 70 countries.[2]

Southeast Asia had more than its share of this. Singapore and Malaya both endured major attempts by an internal Communist Party to take over their countries over the period 1945-63. The same Party attempted both these takeovers - the Malayan Communist Party (MCP) - but it used two very different techniques. In Singapore the technique was Lenin's - an attempt to gain control of student and labour organizations and of a leading political party (in Russia the Social Democrat Party and in Singapore the People's Action Party); the process being assisted by strikes, student demonstrations and riots. In Malaysia the technique was that of Mao Tse Tung, the MCP being based in the jungle and trying to work inwards to the populated areas, by organizing popular support and by terrorising local officials and those who collaborated with them.

Both of these techniques have achieved many successes all over the world since Lenin's triumph in 1917 and Mao's in 1949. Other theories of revolution developed since the 1950s, and spelled out by philosophers like Sartre, Marcuse and Debray, have been far less successful. Their disciples have sometimes achieved considerable erosion of the stability and authority of their governments but they have not so far succeeded in overthrowing one.[3] This is chiefly because of their belief that public support will come spontaneously whereas in fact it comes only as a result of organization. This organization was the decisive ingredient in the victories of Lenin and Mao.

INTRODUCTION

Parts I and II of this book examine how these techniques for organizing support were applied in the urban setting in Singapore and in the rural setting in Malaya. The primary focus in each case is on the point of contact between the revolutionaries and the public, and on the way in which the police concentrated on these points of contact to acquire the intelligence which enabled them to defeat the bid to take over.

Part III follows the fortunes of the two countries in the 20 years following the defeat of these attempted revolutions. Both emerged strengthened by the ordeal, with stable democratic structures, experienced security forces and, above all, highly efficient intelligence services.

Their successful techniques were developed in the latter stages of the challenge, after 1954. The earlier years of the Malayan Emergency, 1948-54, have already been fully described in many books.[4] By 1954 the MCP guerrillas and their supporters in Malaya had been refined and hardened into a really tough and professional revolutionary organization. Similarly, by 1954 the MCP in Singapore had achieved a powerful hold on the Chinese student organizations and the trade unions and had penetrated the Central Executive Committee of the People's Action Party from its foundation in that year. At the same time, however, by 1954 the two governments had refined their own techniques for mobilizing public cooperation, for riot control, and especially for acquiring intelligence. The result was probably the most skilled contest of its kind in the world, on both sides, fought simultaneously in an urban and a rural setting. The governments prevailed because they fought on all fronts, political, social, economic, military, intelligence and public information.

Urban and Rural Revolution

Urban and rural revolution have the same aim – to bring about the overthrow or capitulation of established authority by means outside the law. They have many other features in common, in their organization, in some of their techniques of terror and coercion, and in their common need to weaken the police and the army by penetration. They are, however, radically different in strategy. In an urban revolution, the strategy is to seize control of the centres of power and of communications, so that the government in the countryside withers on the vine. In a rural revolution the strategy is to oust the government from the remotest areas first, work inwards and finally isolate the cities so that they fall like ripe plums.

The fears and aspirations of the people who form their raw material are also radically different. City people live from week to week, relying for next week's food on work, wages and a continuing system of wholesale and retail distribution; they also fear the failure of public services, such as water, sewerage, electric power and transport; they therefore have a vested interest in law and order; faced by chaos and a choice between two claimants to power, they will rally to the one which gives them most confidence of a return to normal life – as the Bolsheviks did in Petrograd in 1917.

On the other hand rural people – that is, those of them who live in the under-developed areas where alone Mao Tse Tung's techniques have succeeded – live from season to season; they rely on access to their land and security for their stocks of food until the next harvest;[5] they fear plunder and abduction; they fear murder, especially in the night or when they are at work in remote places; they usually have little use for government officials or policemen whom they regard as agents sent to squeeze taxes or bribes out of them, or to force them to move from their land; they do not want law and order so much as to be left in peace.

Because in every revolution victory depends ultimately on winning popular support – with varying degrees of willingness or compulsion – these differences in popular fears and aspirations demand that revolutionary leaders must handle urban and remote rural people very differently. If they fail to assess popular reactions correctly they will have little success – and there were examples of this both in Singapore and Malaya.

How a Revolution Ends

Most revolutionary attempts fail. In those which succeed, the transfer of power can only come in three ways – by cooperation with an invasion from outside, by civil war or by *coup d'état*.

In the case of invasion or civil war, a foreign army or a revolutionary army gains undisputed control of part of the country, from which it advances to drive the government forces from the remainder and places its own leaders in the seats of power. This was Mao Tse Tung's way.

Coups d'état can be subdivided into three types. First is the

'Palace revolution', in which a new team of leaders ousts the old and acquires the practical support of the existing power structure of the country: the civil service, the police, the army etc. Second is the 'Military coup' in which significant sections of the power structure are supplanted by a military hierarchy. In a Palace revolution the power structure is (initially) untouched and in a military coup the military hierarchy already exists, so either of these can happen with little warning, little bloodshed and little disruption of daily life. They may or may not be followed by changes and reforms.

The third form of *coup d'état* can be best described as a Party revolution. This kind of coup is preceded by a prolonged period of dislocation and erosion of authority during which the revolutionary party builds up a parallel hierarchy of government (usually clandestine, but not always) which is ready to replace those sections of the power structure which do not seem likely to cooperate with the revolutionaries. If such replacement is unnecessary, then one of the quicker, simpler methods (a Palace or Military coup) would have been used rather than the more prolonged and disruptive Party revolution. It therefore follows that a Party revolution will always be accompanied by considerable changes and reforms.

This was the method used by Lenin and was also the target in both the Singapore and the Malayan insurgencies – though the latter might alternatively have ended in civil war. The evolution of this kind of revolutionary technique has often been described and will be considered only briefly here as a historical process in which the Singapore and Malayan attempts have played their part.

The Developing Pattern of Urban Revolution

Modern urban revolution made its practical début in the French Revolution[6] which established a pattern of events which has reappeared in many subsequent revolutions. A tyrannical *ancien régime* was first ousted by moderate politicians who were committed to liberal reforms and to dismantling the suppressive apparatus of the State. Extremists then took advantage of this relaxation to oust the moderates. To hold power they had to resort to terror. Terror bred a 'Thermidorean Reaction' which carried a powerful and authoritarian ruler (Napoleon) to power. This sequence has been lucidly analysed by Crane Brinton in *The Anatomy of Revolution*.[7]

After the defeat of Napoleon in 1815 Europe was quiescent for a time, apart from the brief explosion of the July Revolution in France in 1830, but revolutionary theorists and conspirators were hard at work. 1848 saw a series of revolutionary attempts – generally unsuccessful except again in France – which provided much of the material for the theories of Karl Marx, but still no successful technique for organizing a popular rising had begun to appear. The Jacobin theory of conspiracy was developed by Blanqui (born in Paris in 1805), who based his ideas on the formation of a highly trained élite which would establish barricades from which they could debouch to seize key points such as arsenals, police stations and centres of government. He was convinced that the workers of Paris would then rise spontaneously and seize the capital. He did not, however, have any organization to lead them. At his first attempted uprising in 1839, his élite had immediate success and he seized the Hotel de Ville and declared a provisional government, but the people, lacking organization, failed to rise. Worse still, Blanqui had also failed to penetrate or neutralize the army, so it was only a matter of time before the insurgents were defeated. Blanqui made thirteen unsuccessful attempts and his theories were finally discredited in the bloody defeat of the Paris Commune in 1871.[8]

The focus then shifted to Russia, which Karl Marx considered to be the least suitable place in Europe for this kind of revolution because it was still a predominantly peasant country. Until the end of the century, passionate outbreaks of violence (such as the assassination of Tsar Alexander II in 1881) were not supported by any organization for a popular rising, so they led simply to decisive reaction and to a strengthening of the government's apparatus of power.

Lenin, from the 1880s onwards, began to develop the theories of Tkachev, who followed Blanqui's belief that power must be seized by a revolutionary élite, but contended that it could only succeed in a situation in which the mass of the people had developed a sense of impunity.[9] This sense of impunity was the foundation of the 'revolutionary situation' for which Lenin urged his Bolshevik party to strive from 1903 to 1917. Lenin was a brilliant propagandist, and in his writing 'his real aim is not to justify theoretically what he wants done but to make men do it'.[10] He was also an organizer and a tactician, but while he roused the masses he had no intention of allowing them to influence the power and freedom of action of the party – Tkachev's revolutionary élite.

INTRODUCTION

Lenin also appreciated the importance of the army which Blanqui had not. He realized that the sense of impunity depended above all on confidence that the army would not react effectively against the revolution. In July 1917, he felt that this confidence had not yet developed, so he restrained his Bolshevik colleagues from trying to seize power.[11] Within less than three months he was convinced that the attitude of the army had radically changed in his favour – thanks largely to the reaction against General Kornilov's attempted military coup – and he had become almost hysterical in his messages from his hiding place in Finland urging his comrades to seize the chance.[12]

The pattern of urban revolution which emerged was a series of techniques whereby a minority[13] can influence a government or a majority of the public to accept changes which they do not want. This was done to a small extent by an appeal to conscience, but to a far greater extent by sheer exasperation. Also, in the case of the mass of the people, by inducing fear for their livelihood – fear that chaos would result in no work, and therefore no wages next week; no food, no water and (with winter coming on) no fuel. Having no confidence that the Provisional Government could maintain these things they were willing to accept the idea of the Bolsheviks – with their impressive organization – taking over the reins, even though politically most of them would have preferred it if the leaders of one of the other political parties – especially the Social Revolutionaries – had been forceful enough to take control instead with similar confidence.

This revolutionary situation had been built up over the previous six months by a calculated erosion of the authority of the Provisional Government, of the civil servants, of army colonels and generals and of factory managements.

Gradually, practical control shifted from the normal power structure of the state to the parallel hierarchy of the Soviets – workers' and soldiers' committees – which the Provisional Government had agreed should be lawfully constituted. Ultimately it was the control of army regiments by their soviets instead of by their colonels which proved to be the fatal weakness of the Provisional Government. The disease began to gallop when Red Guards in the factories were armed by Trotsky, and in the final stages many of the officials of the government lost heart and waited apathetically to be relieved of their responsibility. The parallel hierarchy – which in this case was the overt structure of Soviets – was already in operation and when

Trotsky announced that the Bolsheviks had taken over in Petrograd this was generally greeted with relief.[14]

Revolutionary Errors Between the World Wars

The twenty depressing years after the First World War – and after the Russian Revolution – might have been expected to be a period of further success for Socialist and Communist revolutionary efforts, but in the event it was one of almost unmitigated failure for them. Perhaps for reasons similar to those for the Thermidorean Reaction to terror and insecurity, people rallied rather to authoritative right-wing leadership, such as that afforded by Mussolini and Hitler.

There were, however, a large number of unsuccessful revolutionary attempts in Europe, by both left- and right-wing groups. These generally failed because they did not appreciate the resilience of a modern state in resisting a *coup de main* – and particularly the need to neutralize or control both the civil and the military apparatus of power, and not just one or the other.

Thus there were, in 1919 and the early 1920s, a number of unsuccessful attempts at a *putsch* (defined by the Oxford Dictionary as 'the seizure of power by a sudden vigorous attack'). In Germany, for example, there was a series of Communist disturbances starting in January 1919 which reached a climax in Hamburg in 1923 when a concerted attempt to seize the post office, railroad stations, and airfields, and to raid all the city's police stations simultaneously was, after some initial success, defeated, because the Communists had failed to shake the control of the trade unions and other mass organizations of the workers by the Social Democrats who supported the government, so that the hoped-for popular rising did not materialize; also because the revolutionaries had failed to neutralize or penetrate the army, or to break the tacit alliance between the General Staff and the Socialist government, which had ensured that the Soldiers' Councils (unlike those in Russia in 1917) were not allowed to prejudice military discipline and the control of units by their officers.[15]

Failure to appreciate the power of trade unions and other civil organizations also led to the collapse of a right wing military *putsch* by the German General Luttwitz in March 1920. Though Luttwitz successfully seized Berlin on 13 March, he failed to secure the support of the trade unions, the banks, the civil service, or even of the leading right-wing politicians. The combination of a general strike, the refusal of the Finance Ministry to sign cheques and of the National Bank to release money paralysed the new regime. Political and military leaders and the police rallied to the legitimate government, and the insurrection collapsed within four days.[16]

These failures were symptomatic of the fallacy of what could be regarded as a post-1917 version of nineteenth-century Blanquism – the 'life-force' theory of revolution propounded by Curzio Malaparte, who, like some contemporary revolutionary theorists, rejected the need for organization and preparation which had been so much insisted upon by Lenin. Malaparte maintained that all that was needed was 'a small company, cold-blooded, violent, well-trained in the tactics of insurrection', which could paralyse any state, however strongly organized the police, by paralysing its 'life-force' or nervous system. 'The key to the state lies, not in its political and secretarial organizations . . . but in its technical services, such as the electric stations, the telephone and telegraph offices, the post, the gas-works and water mains'.[17]

Malaparte, however, like Blanqui, failed to appreciate on the one hand the power of political and civil apparatus (including the trade unions) and the vital importance of the army, as had been so amply demonstrated in Petrograd. 'First and foremost' wrote Sukhanov, 'the military apparatus had to be liquidated. The telegraphs, bridges, stations and the rest would take care of themselves'.[18]

The Reaction Against Leninism

In view of the success of revolutions which have used Lenin's techniques and organization, and the almost invariable failure of others, it seems surprising that the need for such organization is still so much questioned by modern revolutionary theorists. This may just be a symptom of the rejection of Russian Communism, and particularly of the reappearance of an 'establishment', in which the once revolutionary party structure appears to lapse back into bourgeois ways.

While the Sino-Soviet dispute arises more from nationalist and doctrinal differences, Mao Tse Tung certainly made vigorous efforts (in his 'Cultural Revolution') to halt this reversion to a bourgeois establishment, but he was reacting not against Leninism but against what he regarded as a Russian betrayal of Leninism. It is true that

Mao himself was initially, in the 1920s and 1930s, reviled even in the Chinese Communist Party for his contention that the revolution could have a peasant rather than a proletarian base, but he always declared and documented his adherence to Leninism,[19] and there is no reason to assume that Lenin, faced with the situation in China, would not have approved of Mao's strategy, for Lenin was always flexible and pragmatic. The essentials of Leninism – the revolutionary élite, the seeking of a revolutionary situation, the weakening of the apparatus of government and of the army, and the imposition of control of all activities of the State by a parallel Communist Party hierarchy both during and after the Revolution – were all reflected in Mao's organization and technique.

Every subsequent successful party revolution – even those (such as in Algeria) in which the revolutionary party was not Communist – have borrowed these techniques, though it is claimed by Regis Debray and some other writers that Castro's revolution in Cuba made significant departures from them.[20]

These writers are amongst a number of modern revolutionary theorists, including Sartre and Marcuse, who contend that the whole pattern of revolution has changed – or should change. They claim that it is wrong to delay the revolutionary process by building up an elaborate organization, as Lenin did, or to wait for a revolutionary situation; that a revolutionary situation can be created anywhere by urban violence or guerrilla activity, and that organization can follow later; that violence in itself is a proper technique even if it fails in its apparent objective, since violence breeds comradeship and commits its participants to the revolutionary cause;[21] also that, in an orderly society, disorder provokes reaction and suppression which inspires greater revolutionary fervour.[22] This is the technique of continued confrontation with the established power structure, administrative, industrial, social and educational, in order to induce it to modify its powers from fear or from sheer exasperation. The eventual hope is so to weaken these powers – especially those of the police and the army – and so to erode public confidence in the established authority that this authority is induced to cede important functions to revolutionary bodies (under such titles as Workers' or Students' Councils) or to abdicate control altogether.

This was the philosophy of the student revolution in Paris in May 1968. It was led by intellectual Trotskyists and anarchists but was not supported by the powerful orthodox Communist Party which was anxious to avoid provoking the destruction of its organization. When the French government showed apparent weakness by making concessions to the students (on 11 May) the Communist and Socialist Trade Unions exploited the weakness by building up the biggest strike in French history involving nearly ten million workers, from which they gained staggering wage increases of 35 per cent and more. This mattered more to them and to their members than an attempt to change the social order. Some of the left-wing intellectual groups in Paris felt that, at this point, de Gaulle might have been overthrown had there been an organized political movement ready to step in. In the event the intellectuals' and the students' revolt collapsed in the face of a firm speech by de Gaulle which rallied the mass of ordinary people who had been shaken by the rioting (which had been greatly magnified by the television cameras). De Gaulle called a snap general election which returned him with a massively increased majority – all the left-wing parties lost over half their seats – less than two months after the rioting had begun.[23]

The theory of the use of violence and confrontation as a means of generating popular support is nothing new. First preached in the mid-nineteenth century, its most famous exposition was in 1906 by Georges Sorel, in a series of articles in *Mouvement Socialiste*, which he later had published collectively in 1908 in his book *Reflections sur la Violence*. Sorel tied his philosophy to the syndicalist theory of the destruction of government and the seizure of control of industry by the workers by means of a general strike.

> 'Strikes have engendered in the proletariat the noblest and the most moving sentiments they possess; the general strike groups them all in a coordinated picture and, by bringing them altogether, gives to each one of them its maximum of intensity; appealing to their painful memories of particular conflicts, it colours with an intense life all the details of the composition presented to the consciousness.'[24]

Like Lenin, Sorel was enraged by 'social reforms', aimed to lure the workers away from militance and violence.

> 'When the governing classes, no longer daring to govern, are ashamed of their privileged situation, are eager to make advances to their enemies, and proclaim their horror of all civil cleavage in society, it becomes much more difficult to maintain in the minds of

the proletariat this idea of cleavage without which Socialism cannot fulfil its historical role.'[25]

He praises the Christian martyrs for provoking the Romans to use force.[26] The Romans, by dealing severely with anyone who showed a tendency to disturb the peace, enabled the Christians – even though their physical martyrdom was in fact rare – to convince people of the superiority of their philosophy so that Christianity eventually captured the Roman Empire.

To inspire such dedication, Sorel insists that there must be a 'myth' believed by its adherents to be certain to prevail in the end, regardless of temporary setbacks. Christianity has for centuries provided one such 'myth',[27] and the certainty of the ultimate overthrow of the hated European settlers by the natives is the 'myth' expounded by Frantz Fanon in *The Wretched of the Earth*. Sorel's philosophy was much admired later by Mussolini and Hitler, both of whom created their own myths on which to launch their political movements.

Sorel's 'myth' was the general strike. Strikes he said, are the means whereby the proletariat asserts itself, and are a phenomenon of war. He compared violent strikes to warfare, saying that, just as war provided most of the ideas of modern culture, so strikes accompanied by violence might engender a socialist society.[28] His writing was understandably diffuse (presumably to avoid giving grounds for arrest) but he leaves no doubt that he considers violence to be the only medium whereby revolutionary fervour can be effectively aroused.[29]

Debray is not so diffuse, and paid for the clarity of his writing by receiving a thirty-year sentence in a Bolivian prison (from which he was released after a subsequent coup). There have been regular reflections of Debray's (and Sorel's) philosophy of violence in Latin America – by both urban and rural revolutionaries. For example, a manifesto of a now defunct urban revolutionary organization in Uruguay – the Tupamaros – declared that

> 'revolutionary action in itself, the simple process of taking up arms, organizing supplies and committing acts that violate bourgeois legality will engender a consciousness, a movement, and the conditions for revolution.'[30]

This has yet to be proved. Where a government or management is weak, the new revolutionaries have proved that its power can be eroded, as was propounded over half a century ago by Sorel. The technique of erosion by confrontation was used in Russia and in every other country where a party revolution has been attempted, including Singapore and Malaya, but it has not yet led to an actual overthrow of power without the accompaniment of a Leninist or Maoist type of organization of popular support. A study of the erosive techniques used in these earlier revolutionary attempts may give indications as to the prospects of 'violence and confrontation without organization' achieving its ultimate aim – either in the cities or in the countryside.

The Pattern of Guerrilla Revolution

Modern guerrilla revolutionary technique was born and developed in East and South East Asia. It has been tried elsewhere, for example in Greece, and success for it has been claimed in Algeria and Cuba. Algeria had more of the ingredients of a civil war than of a guerrilla revolution, and the French soldiers claim to have won the military war, only to have their victory tossed aside by their own politicians and economists.[31] And in Cuba, despite the folklore arising from the revolution, the activities and achievements of the urban revolutionaries had more significance in overthrowing Batista than those of the guerrillas[32] in the Sierra Maestra.[33] Rural guerrilla technique has more often than not failed in South America but has had a better record of success in Central America, notably in Nicaragua where the Sandinistas followed the Maoist pattern as the Vietminh did in North Vietnam. Starting from bases in neighbouring countries, the Sandinistas gained control of remote frontier districts, extended it inwards until the country was in a state of civil war, whereupon President Somoza fled into exile leaving his demoralized National Guard to surrender. Guerrillas in other Central American countries tried to follow suit with varying degrees of success, always operating from secure bases beyond their frontiers.

Outside-based guerrillas had similar successes in Zimbabwe and the three Portuguese African colonies Mozambique, Angola and Guinea, where the strains of the guerrilla wars brought about an internal revolution in Portugal itself. Apart from China, however, the greatest success for the technique was in South Vietnam where a successful guerrilla war developed into civil war and created a situation ripe for invasion by the North Vietnamese army.

Mao's guerrilla revolutionary organization was no less extensive than Lenin's. In fact, the guerrilla army encompassed the party structure. This was also true in Malaya, where the two structures, though in theory separate, were intermingled and shared the jungle.

The pattern of Mao's and Ho Chi Minh's protracted war has been amply described in many books.[34] Briefly, the revolutionary organizations, guerrillas, village cadres and open front associations, are built up from the bottom. The guerrilla army begins with local village platoons, often part-time. From these full-time soldiers are selected for regional forces, and from these in turn the main force of regular battalions and regiments are formed and trained. The guerrillas dominate the fields, plantations, mines etc. where the people work so that they have little option but to provide money, supplies and information to the revolutionaries, but dare not betray them to the government. Selective terror is used to deter or punish government informers, to gain popularity by murdering unpopular bosses and administrators, and to intimidate local officials and policemen so that they have to 'live and let live' or face death. The village cadres are then able to control the village at least by night, which means that no villager who betrays them can expect to sleep in peace. Eventually the revolutionaries hope that the government officials will either become totally subservient or will be withdrawn, leaving the cadres in control by day as well.

As this control spreads whole areas are 'liberated', and in these the guerrilla forces can live openly to be retrained as a conventional army to drive the government forces back, first from the remote areas, and then from the more populated agricultural areas, finally isolating them in the cities. Deprived of food from the countryside, harassed by urban violence and attacked from the outside, the cities finally succumb and the revolutionaries, in what has by now become civil war, gain complete control.

Popular Support

Almost every revolutionary and counter-revolutionary has drawn attention to the need for popular support. Mao Tse Tung, for example, wrote that:

'The army must become one with the people so that they see it as their own army. Such an army will be invincible . . .'[35]

INTRODUCTION

Che Guevara wrote:

> 'For the individual guerrilla warrior, then, wholehearted help from the local population is the basis on which to start. Popular support is indispensable.'[36]

On the other side, General Templer is quoted as saying:

> 'The answer lies not in pouring more troops into the jungle, but in the hearts and minds of the people.'[37]

This thought, however, had already been expressed 134 years earlier by the American John Adams:

> 'The revolution was effected before the war commenced. The revolution was in the minds and hearts of the people.'[38]

Regis Debray puts a different slant on popular support. Though he does not underestimate the eventual need for the masses to rise, he gives a passionate warning against premature involvement of the population by the guerrillas, both because it will invite repressive measures and because of the risk of betrayal. He denounces the 'Trotskyist' techniques of dual power, agitation for factory and peasant committees etc. because, he says, they invite the destruction of the workers and peasant supporters by the government.

> 'The revolutionary guerrilla force is clandestine ... is independent of the civilian population, in action as well as in military organization; consequently it need not assume the direct defence of the present population. The protection of the population depends on the destruction of the enemy military potential ... the populace will be completely safe when the opposing forces are completely defeated. ... This objective requires that the guerrilla *foco* be independent of the families residing within the zone of operations.'[39]

While he accepts that the people must be activated and led, he visualizes this being done by small 'armed propaganda patrols', i.e. by the guerrillas rather than by cadres who live in the villages.[40]

He sees the guerrillas themselves as the nucleus of the party, not vice versa. He scornfully rejects the building up of a revolutionary political organization which, he says, merely delays the armed struggle, adding that 'insurrectional activity is today the number one political activity'. His theory is based, not on fixed bases but on a number of guerrilla *focos* or centres of activity, each based on an active and mobile band of guerrillas.[41] The impression he gives is of a swarm of bees, sometimes buzzing for a time in the area, but, when necessary, shifting its focus, still buzzing around. As the enemy swipes, the focus dodges elsewhere. As it buzzes it gathers other insects around it. Soon the whole air is alive with insects everywhere and the enemy swipes in vain until he is stung to death.

Whether the activation of the people is done primarily by guerrillas from outside or cadres from inside the villages, it is questionable how widespread the contacts with the population need be. How big a percentage need to be trained and prepared for local leadership, and to provide the support the guerrillas need? And is the support of the remainder necessary at all? What is required of the majority is 'acquiescence' or even 'indifference' rather than 'support'. It is true that neither side can succeed without *active* support from *part* of the population, but this part need not be more than about 10 per cent. If a much larger percentage, say 30 per cent, gives *active* support to one side, then this may well prevent the other side from winning. In either case, however, a large proportion, usually some 80 per cent, of the population will nearly always be neutral, aiming to keep out of trouble by not giving active support to either side.[42] This hypothesis was particularly worthy of examination in the Malayan Emergency, and in Northern Ireland where, in the elections in 1982, about 10 per cent voted for Sinn Fein candidates supporting the IRA.

Escalation

Since urban violence and guerrilla warfare have become prevalent forms of conflict, the prevention of their escalation into something bigger is of some importance to the world. Malaya provided a good example of this prevention. The British can claim a fairly good record in keeping revolutionary conflict from becoming unduly bloody both internally[43] and in the decolonization of her Empire. The aftermath, when law and order has been in the hands of a newly independent government, has often been a great deal bloodier, as it was in India and Pakistan, Palestine and Nigeria. Some would say that this aftermath was an inevitable result of a divide-and-rule policy and that Britain was cleverer in abdicating responsibility in time. For over twelve years after Independence it seemed as though the highly explosive racial mixture in Malaya might be kept cooler than the flash point, but the carnage in Kuala Lumpur after the general election in May 1969 put a sharp stop to any complacency about this. The most cursory comparisons of Malaya, Cyprus and Kenya with Indochina, Indonesia, Algeria and the Congo suggests, however, that, during the period in which Britain remained responsible for law and order in her emerging colonies, there was much less escalation of violence than in most others.

Sir Robert Thompson contrasts the escalation in Vietnam with that in Malaya. Though there were very marked differences in the situation and in the background, there were also some striking similarities. The insurgents in each had roughly the same plan and used similar techniques. In Malaya in 1949 there were some 4,500 guerrillas, with about 50,000 supporters. In Vietnam in 1959 there were about 5,000 guerrillas and 100,000 supporters in a population twice the size. At that time Thompson suggests that government methods which had succeeded in Malaya could also have succeeded in Vietnam, but they were not applied.[44] In any event, the number of civilians killed in Malaya, having risen over these three years 1948–50 (500, 700 and 1,200 respectively) fell away in 1951 to 1,000 and continued to fall; whereas in Vietnam, they started to rise on a similar scale in relation to the population in the years 1957–9 (700, 1,200, 2,500) but soared in the following year, 1960, to 4,000 and went on rising until the guerrilla war escalated into a civil war.[45]

Malaya and Singapore – The Background

There were, however, very important differences between the settings of the insurgencies in Malaya and in Vietnam: differences in their terrain and in the positions and attitudes of their neighbours; in their ethnic structure, history (including colonial history) and, arising from these, in their type of government, and in their relationship with, respectively, Britain and the United States. All these things have been described and analysed in several books,[46] so there is no need for more than a brief mention of some of the more important background here for reference.

Malaya is a peninsula of about 50,000 square miles of which 80 per cent is uncultivated jungle. After the formation of Malaysia in 1963 it became known as 'West Malaysia' or 'Peninsular Malaysia' and is so described in Part III of this book. All these terms exclude Singapore.

Before the Federation of Malaya became independent in 1957, it contained nine Malay States ruled by Malay Sultans with British Advisers, and two settlements (Penang and Malacca) governed by British officials (Fig. 1). Singapore, which was separate, also had a British Governor.

Though a few aborigines remained, the peninsula had been occupied and ruled by Malays for many centuries. The Malays were originally immigrants from Melanesia, possibly via Southern China. The word 'Malay' denotes a man of this race, whether he lives in Malaya or not. A 'Malayan' or 'Malaysian' refers to a person's domicile or citizenship and he may be of any race e.g. a Malayan Chinese. From the sixteenth century onwards Portuguese, Dutch and British traders made contact with them, and coastal settlements were established, which eventually became British (Penang, Malacca and Singapore). Treaties were made with the Malay Sultans who accepted British advice, British officials and British defence, but remained, as they still remain, rulers of their States.

During the late nineteenth and early twentieth centuries the development of the rubber and tin industries led the British to bring in large numbers of Chinese and Indian immigrants since the Malays never took kindly to working in these industries, preferring their traditional way of life in agriculture and fishing.

By the 1940s, the Malays had ceased to have an overall majority of the population in the Federation though they were the largest single race. Figures were about –

Malay	2,600,000	– 49%
Chinese	2,040,000	– $38\frac{1}{2}$%
Indian*	578,000	– 11%
European	12,000	$1\frac{1}{2}$%
Others	70,000	

5,300,000[47]

* including Indian, Pakistani, Bengali or Sri Lankan, etc.

In Singapore, however, there were over one and a half million people, of whom 75 per cent (over one million) were Chinese. Had Singapore been joined, like the other Settlements, to the Federation, the Chinese would have had an overall majority. Though at this time very few Chinese had citizenship rights, being regarded as temporary residents from China, this would have been unacceptable to the Malays and their Sultans. That is why Singapore remained separate.

INTRODUCTION

Figure 1 Federation of Malaya, showing States

Even so, only two of the Malay States had an overall Malay majority: the two East Coast States of Kelantan and Trengganu in which rubber and tin had not been appreciably developed.

In the Federation as a whole, and sited mainly astride the main road and railway from Singapore through Kuala Lumpur to Thailand, there were 720 tin mines and three million acres of rubber (Fig. 2). Other crops included pineapple, oil palm and rice, and there were many small peasant farms and market gardens. The rubber estates were worked largely by Indians, with some Chinese but very few Malays. Tin-mine labour was virtually all Chinese, as were the market gardeners and pig and poultry farmers. The Malays grew most of the rice, but most Malays lived peacefully by fishing and subsistence agriculture in their kampongs (villages).[48] Despite this, however, only half the total rural population of all races was employed in growing food, and the remainder, i.e. most of the Indians and Chinese, in producing cash crops and tin.[49]

Thus the Chinese and Indians were far more economically effective than the Malays. Average incomes per head in 1947 were: Chinese $656, Indian $560 and Malay $258.[50] (Note. $ are Straits Dollars, of which 3 went to $US1 and 8.57 to £1 in 1947.) Even more significant were their contributions to taxation. The only figures available include both the Federation and Singapore. In 1950

```
 9,624 Europeans paid a total of $136,071,000 Income Tax
10,037 Chinese       „  „  „  „  $117,812,000     „      „
 2,610 Indians       „  „  „  „   $17,569,000     „      „
   876 Malays        „  „  „  „    $8,836,000     „      „[51]
```

Thus only one Malay in 3,000 earned enough to pay any Income Tax at all, compared with 1 in 200 Chinese. But these 1 in 200, that is the 10,000 Chinese merchant landowners, tin miners and industrialists, paid, head for head and in all, almost as much as the British.

As a further indication of Chinese economic involvement Donnison records that, out of $130 million invested in Malaya before the war, $50 million was British and $40 million Chinese, again almost equal.

Even so, throughout the Emergency, the British found it hard to convince the bulk of the Chinese working population that they had a stake in Malaya as Malayans.[52] Many remitted money to China, and many returned there, or had planned to do so until China was taken over by Mao Tse Tung.

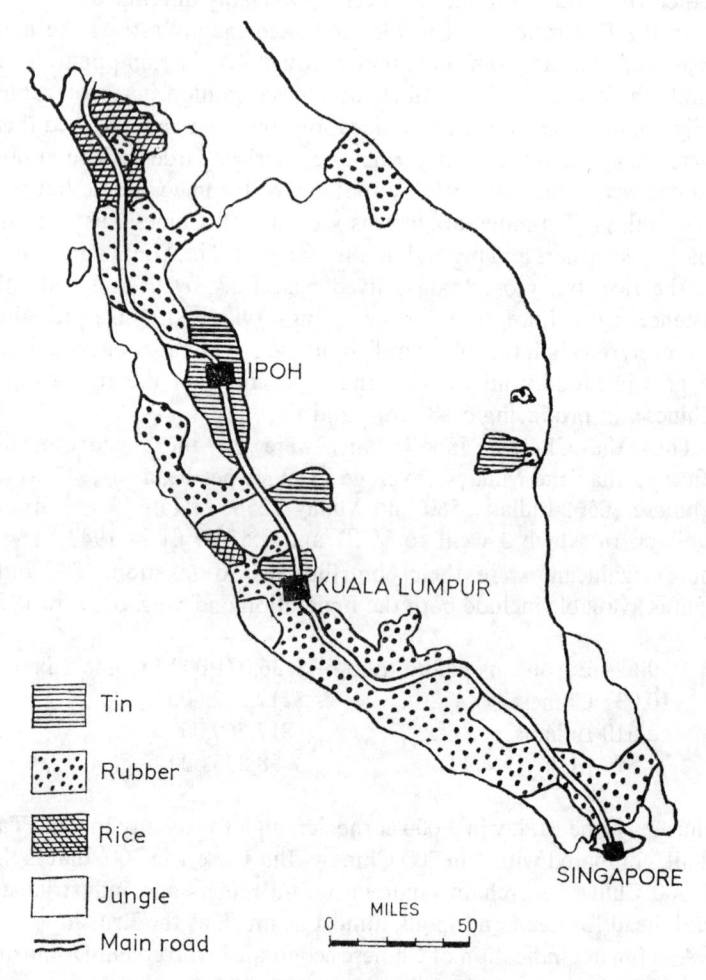

Figure 2 Federation of Malaya, showing main rubber, tin and rice growing areas

The bulk of the Federation army and police force were Malay, initially with British officers. At the start of the Emergency there were two Malayan battalions, rising to eight by 1955, of which seven were wholly Malay, and the eighth of mixed race – but still mainly Malay. In the police force, almost all the constables were Malay, though its most vital element proved to be the small Special Branch formed during the Emergency, which was largely Chinese with senior posts held by the British.

The Malayan Communist Party and the Japanese Occupation

Little need be said about the formation of the Malayan Communist Party (MCP) which has again been described in many books.[53] It had an urban beginning in Singapore where Communist agents from Shanghai started work in 1924, and where the MCP was formed in 1930. The party was, however, set back by a brilliant Special Branch coup in its first year. In 1934 a young Vietnamese communist, Lai Tek, joined the Party and by 1939 had become Secretary General, remaining so throughout the Japanese occupation and thereafter until 1947. It is now generally accepted that he was originally planted by the British Special Branch, though his subsequent loyalties are more doubtful.[54]

During 1941 the British in Malaya were blissfully sure that the Japanese would not invade Malaya, and that, even if they did, they would not attempt to advance on Singapore from Thailand through the jungle-covered Malay peninsula. Though a small irregular warfare training school was started in Singapore early in 1941 by Lieutenant Colonel (now Major General) J. M. L. Gavin, R.E., later joined by Major (later Colonel) F. Spencer Chapman, the British High Command in Malaya in October that year turned down a proposal to train locally enlisted stay-behind parties. Only after Pearl Harbour did they change their minds, and on 18 December 1941 there was a clandestine meeting between British officers and Lai Tek in a back-street room in Singapore. Thereafter, during the few weeks remaining before Singapore fell, under arrangements made with the MCP, 200 Chinese were trained as guerrillas. These took to the jungle behind the advancing Japanese, and during the next three years they grew into a force of 7,000 men, under Communist leadership and control, known as the Malayan People's Anti-Japanese Army (MPAJA). They were supported by a strong, largely spontaneous and loosely organized body of Chinese villagers and squatters on the jungle fringe, known as the Malayan People's Anti-Japanese Union (MPAJU).

The MCP concentrated on building up its organization, both for use against the Japanese, and eventually for use against the British after the war. Meanwhile, they avoided provoking Japanese interference with this organization and took little aggressive action.[55] Spencer Chapman remained with them, though virtually a prisoner, until 1945.

The MPAJA operated in patrols of about 100, which included a few girls (who apparently caused no disharmony). Each unit had a Military Commander, but he in turn was a subordinate to a Political Leader who was a Party Member and had absolute power. The army was almost wholly Chinese. (Spencer Chapman mentions one Indian in a group or regiment of 216 and no Malays.) In addition to the full-time guerrillas, the MPAJA trained 100 per cent reserves, who came into the jungle for a two-months' course, and returned to their villages or squatter-huts to await recall when enough weapons had been acquired to arm them.[56]

Though the MPAJA killed few Japanese, they killed many 'traitors'. Spencer Chapman found himself for a time with a special Traitor Killing Squad in the jungle near Ipoh, which was credited with killing over 1,000 people of all races, mainly by descending on the towns and villages and picking out its victims in houses, coffee shops or police posts. The killer-squad was never given away to the Japanese by witnesses.[57] Executions such as these were always done by guerrillas from the jungle rather than by supporters in the villages who were too vulnerable.[58]

On the other side, the Japanese treated the Chinese with extreme ruthlessness and, for example, slaughtered 5,000 in February 1942, mainly picked out by hooded informers. Many Malay officials and police continued in their posts under the Japanese, on the not unreasonable grounds that it was better for them to maintain some semblance of order in their own land rather than abandon it wholly to Japanese officials, but, because of the Japanese butchery of Chinese, the relations between Chinese and Malays, which had been good before the war, were ruined.[59] This resulted in some appalling massacres of Malays by Chinese after the Japanese collapse.

Nevertheless, some of the Chinese did betray their own people to the Japanese – as they were later to do to the British and Malay soldiers and police in the Emergency. The explanation of this surprising attitude is discussed later in Chapter 9.

In May 1943, a new element entered the jungle war in the form of a British army liaison team, Force 136, under Colonel John Davis, which was landed by submarine in August 1943 after an in-and-out reconnaissance in May.

Their function was to contact the guerrillas (and rescue Spencer Chapman), to send radio reports to the Allied Command in Calcutta, to arrange the supply of British arms and equipment, and, in due course, to guide the guerrillas in cooperating with the Allied reoccupation forces.

Davis made contact with Chin Peng, at that time the MCP leader in Perak, in September 1943, and an agreement was reached with the MCP in December 1943.[60] (Chin Peng was later to become Secretary General of the Party, and remains so to this day, while Davis was to play a major part in running the government's Emergency effort. They never lost their mutual respect, and when Chin Peng emerged for the abortive truce talks in 1955, it was Davis who met him at the jungle fringe and escorted him back there after the talks broke down.[61])

Thereafter there was much frustration, largely caused by the failure of the radio and the difficulty of repairing it. The first airdrop of supplies was not received until December 1944. Eventually, between June and December 1945, over 1,000 airdrop sorties were made, delivering 510 men and one and a half million lb. of equipment and supplies, in preparation for the support of the Allied invasion[62] – which in the event was unopposed due to the Japanese surrender after the dropping of the two atomic bombs.

During the period 1943–5 there were several meetings between Davis and senior MCP representatives including Lai Tek. The MCP was prepared to cooperate in ousting the Japanese but left Force 136 in no doubt that they intended to make Malaya a Communist Republic after the war.[63] The British, on their side, agreed to pay the MCP £3,000 per month, which they said was not to be regarded as wages but as provision for the food and upkeep of the guerrillas.[64]

Reoccupation by the British

The British South East Asia Command (SEAC) in Calcutta had been planning to reoccupy Malaya in November 1945, and to assist in planning this operation (code named ZIPPER) Spencer Chapman was taken out of Malaya by submarine on 13 May. The planned date of the landing was then brought forward to mid August.

On 6 and 9 August the atomic bombs were dropped on Hiroshima and Nagasaki. By 11 August it was clear that the Japanese were about to surrender. On 17 August SEAC ordered Force 136 to cease fire.[65]

Meanwhile, there was real concern in SEAC that the MPAJA might usurp the government. Many guerrillas entered the towns and villages and confusion was caused by bandit gangs also doing so and claiming to be MPAJA. The MPAJA seized most of the police stations and barricaded the others. On 22 August, SEAC authorized Force 136 to reoccupy areas vacated by the Japanese and a few days later to enter Japanese-occupied areas as well as to maintain order if the Japanese were not doing so.[66] Singapore was reoccupied on 8 September, but it was 28 September before the Japanese on the East Coast surrendered.[67]

During this period and for some months afterwards there was communal violence on an appalling scale. In August, when the MPAJA began to seize control, the Japanese provoked the Malays to kill 400 Chinese in the predominantly Malay Coastal towns of Muar and Batu Pahat, and many Malays, accused of collaboration, were slaughtered by the Chinese. Between September 1945 and 1 April 1946, 600 murders were actually recorded by the police but there were undoubtedly many more.[68]

The occupation force commander in Malaya (General Dempsey) decided to keep the guerrillas under military control, and to this end they were paid $30 a month, given clothing and rations, and employed on guard duty. Any who wished were allowed to opt out of this by handing in their weapons and collecting an immediate payment of $150.[69]

Meanwhile, negotiations began for disbandment of the MPAJA. The British were afraid that too high a gratuity would encourage inflation, and decided upon an award of $350 at the final disbandment for each guerrilla who handed in a weapon. A disbandment ceremony was held at the beginning of December 1945, and 5,497 weapons were handed in. This was more than the number issued through Force 136 (4,765), but certainly not as many as were at large. The MCP already had a substantial clandestine stock of weapons left over from the war in abandoned dumps and taken from dead bodies, and they knew well that they could get more from the same sources.[70]

The Party structure and the Party branch organizations established in the villages remained intact. Only the uniformed guerrillas handed in their weapons, and registered their names with the MPAJA Old Comrades Association (OCA). Secret members, however, hid their arms and did not register.

Nevertheless, the MCP were not as prepared either for the take-over which had been their intention, nor for launching the campaign to oust the new and weakly established British Military Government. The British, all powerful and godlike before the war, had been humiliated by the Japanese and were no longer regarded by the people as invincible. A concerted take-over bid by the MPAJA might have aroused a response from the Chinese at least, though the Malays might then have rallied to the British as the only hope of preserving their position in the country. As it was, the MPAJA was taken as much by surprise by the atomic bombs and the surrender of the Japanese as was the rest of the world. Hating the Japanese and relieved of their terror, many of the Chinese 'literally wept with joy' when the first British soldiers reappeared.[71]

So the British were back. Though the MPAJA had earned great credit for their resistance to the Japanese, there was a slightly hollow ring about their claim to have finally defeated them. Spencer Chapman (writing early in 1948, just before the Emergency began) considered that if only the atomic bomb had come late enough to allow the MPAJA to play their part in driving the Japanese out of Malaya, its resettlement might have proved easier than it did.[72] As it was the MCP had to decide all too quickly whether to oust the British by a rural or urban revolution, and started work on it without proper preparation.

Part I URBAN REVOLUTION – SINGAPORE

Chapter 2 The First Attempt at an Urban Revolution – 1945–8

The Decision to Adopt an Urban Strategy in 1945

When the MCP took to the jungle on the arrival of the Japanese in 1942 only a small minority had stayed underground in Singapore, including the Secretary-General, Lai Tek. Their organization in the city had then been smashed by the Japanese in August 1942,[1] and thereafter it was virtually impossible for the Communists to operate in Singapore for the remainder of the Japanese occupation.[2]

In 1945 the Party set its sights on gaining control of Singapore first, i.e. by means of an urban revolution on the Russian model. This may now seem surprising but in 1945, though Mao Tse Tung's theories had been put on paper, and to some extent practised against the Japanese and the Kuomintang, they had not yet been proved to the world. His victory in China was still four years ahead. In any case, the Communists seemed to have a good chance of a quick victory in Singapore in 1945–7. Everything was in their favour at the time of the Japanese surrender. Their prestige was at its peak, and that of the British very low after their humiliation by the Japanese in 1943. Two Communists sat on the Advisory Committee established in 1945 by the British Military Administration. They were the only organized vocal opposition, and there were causes enough for complaint. The Chinese were an urban people, and urban discontent was greater because of the difficulty of getting going again quickly in a basically commercial community.[3]

Their hope of gaining control by constitutional means was based on a not unreasonable estimate of the British ability and determination to resume effective colonial government. During the war they had hoped that the Japanese army, weakened and overextended by the Americans and the British, would find itself strangled by a popular rising in China enabling the MPAJA to lead a similar rising by the Chinese in Malaya. The sudden ending of the war found them unready everywhere. They expected, however, that the British reoccupation forces would do no more than maintain some kind of order under which the MCP could build up its organization,[4] especially in the urban areas, and it seemed inconceivable to them that the people would not rally to their call for freedom from colonial government, or that the British government would be able to resist the flood of national feeling led by a recognized political party which would quickly prove itself ready to take over. Indeed, there was no other political party which could remotely have stepped in and, although their hopes may now seem to have been naive, they did not seem so to themselves at the time in the light of the chaos which inevitably followed the collapse of the Japanese administration.

A victory in Singapore would have been followed by others in Kuala Lumpur, Ipoh and Penang, with Communist control thereafter spreading to the mines, estates and rural areas.

On the other hand it is arguable that, had the MCP maintained its strong guerrilla army in the jungle, supported as it was by a large majority of the rural Chinese on the jungle fringe, the British could never have re-established control over the rubber estates and tin mines and, with no prospects of profits from these industries, would soon have abandoned both Singapore and the Federation. Perhaps either strategy could have succeeded if the sudden Japanese collapse had not given them so little time to think it over.

The urban revolutionary effort in Singapore was doomed to fail in 1948. It was to be resumed with some intensity during the critical years in which Singapore was progressing through the interim phase of self-government under British sovereignty to full independence (1955–63), but by that time the party was illegal, while the government and its police force had gained greater experience and stronger powers with which to deal with it.

In 1945, however, the MCP was legal, and the time seemed ripe for action in the cities. It therefore sent most of its best men to Singapore and the other big towns to work for the seizure of power. This was an 'Open Front' period, i.e. they worked through a number of legal organizations, especially the trade unions which had been revived under the pre-war General Labour Union (GLU) of which the Communists rapidly gained control. Other legal Front Organizations under MCP control included the New Democratic Youth League (NDYL), the Singapore Women's Association (SWA), the MPAJA Old Comrades Association (MPAJAOCA) and the Malayan

Democratic Union (MDU).[5] All of these were gradually taken under a dual system of open and secret direction as will be described in the next chapter. At the same time, the MCP emerged as a legal political party, with a Party platform for running the country. The Central Committee itself, led by Lai Tek and including Chin Peng, remained underground, but two senior Party members, both already well known to the British, established themselves in the Party's headquarters offices in Kuala Lumpur – Liew Yit Fan at the head of the Political Committee and Lau Yew of the Military Committee. They made speeches and attended public functions alongside British and other Malayan dignitaries as leaders of a normal political party.

The Difficulties of the MCP as an Open Political Party

The MCP was not alone in operating as a legal political party at this time. In 1945 there were many others, for Britain, America and Soviet Russia had emerged as Allies, and Communist Parties did (and still do) operate freely in the democratic process.

In Eastern Europe, under Soviet occupation, 'Coalition' governments were formed, but their other member parties were given short shrift by their Communist factions. Czechoslovakia, however, was not occupied by the Soviet Army, and the Coalition lasted until 1948, when the world was given a classic example of the ability of an open and legal Communist political party to seize power through 'constitutional' means, even though in a minority. With 38 per cent of the popular vote in the 1946 elections the Communists secured a number of key ministries in the Coalition cabinet, including those of the Interior, Defence, Labour, Education and Information. Before long they also had the Premiership, though they held only nine of the twenty-six cabinet posts.[6] By clever and ruthless exploitation of the power of the ministries they held, particularly the control of the police, they manoeuvred twelve anti-Communist ministers into resigning on the tacit understanding that President Benes would ask them to resume their ministries. The Party then intimidated the President into replacing them instead with twelve pro-Communists, thereby giving the Communists control of the Cabinet.[7] With any other Party, such control might have been temporary, but the Communists at once disarmed the Constitutional machinery for political change, and have held power ever since. An attempt to liberalize the Party from within was ruthlessly suppressed by a Soviet Army invasion in 1968.

The intimidation of President Benes and of the general public into acquiescence was greatly helped by the Front organizations, especially the Labour organization, and by the Information Services, which created a terrifying prospect of chaos and violence. These organizations were, however, already operating quite openly under Communist control, since there was no need for them to use false colours.

This demonstration of the final stages of a Russian-pattern urban takeover gave encouragement to other Communist parties, but it was probably more significant in the long run in alerting anti-Communists to this particular Communist technique.

There are many advantages for a Communist Party in having legal status and operating within the nation's constitutional system. Its more respectable image helps it to attract broadly-based support, and should result in less shock and reaction if and when it gains power. Meanwhile, the Party has a better platform for propaganda. But there are disadvantages. Although the members of the open political Party are in theory quite separate from the secret Party structure, some contact, even though indirect (i.e. through couriers and cut-off men) is inevitable. This gives the police Special Branch more chances of detection and penetration. That also applies if, as happened later in Singapore, the open political Party operates under a transparently false name (see Chapters 5 to 8). And if the Party (whether under its own or some other name) is declared illegal, it is difficult for men who have become well known publicly as politicians to disappear underground. The Party's dilemma is to pick men good enough to attract public support and to govern if power is gained by 'constitutional' means but whom it can also afford to lose. Even in states where the Communists have gained full power the tradition persists that ministers and officials of the government remain subservient to the parallel hierarchy of the Communist Party structure.

Liew Yit Fan and Lau Yew were both, in fact, men of considerable ability, and their 'expendability' was presumably founded on the fact that both had already become well known to the British. Lau Yew was one of the Party's foremost strategists and military organizers, and had led the MPAJA contingent in the Victory Parade in London. Liew Yit Fan was a Eurasian who looked more European than Chinese, had great charm, and could easily be envisaged emerging as a constitutional prime minister. In the event, Liew Yit

Fan was arrested on 9 June 1948, just before the State of Emergency was declared, and later deported to China. Lau Yew went underground and was the first major Communist casualty of the Emergency, being killed on 16 July 1948 in a raid by the police (acting on a tip-off) on a hut in the country in which he had set up his military headquarters.[8]

During their three years as open political leaders they had had few of the opportunities enjoyed by the Party in Czechoslovakia. The reimposition of British Colonial Government meant that there were no ministries within their grasp. Also, their Front organizations were not difficult to recognize as Communist,[9] and it was possible for the Government to frustrate their activities by legislation before they could get the situation out of control.

The British Military Administration

During the Japanese occupation the British had not maintained a Government-in-exile for Malaya as they did for Burma. Late in 1943, however, they did form a Malayan Planning Unit, which included Sir Edward Gent, a Colonial Office civil servant who was to become Malaya's first post-war High Commissioner. It was decided that in place of the pre-war mixture of Federated and Unfederated Malay States, a Malayan Union should be formed, in which the immigrant races (mainly Chinese and Indian) would be granted similar citizenship rights to those enjoyed by the Malays, provided that they were born or ordinarily resident in Malaya.

The majority of the Unit also recommended that Singapore should be included in the Union but the Government decided that it should remain separate.[10]

The Malayan Union was to have a short, unhappy life from 1946 until 1948. This coincided with the attempted urban revolution which is described hereafter in this chapter, but had little effect on the attitude of the predominantly Chinese population in this attempt except in providing one more issue of dissatisfaction which the MCP could exploit.[11] It did, however, have a disturbing effect on the Malay population, and on Malay government officials, soldiers and policemen, which greatly strained their loyalty to the British, whom they had trusted to defend their rights against the alien Chinese and Indians whom they (the British) had brought into their country.

For the first six months of reoccupation, the Malayan Union was still only a paper plan in London, and the Malay States and Singapore were all under a British Military Administration (BMA)[12] responsible to the Commander-in-Chief South East Asia Command, Admiral Lord Mountbatten.

The first urban trial of strength was not long in coming, and started not in Singapore but in Kuala Lumpur. On 29 October 1945 the General Secretary of the Selangor MPAJU – Soong Kwong – was arrested on a charge of extortion. He was accused of having threatened a Chinese victim and his family with death unless they wrote a promissory note for $300,000 as compensation for alleged collaboration with the Japanese. A British judge presided over the court, with two Malayan assessors. There was a split verdict, the judge finding for conviction and the two assessors for acquittal. A second trial had the same result, and it was deemed that the assessors were intimidated. On 3 January 1946, at a third trial (this time all-British) the accused was found guilty and sentenced to four years' imprisonment.[13]

There were immediate petitions for his release, and a threat of a general strike. Meanwhile the sentence was reviewed, and it was decided to release the prisoner, but to withhold the announcement of the decision lest it be interpreted as bowing to threats.

On 29 January the strike began. Over 150,000 took part in Singapore alone, but the great majority did so unwillingly, under intimidation from a well organized cadre of 3,500.[14]

The strike was called off on 30 January, probably because of the fear of banishment of the leaders, but it had given an awesome warning of the strength and organizing capability of the MCP.[15]

On 3 February, the review of Soong Kwong's sentence was published[16] and he was released on sureties.

The General Labour Union (GLU) thereupon applied for a public holiday on 15 February 1946, avowedly to commemorate the day the MCP had 'taken over' in 1942 as an underground movement,[17] but it was obvious that the real intention was to rejoice over the anniversary of the British defeat on 15 February 1942. The Military Government declined to grant a public holiday, commenting that it would be better to hold such a celebration in August, the date of the Japanese defeat.[18]

On 13 February the Government published a warning against applying pressure with a view to using the strike weapon to interfere with the course of law, to endanger the peaceful living of the population by 'extortion, intimidation or other illegal means', adding that persons so doing would be 'arrested and prosecuted and, if aliens, may in addition be repatriated . . .'[19]

This was a clear threat that the government intended to use its power of deportation to China, which was greatly feared, since any Chinese deported for Communist activities could expect little mercy from the Kuomintang.

On the morning of 14 February, all Chinese-language newspapers called upon the public to demonstrate. The crowds, armed with sticks, bottles and crowbars, became violent. The police opened fire, killing two and wounding a number of others, including one of the leaders. On the night of 14/15 February there were a number of arrests, and nine were named for deportation.[20]

Lord Mountbatten, however, refused to approve the deportation orders on the grounds that the accused had had only thirty-six hours to heed the warning, and that there had been no judicial proceedings against them.

The case was deferred until the civil government took over one month later. The nine accused, plus one more, were then deported without legal proceedings and without fuss. It was ruled that the expulsion order was valid provided that it was in the public interest, and could be based on evidence of past behaviour (i.e. before the warning).[21] Though somewhat harsh, this was a realistic decision in the circumstances since judicial proceedings would clearly have been impracticable on account of intimidation of witnesses.

'Peaceful Agitation'

This was the kind of problem which was to plague Singapore and the Federation of Malaya for many years to come, and to some extent does so to this day. How far was it possible to maintain a liberal legal system, with the traditional safeguards of English law for the rights of the individual, in the face of an organized and widespread conspiracy to interfere with the processes of the law?[22] Alan Blades commented in 1969 as follows:

> 'There was, however, nothing unusual in banishment without judicial proceedings. This had been the practice for many years before the war in dealing with all kinds of Secret Society pressure tactics, including especially the MCP, which defeated the process

of justice through intimidation of witnesses ... It is salutary to note that detention without trial in open court has been continued ... and is still in force in 1969.'[23]

A similar problem developed over the trade unions. The newly elected British Labour Government was reluctant to inhibit the revival of the unions, but they were clearly being used by the MCP for purposes much wider than those of labour negotiations. The Party was fully prepared for the task of organizing and controlling them. Industry, both urban and agricultural, was disorganized and unemployment was high. Labour tended to move freely, seeking work wherever a new rubber estate or tin mine was restored to operation. By re-establishing the General Labour Union (GLU) the Party was able to offer valuable introductions to itinerant workers. The GLU also incorporated many guilds and labour-contracting gangs, and attracted numerous individual workers, such as trishaw riders, barbers and cabaret girls.[24]

The Party was well placed and well prepared to assume the leadership of the whole Chinese community which, in Singapore and the Federation of Malaya added together, was the biggest single racial community, having 45 per cent of the total compared with 43 per cent Malays.[25] (The Malays had the majority in the Federation and the Chinese in Singapore.)

In addition to its labour and other activities, the Party sponsored numerous schools. Though most of these were only small elementary schools, they offered Chinese children an opportunity for education to which until the pre-war educational system had been re-established, there was often no alternative. These schools improved the party image, provided a splendid opportunity to influence the young Chinese, and gave employment for Party members.[26]

This last is a point often overlooked by Europeans. Like most Asian Communist Parties, the MCP had always expected many of its members to be full-time Party workers, and in the post-war period there were particularly good opportunities for this, not only in the legal party organization, but in unions, front groups and schools; also in running Communist-sponsored business enterprises such as book-stores, coffee shops and small general stores. The Party membership in the Federation and Singapore was nearly 3,000 (as high as it was ever to be throughout the Emergency – remembering that no more than a minority of guerrillas or supporters ever became

Party members), and their activities enabled the Party to meet its budgetary needs. By controlling the income of most of its members, the Party was also able to maintain discipline. Indeed, it discouraged its members from finding outside employment.

It soon became clear that the activities of the GLU were too wide to be adjusted to the registration requirements of the Trade Union Ordinances, particularly as the governments of Singapore and the Federation of Malaya were separate. The Party desired at this time that its open activities should have legal status, so the GLU split into two Federations – the Singapore Federation of Trade Unions (SFTU) and the Pan-Malayan Federation of Trade Unions (PMFTU) both of which were duly registered with their respective governments.[27] They made little secret of their Communist affiliation. Indeed, in Singapore, the SFTU played a more prominent part in running Communist affairs than the Open Party organization.

Their preoccupation with legality, and the desire to attain power by constitutional means (or by nothing more violent than 'peaceful agitation') was a dominating factor in the activities of the MCP during 1946. This is by no means inconsistent with the fact that the Secretary-General, Lai Tek, almost certainly was (or had been) a British agent. This fact would only have been known to a very small number of Police Special Branch officers and senior government officials, and it would have been normal intelligence practice for them to allow him full rein to organize as much 'peaceful agitation' as was necessary to maintain the credibility of his position as Secretary-General.[28] Indeed, in the post-war period, some may have been content that he, as a 'moderate', should lead the MCP into respectable participation in the political life and even the government of the country, rather than have the Party led by a firebrand into its more normal revolutionary opposition.[29]

Fong Feng, one of Mao Tse Tung's Central Committee, may well have been influenced by hopes of British gullibility when, at a meeting in Hong Kong in 1946, he advised Lai Tek not to embark on armed insurrection, but to organize a United Front and work for self-government by constitutional means.[30]

A Change of Leader

Nevertheless, Lai Tek did not last for much longer. Within the MCP there was growing dissatisfaction with progress. Although the Party was confident in early 1947 that it had achieved control of labour, this power did not seem to be used to much effect. In the face of economic recovery and social progress in Malaya, the MCP appeared to be losing its position of leading the people towards a better life. Moreover, the rank and file were complaining that too much of the Party's income was going into providing Western-style homes, cars and other bourgeois comforts for its open leaders.[31]

Lai Tek's treacherous dealings with the Japanese, moreover, were now proven beyond doubt in the eyes of the Central Committee. Once his Japanese protection had been removed, and communication between the city and the rural areas had become free, he was bound to be found out. His remaining unexposed for so long is a testimony to his cleverness, and to the legendary reputation he had built up in 1943–5 amongst the guerrillas – most of whom had never seen him. The problem facing the Central Committee in 1947 was how to expose and dispose of him without doing irreparable damage to party morale. The Party document which finally set out his misdeeds had to be most clearly and convincingly stated as its authors obviously feared that it might be impossible to believe.[32]

It was hoped initially, however, not to raise the dangerous issue of his treachery at all, but to oust him on grounds of inefficiency. At a meeting of the Central Committee in February 1947, his leadership was openly attacked. The meeting broke into uproar, and was adjourned until 6 March. Lai Tek never reappeared and was found later to have decamped with the bulk of the Party's funds.[33]

Chin Peng was unanimously elected as the new Secretary General, and wasted no time in responding to the desire of the Party for more militant action. 1947 has been described as 'The Year of Strikes'. There were no less than 300 major strikes involving the loss of 696,036 working days.[34]

These strikes continued, with growing use of violence, through into 1948, under the open and militant leadership of the PMFTU and SFTU. Of the 289 unions in Malaya only 86 were fully independent. Another 86 were of doubtful allegiance and the other 117 were federated in the PMFTU.[35]

Similar domination had been achieved in Singapore by undisguised violence and intimidation. For example, the Singapore Harbour Board Employees Union (SHBEU), an unfederated union, had in May 1946 successfully negotiated a 20 per cent wage increase for its men. This kind of success by an unfederated union was not acceptable to the MCP and feelings ran particularly high because the Kuomintang was behind the SHBEU.[36] The president of the SHBEU was repeatedly beaten up until in September 1946 he was driven out of Singapore. On 25 October harbour workers were kept out by pickets while the SHBEU offices were destroyed. An unregistered Communist-run body calling itself the Singapore Harbour Labourers Union (SHLU) announced that it had taken over from the SHBEU, which in fact remained out of action until late in 1947. In January 1948, the SHBEU reappeared and, with another unfederated union, opposed a strike called by the SHLU, and initially succeeded in persuading 30 to 40 per cent of the total labour force to continue work for the first night shift. Next day, however, they too were intimidated into stopping work.[37]

The SHLU was again prominent when the SFTU called a general strike on 23-4 April 1948. A police raid on their premises uncovered documents concerning a 'Singapore Workers Protection Corps', which gave clear evidence of the use of threats to intimidate people who did not support their activities. Four men were arrested, and at their trial one of these was reprimanded by the judge for giving the clenched fist salute to his supporters in court.[38]

Immediately after the General Strike, in which they claimed that 52,000 had participated, the SFTU planned a May Day rally of 100,000, to be followed by a march in procession five miles long.[39] The SFTU demanded that they, and not the police, should be responsible for controlling this procession. Had the government agreed to this, it would have been interpreted as a sign of weakness.[40] The police, however, while agreeing to the rally, forbade the procession on grounds of interference with traffic. The SFTU announced that they would defy the ban on the procession, and the government thereupon banned the rally as well, making it clear that this ban would be enforced by the police, if necessary supported by troops.[41] Next day, the SFTU decided to call off the entire demonstration.[42]

There was no doubt that the majority of the people of Singapore were relieved that the Government's firmness had averted a violent demonstration. There was little sign of public resentment at the threatened use of troops, since the Communists had, as on every previous occasion in which there had been use or threat of use of troops, provided ample reason for expecting a breach of the peace, and the people were getting tired of it.[43]

The people were also getting tired of the constant interruption of their livelihood by strikes, and with the intimidation of those who failed to support these strikes. They had few financial reserves, and cared more about earning a reasonable living than they did about the wider social and political issues.[44] The unions, too, were themselves becoming exasperated with the dictatorial attitude of the two Communist Federations,[45] who had demanded that 20 per cent of the union contributions be paid into their funds.[46]

The Government Reacts

In June 1948 the Government felt confident enough of these sentiments to introduce some fairly drastic legislation to curb the Communist penetration and manipulation of the trade unions. First, no one was permitted to hold office in a trade union, except as Secretary, unless he had had at least three years' experience in the industry or trade concerned. Secondly, anyone convicted of extortion, intimidation and similar crimes was prohibited from holding office. Thirdly, no federation of trade unions could be registered except on an industry or occupation basis.[47] These measures, which were introduced only a few days before the declaration of the State of Emergency, proved effective and were accepted with equanimity by the bulk of the working population. Within two weeks, the officers of the two de-registered Federations had taken to the jungle,[48] to join the MPAJA, now renamed the Malayan Peoples Anti-British Army (MPABA), which had already launched a growing wave of violence in the rural areas of the Federation (see Chapter 9).

Peaceful agitation had failed. At a meeting of the Asia Youth Conference in Calcutta in February 1948, delegates from all Asian Communist Parties, including the MCP, had meanwhile been urged to seize power 'by any means'.[49] It is notable that within a few months, armed rebellions had broken out in Burma, Indochina, Malaya, Indonesia and the Philippines. While there were other powerful reasons for their doing so, the Calcutta conference no doubt played some part in prompting the MCP to remobilize the guerrilla army and to go over to the phase of the 'armed struggle' in Malaya.[50]

The effect of this mobilization was to switch the revolution firmly from the urban to the rural strategy. This rural campaign will be discussed in later chapters. The effect of the decision on Singapore was to reverse the change of 1945, and the strength of the Singapore Communist Town Committee, District and Branch organization, which had been raised from fifty to three to four hundred in 1945–6, now fell again to about a hundred.

This chapter has broadly described the sequence of events during the Communist attempt at an urban revolution in the period 1945–8. The next chapter describes the Communist Party's internal structure in Singapore, and the technique for activating the public which it used during this same period.

Chapter 3 The Communist Party Structure in Singapore – 1946–50

The Open and Secret Organizations of the Party

The Singapore Town Committee of the MCP was responsible directly to the Central Committee of the Party, and ranked equally with any of the dozen or so State and Regional Committees in the Federation.

The Party structure under the Town Committee was in line with the main Front Organizations: the trade unions, the Women's Organizations, the Democratic Youth League and the ex-MPAJA Old Comrades Association. These provided a machinery for organizing and activating working men, women and students – a comprehensive cover. All were open and legal, and not difficult to recognize as Communist – indeed, people joining them had little doubt about the source of their direction.[1] The SFTU and PMFTU and the unions they controlled again left no one in any doubt, by their militancy and their methods, that they were Communist organizations, but even they made perfunctory denials of this for the public record, presumably to avoid handing the government a ready-made reason which would be accepted by the public for banning them if the Party itself were banned.

Paradoxically, the secret elements of the Party were far stronger in 1947 when the Party was legal and its Front organizations militantly Communist in everything but name, than they were later when the Party was illegal. This is in fact more sensible than it looks at first sight. Like the leaders of the open political Party (see Chapter 2), the semi-secret members were also vulnerable. For example, the legal Committees of the federated trade unions, and of the other Front organizations, were heavily penetrated by Party members who held many of the key posts on the Committees often including that of Secretary. These Party Groups, as they were known, were supposed to conceal their Party membership. Apart from study, they did no underground work and attended no Party meetings, but simply received instructions to influence the decisions of the legal Committees in which they worked to suit the Party's plans. Nevertheless these decisions were often so militant that the Party Groups were not difficult to detect.[2]

Within the rank and file of the unions and other Front organizations, therefore, there was an entirely separate structure of Party workers operating in cells which held regular clandestine meetings but whose members held no overt office in the unions or associations concerned. They concealed their Communist affiliation and their links with each other, and their work was wholly secret. The lower their position in the hierarchy the more directly they worked on the masses, and therefore the greater was their risk of compromise. To reduce this risk, however, the members of the Party Group on the legal Union Committee themselves did not know the identity of the underground workers within their own unions.[3]

The control of these two structures is shown in Figure 3, which also traces as an example the chain of command from Town Committee to one particular trade union, the Trishaw Riders Union.

The total number of Party members in Singapore reached a peak of 300 to 400 in 1947. Six of these were members of the Town Committee, each of whom was personally responsible for (and the sole contact with) one or more of the Guidance Committees, whose meetings he would attend.

In turn, each member of a Guidance Committee would be responsible for one of the unions etc. in his group, e.g. one of the three members of the Transport Workers Guidance Committee was responsible for the Bus Workers Union, another for Taxis and miscellaneous workers and the third for the Trishaw Riders Union.

The responsibility of this member was exercised through the two separate arms which he controlled – the Party Group which dominated the legal and open trade union committee and the underground Party workers within that union. In the case of the Party Groups, because of the open nature of their work, these contacts would normally be through a courier or cut-off man to protect the Guidance Committee Member.

The underground Party workers were organized (Fig. 4) in Party cells, normally only one within each trade union. Each cell member would control the work of one or more 'Anti-British League' (ABL) cells, perhaps one in each branch of the union, each of which would in turn recruit and control a number of 'sympathizer' cells or committees. These three grades of cell can be compared with 'University' (Party), 'High School' (ABL) and 'Primary School' (Sympathizers). Lee Kuan Yew wrote that 'the ABL relation to the MCP is like that of the volunteer force to the regular professional army'.[4] The sympathizer cells were the most expendable, and would handle

SINGAPORE COMMUNIST PARTY ORGANIZATION – 1947

Town Committee

Transport Workers Guidance Committee

Similar Guidance Committees for

Rubber Workers | Water Front and Harbour Board | Misc. Workers (Barbers, Shopworkers) | Women's Association | Youth | Schools

each with a similar structure

Members responsible for:
Buses   Taxis   Trishaws
and misc.

Party Group (B) comprising Secretary and two members of Trishaw Riders Union Committee
|
Normal Trade Union Machinery (1,000 members)

Branch cell (C) of MCP for Trishaw Riders Union
|
Anti-British League (ABL) and Sympathizer Cells
(not Party Members)

Propaganda Committee
|
Editing Committee for Party News

Committee Supervising Open Legal Activities of the Party
|
Open Political Leaders of the Communist Party

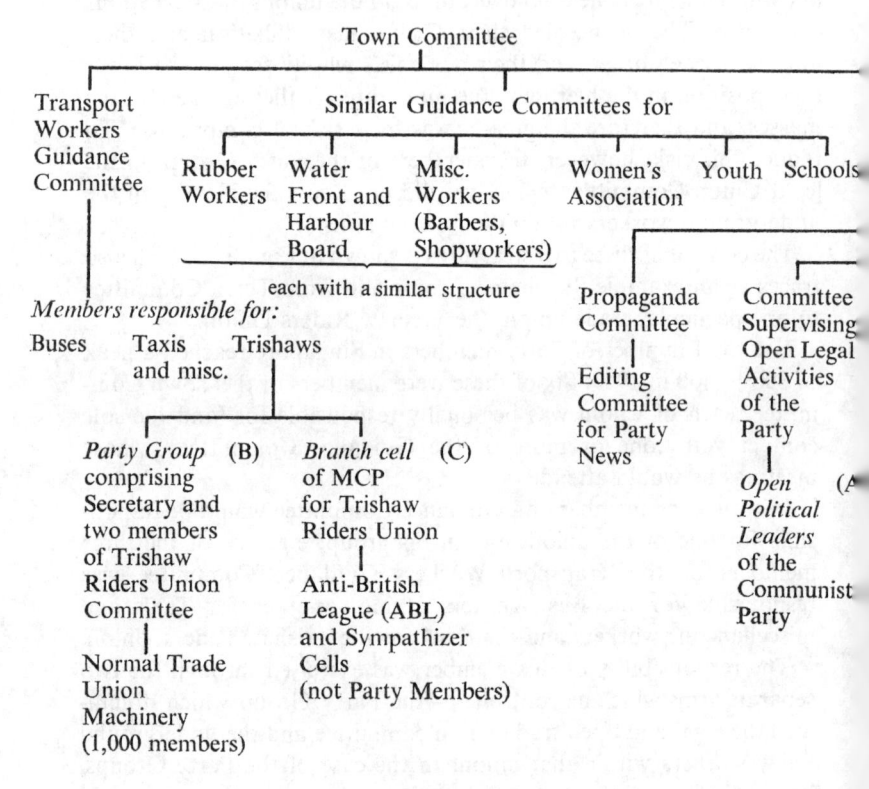

(A)

Figure 3

The three main elements of the Party organization at working level are shown at (A), (B) and (C).
(A) The Open political leaders (when the Party was legal)
(B) The semi-secret Party Groups – holding public offices which they could manipulate to suit the Party, but concealing their Party membership.
(C) The secret Party cell members. Their existence was known, but the identity of individual members was not known to (A) or (C).

as much as possible of the contact with the masses. Their tasks were threefold: first, to detect and report grievances amongst the workers which had potential for exploitation; secondly to activate the workers to demand redress for their grievances; and thirdly to recruit others into the cell system who had leadership potential. Thus the cell system grew downwards, whilst its more successful members graduated upwards through the ABL cells to probationary, and finally to full Party membership. The top Party cells organizing the underground workers reported directly to the responsible member of their

MCP CELL ORGANIZATION IN SINGAPORE – 1947–50

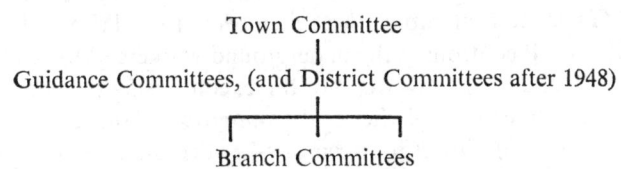

Town Committee
|
Guidance Committees, (and District Committees after 1948)

Branch Committees
Supervised by one member of Guidance or District Committee
Branch Committee Secretary (BCS)
2 or 3 Branch Committee Members (BCM)

Party Cell	Party Cell	Party Cell	Party Members
ABL Cell	ABL Cell	ABL Cell	Anti-British League Future
Sympathizer Cell	Sympathizer Cell	Sympathizer Cell	Party Members

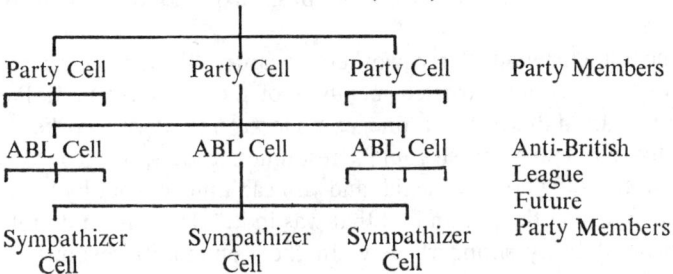

Figure 4

1. BCS and BCMs each attend and supervise meetings of one of their subordinate cells. Size of cells normally 3, but not rigid.
2. Similarly each Party cell member and each ABL cell member supervises one subordinate cell.
3. In theory, the maximum number of people any member knew was about 6 – one supervisor from above, two fellow cell members and three in the cell he supervised.
4. In practice, there were large gaps in this structure, of which both those above and below were often unaware.

Guidance Committee, who would, when appropriate, warn the Party Group on the legal union committee to be ready to receive and back the demands activated by the cells as coming from the 'grass roots'.[5] Meanwhile, the Guidance Committee would keep the Town Committee informed, so that they could judge the potential of the grievances and the temper of the workers in particular industries, and decide how and when to provoke and co-ordinate strikes and demonstrations.

This system was particularly effective in the control of transport and the Town Committee was able in 1946 and 1947 to bring the whole transport system of Singapore to a halt at its command. The total number of full Party members involved in the entire transport field was probably less than twenty-five. In the case of the Trishaw Riders Union the number was seven: the responsible member of the Guidance Committee, three members of the Trishaw Union cell of the MCP controlling the underground workers (ABL and sympathizers), and the Party Group of three, comprising the Secretary and two other members of the legal Committee of the Trishaw Riders Union (Fig. 3). Given fourteen days' notice by the Guidance Committee, this team was able to bring grievances to a head and bring all the 1,000 Trishaw Riders out on a 'bona fide' strike on a pre-arranged date, together with the bus, taxi and other transport drivers.

The underground Party workers regarded themselves as more important and more trusted members of the Party than the Party Groups. In the words of one ex-underground Party worker: 'It was like a pot; the British could arrest union leaders, but they would just be grabbing hold of the lid, and you can't move a pot by holding its lid. We held the pot and all that was in it.'[6] There is no doubt an element of Party snobbery here. In the Communist revolutionary tradition secrecy is a status symbol. Nevertheless, the more open elements, the open leadership at the top and the sympathizer cells at the bottom, were the ones which activated the masses and led the strikes, demonstrations and riots which were the main weapons whereby the Party tried to coerce the government into making concessions. As will be seen later, when the Party made its second major attempt at an urban revolution in Singapore in 1954–6 it concentrated almost all its efforts into Party Groups running the Front organizations and spared little effort for an élite Party cell structure barred by its secrecy from any positive leadership of the people. Ideally, the Party has both, but the more open elements should not be too contemptuously dismissed as mere 'front men'. It is equally wrong, however, to underestimate the tremendous strength and resilience provided by the secret organization, which enables it to survive drastic government action against the open organization, and to go on building up the strength of the Party from below through its clandestine sympathizer cells.

Recruitment and Advancement

Recruitment to sympathizer cells was done mainly by encouraging the livelier spirits to join the team of active leaders of generally popular causes; for example, amongst students, the safeguarding of Chinese education and, later, opposition to conscription; for workers, the seeking of better wages and conditions; for rural smallholders, opposition to eviction or, when this failed, obtaining fair compensation; for women, the campaign for equal treatment and pay; and for all, the crusade against colonialism and oppression (Fig. 4).

Sympathizer cells met for indoctrination and study, also to plan and report on Party work. Their work included the more recognizable and vulnerable activities, such as slogan-painting and (later) the destruction of identity cards and the distribution of propaganda. It also included supply work (when necessary) and the acquisition of information about the Security Forces and 'Traitors'. Cell members who were doing full-time paid work for the Party in fact generally lived on the subscriptions collected by their subordinates from Party members and sympathizers. (This is also a quite normal method of taxation and payment of government officials in many parts of Asia.) Children and teenagers were also brought in, to carry local messages and acquire information.

The feeling of being members of a secret brotherhood is exciting for anyone young, and particularly for the Chinese, who have always felt the need to join some kind of secret society. To many of them the MCP was a more attractive alternative than the traditional and now largely criminal Chinese Secret Societies.[7] It would be wrong to picture them as taking part in some dark and destructive conspiracy – at least in their own eyes. There were plenty of things that needed putting right in post-war Singapore and Malaya, and there was much genuine idealism in their attitude. To join a club or society or union was often to fulfil a desire to join an active group of kindred spirits who knew where they were going. To join a sympathizer cell was to join the élite of this group.

Lee Kuan Yew,[8] though writing of a later period (1953–6), frankly admits their idealism and their strength.

'The strength of the MCP lies in the propagation of Communist theories and ideals to recruit able and idealistic young men and women to join them in their cause . . .

'The Communists, though they had only a few hundred active cadres, could muster and rally thousands of people in the unions, cultural organizations and student societies . . .

'By working and manifestly appearing to work selflessly and ceaselessly, they won the confidence and regard of the people in the organizations . . .'[9]

'The strength of the Communist Party lies not in their mass as such but in the band of trained and disciplined cadres who lead the masses into Communist causes, often without the masses knowing they are Communist . . .

'The Communists always do this. Exploit a real or imaginary grievance through cadres and sympathizers not generally known to be connected with them.'

There was also a strong element of reaction against the older generation of Chinese. Many young people despised their parents because they were illiterate, or because their ideas seemed outmoded and subservient. Even children from middle-class homes found the lively political discussions amongst their friends in the front organizations a great deal more stimulating than conversations at home. Marxism seemed a dynamic and positive philosophy. They gradually became aware that most of the leading spirits, the people they most admired, were Marxists. To find themselves invited to take part in clandestine cell meetings with one of these people was exciting and rewarding.[10]

Graduation to a higher cell (of the Anti-British League) was the next stage. This involved more secret indoctrination and training, and after one or two years a promising candidate would be invited to become a probationary member of the Party. After a further six to twelve months, he might be initiated as a full Party member.

This was a typical pattern of recruitment and graduation, but it would be wrong to visualize it as the standard or sole procedure for getting people involved in Party affairs. The Party Group, for example, also attracted promising members of the ordinary committees of trade unions and other organizations into supporting them at committee meetings. These people became well aware that the 'activists' on the committee were Communists, but neither of them would mention this until the Communist felt sure enough of his man to tell him of his affiliation and invite him to join a secret study group.

Douglas Hyde has described an interesting parallel from his own experience as a Communist in subverting members of a local branch of the British Labour Party in the 1930s. On arrival in the area he joined the branch, attended meetings, spoke and attracted friends. After a time he was elected to the Executive Committee. Amongst his friends he selected those whom he considered worth converting to Communism and worked to get them elected to the Committee. Meanwhile, he converted them to Communism secretly, one by one, unknown to the others. At the meetings of the Committee these converts formed a 'Ginger Group'. One day, when he judged the time ripe, he assembled the Ginger Group and announced, to their surprise, that all present were members of the Communist Party. Thereafter they acted as a secret Party Group, retaining their executive positions on the Committee.[11]

He also described how similar secret Party factions operated within trade union committees, planning strategy and tactics for meetings, getting members onto committees, and organizing majorities for snap votes on key issues. These factions would meet as much as nine months before the annual conference to select resolutions to be fostered and plan how to get them through.[12]

The Student Organization

Subversion in the schools had certain differences from that in labour and other front organizations, chiefly because the population was constantly moving: a boy scarcely had time to graduate through the sympathizer and ABL cells before he was in his last year. For this same reason, it was also more difficult for Special Branch to keep track of the cell members so that the student organization in the event proved the most resilient of all in surviving disruption by the government. The student organization was not really laid bare until 1956, after a major showdown, and its description will therefore be deferred until that period is discussed, in Chapters 4, 5 and 6. It was to play a vital part in the survival of an element of the Party structure in Singapore through the very difficult years following the outbreak of the Emergency and the proscription of the MCP in 1948, and really came into its own in 1954, when it provided both the leadership and the organization for the second attempt at activating an urban revolution in Singapore.

There was a small but very important element of the student organization amongst the English-speaking students at the University of Malaya (which was in Singapore). This had originated from the Malayan Democratic Union which had been formed in 1945, and it attracted a number of very able young lawyers, teachers, etc. (known to the Special Branch as the 'English-Speaking Intelligentsia' (ESI)) who would undoubtedly have provided a most effective team of open-front political leaders, able to argue with the best and to present their case to the world press. Though the ESI was successfully unearthed and broken up by the Special Branch in 1951, many of its members reappeared as Open Front leaders in 1954, including James Puthucheary, S. Woodhull and Devan Nair.[13]

1948 – A Drastic Reorganization

In June 1948, the combined effect of the Government's trade union legislation (see Chapter 2), the MCP's decision to mobilize in the jungle, and the imposition of Emergency Regulations left the Singapore Town Committee with only forty to fifty members, and forced it to undertake a drastic reorganization. Its main structure in the trade unions was replaced by a district organization. There were four District Committees, one District covering the Western part of the island, and particularly the Bukit Timah factory area, the second covering the naval base and the villages and factories in the north part of the island, and the other two covering the city itself, divided by the Singapore river into North and South. In addition, there were Women's and Students' Committees. The Town Committee was reduced to five and later to three members, each of whom, including the Secretary, supervised the work of one or more of the District or other Committees (Fig. 5).

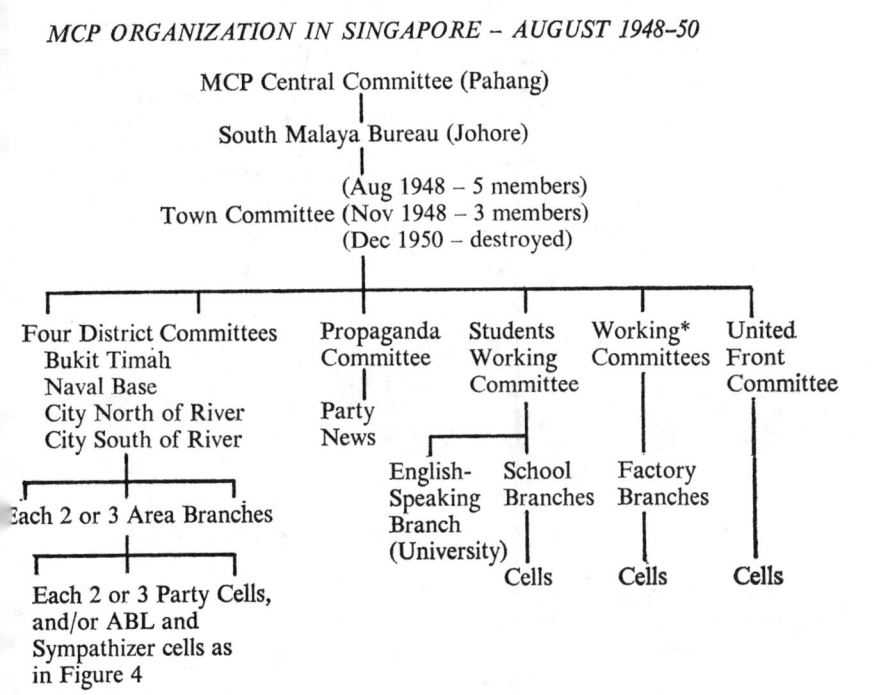

MCP ORGANIZATION IN SINGAPORE – AUGUST 1948-50

```
                MCP Central Committee (Pahang)
                            |
                South Malaya Bureau (Johore)
                            |
                    (Aug 1948 – 5 members)
            Town Committee (Nov 1948 – 3 members)
                    (Dec 1950 – destroyed)
```

Four District Committees	Propaganda	Students	Working*	United
Bukit Timah	Committee	Working	Committees	Front
Naval Base		Committee		Committee
City North of River	Party			
City South of River	News			

```
                        English-    School      Factory
                        Speaking    Branches    Branches
                        Branch
                        (University)
                                    Cells       Cells       Cells
Each 2 or 3 Area Branches

Each 2 or 3 Party Cells,
and/or ABL and
Sympathizer cells as
in Figure 4
```

Figure 5
Total Party Strength in Singapore – August 1948 – 40 to 50.
November 1948 – About 100.

* The Working Committees had a rather sporadic existence and factory branches often operated under the district organization.

A Tightening of Security in the MCP in Singapore

In July 1948 the Party was declared illegal, and the police had the power to detain without trial. Most of the known Communists had taken to the jungle, and many others had been arrested. A Front organization leader could no longer enjoy the luxury of letting it be generally known that he was pro-Communist with no more than a

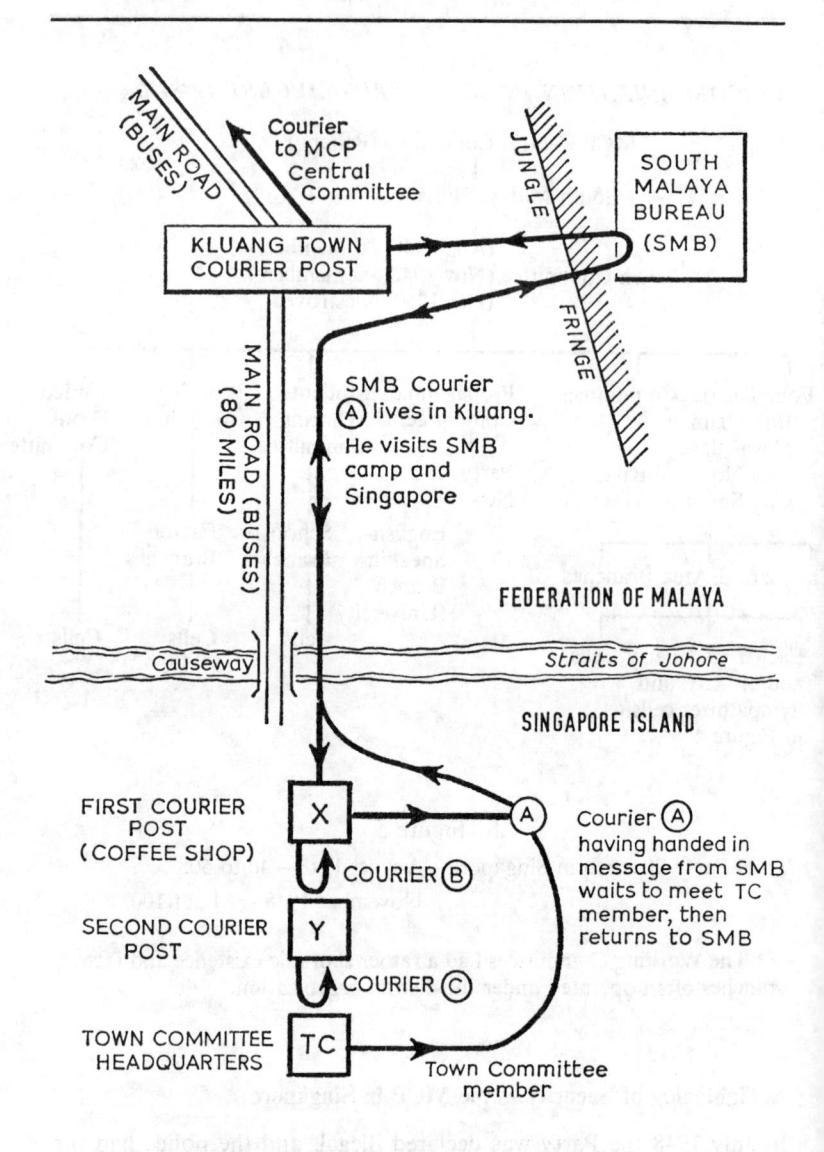

Figure 6 MCP Communication System from the Jungle to Singapore, 1948–50

perfunctory public denial. He now had to conceal it – or go into hiding. A marked increase in security was necessary.

The Singapore Communist Party was, of course, part of the MCP and had its links with the Central Committee in Malaya. These links were through the South Malaya Bureau (SMB) to which the Singapore Town Committee was subordinate. The SMB was located in the jungle near Kluang, about seventy miles north of Singapore. Communications between the SMB and Singapore were by a system of couriers and cut-outs shown in Figure 6. Nearly all the couriers were women. Only one courier (A) knew the location of the SMB camp and she lived in Kluang town.[14] She would travel by bus to Singapore where she would go to a Courier Post (X) – usually a coffee shop. She would wait here while her presence was reported by another courier (B), to a second Courier Post (Y). From this, a third courier (C) would pass the word to the Town Committee (TC).

A member of the Town Committee would then go direct to the first Courier Post (X) to meet the SMB Courier (A) face to face to enable her to transmit at least some of the personalities of the respective Bureau and Committee members to each other, and either to develop a little of the theme of the written messages, or give direct verbal messages, thereby avoiding the risk of carrying any written messages at all.

A few years later these security measures became tighter. Nevertheless, the personal meetings between the Town Committee Members and the SMB Courier did not compromise the complex security barriers imposed by the multiple courier posts as much as they would seem to at first sight. The aim of these barriers was to avoid compromising the base, or headquarters of the Town Committee, where it held meetings every two to four weeks. A raid on this could wipe out the whole Committee at one blow, unknown to the rest of the party, as did indeed happen later, but the hazarding of a single member was worth while to gain the advantages described in the previous paragraph.

In the cell system itself, security was always intense. With the experience of several generations in clandestine revolutionary activity, the Communist Party always assumes that some amongst its ranks will defect or be captured, and that they will talk. As soon as a cell member (M) made a slip (Fig. 7), or his supervisor (L) from the cell above suspected that he might be compromised, he (M) would be

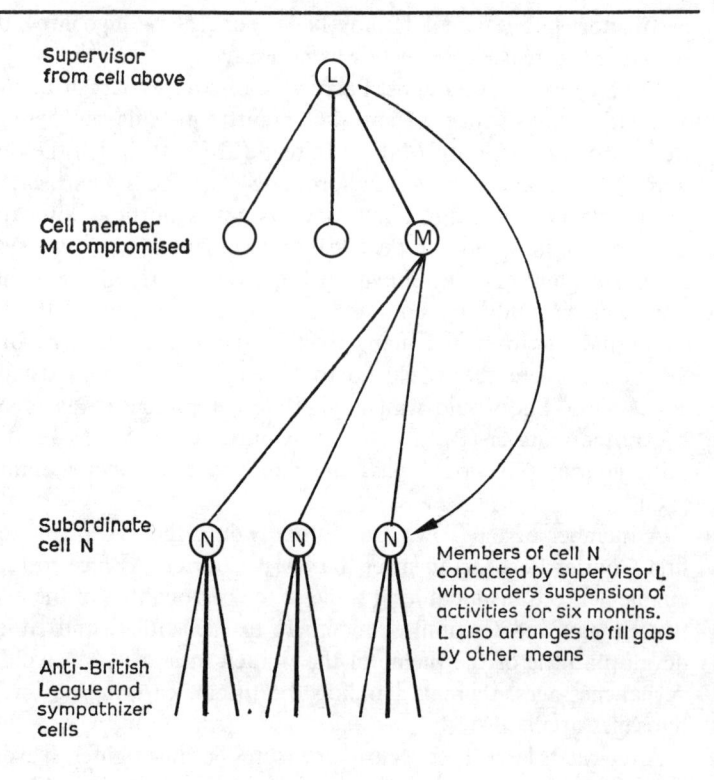

Figure 7 Security Procedure if MCP Cell Member Compromised

Supervisor from cell above: L

Cell member M compromised

Subordinate cell N

Members of cell N contacted by supervisor L who orders suspension of activities for six months. L also arranges to fill gaps by other means

Anti-British League and sympathizer cells

dropped and never trusted again. The supervisor would warn the subordinate cells under M's direction (N) to cease operating, usually for about six months.

If M then betrayed them to the police, the police would start watching the members of this subordinate cell, but would find them doing nothing, and giving no leads into the ABL or sympathizer cells below them.

Supervisor L would at the same time organize the filling of the gaps, to replace M, and to continue the activities of cell N, including the direction of its three subordinate cells. This would not be easy, because L would not know the names of the members of cell N. He would, however, know their places of work and their party names, and would have other information about them from past reports on their activities by M. With or without M's assistance (depending on the nature of his compromise) L would establish contact with the members of cell N, and find out enough from them about their subordinate cells for him to arrange for someone else to take over their supervision – probably with sufficient alteration to guard against their compromise in the event of members of cell N being questioned by the police as a result of betrayal by M. The other various overlapping and cross-checking systems (such as Party Groups, and Party members who have moved from elsewhere to work in the same factories etc. as cell N members) would also be of some assistance to L.

Nevertheless, the security precautions were so complicated that not only were there large gaps in the MCP cell organization, but also the leaders at the top and the rank and file themselves often unaware of them. People such as L would, if they could, conceal the shortcomings and defections amongst their subordinates, as the image of a solid, loyal, well-recruited structure under them would most impress their superiors. Similarly, the morale of Party workers in the cells subordinate to N would be better for not knowing of M's defection or arrest. They too were, therefore, presented with the image of a solid structure above them.

The Arrest of the Town Committee

The Communist organization in Singapore, however, was shattered in December 1950 by the arrest of the entire Town Committee. An alert police detective spotted two men at a bus stop exchanging newspapers in a rather suspicious manner, as if there might be messages inside them – which in fact there were. He pursued and arrested them, finding them in possession of incriminating documents. One was the Secretary of the Town Committee himself and the documents gave leads to the remainder of the Town Committee.[15] Their arrest left the MCP in Singapore leaderless through the most critical period of the Malayan Emergency, and it was not until 1954 that it resumed any significant part in the revolution.

The Hertogh Riots

In the same month of December occurred the most unexpected riots in Singapore during the whole of the period under review, and the most serious in terms of bloodshed. These riots had nothing to do with the Communists. Their significance lay in the weaknesses which they revealed in the Singapore police force. The action to remedy these weaknesses produced a force whose control of the organization became the envy of visitors from all over the world,[16] and which was to prove itself in the later riots in 1954–6.

The riots in December 1950 arose out of a lawsuit over the custody of Maria Hertogh, the thirteen-year-old daughter of Dutch-Eurasian parents, who had been born in 1937 and baptized as a Catholic. In 1943 her parents had been arrested in Java by the Japanese, and Maria had been cared for by an Indonesian/Malay family who had subsequently moved to north-eastern Malaya and had brought up the girl as a Moslem.

Her parents discovered where she was in 1948 and claimed her back. In May 1950 the Dutch Consul in Singapore obtained a Court Order for her custody. This order was, however, reversed on a legal technicality in July. Maria returned to her foster parents and was rushed through a marriage ceremony with a Malay, which was within Moslem law, but contrary to Dutch and British law, and aroused great indignation in Holland and amongst many Christians in Singapore. A further Court hearing led to Maria's removal from her Malay 'husband' to a Catholic convent in Singapore. He in turn appealed, and it was the hearing of this appeal at the Singapore Supreme Court which led to the rioting. By this time, the Singapore Moslems (both Malay and Indian/Pakistani) had been aroused to high passion over the issue, and in particular against the European and Eurasian communities.

The seventy constables deployed outside the Supreme Court were Malays. This was both unwise and unnecessary because, although the Singapore police force was 90 per cent Malay, it did include about 400 Indians (some admittedly Moslem) and a contingent of 119 Gurkhas especially trained for dealing with riots – a force of particular value in a multi-racial city.

The Malay constables, who had been subjected to considerable propaganda by the Moslem 'Action Committee' which led the campaign for Maria Hertogh's custody, allowed a small crowd of demonstrators to pass through their ranks unopposed. The demonstration thereupon gathered momentum, and after one and a half hours a force of forty-eight Gurkhas was brought in. A number of the British police officers, however, showed the most deplorable indecision and misjudgement, and the Gurkhas were repeatedly moved up and then withdrawn (at the request of the demonstration leaders) in full view of the crowd. As a result, all respect for the police – Malay and Gurkha – disappeared. By the afternoon, mobs were ranging all over the island, dragging Europeans and Eurasians from cars and buses. During the evening and the night, they killed nine people and seriously injured another twenty-six. The army was called in just after dark, and next day had to open fire to restore order. In all, nine people were killed by the army and the police, bringing the total death toll to eighteen. It is a tribute to the normal efficiency of the police that, throughout the disturbed years of 1946–63, this was the highest death toll of any of the outbreaks of rioting during the whole period. In addition to the 18 killed, 173 were injured, 72 vehicles burned and another 119 damaged.[17]

Reorganization of the Police

It was clear that the demonstrations should never have developed into serious rioting, and the British Government sent out a Commission early in 1951 to investigate the matter. As a result of the Commission's Report, widespread changes were made in the police force. The establishment of junior officers (Inspectors) was trebled, and the increase was rapidly implemented by direct recruiting instead of only by promotion from the ranks. The number of Inspectors thus reached well over 300 during the next few years, many of them younger and better educated than before. In addition, sixty Police Lieutenants were recruited on short contracts. This rank was roughly equivalent to Sergeant-Major in the army, ranking below the Inspectors. Most of them were Europeans or Eurasians, some being British ex-Sergeants from the Palestine Police and from the army. Multi-racial Reserve Units were also formed, especially trained and equipped to reinforce the regular police in riots and other emergencies. The final (and perhaps most significant) improvement was the development of a highly efficient radio patrol system with a central Control Room manned for twenty-four hours. The Control headquarters had space to accommodate an army brigade command post to operate jointly with the police if needed. Each radio patrol car had a crew of five, often headed by a Police Lieutenant.[18] This joint control headquarters with its team of forty patrol cars was to prove a decisive weapon in the much more dangerous riots of 1956 (see Chapter 7).

Chapter 4 The Survival of the Student Organization – 1950–4

Resilience

At the time of the events described in the last chapter (December 1950) the tempo of the Emergency in the Federation was rising to its peak, and little attempt was made to rebuild the shattered Party organization in Singapore. During the following three years it suffered a further series of disasters, but through all these the student organization survived, even though the Town Committee member responsible for students had been captured in 1950. Its structure was as in Figure 8.

The organization was confined to schools using the Chinese language as the medium of education (i.e. the Chinese Middle Schools)[1] with the exception of a short-lived but influential English-speaking branch in the University of Malaya, which was broken up in 1951.

The Chinese schools were particularly vulnerable to Communist propaganda. There were no Chinese schools provided by the Government, and they were run with the voluntary support of rich Chinese philanthropists, and by governing bodies whose members were selected more on grounds of prestige than of knowledge of education. Teachers were underpaid and had little security in their jobs. The Chinese boys and girls in turn knew that, by being educated in their own language, their opportunities in Singapore would be less than those of their neighbours' children who were being educated in English. This caused an obvious feeling of resentment. Since their culture, and many of their teachers, emanated from a land which was now Communist, and whose Communist government enjoyed very high prestige at this time, these boys and girls made excellent material for MCP leadership against the injustices of their situation in Singapore. Little was done to tackle this situation until 1956 when a Commission on Education in Singapore was established, which was to get the Chinese schools within the national education system.[2]

THE SURVIVAL OF THE STUDENT ORGANIZATION

MCP STUDENT ORGANIZATION UP TO 1953

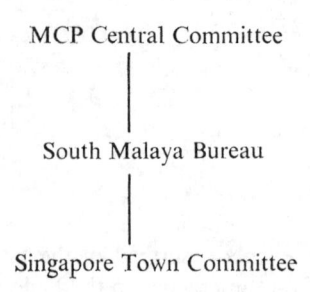

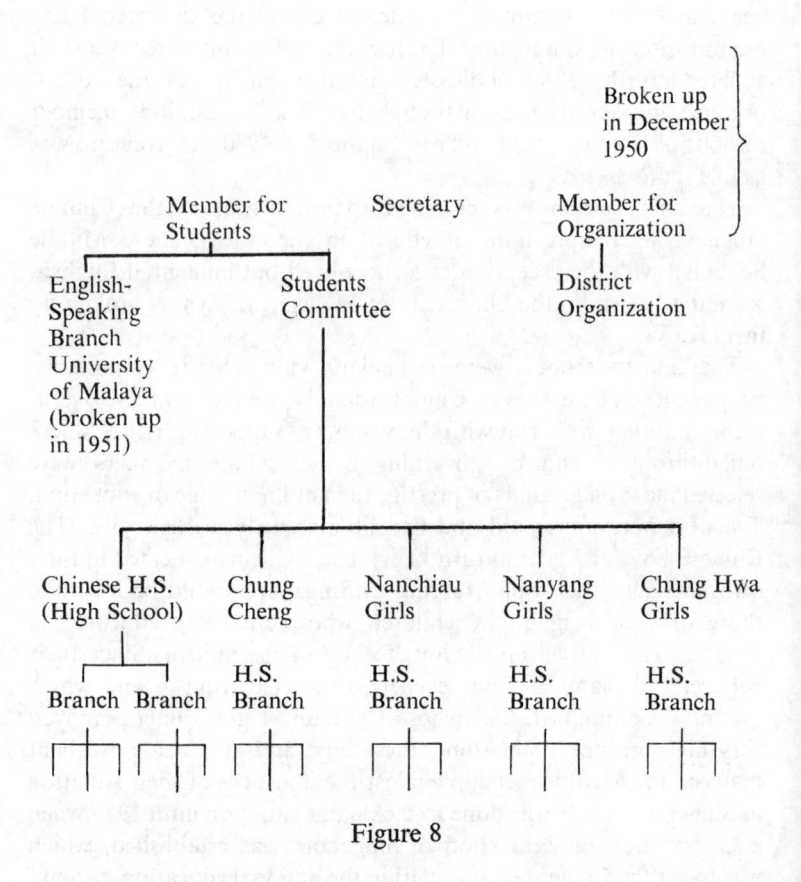

MCP Central Committee
|
South Malaya Bureau
|
Singapore Town Committee

Broken up in December 1950

Member for Students — Secretary — Member for Organization

English-Speaking Branch University of Malaya (broken up in 1951) — Students Committee — District Organization

Chinese H.S. (High School) | Chung Cheng | Nanchiau Girls | Nanyang Girls | Chung Hwa Girls

Branch Branch | H.S. Branch | H.S. Branch | H.S. Branch | H.S. Branch

Figure 8

But by this time the Communists had been able to use the Chinese schools as a focus for the most dangerous riots in Singapore's history.

After the destruction of the Town Committee in December 1950, all attempts to revive it were disrupted by Special Branch, but the Students' Committee and the District Committees did manage to reestablish tenuous contact with the Central Committee in the jungle. In 1953 Special Branch managed also to smash the entire District organization, but the Students' Committee and the Middle School branches still kept alive, and they continued to survive right through the defeat of the armed revolt in the jungle and the smashing of the second attempt at an urban revolt in Singapore in 1956. Indeed, they remain to this day a most active section of the Party in Singapore.[3]

This remarkable resilience was also described much later by Lee Kuan Yew, Prime Minister of Singapore:

'For years since the beginning of the Emergency in 1946, Communism has been painted in terms of violence, terror, brutality and evil. There was violence, there was brutality and there were evil men. But that is not the whole story. For if it was as simple as that, the Communists would have died and perished with the collapse of their armed revolt.

'It is because, together with these weaknesses, they have some strong qualities, that they have been able to survive in spite of the collapse of their armed revolt.

'... New recruits have been found. These are idealistic young men and women, largely from the Chinese Middle Schools of Malaya, both the Federation and Singapore . . . Partly by persuasion, mainly by fanaticism and faith that the future belongs to the Communists. These new recruits are continuing the struggle. They press on capturing the leadership of trade unions, cultural organizations and Old Boys' associations. Most important of all they try to capture the power to manipulate the lawful political parties.'[4]

Security – Strengths and Weaknesses

Another reason for the survival of the student organization, both as an activist organization and as a training ground for future party workers, was that its constant turnover of members made it very difficult for Special Branch to identify its leaders before fresh ones had taken their places, which compensated for the inevitable amateurishness of student Communist activities compared with those outside.

Security also was much looser amongst schoolboys, not only from lack of experience and restraint, but also because the penalties of discovery were far less, i.e. expulsion or, at worst, detention; whereas those organizing supplies or intelligence for the Party outside were liable to the death penalty.[5]

Party members inside the schools were rare, since it was almost impossible for a boy to graduate to full membership before leaving. Those who did were invariably over-age students of twenty or more, who were being allowed to make up for missing their schooling in the war. Furthermore, a student would rise out of the cell organization during his final year, confining his activities to the supervision of his successor who was in his penultimate year. This made him still harder to catch, and if the cell he supervised was compromised he was available to rebuild it.

ABL cell members maintained fairly tight security outside and did not tell their own families – even their wives (unless they were members also). On the other hand, they were not difficult for those on the fringes of the organization to recognize within the schools, as they were seen distributing Party News etc.[6] The Open Front leaders were even more generally known because of their constant exhortations and spouting of propaganda, though they did not openly admit to being Communists. The security of the remainder of the open organization was also poor, as will be described later in the chapter.

As outside, a boy who came under suspicion was ostracized by the Party as a matter of security. For example, 'Ching',[7] after three years of working up the school front organization and study cells (see Chapter 5), was found in possession of an incriminating document rolled up in a tiny gramophone-needle box. He was held and questioned by Special Branch for a month. On his return to school his friends in the cell system no longer trusted him, and he was also regarded askance by the staff. He therefore switched to an English school before going on to Nanyang University. He is now educated in both cultures and is strongly anti-Communist, so the Communists have been the losers.

The security at the top, however, was excellent, and the Party direction particularly difficult to spot as it came from outside the school. The outside supervisor had contact with a very select number of boys and girls at the top of the structure in the school, and these changed every year. Moreover, since subversive activities, unlike the organization of supplies or intelligence, could be carried out under general guidance promulgated in Party News, Wall Newspapers or even, in guarded terms, in the left wing press, direct contact between the Party supervisor and the cell structure inside the schools needed only to be rare.

The Schools as a Training Ground for Party Workers for the Jungle War

During 1951 the tide in the jungle war began to turn and the Central Committee issued its Directive of October 1951,[8] recognizing that unbridled violence was being counter-productive, and ordering a switch of emphasis to building up the popular base outside the jungle. The Middle Schools were specifically encouraged to play their part – though still with an eye on the rural rather than the urban campaign:

> 'Town organizations must train up working personnel to send out to operate in the rural areas. To this end it is very necessary for the Party to be active among Middle School Students . . .'[9]

There was an interesting example of this policy in action, which also presents a microcosm of open front student subversion in Malaya. In 1951 an over-age student in his twenties, 'Hong', came under suspicion for his Communist activities at the Chinese High School in Penang and decided to move to Singapore. Here his father, who was headmaster of a Primary School in Singapore, bought Hong a false School Certificate, thereby qualifying him to apply for a teaching post himself.

Hong met another Communist whom he had known at school some years previously and who was now headmaster of a Primary School at Ayer Baloi – about sixty miles away in South Johore. Hong, and later also his wife, were taken on as teachers. It was a small school, with only four teachers in all – the Headmaster, Hong, his wife and one non-Communist.

Hong, as well as teaching the primary school children, organized evening classes for Chinese boys of Middle School age. Most of these boys did daytime jobs, so this filled a need that could not be filled for most of them in any other way. Moreover, if they had found time

THE SURVIVAL OF THE STUDENT ORGANIZATION

to study at the nearest High School – in the small town of Pontian eight miles away – it would have cost $15 a month, whereas Hong only charged them twenty cents a month for paper etc. He attracted sixty boys from Ayer Baloi alone.

Thus far one could have nothing but praise for the spare-time service he was giving to the young Chinese in his district, but before long, inevitably, their academic studies were supplemented by political instruction, initially innocent enough, but gradually becoming more subversive.

The next step was for Ayer Baloi students to attract brothers, sisters and friends from Pontian to help as part-time instructors. They made a basket-ball pitch and invited teams from other schools. A liaison was established with Pontian High School, and likely sympathizers were sought out by asking seemingly innocent questions about social life in the school. Bacon and egg parties at Ayer Baloi and moonlight beach parties soon became the occasion for handing out propaganda publications. The next step was the formation of a secret cell system.

So far, Hong had acted entirely independently in accordance with his Communist training, but in 1952 he met an ex-MPAJA man who offered to put him in contact with the MCP in the jungle. Hong therefore addressed a letter to a member of the South Johore Regional Committee, Lee Hoi Fatt, asking for guidance.

The letter was in fact routed through the Pontian District Committee whose Secretary, Ah Chiau, was a young woman of great ability whose District was a model of Communist clandestine administration (see Chapter 14). She consulted Lee Hoi Fatt, who wanted to hear more. Ah Chiau therefore sent a message to Hong, asking him to park his car at a certain time a mile along the track into a pineapple estate from a certain milestone, and there to await instructions. She sent one of her contacts amongst the estate workers to fetch him, and handed him various Party publications (including, presumably, the appropriate portions of the October 1951 Directive). She congratulated him on what he had achieved, encouraging him particularly to develop the study cells,[10] and the secret side of his activities. There is little doubt that Hong's school thereafter turned out a considerable number of trained party workers well briefed on the strategy and tactics of the jungle war.

Special Branch knew nothing of these activities until the Regional Committee Member, Lee Hoi Fatt, was killed and a letter was found on his body. The handwriting was identified as Hong's by one of his former headmasters. Special Branch arrested Hong, his wife and the Ayer Baloi headmaster, together with twenty or thirty others. They told their story, but opted to be deported to China under the current surrender terms rather than become Special Branch agents to betray their comrades. Hong's wife has since returned to Malaya, and that is why he has been referred to by a pseudonym.

The Revival of the Urban Campaign in Singapore

By 1953 the war in the jungle was going very badly for the Communists, and the Politburo began to give more thought to the subversive campaign in the cities. Here too, however, they were having their troubles. In that same year the Party in Singapore, still a poor relation whose primary role was the support of the jungle war, suffered a series of further blows from Special Branch, who smashed up the entire district organization, leaving the resilient students' organization as virtually the only functioning element of the Party.

From 1954 onwards there was a marked revival of positive action towards an urban revolutionary situation in Singapore, though the weakness of the Party organization in the city necessitated concentrating most of the talent on open or semi-secret activities rather than on rebuilding a strong secret Party cell structure.[11]

It would be misleading to regard this as the result of a conscious appreciation of the situation in the Central Committee in the jungle, resulting in a decision to switch from a rural to an urban strategy, followed by an orderly promulgation of that decision to subordinate units. This would be to credit them with a sophisticated communication system (upwards for information and downwards for orders) such as exists in an established government but not in a clandestine guerrilla movement.[12] Nor would this be a normal practice for a Communist revolutionary movement – particularly one on the defensive. The MCP had no 'Master Plan', either regarding the emphasis on city or guerrilla revolution, or for Singapore itself. The Communists were never fully prepared, and their actions were dictated by events. The Party's policy (if such it can be called) was to expect all its workers to keep up the pressure in their own particular spheres reacting to 'objective conditions'.[13] The commonly used analogy of the rising tide creeping up the creeks and lapping at the sea walls does not really apply. The party workers can better be compared to an army of ants surrounded by water, each hunting persistently for a crossing, largely unaware of the activities of his comrades elsewhere on the perimeter. Even this analogy falls short, because as soon as a crossing is found – or more probably the water pushed back – not only do the other ants converge upon it, but many other less committed insects also join the successful ants and some become ants themselves.

Thus the swing towards an urban strategy should be regarded as a reaction to events and an exploitation of opportunities. Amongst the more important of these events and opportunities were:

(a) The massive reverses suffered by the Communists in the rural areas between 1951 and 1954, during which they lost two-thirds of their fighting strength, and support in the Chinese villages fell even more than that (see Chapter 9). The Central Committee had shown considerable foresight in attempting to forestall this by their October 1951 Directive, but they had failed to do so. In other words, there now seemed little hope of breaking out on the rural flank.

(b) The imminence of self-government, common talk through 1953, and culminating (in the case of Singapore) in the Rendel Constitutional Commission Report on 22 February 1954. This gave rise to the hope of the election of a weak liberal government, committed to relaxing irksome security restrictions, and thereby giving the Communists their chance – the 'fat bunny' regime which is the historic appetizer for urban revolutionaries.

(c) The relaxation of restrictions on trade union activities – also announced in the Rendel Report.

(d) The enforcement of the National Service Ordinance, under which Singapore students were required to register for conscription by 22 May 1954, on pain of six months in gaol or a fine of $2,000 or both.[14]

Only the student organization was in a position to lead the exploitation of these opportunities. This they did on 13 May 1954 in a violent demonstration against the National Service Ordinance. Five hundred demonstrated and twenty-six were injured (six police and twenty students). Forty-four boys and one girl were arrested, all over sixteen.[15] All were released next day on bail. Later, 1,000 locked themselves into the Chung Cheng High School, and were forced out next day.[16]

On 18 May a delegation fifty-five strong demanded that students be exempted from National Service. Their request was refused.[17]

A week later, the threat of further demonstrations led the Directors and Principals of ten[18] boys' and girls' high schools to close them by advancing the summer vacation by two weeks. Over 15,000 Chinese boys and girls were affected.[19]

On Saturday 22 May, the day after this announcement, 2,500 boys and girls locked themselves into the Chung Cheng High School.[20] At dawn next morning (Sunday) their parents, mainly mothers, came to fetch them out. The student leaders initially tried to prevent the parents from entering the school, but were later persuaded by the police to allow them to pass. The school was cleared without violence by 11 a.m.[21]

The National Service issue was a godsend for the MCP. To mobilize boys who, because of their Chinese education, would be given the poorest chances in the alien colonial society which they were being called upon to defend was a gift to Communist slogan writers. Moreover, it offered an anti-colonial issue on which the English educated Chinese would join them. It was in this climate that Lee Kuan Yew's Peoples Action Party (PAP) was founded.[22] The demonstration in May 1954 was hardly a success, but it did much to awaken students' consciousness and corporate spirit and to strengthen the position of their leaders. Moreover, the Chinese public were always sensitive about any interruption of the process of education in the Chinese schools, and their sympathy was strengthened by the use of violence by the police against schoolchildren.

Chapter 5 Subversion in the Chinese
Middle Schools 1954–6

Formation of the SCMSSU

The demonstration against National Service in May 1954, with its popular cause and its provocation of the use of force by the police, gave a tremendous boost to open left-wing activity in the Chinese Middle Schools. The Party recruiting and selection process had drawn many of the most able leaders into this Open Front Organization, and these became popular heroes.

This led in October 1954 to a public proposal to form a Singapore Chinese Middle School Students Union (SCMSSU). On 7 January 1955 the Preparatory Committee of the Union filed its application for registration, but this was rejected on the grounds that its aims were political.[1]

In April 1955 the first elections under the Rendel Constitution put Mr. David Marshall into power as the first Chief Minister, with limited power of self-government,[2] and an elected majority in the Legislative Assembly. As expected, at the first meeting of the new Parliament on 22 April he announced the removal of certain of the powers used by the police for controlling riots and demonstrations.[3]

This was followed almost at once by the Hock Lee Bus Strike, leading to rioting on 10 to 12 May in which three people were killed. These riots, and the restoration of some of the police powers afterwards, will be discussed more fully in Chapter 6 which is concerned with rioting and riot control. For the time being, only their effect on the process of student subversion will be considered.

During the strike, large numbers of dismissed bus workers locked themselves into the Hock Lee Garages in Alexandra Road, posting pickets on the gates. From 28 April onwards, thousands of school children brought them food and entertained them with singing and dancing.[4] On 10 May the pickets were removed by the police, and rioting began. On 12 May twenty lorry loads of Chinese Middle

School Students joined the demonstrating strikers, and seventeen more were intercepted by the police.[5] These lorry loads converged with military precision and timing from schools all over Singapore.[6]

On 13 May the Government closed three Chinese schools for a week[7] and ordered the expulsion of some of the ringleaders.

On 14 May the Hock Lee bus strike was settled by government arbitration on terms generally favourable to the strikers.

The focus then shifted to the schools, where the students had locked themselves in to protest against their closure and the expulsion order. The Chief Secretary,[8] Mr. Goode, said in the Legislative Assembly that the part played by the students in the demonstrations was highly organized, and that the School Principals feared assassination. The London *Times* correspondent reported, however, that the School Management Committees (composed of leading and generally conservative Chinese citizens) refused to take a line at all and seemed to be frightened of the students.[9] The police, who had no legal power to enter the school except at their request, were never asked in until violence had actually begun, so subversion and mass meetings went unchecked.[10]

On 22 May the stay-in strike in the high schools ended when the Government withdrew its demands for the expulsion of the student ringleaders.[11]

The newly elected government had shown some resistance to mass coercion in its use of the police to break up the riots, and in restoring some of the suspended police powers on 16 May.[12] Nevertheless, it had made concessions both to the strikers and to the students, and the students had successfully intimidated many of their school management committees and teachers. The struggle had polarized into the familiar one of the students versus the establishment, and the students rallied to their open front leaders. Their blood was up.

Meanwhile, the MCP had instructed the Preparatory Committee of the SCMSSU to reverse their earlier attitude and to seek registration by accepting the government's condition that they undertake not to take part in political activities or to interfere in labour disputes. They were to give their undertaking without any intention of carrying it out[13] – a normal Communist tactic for getting the advantages of legal recognition. This they did on 28 July 1955 and on 6 October their registration was approved.[14]

Fourteen days later they launched a campaign against the condition that they had been asked to sign, and at their inaugural meeting

SUBVERSION IN THE CHINESE MIDDLE SCHOOLS 1954-6

on 30 October they attacked the Public Security Ordinance and government educational policy. On 11 November they were warned that they would be dissolved if they continued such political activities, but they rejected this warning at a protest meeting.

On 13 December there was another bus strike (this time against the Singapore Traction Company) and once again the students gave organized support to the strikers.

In March 1956 the SCMSSU leaders became more openly pro-Communist. They protested against the banning of a concert whose programme contained pro-Communist items, and their President, Soon Loh Boon, spoke from the platform at a meeting celebrating the Communist Women's International Day.[15] Their flag bore a five-pointed Communist red star on a yellow background, in calculated similarity to the MCP flag – a yellow star on red ground.[16] In June and July 1956 they held holiday indoctrination classes for over three hundred trade union executives.[17]

The dissolution of the SCMSSU was to be the main pretext for the trial of strength in the October 1956 riots, so this and the events surrounding it will be described in Chapter 6. The current chapter is concerned with the subversive action, open and secret, carried on in the Chinese Middle Schools from the time of its conception after the National Service riots of May 1954 until its dissolution and the arrest of its leaders in October 1956.

Party and Open Front Structure in the Schools

The SCMSSU incorporated ten Chinese Middle Schools, with a total student population of nearly 16,000 boys and girls, aged from ten to twenty-three, and claimed in 1956 that it had 10,000 members.[18]

Each school had six standards or grades – Senior 3, 2, and 1 and Junior 3, 2 and 1.[19] The Open Front Organization (Fig. 9) was run by six Standard Committees, one for each standard. In a large school, a standard might contain several hundred children, mainly of the same age group (though with some over-age students amongst them). The Standard Committee normally contained six or seven members from that standard, plus two or three from more senior standards to give guidance and supervision. The Presidents of the six Standard Committees formed the School Committee, which was the 'GHQ' of the Open Front in the school, receiving secret guidance from the Party Supervisor outside the school.

PARTY AND OPEN FRONT STRUCTURE IN THE SCHOOLS

PARALLEL OPEN AND SECRET PARTY ORGANIZATIONS IN THE CHINESE MIDDLE SCHOOLS, 1954-6

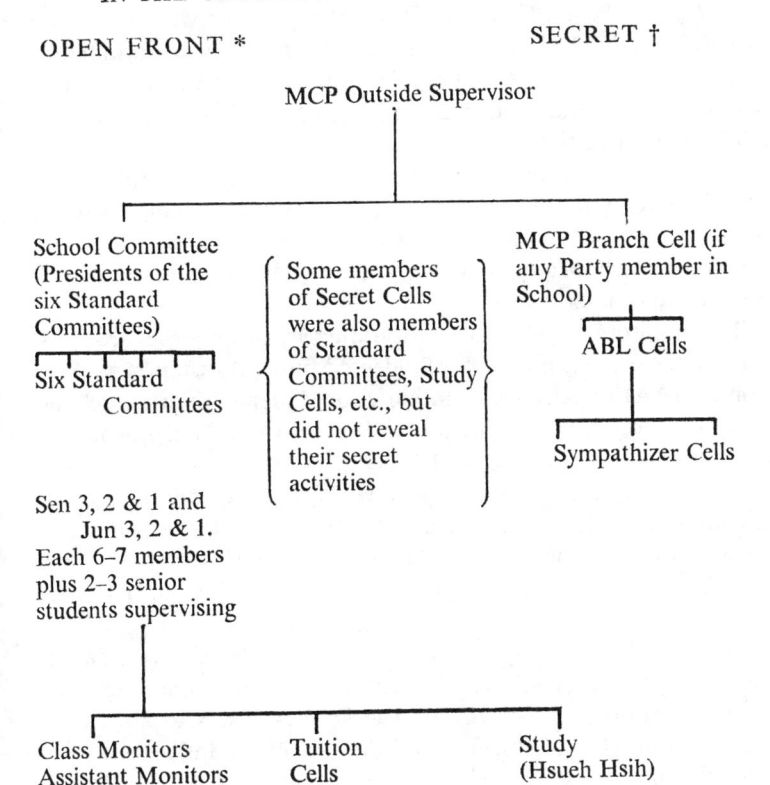

OPEN FRONT *　　　　　　　　　　　SECRET †

MCP Outside Supervisor

School Committee (Presidents of the six Standard Committees)

{ Some members of Secret Cells were also members of Standard Committees, Study Cells, etc., but did not reveal their secret activities }

MCP Branch Cell (if any Party member in School)

ABL Cells

Sympathizer Cells

Six Standard Committees

Sen 3, 2 & 1 and Jun 3, 2 & 1. Each 6–7 members plus 2–3 senior students supervising

Class Monitors / Assistant Monitors　　Tuition Cells　　Study (Hsueh Hsih) Cells

† *Tasks*
 . Study Communist Theory
 . Train for Leadership
 . Influence Open Front Activities from within
 . Select recruits.

* *Task*
 . Organize Open School Activities

Figure 9

87

In a school of 1,000 boys and girls, there would normally be about six classes in each of the Junior 1, 2, and 3 standards with dropouts narrowing the size to about three classes in Senior 3 – the final year. At the Chinese High School (2,000 boys) there were about fifty classes in all. Each class elected a monitor and an assistant monitor, so there were about 100 of these in all at the Chinese High School and perhaps 150 at Chung Cheng High School, which contained 3,000 boys and girls.

One of the functions of the Standard Committee was to sponsor the election of its own nominees (often over-age students) to be monitors and assistant monitors. This not only gave them a stranglehold on the school's disciplinary structure, but provided them with a structure of their own.

The monitors established their position by genuine welfare work such as the establishment of a Students Mutual Assistance Association (SMAA) to raise funds to aid poor students, though such aid was not always entirely disinterested. They also organized propaganda meetings and published a Wall Newspaper, whose aim was to promote political consciousness. The Wall Newspaper criticized the Government rather than the school staff, since the editors were anxious to avoid prohibition. Many of the staff, certainly at the Chinese High School, knew very well what was going on, but dared not interfere.

Indoctrination and 'agitation of the young masses' was probably the most important task of the School and Standard Committees and of the monitors they controlled. The first thing was to attract the maximum number of students into their sphere of influence. As an example, the Chung Hwa Girls High School Branch of the SCMSSU reported that they were using

'Lively and subtle working methods to carry out resolutions on propaganda work, more especially by the various small-scale activities, such as lunches, tea-parties, in acting plays, collective visits to a cinema etc.

'All these small-scale activities suit the taste of fellow students very much. Consequently the majority of the fellow students were organized in this way.'[20]

The same branch later described the next stage of its 'Programme' in publicizing resolutions (of the SCMSSU).

a. Meeting held by the working personnel of the branch (i.e. the School and Standard Committees) to review and study the resolutions.
b. Issue an "Express News."
c. Meeting of fellow-students [i.e. the 'young masses'].
d. Meeting of working personnel of the classes [i.e. of monitors sponsored by the Standard Committee].
e. Issue Wall Newspaper and Blackboard News.
f. The various classes proceeded with small-scale activities and studied the resolutions.
g. Reunion dinner.'[21]

The Chung Cheng High School reported similarly, and also included visits to tutors as well as to students, and a broadcast to the whole school, of which the script was afterwards distributed. This was with permission of the school authorities (see below).[22] They also reported holding tests on current affairs and 'Fill the Blank' games.

The questions in these tests were often naïve, but made no attempt to conceal their propaganda purpose. For example:

'Out of the various newspapers in Singapore, which one contains news which is most untrue and with most distortion of facts? (List given, say WHICH.)

'The people in the New Villages in the Federation of Malaya are leading a very free life. (YES or NO.)

'Malaya is situated in South-East Asia or North-East Africa or South-West Europe. (WHICH.)'

The 'Fill in Gap' questions were on similar lines, for example:

'Malaysia has been ruled by the British Colonialists for . . . years.

'The tragic incident of 13 May occurred in . . . (year) at . . . Park and . . . Road.'[23]

The SCMSSU also made subtle efforts to represent its views and policies as coming from students:

'Similarly, after the SCMSSU has collected the numerous but loose and unsystematic views, they will be adjusted into complete systematic common views which will be handed back to the fellow students. The School Committees will lead the fellow students in carrying them out.

'Of course before carrying them out, the School Committees should first patiently and carefully make propaganda among the fellow students about the meaning and contents about the resolution passed. The fellow students are then allowed to give the matter consideration and discussion so that thereafter the resolution may be turned into the students' own views and demands and carried out accordingly.'[24]

The 'meetings of working personnel' were the mainspring of these activities, and were used to check on their work. Being part of the Open Front, each member of the School Committee knew all the working personnel under his command (i.e. in his own standard) and was kept informed of their statements and answers to questions at their self-criticism meetings. He did not, however, know members of other standards, except in so far as their leadership made itself obvious on demonstrations, etc.

There was also, however, an element of 'strength through joy' in some of the activities of the working personnel – particularly in the joint meetings between equal ranking Standard Committees from brother and sister schools. For this purpose neighbouring schools were affiliated, where possible, to make an added attraction by mixing boys and girls. For example, the Chinese High School (2,000 boys) in Bukit Timah Road was affiliated to Nanyang Girls High School (1,000 girls) which was only a few hundred yards away, and with the Chung Hwa Girls High School (1,200 girls) which, though several miles away, was easily accessible by the ring road. The three Standard Committees of, say, Senior 2 Standard would meet for picnics in the park around the nearby MacRitchie Reservoir – an ideal site with its large surrounding jungle reserve into which the party, some thirty boys and girls in all, could withdraw to complete seclusion if they felt that they were being watched. They would hold discussions on current affairs generally, or on the specific tactics to be adopted in resisting the government education policies or the National Service Ordinance. Unlike those in the secret and earnest ABL cells, these boys and girls did not yet have to endure the dreary catechism of the more theoretical Communist studies, so they generally enjoyed themselves and got satisfaction out of being members of a lively élite, the thirty of them holding power over about 1,000 of their fellow students, through the monitors, and the study and tuition cells. The three Presidents in particular would look forward to making their rather priggish reports of their activities to their School Committees.

The Secret Organization

The members of the School Committee, as the open front leaders, were, of course, the 'ringleaders' whose arrest was threatened in 1955 and carried out in 1956. Nevertheless, many of them were also members of the parallel secret organization. According to rigid Communist theory, these potential or probationary party members should not have risked arrest by open activities, but should have concentrated on their theoretical studies of Communist doctrine and revolutionary techniques, and on training themselves to emerge unsuspected by the police, as party workers for the secret organization outside. In practice, however, the importance of good leadership and organization in the schools and in demonstrations, and the weak state of the Party's secret structure as a whole in Singapore, meant that most of the leaders joined in the Open Front Activities.

All the same, the secret ABL structure did exist, and in some schools was very strong. These cells were, of course, avowedly Communist,[25] and members addressed each other as 'comrade' whereas in the Open Front Organization (including the semi-secret study cells) the members called each other 'fellow students'. ABL members also used party names, and distributed amongst themselves (and amongst trusted sympathizers whom they hoped to recruit) a clandestine 'Free Press' which is not to be confused with the Wall Newspapers, Express News, etc. which were distributed as open propaganda to the whole school.

Recruits for the ABL cells were found, after the usual apprenticeship in a sympathizer cell, by selection from amongst working personnel in the Open Front Organization. As well as ability, power of leadership, popularity, etc. the boy's background was also carefully checked.

There was, however, an element of Communist snobbery here. It was Party philosophy that a boy of middle-class background, however dedicated a Communist, might one day be attracted back to his bourgeois tastes and ambitions, and, if entrusted with the innermost party secrets, might betray them. A boy of proletarian origin, however, should in theory have neither the desire nor opportunity to acquire bourgeois tastes or ambitions, and, if he attained a responsible position in the MCP structure, should feel that he would never have been allowed to attain such a position in a capitalist society, and that he therefore owed everything to the Party, and would have everything to lose by betraying it. Though there were some notable examples of boys of middle-class background joining the ABL and reaching high positions later on, there was at school a definite prejudice against them.[26]

So 'Ching', son of a prosperous contractor, was drawn into the Open Front structure of the Foon Yew High School, and became treasurer of the SMAA, but received no overtures from the secret organization. On the other hand, 'Yung', one of seven children of an unemployed father and of a mother who supported the family by working as a hawker for three or four dollars a day, was under constant pressure to join the ABL. He resisted this, though he was a member of his Standard Committee all the way from Junior 1 in 1955 to Senior 3 in 1960, and well knew that these were Communist sponsored. Indeed, one of his supervisors was Cheng Yew Leng, who was arrested in 1956 and deported to China. Many of his friends were ABL members, and gave him copies of their clandestine Free Press, but he did not join, because he realized that it would place him between two grave hazards. If discovered, he would sacrifice his chance of education. If, on the other hand, he were to leave when once he had joined, he would risk being assassinated.

He had experienced a frightening demonstration of Party ruthlessness when he was only twelve or thirteen, before he had left Primary School to join the Chinese High School. On 17 April 1955 he was attending a rehearsal of a folk dancing performance to be staged by a front organization.[27] The conductor of the band was a twenty-one-year-old Chinese high school student, Lee Ta Lim. He was called from the rostrum and shots were heard outside. Lee's body was found in a pool of blood. He was suspected of having betrayed the Party, so there was little expression of sympathy for him, and no one came forward when the police offered a $20,000 reward for information (see Chapter 8).

So 'Yung' never became a Communist, though, with his strong powers of leadership and working-class background, the Party worked hard to get him. Indeed, when he went on to Nanyang University, he led the opposition to the Communist attempt to take over the Students Union,[28] and later became a teacher at the Chung

Cheng High School and an active member of Lee Kuan Yew's Peoples Action Party. His experience in the Communist Open Front Organization stood him in good stead.

Study and Tuition Cells

The third sphere of influence of the Party in the Chinese Middle Schools was the twilight world of the 'Hsueh Hsih' (study) Cells, and of the Tuition Cells which fed them.

When the SCMSSU Preparatory Committee drafted its Constitution in 1954, there were two significant aspects which were noted by Special Branch. The first was that membership could be extended one to two years after leaving school which added great strength to the continuity and supervision of Open Front activities. The second was the inclusion of 'the betterment of education' amongst its aims, in such a way as to leave no doubt that it planned to use a comprehensive organization for assisting students in their academic studies as a cloak for political indoctrination, even though the mutual help element was none the less real.[29]

The nearest translation of Hsueh Hsih is 'Study-Action' or 'Study-Practice', and it incorporates the Communist idea that study without practical work (the student in an ivory castle) is no good. The Hsueh Hsih cell is in fact an adaption of an old Confucian analect about how the young should educate themselves, and now provides the basis for the lowest cell of Maoism, first introduced by Mao Tse Tung in October 1938.[30] It is a Communist vehicle for assessing and educating the 'Grey Masses' (i.e. potential sympathizers) and, though part of the Open Front Organization, its activities are conducted with discretion. These Hsueh Hsih cells will hereafter be referred to as Study Cells.

Prior to being invited to join Study Cells, promising boys were attracted into wholly open Tuition Cells. These were precisely what their name implied. A senior student would offer to form a 'seminar' of young students to help them with their studies – in itself a laudable activity. Indeed the SCMSSU claimed that this was their chief function, and used it to inflame public opinion when threatened with dissolution.

These Tuition Cells might be anything from a handful to fifteen strong. In Chung Cheng High School they were about nine strong, each class being divided into three or four cells as some students were shy of speaking their minds in front of the whole class.[31] Sometimes the Tuition Cells arrogated to themselves wider functions. One school branch, for example, reported the formation of a fifteen-man cell to 'assist' the class executives elected by the students who were found to be inefficient.[32] Detailed methods varied.

In the Tuition Cells, young students were helped to pass examinations, made friends and gained respect for the senior student who was helping them. He, of course, was also a party worker, either in the Open Front or the Secret Party organization, or both, and it was his duty to discover background data about his students to decide whether they were suitable as recruits for the Study Cells.[33]

While he might join a Tuition Cell in his first term, a student would not normally be considered fit to join a Study Cell until he reached Senior 1 Standard, i.e. at the age of fifteen or sixteen. He might then become a Study Cell leader in his penultimate year. In his final year (Senior 3), he would rise out of the cell system altogether and act as a supervisor. This, of course, was without prejudice to his continuing wholly open activities (e.g. on a Standard Committee) or leading a double life as supervisor of an ABL cell.

Indoctrination in the Study Cells would usually begin with Communist folk stories[34] and an introduction to Chinese literature and history. This would include stories of heroes of past dynasties, and, for example, of the heroic resistance against Japan, and of Communist China's feats of reconstruction. There would also be discussions on the philosophy of life, leading to study of standard works on Communism (Marx, Lenin, Stalin and Mao Tse Tung). The cell leader would be provided with material from outside the school, and would conduct the meetings in a deliberately conspiratorial atmosphere.[35] In all these activities, criticism and self-criticism played an important part.

Self-criticism and Intimidation

Self-criticism was primarily a technique for Party discipline. For example:

> 'The functions, feelings, actions, beliefs and speech of a Party member are all of concern to the party . . . Party organizations and individuals . . . if they uncover the tendency of a comrade which is injurious to the party affairs, must never compromise or keep such a discovery secret.'[36]

It went wider than that, however, and was used as a weapon to bring pressure to bear on individuals. For example:

'In order to consolidate their own organization, the entire body of members of the Chinese New Democratic Youth Corps must learn how to *manipulate*[37] the method of criticism and self-criticism so as to carry on a struggle against all the bad phenomena which are harmful to the enterprise of the people and the undertakings of the party.[38]

'Criticism and self-criticism are the powerful *weapons* of the Youth Corps when educating its members and the young masses . . .'[39]

The SCMSSU made use of this weapon in 1954–6 to exert psychological pressure on its members (who comprised a majority of the 'young masses' in the Chinese Middle Schools) to swim with the stream. The Secretary-General of the SCMSSU, in his message 'Welcome the Year 1956' wrote:

'We must lay stress on the importance of the unity of members [of the SCMSSU] and the development of the union. All members should be able to reach mutual understanding and have *a correct hold on the weapon* of criticism and self-criticism.'[40]

Amongst working personnel, the discipline was naturally stricter than amongst the 'young masses'. The SCMSSU Study Outline for 1956 defined criticism and self-criticism as:

'. . . just like a searchlight enabling us to check at once the actual conditions of a certain working department or section,'

and any who might have the effrontery to fight back were deterred with a threat to which a young Chinese feeling himself entering the élite would be particularly sensitive:

'. . . everyone can see that standing before them is a weakling who has not the courage to admit his mistakes, a bad worker who is unwilling to rectify his defects . . . he is decidedly not a person who possesses the quality of a leader.'[41]

Thus, public criticism and self-criticism become a subtle form of intimidation, playing on the normal desire of a boy or girl to be accepted as one of a group. 'Public' (i.e. in the presence of other members of the group, be it open or secret) was the operative word.

Group loyalty was placed above personal loyalty.[42] Carried as far as it was, however, it had something of a backlash in denying boys and girls the normal solace of sharing their thoughts with their really close friends, and casting a shadow which took a lot of the warmth and humanity away from their lives,[43] despite the 'strength through joy' picnics and the exhilaration of conspiratorial teamwork.

The intimidation of the 'young masses' was often direct and brutal, just as it is in schools anywhere in the world in which there is strong and organized leadership against authority. In the Chung Cheng High School, for example, 'traitors' were listed on the blackboards, and when one boy in the Chinese High School tore down a poster, he was confronted by a large gang, which announced that it would enforce his immediate ostracism, and hinted worse to come if he persisted.[44] The murder of Lee Ta Lim in April 1955, and the reluctance of anyone to come forward to give evidence, were an indication of the degree to which this intimidation was sometimes carried, though it was seldom necessary to go as far as this.

The Position of the Teachers

Some of the teachers were openly or discreetly sympathetic to the SCMSSU in the battle for Chinese rights and Chinese culture under the British (and, in the Federation, Malay) domination.[45] Until the foundation of Nanyang University in 1955, there was no Chinese language education available in Singapore or the Federation above Middle School level. Thus, most of the Chinese graduates teaching senior classes in the Chinese Middle Schools in 1954–6 had spent three years at University in China.[46] The older ones had done this before or during the Second World War, under the Kuomintang, and were generally anti-Communist, but many of the younger ones had Communist sympathies.

The school staffs not unnaturally welcomed the Tuition Cells, and sometimes also welcomed the Study Cells, of whose existence they were generally well aware. In one girls' school, the principal suggested the formation of a study section for student teachers to study teaching methods, and offered prizes. This, of course, was accepted with glee by the School Committee. In another school, after some initial opposition to the 'Hsueh Hsih' concept, the school authorities changed the extra-curricular programme to enable students to take part in it.[47]

THE POSITION OF THE TEACHERS

Politics apart, many of the teachers got on well with the students and particularly with the best amongst them, and it was from amongst the best that the Communist Open Front or secret leaders were recruited. The SCMSSU and the ABL, combining progressive politics with the opportunity for patriotic leadership of the rising generation of Chinese, were particularly attractive to the cream of the students, like 'Yung', for example, who was equally popular amongst the staff, his fellow students and the ABL and SCMSSU. The teachers knew about the School and Standard Committees and propaganda indoctrination, but generally (whether from sympathy or intimidation) kept out of campus activities, and the ABL and SCMSSU went out of their way to be friendly to them provided that they did not interfere.[48]

Those who did interfere at once became targets for intimidation of a particularly vicious kind, since the domination of the 'young masses' by the SCMSSU gave it a mob flavour. 'Yung' witnessed such an occasion when he was representing the Chinese High School at a mass rally of the Chung Cheng High School branch of the SCMSSU in March 1956. The meeting set itself up as a 'Peoples' Court', with over 1,000 boys and girls present One of the teachers, Song Choh Eng, was hauled from his office on to the stage, and students shouted accusations from the floor: '... distributed Kuomintang propaganda! ... spoke against the SCMSSU! ....' etc. The 'Peoples' Court' demanded that he be sacked, and the School Management Committee complied. Song went to teach in the Federation.

In August 1956 the Nanyang Girls' High School went on strike because of the refusal to dismiss their English-language teacher, and only returned to work when the Principal promised that the teacher would change her attitude.[49]

Personal violence (apart from manhandling) was again relatively rare, but not unknown. In 1954, for example, the Principal of Nanyang Girls' High School, Madame Lau Ing Sien, had acid thrown in her face and had to go to the United Kingdom for treatment. Other teachers were pelted with rotten eggs, but the commonest form of coercion was the mean and impersonal one of damaging the bodywork of their cars or putting salt or sand in the petrol tanks.[50]

Eventually the intimidation of the teachers, principals and management committees was one of the main factors which led the government to take positive action against the student organization in

October 1956, thereby providing the spark for the riots in that month, which are described later.

The Baling Truce Talks and the Razak Report

In June 1955 the MCP in the jungle made overtures for peace talks, and in December of that year Chin Peng met the Chief Ministers of the newly elected governments of Singapore and the Federation – Mr. David Marshall and Tunku Abdul Rahman. After the breakdown of these talks, the MCP issued a fresh Directive which included the following admissions:

> 'Especially in circumstances where the enemy is stronger than we are, the work of winning support from schoolchildren and organizing them to struggle is more important than military activities.'[51]

Also in 1955 a new government report on Education was published by Dato Abdul Razak, the Minister of Education in Kuala Lumpur. Although applicable only to the Federation, it raised a tremendous outcry in the Chinese Schools, including those in Singapore. Among other things, it announced that now, eleven years after the end of the war, the time had come to make more room for the rising generation by ceasing to accept over-age students. This was, of course, a devastating blow to the MCP, since both their secret and Open Front activities were largely run by over-age students, whose experience and Communist training were indispensable to them. Opposition to the Razak Report provided a fresh focus for the Study Cells and for Open Front propaganda.

Thus, coinciding with the Government's reaction to the erosion of the authority of the school staffs, the SCMSSU and the ABL cells intensified their activities in response both to the post-Baling MCP Directive and the Razak Report. By the autumn of 1956 the situation was ripe for a head-on clash.

By the time this clash came, however, Singapore was a self-governing State. Before examining this clash, therefore, we must look back at the development of this self-government which had begun in April 1955 and had proceeded, in conjunction with a sharp rise in strikes and riots, in parallel with the development of the power of the SCMSSU.

Chapter 6 Self-government

The 'Middle Road' Group of Trade Unions

Amongst the student organization in the Chinese High School, one of the leading figures from 1949 to 1951 had been Lim Chin Siong, who was to play a major part in the affairs of Singapore from 1954 to 1962. Expelled from the Chinese High School for organizing agitation in 1951 at the age of eighteen, he had continued his underground work in a supervisory role in the ABL. He became a paid trade union Secretary, was elected to the Assembly in 1955 and played a leading part in the 1956 demonstrations, after which he was in detention until released on Lee Kuan Yew's election to power in June 1959. During the next four years he made a determined bid to oust Lee Kuan Yew before being placed again into detention in February 1963. He was eventually released in 1969 and went to England, where he resumed the education which had been interrupted in 1951, getting down to taking 'A' levels in his late thirties and going on to university.[1]

Lim Chin Siong has never publicly admitted to being a Communist. Douglas Hyde, who spent a number of periods of several days in Lim's cell in Changi goal between 1964 and 1968, is convinced that Lim was never a Party member, but that his aims did coincide with Communist Party aims. Lim claimed that he used the Party to further his aims, and admitted that he was prepared to fall in with Party plans, but denied that he had any contact with the Party underground.[2] Lee Kuan Yew, however, has stated categorically that 'he is... what he always has been, a Communist Open Front leader',[3] and produces documentary evidence to prove this. At the height of the constitutional battle for power in September 1961, whilst Lim was still a member of the Assembly, Lee Kuan Yew described him in a broadcast over Radio Malaya as follows:

'Lim was the most important Open Front leader the MCP had built up. By 1955 he knew that I knew this. He is a friendly and quiet person. He is prepared to devote his whole life to working for the creation of a Communist Malaya. But once you resist and fight the Communist cause, then you can expect all that personal friendship to mean nothing in the ruthless and relentless struggle for supremacy.'[4]

In 1954, Lim was still only twenty-one, but was already emerging as a powerful figure in Singapore. In view of the generally improving Emergency situation, the British Government was anxious to allow more rein to legitimate organization of labour and in 1954 the trade unions in Singapore recovered some of the freedom of action which they had lost in 1948. The MCP lost no time in establishing control over a number of key unions, enabling them to wield the same power over labour as they had in 1946-8 (see Chapter 2). In the light of the immediate consequences, the British Government's liberality may seem surprising, but at the time the greatly improved Emergency situation seemed to justify this calculated risk – and in the long run there is little doubt that the policy paid off, both in the Federation and in Singapore.

The grouping of unions in 1954 was much looser than it had been in the Singapore Federation of Trade Unions in 1948. It was simply an informal arrangement whereby the executives of a number of unions met from time to time on the premises of one of them, the Singapore Factory and Shopworkers Union (SFSWU) of which Lim Chin Siong became Secretary-General. The SFSWU head office was in Middle Road, near the centre of the city of Singapore, so this association became known as the 'Middle Road Group'. Though, as in 1948, there was a more moderate constitutional group of unions (the Singapore TUC) which generally aimed to attain better conditions by some degree of cooperation with management and government, the Middle Road Group controlled the unions in many complete sectors of industry and the public services, including all public transport systems. The control of these unions was closely linked with the People's Action Party (PAP), or rather to its militant left-wing faction which was led by Lim Chin Siong. Their success can be measured by the fact that, whereas in 1953 and 1954 there was a total of 13 strikes in two years, there were 213 in the five months from April to September 1955 – 162 of them attributed to the Middle Road Group.[5]

Self-government

Meanwhile, the Constitution for self-government proposed in the report of the Rendel Commission was being put into effect. The Assembly contained thirty-two members of whom twenty-five were elected. The other seven consisted of three British officials holding Ministerial appointments and four unofficial members nominated by the Governor.

The Executive consisted of a Council of Ministers over which the Governor presided. Of the nine Ministers, six were found from the twenty-five elected members of the Assembly, and the other three were the British officials mentioned above. Portfolios were as follows:

Elected Ministers (who included the Chief Minister):
No. 1 Commerce, Industry, Shipping, Agriculture and Fisheries.
No. 2 Labour, Immigration and Social Welfare.
No. 3 Education.
No. 4 Housing, Lands, Administration of the adjacent Islands, Town and Country Planning and Local Government.
No. 5 Civil Aviation, Communications and Public Works.
No. 6 Health

British Official Ministers:
No. 7 Finance Minister.
No. 8 Attorney General.
No. 9 Chief Secretary, responsible for:
    (a) External Affairs.
    (b) Internal Security, including Police and Prisons.
    (c) Defence.
    (d) Public Relations, Broadcasting, Civil Service.[6]

In the light of subsequent events it is hard to remember that Singapore attained this degree of Constitutional Self Government before the Federation did (in April and May 1955 respectively), because thereafter, whereas the Federation attained full independence from the British in a little over two years (August 1957), Singapore had to wait eight years (September 1963) for hers. Two of the reasons for this were related: first, the MCP in the Federation, though far bigger than in Singapore, was spread about the jungle and had little means of influencing political development in the cities; and secondly, whereas the non-Communist political factions in the

Federation formed an overwhelming Alliance Party holding fifty-one out of the fifty-two elected seats, those in Singapore were split in continuous rivalries, which were not resolved until 1963. Which of these, in the long-term, will have proved to be the healthier political apprenticeship will have to be deduced later by historians who will have many other factors to take into account. Certainly the circumstances mentioned did give Singapore a much more stormy period of transition to full independence than the Federation, though Singapore subsequently attained a remarkable degree of internal political stability.

The 1955 elections in Singapore provided a shock for the British, who had since 1947 been grooming the leaders of the Progressive Party, made up mainly of English-educated commercial Chinese, to take over when the time came for self-government. Unlike the Alliance Party in the Federation, these leaders were decisively rejected at the polls.[7] Power instead went to a coalition headed by David Marshall, a successful lawyer who had switched to politics in 1954 after a six-weeks' course in electioneering at Transport House in London.[8] The Coalition supporting him as Chief Minister held only thirteen out of the twenty-five elected seats. Thus, if the twelve opposition members did not support him on any particular measure, he had to rely on the concurrence of the balance of seven official and nominated members and vice versa. Marshall's thirteen were from his own Labour Front (ten) and the Alliance Party (three) – while the 'opposition' comprised four Progressives, three People's Action Party (PAP) and five Independents, one of whom in practice always voted with the PAP. The PAP members included Lee Kuan Yew (the party leader) and Lim Chin Siong.[9] It is an interesting reflection on the racial complexion of Singapore that the six elected ministers included men of five different races; Chinese, Malay, Eurasian, Indian and Jewish.[10]

The new Assembly met on 22 April 1955. Its mood above all else was anti-colonialist. The 1955 Constitution was a landmark, but it gave them only a limited degree of self-government. In the last resort, for example, responsibility for Internal Security lay with a colonial official (the Chief Secretary) served by a colonial Commissioner of Police and a colonial Head of Special Branch. The three colonial Ministers (all of British race) also retained control of finance, of the judicial system and of the information services, including radio. In practice, as Marshall publicly acknowledged in the

Assembly,[11] the three British Ministers deferred to the vote of the six elected Ministers in the Council, but there was no guarantee legally that they would do this and Marshall resented the fact that he was not always privy to Special Branch secrets and did not have access to their files.[12] Even the departments wholly controlled by the elected Ministers (such as education and housing) were subject to a budget controlled by a colonial Finance Minister, and the appointment of the Ministers themselves was made by the Governor – albeit from amongst the elected members of the Assembly, and on the advice of their majority leader.[13]

In the circumstances, with an Assembly containing Open Front Leaders, who might become members of a majority party or coalition, these safeguards were not unreasonable, but of course they were unpalatable to the elected members. While the Assembly did give them a forum from which they could influence public opinion, they did not have real independence and they were not prepared to wait too long for this. They wanted to govern themselves, not to wait for their sons to govern.

In the Assembly, during this transition period, they had individually to establish themselves as leaders, and this depended on their presenting a progressive, anti-colonialist image. The most wounding jibe that could be flung across the floor was 'Colonialist stooge'.

Neither Marshall nor his deputy, Lim Yew Hock (who had been a member of the Rendel Commission) seemed to have any illusions about Communism, and Marshall was to give a convincing demonstration of this at the abortive truce talks with Chin Peng at Baling later in the year. Nevertheless, the mood of the Assembly and of the Singapore public was anti-colonialist rather than anti-Communist. Marshall had to ride along a knife-edge between appearing to merit the 'stooge' label or allowing the Communists to gather strength and unseat him. He knew that this was the last thing the British wanted, but he was highly critical of the powers they gave him to prevent it. Inevitably, this responsibility cast him as a 'moderate' enabling the PAP to claim the radical leadership, and they exploited this situation to the full.

The People's Action Party

The PAP, with only three members (or four with their Independent supporter) was itself split. Its extreme left wing, represented in the

Assembly by Lim Chin Siong, made no secret of its leadership of the militant Middle Road Group of unions, and of the dissent amongst the Chinese Middle School Students (described in the previous chapter).

The other faction was led by the Party Leader, Lee Kuan Yew, who knew well that the extremists in his party were Communist.

'Some', he said later,[14] 'were my personal friends. They knew that I knew they were Communists, for between us there was no pretence. They believed that I should join them.'

He was, however, quite convinced that independence from the British required the concerted efforts of all progressive political factions in the Colony, including the Communists. He was confident that he could handle them and in this he proved right. He will go down in history as one of the few democratic leaders who has risen to power astride the Communist tiger without ever losing control of it and who has been able to discard it as soon as it seriously challenged his leadership. In 1961, at the height of this challenge, he described his past relations with them in a series of startlingly outspoken broadcasts over Radio Malaya, the published version of which (in *The Battle for Merger*) now forms a colourful and illuminating reference book on Communist political subversion.

In 1955 he was cooperating with them broadly for three reasons. First, as already mentioned, to accelerate independence from the British; secondly, because he was largely sympathetic with the aspirations of Chinese trade unionists and students; and thirdly because he was determined to bridge the gulf between the Chinese educated in the English-speaking schools (such as himself) and those educated in Chinese schools (such as Lim Chin Siong).

Lee Kuan Yew had since 1950 been most active as a barrister in representing the trade unions (he was a brilliant lawyer, with double first-class honours at Cambridge). In so doing he had made many friends amongst their left-wing leadership. It was, in fact, the court charges arising from the student riots which gave him the chance to bridge the gulf. He describes it thus:

'Then one day, in 1954 we came into contact with the Chinese-educated world. The Chinese Middle School students were in revolt against national service, and they were beaten down. Riots took place, charges were prepared in court. Through devious ways they came into contact with us.

'We bridged the gap to the Chinese-educated world – a world teeming with vitality, dynamism and revolution, a world in which the Communists had been working for over the last thirty years with considerable success.

'We, the English-educated revolutionaries . . . were considered by the Communists as poaching on their exclusive territory.

'In this world we came to know Lim Chin Siong and Fong Swee Suan. They joined us in the PAP. In 1955 we contested the elections. Our initiation into the intricacies and varifications of the Communist underground organization had begun.

'It is a strange business working in this world. When you meet a union leader you will quickly have to decide . . . whether or not he is a Communist. You can find out by the language he uses and his behaviour, whether or not he is in the inner circle which makes the decisions. These are things from which you determine whether he is an outsider or an insider in the Communist underworld.

'I came to know dozens of them. They are not crooks or opportunists. These are men with great resolve, dedicated to the Communist revolution and to the establishment of the Communist state believing that it is the best thing in the world for mankind.

'Many of them are prepared to pay the price for the Communist cause in terms of personal freedom and sacrifice . . . often my colleagues and I disagreed with them and intense fights took place, all concealed from the outside world because they were Communists working in one anti-colonial front with us against the common enemy and it would not do to betray them.'[15]

In the early stages of the wave of strikes which followed the inauguration of self-government (see below) Lee Kuan Yew showed how far he was prepared to go at this stage. Though he repeatedly stressed that he was not a Communist, he was quoted in an interview with the *Straits Times* on 5 May 1955 as saying:

'In Malaya we are sitting on a powder keg . . . The Communists are certain to win . . . Any man in Singapore who wants to carry the Chinese-speaking people with him cannot afford to be anti-Communist . . . If I had to choose between Colonialism and Communism, I would vote for Communism, and so would the great majority of the people.'[16]

This is the most extreme statement attributed to Lee Kuan Yew – particularly his alleged remark that 'The Communists are certain to win'. It is in fact at variance with his other public statements, either then or later. A study of his speeches in public debate in the Assembly from 1955 until 1963 shows a general consistency in his attitude towards the Communists.

On the following day he qualified his statement, saying that he would vote for Communism only if it were the *only* alternative to Colonialism.[17] Nevertheless, this period was the highwater mark of Lee's cooperation with the Communists, though this cooperation was from political necessity rather than from choice.[18] Six years later (1961), whilst he was at the crisis of his political battle to throw them off, he explained this in one of his broadcasts over Radio Malaya:

> 'You may ask: If the Communists are such a danger to our society, why did we work with Lim and his Communist friends in one anti-Colonial united front? This and other questions have to be answered. However uncomfortable the truth may be to me and my colleagues, you must know it . . .
>
> 'We came to the conclusion that we had better forget the differences between our ultimate objectives and work together for our immediate common objective, the destruction of the British. Whether you wanted a democratic Malaya or a Communist Malaya, you had first to get rid of the British . . .
>
> 'But we never forgot that once the British were out of the way, there would be trouble between us and the Communists as to what kind of Malaya we wanted to have in place of the old British colonial Malaya.
>
> 'We were quite clear as to what we wanted – an independent, democratic, socialist Malaya, which by democratic means could bring about a more just and equal society. On the other hand, they wanted a Communist Malaya. This is what the Communists mean when they say "seeking concord whilst maintaining differences".'[19]

The Emergency Regulations

Such was the Assembly which met in Singapore on 22 April 1955. David Marshall, with his coalition government, determined to evade the 'stooge' label, faced Lee Kuan Yew and Lim Chin Siong, both working for the left-wing vote, but each aware that he would eventually have to fight the other for its leadership.

All three (indeed, all the elected members) demonstrated their rejection of colonial pomposity by wearing open-necked shirts.

The government had in fact taken office on 7 April, and the Council of Ministers had therefore been meeting for two weeks before the Assembly itself met. After an exhaustive examination of the Emergency Regulations, they had agreed to revoke certain of them and to extend the remainder for three months. David Marshall, with some courage, chose himself to move the adoption of the three months' extension, rather than to leave it to the Chief Secretary, to underline that this was a decision of the Council of Ministers. Behind the scenes the Governor had shrewdly encouraged Marshall to oppose the extension of Emergency Regulations, so that the odium of extending them would then fall on the British, using their overriding powers, without damaging Marshall's 'progressive' political image. Marshall scorned this offer, preferring not to start his first weeks of power by becoming beholden to his Colonial Governor.[20] In the Assembly, Marshall said that the three British Ministers had shown that they were willing to abide by the majority decision of the Council, no matter how strongly they had expressed their views in arriving at it.[21]

The British Chief Secretary, Mr. Goode, reminded the House during the debate that a young Chinese had been shot dead on Sunday 17 April, called out from a Club and butchered in a public street (see Chapter 5). 'Unless the police have some special powers,' he said, 'these killers are unlikely to be found and locked up, because no one dares to say what he knows until he is sure that he is safe from retaliation.'[22] (This offers an interesting parallel to the situation in Northern Ireland in 1971/72.)

Nevertheless, it must have been with some misgiving that the British officials had agreed to the removal of certain very important police powers – some of which had before long to be restored. The police were deprived of the power to close roads, to enforce curfews and to search premises, vehicles and persons suspected of having weapons.[23] But the power of detention without trial remained, and this was strongly attacked by a number of members, including Lee Kuan Yew, who said that if the government would 'remove the Emergency Regulations in so far as they affect arrest and detention without trial in open court, restrictions on freedom of speech, assembly and publication' the PAP would rest content.[24] Once again, similar views were to be expressed about internment in Northern Ireland in 1971.

The Hock Lee Bus Strike

The relaxations of police powers were debated and approved by the Assembly on 27 April, but they had been announced in the Governor's address at the Opening of Parliament (the 'Speech from the Throne') on 22 April. These relaxations, together with greater freedom of action enjoyed by the trade unions, gave the Communists their best chance of stirring up trouble in Singapore since 1948, and the Middle Road Group wasted no time in launching a challenge by means of their control of the public transport system. On 23 April the Singapore Bus Workers Union (SBWU) served strike notices on the Chinese-owned Hock Lee Amalgamated Bus Company, by virtue of a dispute which had been going on for some weeks.

The PAP version of the origin of the dispute was that when the SBWU was formed in February 1955, 250 of the Hock Lee workers had joined it. The company, however, had simultaneously formed a rival union, and had recruited 200 redundant men into a pool of spare drivers, with a retaining fee of $2 per day paid on condition that they joined this union. This pool would then be available 'to meet any trouble'.[25] The dispute came to a head in April over the introduction of new working rosters. The management replied to the strike notice by dismissing a number of workers, who thereupon locked themselves into the company's garages in Alexandra Road and picketed the gate.[26]

On the mornings of 25 and 26 April the strikers tried to prevent the buses from leaving the garage by sitting on the ground across the gates. On these two days they were persuaded by the police to get up without trouble, but on 27 April 150 strikers blocking the gate threw stones at the police, who had to remove them physically though 'without undue force'. Some strikers feigned injury, but made off when an ambulance was called.[27] On 28 April the police used batons to clear the gate and fifteen people were injured. On 29 April thousands of students converged from Chinese Middle Schools all over the island in a highly organized operation to bring food and to entertain the strikers with singing and dancing.[28]

30 April, the eve of May Day, brought a wave of other strikes by unions of the Middle Road Group. These strikes extended to the Docks, on which, with 100 or more ocean going ships lying in the harbour at any one time, the life-blood of Singapore depended. The familiar pattern of a widely organized stoppage of the transport of

passengers and freight into and within Singapore began to re-emerge. Both Lim Chin Siong and the Secretary of the SBWU, Fong Swee Suan, were accused by the Chief Secretary of instigating the use of violence at a May Day Rally.[29]

Thereafter large numbers of students from the Chinese High School, Chung Cheng High School and the Chung Hwa, Nanyang and Nan Chiau Girls' High Schools arrived day after day in lorries, regimented and organized, gave large sums of money to the workers, danced for their entertainment and sang what were described as inflammatory songs. Some students from the two boys' schools stayed overnight with the strikers.[30]

On Monday 9 May negotiations between the company and the SBWU broke down and the police were ordered to take necessary action to ensure the right of passage of buses from the garage. On 10 May the human barrier across the gate was cleared with fire-hoses. Eight strikers were carried with some drama to ambulances on stretchers, but on arrival at the hospital one was found to have no injuries at all, another to be suffering from mild concussion, and the remainder from minor abrasions only.[31]

On 11 May the strikers cleared the gate on the arrival of the police, but on 12 May they stoned the police and damaged some of the buses and were again dispersed by hoses.

During 12 May the trouble built up. Large numbers of workers and students converged on the Hock Lee garages by lorry and bus. Seventeen lorry loads were diverted by police, but another twenty got through. Rioting crowds were estimated at 2,000.[32] Between 4 p.m. and 7 p.m., mobs of up to 1,000 attacked the police and were dispersed by tear gas. During the night, four people were killed in rioting of exceptional viciousness exacerbated by the fact that the SBWU was Communist-oriented, whereas the Chinese owners of the company were regarded as Kuomintang supporters. The bitterness of the feeling can be gauged by incidents such as when the mobs sprayed a Chinese police officer with petrol and burned him alive.[33] They also beat to death an American Press Correspondent (Gene Symonds) who was covering the strike; and a Chinese volunteer Special Constable, Andrew Teo, was also beaten to death by a mob which set fire to his car. A British police lieutenant in command of another police vehicle opened fire when it was attacked and a sixteen-year-old Chinese student was hit in the lung. The wounded boy was then paraded round by rioters attempting to whip up the crowd for two and a half hours before he was taken to hospital, where he died. It was stated that if he had been taken there direct he might have lived.[34] In addition to the four dead, thirty-one were injured.[35]

The rioting subsided by 3 a.m. and 13 May was generally quiet, though there was an almost complete strike of bus workers throughout Singapore. On Saturday 14 May a government arbitrator gave a ruling which was signed by the Hock Lee Bus Company and the SBWU under which the pre-strike rosters were restored. The Bus Company objected that these rosters were unfair to non-SBWU employers, but stated that they would accept the ruling in the public interest. Bus services were resumed on Monday 16 May.[36]

On the face of it, the Middle Road Group had won the day in that the employers were directed by the government to meet the strikers' demands. Marshall's problem was that although the SBWU was Communist controlled and was using the dispute for political rather than industrial purposes, the merits of the dispute did appear to put justice on its side, particularly in the eyes of the Chinese-educated public for whose leadership Marshall was competing.[37] On the other hand, the outbreak of violence and the deaths and injuries on the streets shocked the public as a whole and caused a reaction in favour of strengthening the powers of the police in maintaining law and order. There was an immediate reversal (approved by the Assembly) of some of the relaxations of the Emergency Regulations, and, for example, the power of the Commissioner of Police to impose curfews by administrative order was restored.[38]

Lee Kuan Yew's dilemma in reconciling his attempts to cooperate with the Communist Open Front with his disquiet at their methods was plain in the Assembly debate on the riots. He said that the PAP could not be responsible for every single member of the Party. They were working for a democratic non-Communist Malaya, but 'would not fight the Communists or the fascists to preserve the colonial system ... we seek to destroy the colonial system and we seek to do so by methods of non-violence ... we are opposed to any group or quarter from which violence comes.'[39]

Lim Chin Siong's contribution to the debate was perfunctory. He said that as an elected representative of the people he was not answerable to a colonial official; that he stood for a free democratic Malaya through peaceful and non-violent methods; that he did not support colonial officials in spreading negative hysteria of anti-Communism; and that otherwise he had nothing to add to what Lee Kuan Yew had said.⁴⁰ He spoke for less than a minute. Both then and later, in the words of David Marshall, Lim Chin Siong 'ostentatiously refused to answer the question as to where his loyalty lies – whether it is to Singapore or to Communism.'⁴¹

David Marshall faces the Communists

On 24 August 1955 the government tabled a new bill for the Preservation of Public Security. This was to replace the Emergency Regulations, though these were meanwhile to be extended (for the last time) for a further three months while the new Bill was being processed by the Assembly. It restored the police powers of search, and of imposing curfews and road blocks, and was finally passed on 12 October 1955 by nineteen votes to four (three PAP and one Independent) with seven abstentions.⁴²

There was a strong reaction, predictably, both from the PAP and from the Middle Road Group of Unions. Workers in all the major hotels went on strike in September, and a strike in the large Singapore Cold Storage Company was defeated only when picketers were arrested for obstruction. The men of the Singapore Traction Company (the only European-owned bus company in the Colony) also came out on strike in September, and remained out for five months. The union's adviser during this strike was Devan Nair, who was later to be detained with Lim Chin Siong, but who subsequently came over firmly to the support of Lee Kuan Yew.

In November the Singapore Bus Workers Union brought out all the rest of the island's twelve bus companies on strike under the leadership of Fong Swee Suan, who was not only Secretary of the SBWU, but also assistant Secretary General of Lim Chin Siong's SFSWU. Fong, who had already been detained for a few weeks in August, was to go into detention with Lim Chin Siong twice more, the second time as a staunch opponent of Lee Kuan Yew in the political struggle that was to come to a head in 1963. It is ironical that in November 1955 it was Lee Kuan Yew who saved the SBWU and the Middle Road group from defeat in this strike by proposing that there should be a public examination of the Bus Companies' books. At the prospect of this, the employers capitulated.

It was at about this same time (October 1955) that the Singapore Chinese Middle School Students Union, on the instruction of the Malayan Communist Party, gave the required 'undertaking' not to take part in political activities, and so became legally registered, as described in the previous chapter.

After seven stormy months in office, David Marshall had no illusions about the threat that the Communists' activities, amongst both workers and students, posed to his authority as Chief Minister. In December 1955 he joined the newly elected Chief Minister of the Federation of Malaya, Tunku Abdul Rahman, in the Truce Talks with Chin Peng at Baling. The main point at issue at these talks was the recognition of the Malayan Communist Party, with freedom to act as a legal political party after the end of hostilities. The PAP urged that this recognition should be given. The Tunku and Marshall, however, both stood firm against this and the talks broke down.

Chin Peng's Central Committee, who knew that they could now do no more at best than hold on to a bare existence as a political nucleus in the jungle, therefore issued further injunctions to the Party branches, both rural and urban, to concentrate their major effort on subversion – particularly in the Chinese Middle Schools.

It should not be imagined that this directive from the Central Committee reached many of the Party branches in time to have much direct bearing on the intensification of the student campaign in the first nine months of 1956. Nevertheless, the normal Communist education and study in party cells will have been enough to lead members to take this action (particularly in view of the well-publicized failure of the truce talks) without further orders. Those responsible for publication of Party News, Wall Newspapers etc. also used these media to exhort their followers to intensify their actions in the urban field, with the effect described in the previous chapter.

The London Talks of April/May 1956

Meanwhile, preparations were building up for constitutional talks in London in April 1956. Marshall took with him an All-Party Delegation which included both Lee Kuan Yew and Lim Chin Siong. The talks opened in a promising atmosphere. The British Secretary of State for the Colonies, the Rt. Hon. Alan Lennox-Boyd, paid tribute to the Chief Minister's fight against Communism. He said that he did not intend that Singapore should become an outpost of Communist China 'where perhaps for a while the essential defence bases might be tolerated because they helped to keep down unemployment, but which would assuredly be crippled in times of emergency by strikes or sabotage.'[43] (Similar things were to be said sixteen years later about the NATO base in Malta in 1972.)

The constitution proposed by the British Government provided that *ex officio* and nominated members of the Assembly would be abolished, and that the Assembly (wholly elected) would be increased to fifty members. The three British official Ministers would be replaced by elected members, and the Chief Minister would preside over the Council of Ministers. The British Governor would be replaced by a High Commissioner, who would preside over a Defence and Security Council, which would include two other representatives of the British Government and two of the Singapore Government. The British High Commissioner would thus have the decisive vote. In addition, the British Government would retain responsibility for external affairs and defence, including the power to make laws by Order in Council and to authorize the High Commissioner to make regulations, both of which would override other laws that might be in force in Singapore. These powers were in relation to external defence and external affairs, but the definition of external defence included 'the preservation or restoration of public safety or public order and the maintenance of essential supplies and services' in so far as they related to external defence or external affairs.[44] The United Kingdom also retained the power to suspend the Constitution 'if in their opinion the internal security of Singapore has so far deteriorated as to threaten Her Majesty's Government's ability to carry out their responsibility for external defence or external affairs; or if the Government of Singapore have acted in contravention of the Constitution as provided in this Order.'[45]

David Marshall applauded the rapid pace at which the Federation of Malaya was advancing to independence despite the continued need for military operations against the Communists; Singapore had no shooting war, and no British troops had had to be used to deal with internal disturbances during the past five years; his Government had now been operating for a full year, and it was their desire to be friends, but their will to cease to be dependents.[46]

He accepted the provisions of the proposed Constitution but for the United Kingdom government's insistence on legislative power to make overriding orders in Council on matters of internal security, and on a British majority vote on the Defence and Security Council.[47] He demanded that internal security should be the exclusive responsibility of the Singapore Government,[48] and also objected to the British retention of the right to appoint the Commissioner of Police, who was also to have direct access over the heads of elected ministers to the British High Commissioner.[49] (This objection was, of course, primarily concerned with the restrictions on his access to Special Branch secrets.[50]) Marshall pointed out that, with his reserve powers, the High Commissioner could, for example, legislate against strikes, processions and student rallies if regarded as prejudicial to external defence, and that, with such powers, the freedom granted by the proposed Constitution was illusory.[51] He said that such powers were unnecessary, since the British Government could always suspend the Constitution even before the eruption of violence if it considered that the deterioration of the internal security situation by subversion affected the efficacy of external defence installations.[52]

The British Secretary of State replied that it was possible to conceive of many disputes between Her Majesty's Government and the Singapore Government which would not call for so drastic an action as suspension. He insisted that the British Government 'must under present circumstance retain an *ultimate* authority in matters of external defence, internal security and external affairs'.[53]

On the twelfth and final day of the Conference, the Singapore delegation offered to accept the United Kingdom retention of overriding legislative powers if, and only if, the Defence and Security Council were composed of equal numbers of British and Singaporean representatives, with a Malayan Chairman appointed by the Federation Government. This proposal was rejected.[54] David Marshall's delegation finally asked whether, if they accepted all the proposals in the new Constitution, the overriding legislative powers could be limited to two years. This too was rejected. The Singapore delegation then took a vote amongst its members, nine voting against acceptance of the proposed Constitution, the other four abstaining. The talks thereupon ended.[55]

According to David Marshall, the left-wing members of his delegation were anxious to accept the proposed Constitution rather than go back with nothing, presumably confident that they could make faster progress under that than under the present Constitution. At the crucial vote on the final day, however, Marshall insisted that he would vote against it, and that if they accepted it he would be established as more radical than they were. On this they agreed to vote with him – including Lee Kuan Yew[5,6]

After the failure of the talks, Marshall resigned and his deputy, Lim Yew Hock, became Chief Minister.

The PAP Central Executive Committee Election

Soon after his return from London, Lee Kuan Yew was faced with a determined Communist challenge for control of the PAP. In July 1956 the Party held elections for a new Central Executive Committee, which resulted in four of the twelve places being filled by pro-Communists.[57] Indeed, Lim Chin Siong himself received more votes than Lee Kuan Yew, though Lee's chairmanship was endorsed by the vote of the eight members of the Committee who supported him.

Having failed to secure control of the Central Executive Committee on the popular vote of the PAP branches, the Communists attempted to have the Party Constitution redrafted so as to allow the branch committee to nominate members to the Central Executive Committee, instead of having them elected by a ballot open to all members of the branch. Lee Kuan Yew resisted this change, considering that it would in effect enable the Communists to capture the party.[58] This is a standard Communist tactic, used to gain control of trade unions and other organizations. Routine branch meetings are not usually well attended except by the more militant members, and by counting heads and springing a well-timed snap vote, it is easy enough to get left-wing members elected one by one to the Committee until they hold a majority. If thereafter this Committee nominates its representative to the next one up, and so on in a tiered system of nominations to the top, the Communists have only to capture the branch committees to capture in due course all the others including the Central Executive Committee. On the other hand, if each member of the Central Committee is elected by a popular vote of all members of the branches, this is far more difficult to manipulate – and more difficult still if the voting is by secret ballot. That is why, from its inception, the Soviet system was based on voting only at the bottom level with a tiered system of nominations above it. In Singapore, the 'Constitutional' Trade Unions (those affiliated to the Trade Union Congress) were generally run on the British system of election of all Committees by popular vote, whereas the left-wing Unions were run on the tiered system. But the left-wing attempt to extend the tiered system to the PAP was successfully resisted by Lee Kuan Yew.

A New Plan for Internal Security

The new Chief Minister, Lim Yew Hock, realized that neither the British Government nor the Federation of Malaya would allow Singapore to advance to full independence, or even to the control of their own internal security, so long as there was doubt about the ability of the government forces, whether directed by the British or not, to control the Communist erosion of their power. The Communist intention at this stage was clearly to coerce the government into making concessions which would give them rein to extend and consolidate their control of the students and workers by subversion and intimidation. Unlike Lee Kuan Yew, Lim Yew Hock believed that this could not be achieved by cooperating with them.[59] He therefore gave his full cooperation to the British Governor and Commissioner of Police.

The Commissioner of Police (CP) anticipated that the failure of the London talks, and the new Chief Minister's firm attitude towards the left-wing, would lead to bigger disturbances within the next few months. In July 1956 he therefore prepared a new Internal Security Plan, in conjunction with the General Officer Commanding (GOC) Singapore Base District. This plan was known as 'Operation PHOTO' (a pun on FOTO – Failure of Talks Operation).

The plan was based on maintaining forty continuous patrols by police radio cars, working in conjunction with army roadblocks and patrols and supported by two RAF helicopters (in the event reinforced to five). The police car coverage was such that from the time of a call, one car could be on the scene within three minutes, and two to three more within another five minutes. Each patrol car had a crew of six armed policemen, equipped also with tear gas and dye grenades (to stain the clothes of rioters as an aid to their subsequent identification).

One of the delicacies of this final period of transition from Colonial rule to independence was that a precipitate show of military force, especially by British units, would certainly be politically exploited, and might therefore do more harm than good. An important feature of Operation PHOTO was a discreet stand-by and deployment stage which enabled a show of force to be made from previously practised vantage points (normally the Police Divisional Headquarter Stations) within minutes of a decision by the Governor – a decision to be reached, it was hoped, together with the Chief

Minister and the Cabinet, unless they themselves were acting as a defiant opposition. This foresight was to pay good dividends.[60]

Working from these vantage points the army planned to establish twenty-six (later increased to twenty-nine) road blocks, covering all roads entering the city, and all the bridges across the river which splits the centre of the city in half. The army also provided vehicle patrols and night patrols to enforce the curfew.

All of these, the roadblocks, the helicopters and the patrols, were designed to prevent small bands of demonstrators from joining up into big crowds. Should they find crowds beyond their power to control, the soldiers could call on riot squads, each fifty strong, from each Police Area Headquarters, and of course, on the rest of the army.

The army garrison of Singapore contained only one British infantry battalion (1st Queens), and even this was normally all deployed in the jungle on the mainland except for one company at a time resting. Two further improvised Internal Security battalions were formed from a Malay-manned artillery regiment and from various units in the Base (also mainly Malay). These soldiers were given part-time training in Internal Security Duties and were known as 'X' and 'Y' I.S. Battalions. They had already proved their worth in the 1950 (Maria Hertogh) riots.

Plans were also made by the Director of Operations in Kuala Lumpur if required to withdraw the balance of the 1st Queens Battalion from the jungle, together with five more British and Gurkha battalions, to reinforce Singapore at very short notice. (In the event all but one of the 1st Queens companies were in Singapore nine hours after the call, and four other battalions within eleven to fourteen hours – a remarkable achievement considering that two were deployed in the jungle over 100 miles away.)

It was decided that, on the threat of serious trouble, the Brigadier commanding the 18th Infantry Brigade would set up his Command Post in the rooms immediately beside the Police Operations Room in Police HQ, Pearls Hill. An office for the CP and the GOC was also set aside in the same corridor. All operations would initially be under the direction of the CP.

The Government's Ultimatum

With these preparations complete, the Government felt better equipped to deal firmly with the Communist challenge. On 18 and 19 September the Council of Ministers ordered the banning of two Front Organizations – the Singapore Women's Association and the Chinese Musical Gong Society, and in the following week (24 September) they dissolved the Singapore Chinese Middle School Students' Union on the grounds that it had blatantly flouted its pledge not to take part in political activities. Special Branch were ready with the draft of the White Paper on the SCMSSU which laid out in detail the subversive activities of the Union as described in the previous chapter.[61] This was published and distributed on 4 October.

Meanwhile, on 1 October, they had arrested the Secretary-General of the SCMSSU, Soon Loh Boon (an over-age student of twenty-three). 15,000 Middle School Students held protest meetings in their classrooms, which coincided with their celebration of Communist China's National Day.[62] A Civil Rights Convention had also been formed on 28 September to protest against the dissolution of the two Front Organizations and the SCMSSU, and this too held meetings at which inflammatory speeches were made.

There was a meeting of the Assembly on 4 October. Lee Kuan Yew proposed a motion 'that this house is gravely concerned over the recent arrests of trade union and civic leaders and the dissolution of two societies.' He warned that 'repression . . . is a habit that grows.' First, he said, the Government attacks only those whom Special Branch say are Communists, even though they have no proof other than hearsay; next, those whom Special Branch say are actively helping, although they are not Communists themselves; then, those whom Special Branch say are aiding the Communists by their intransigent opposition to any collaboration with colonialism, thereby encouraging the spirit of revolt and weakening constituted authority; then finally 'you attack all those who oppose you'.[63] He concluded:

> 'I agree with the Hon. Gentleman opposite that if any act is done to overthrow a government by force, that act must be suppressed.[64] But if we say that we believe in democracy, if we say that the fabric of a democracy is one which allows the free play of ideas, which avoids revolution by violence because revolution by peaceful methods of persuasion is allowed, then, in the name of all the gods that we have in this country, give that free play a chance to

work within the constitutional framework. If you do not, then you will face outright opposition, an armed revolt, and eventually an armed victory. Then the whole social fabric of this society will collapse.'[65]

Later in the debate, he expanded further on this theme:

'In Britain, for 400 years, there have been no violent revolutions because one had this interplay within a system which allowed changes to take place by peaceful persuasion... The theory is that if the British Communist Party could put up a sufficient number of candidates and be able either by political persuasion or propaganda or other constitutional means of political leadership to get the majority of the people to vote for them, then they would become the lawfully constituted and elected government of the people.'[66]

He suggested that it was immaterial whether Special Branch were right or wrong about the guilt of the six men detained.

'Even if, in fact, these six men believe in Communism – the question remains whether they are prepared to compete constitutionally and peacefully. If they have never done anything which is not peaceful or constitutional, then you are negating your whole political philosophy when you say "I will arrest you because I think you are propagating an idea which I consider pernicious"...'[67]

Lim Chin Siong, seconding the motion, challenged the government to try the detained men in open court, and questioned Lim Yew Hock's authority.

'The Chief Minister proudly talks about "My Government"! Whom is he trying to bluff? Everybody knows that under the Rendel Constitution the Colonial Office controls all the key positions and retains ultimate control.'[68]

He criticized the government's 'anti-Communist hysteria', but at no time in his speech did he directly reject Communism or dissociate himself from subversion or violence. The difference between the philosophies of the two wings of the PAP comes out very very clearly in the two speeches, and Lim Chin Siong even made a back-handed reference to draw attention to Lee Kuan Yew's westernized, bourgeois habits.

'According to our Minister for Education, the collective study groups among Chinese students are Communists because the Communists also have such study groups. By this logic study group movements throughout the world must be Communist... Englishmen prefer their tea at 4 p.m. Asians who drink their tea at 4 p.m. are therefore Englishmen! Americans drive about in American cars. Harry Lee also drives an American car. Therefore Harry Lee is an American!'[69]

It was an unimpressive and rather immature speech and it proved to be the last he would make in the Assembly.

Meanwhile, however, trouble was building up in the schools and the government continued to act firmly. On 10 October, 4 student ringleaders from the Chinese High School and the Chung Cheng High School were detained, and 142 others expelled by the Committee of Management on the order of the Government.[70] 4,000 students gathered at the two schools and set themselves up for a siege – 1,000 at the Chinese High School and 3,000 at the Chung Cheng. These comprised the majority (indeed at Chung Cheng the overwhelming majority) of the students. The principals and most of the teachers went away, leaving the students in complete control.[71]

On 12 October the Government closed the two schools, upon which the busmen supplied the barricaded students with food and other comforts, repaying the support which they had earlier received from the students in the Hock Lee strike.

Meanwhile a minority of students defied the SCMSSU, and on 12 October six boys from the Chung Cheng High School called on the Minister of Education and presented him with the signatures of 725 students supporting the government action.[72] Next day the government announced that two temporary schools would be opened on 16 October, and began re-registration of students for these schools.

On 22 October students from the Chung Cheng and Chinese High Schools picketed the other Chinese Middle Schools, and it became clear that the trouble would spread unless firm action was taken. The Government therefore gave warning to parents on 24 October that, unless they removed their offspring from the two barricaded schools by 8 p.m. on 25 October, they would be removed by force.

Zero hour for the October 1956 riots had been set.

Chapter 7 The Riots of October 1956

Clearing the Schools

On the morning of 25 October parents began to gather outside the two schools, and the police removed the outer barricades. Government attempts to address the students by loudspeaker vans outside were drowned by clapping and singing, while the SCMSSU organization used their own public address system to keep up the students' morale, and set up an effective organization to deter any of them from leaving. It was clear that force was going to be necessary. All police and army units were therefore alerted and briefed, though none were moved at this stage, and preparations were confined to those which were not visible to the public.

Lee Kuan Yew, when he became Prime Minister some years later, criticized Lim Yew Hock's government for allowing themselves to reach this situation in which they had to use force to pluck out thousands of non-Communist Chinese educated students in order to immobilize the handful who were responsible for the stay-in strikes. He regarded this as a Communist trap to get them to be presented as anti-Chinese culture and anti-Chinese education, and as stooges, and that this in the end resulted in their downfall.[1]

At 5 p.m. Lim Chin Siong ran a protest meeting in Bukit Timah village, in the centre of the constituency which had elected him to the Assembly. It lies in the middle of one of the main factory areas, and is on the Bukit Timah Road which is the dual carriageway trunk road from the city to the causeway linking Singapore to the mainland. The village is about six miles from the city centre, and the Chinese High School is only two miles away, closer in along the main road (Fig. 10).

This meeting was held under the auspices of the Civil Rights Convention which had originally been formed on 28 September to protest against the dissolution of the SCMSSU and of the two front organizations. Inflammatory speeches were made by Lim Chin

THE RIOTS OF OCTOBER 1956

Siong and others, and when the meeting ended at about 7 p.m. some of those present moved off down the Bukit Timah Road to join the crowds assembling outside the Chinese High School.[2]

Lim Chin Siong's plan was to present a crowd big enough to be beyond normal control, so that the Government would be forced either to capitulate or to be the first to use force.

Lim Chin Siong had built up a strong Students/Parents Association to cement his United Front, and this introduced powerful emotions.[3] The 'cause' was one with a good deal of popular sympathy, and had no obvious connection with Communism. If the situation could be used to bring about the use of violence by big policemen against small schoolboys with a large audience lined up along the Bukit Timah Road, the Communists would have scored a major tactical victory.

Though this was the overt purpose of the Bukit Timah protest meeting, it was also used to brief, on the sidelines, the trade union branch leaders of the Middle Road Group, with orders to engineer 'spontaneous' strikes at all the Bukit Timah factory gates at clocking-in time next morning, and to lead the strikers later in the day to the centre of the city for a mass demonstration of strikers and students from all over the island.

By 8 p.m. the crowd outside the Chinese High School had grown to 3,000 (parents, busmen, workers and other students), many of them, including the ringleaders, fresh from the Bukit Timah protest meeting. A large traffic jam was building up on the Bukit Timah Road.

The police were there in force, but the CP had shrewdly ordered them to take no action to remove the students until 6 a.m. the following morning. As he expected, the hotheads amongst the crowd were unable to restrain themselves, and began overturning and burning cars and stoning police vehicles. Violence had begun, but it had been started – and publicly seen to be started – by the revolutionaries. So the first tactical point went to the police.[4]

Meanwhile, now that it was dark, more positive action was being taken by the Security Forces to prepare for what was clearly going to be a day of violence. At 9 p.m. the CP requested that the army units should move discreetly to their vantage points as planned in operation PHOTO (see Chapter 6). At 10 p.m. the Brigade Commander established his Command Post in the police headquarters in Pearls Hill.

Although all was now quiet on the Bukit Timah Road, sporadic outbreaks of violence continued elsewhere in the city, with crowds up to 300 strong. In the Kallang area (near the Chung Cheng High School) the crowd began to attack Police and European cars, and just before 11 p.m. a police radio car opened fire in its own defence – firing the first shots of the riots.

At this stage, the CP and GOC decided to ask for some of the reinforcement battalions to start extracting themselves from the jungle, and soon after 11 p.m. the orders went out to the balance of three companies from the 1st Queens, to one other battalion and to two squadrons of armoured cars.

Just after midnight, the CP used his existing powers to clamp down a curfew until 6 a.m., the time at which he planned to clear the two schools, and at 3.30 a.m. the Chief Secretary declared an 'Immediate Threat to Public Peace' under the Preservation of Public Security Ordinance, which, among other things, empowered the police to disperse any assembly of more than ten people, including assemblies in private premises such as school grounds, an important feature.[5]

At 6 a.m. on 26 October the police broke down the barriers and flushed the students out of the Chung Cheng and Chinese High Schools with tear gas. In the grey dawn, with no crowds, no audience, the students put up little resistance. At the Chinese High School there were no serious casualties at all. At the Chung Cheng, three were injured, one dying later from a fractured skull, either from a blow or a fall. Both schools were clear in twenty minutes.

Keeping the Crowds down to Manageable Size

By this time, the curfew had ended and parents were beginning to arrive outside the schools. The majority of the students, separated from their ringleaders, were glad enough to go home for a good meal, a wash and a rest after their sixteen-day sit-in.

The more militant ones, however, headed towards the city, mainly in small gangs of about two dozen, throwing stones and bottles, over-turning cars, and smashing up traffic lights, islands, and anything else that was obviously government property. One citizen's impression was that these bands of students had no particular aim or guidance, but that individuals were trying to show off to each other. As they made their riotous way along the streets, others were drawn by the noise and excitement, and joined in the fun of smashing and shouting.[6] Shortly before 8 a.m. the student gangs from the Chinese High School, joined by a number of strikers from the factories, starting setting up road blocks by sitting with arms linked across the road at Newton Circus, about a mile from the centre of the city, but they dispersed on the threat of force by a police riot squad. They continued towards the city centre, and some of them called in at the SFSWU Headquarters about half a mile on where they were met and encouraged to carry on by Lim Chin Siong, Fong Swee Suan and other union leaders, and were provided with sticks, bottles and missiles.[7]

Some gangs of students, however, were already penetrating to the city centre, and three foci of activity were beginning to form, as envisaged in the police/military plan prepared in July – first in China Town (south of the Singapore river), second around Victoria Street/Middle Road (north of the river) and third in the Geylang/Katong district near the Chung Cheng High School (Fig. 10).

By 8 a.m. a crowd of students had barricaded themselves into the Hokkien Association in Telok Ayer Street (China Town) and others were beginning to converge on Victoria Street via the Bukit Timah Road and also from the Chung Cheng High School. All public transport was at a standstill.

By this time, large crowds of workers were gathering outside the factory gates around Bukit Timah, where they had been met by pickets who informed them that there was to be a 'spontaneous strike'. The plan was that there should be protest meetings to whip up support during the morning, but that the demonstrators should not march on the city centre until 2.30 p.m. This would give the Middle Road Headquarters time to co-ordinate the convergence of huge crowds simultaneously from all quarters into the city, presenting the police again with the alternatives of giving way or using force.

As before, however, the hotheads could not wait, and set off in somewhat disorganized columns down the road soon after 8 a.m. joining up with gangs of students on the Bukit Timah Road.

At this stage the Commissioner of Police decided to put the full joint plan into operation.

The Brigade Commander had notified him at 7 a.m. that all the army roadblock teams were standing by in the immediate vicinity of their tasks. Thus far they had remained out of sight to avoid provoking the crowds; they were, however, observing and reporting

KEEPING THE CROWDS DOWN TO MANAGEABLE SIZE

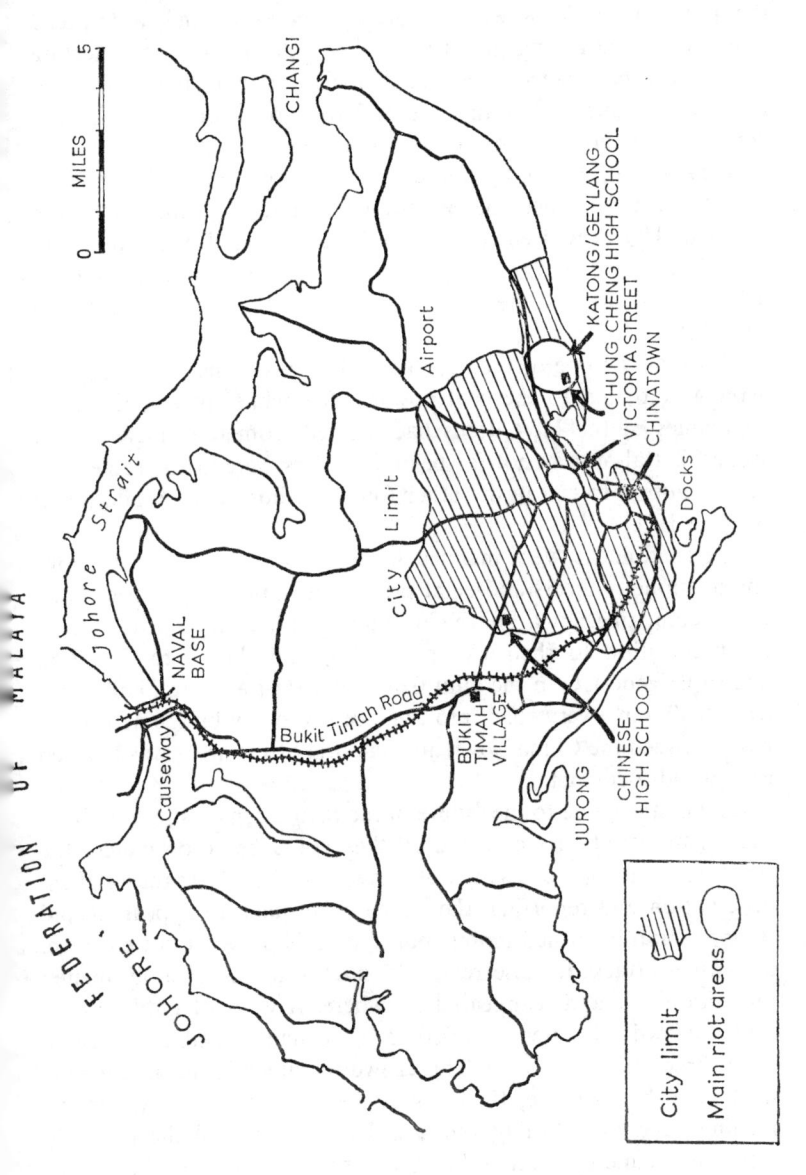

Figure 10 Singapore General Map

the crowds streaming through towards the city. At the same time, the police radio cars were reporting increasing and widespread violence by the roving gangs of students. A crowd was collecting outside the barricaded Hokkien Association in China Town and two crowds, one of 400 and one of 200, were stoning vehicles and erecting barricades in the Victoria Street area.

At 8.15 a.m., the CP therefore made a formal request for military assistance, and handed the Brigade Commander (in the next room at Police HQ) a written requisition for troops to disperse unlawful assemblies. By 8.20 a.m. the orders had gone out by radio, and by 8.30 a.m. all twenty-nine road blocks were established and manned (Fig. 11).[8]

This must be one of the quickest military responses on record to a request for aid to the civil power. Meanwhile, two of the extra companies of the 1st Queens had arrived from the jungle, and a second battalion was not far behind. Orders were at the same time put in motion to call in the other four battalions and an additional Brigade HQ.

The roadblocks were manned by teams varying from two non-commissioned officers and eight privates up to a full platoon. Each was accompanied by a Police Constable. All had radio or telephone communication to their Company HQ, and thence to Battalion and to Brigade HQ in the joint Command Post at Pearls Hill. Thus from 8.30 a.m. every road into the city and every bridge across the river between the China Town and Victoria Street areas was blocked and in radio contact.

At this stage, due to the failure of the revolutionaries to hold back their demonstration marches until they could be co-ordinated, the sizes of individual crowds did not exceed 400. Thanks to the excellent observation and reporting, the police were quick to appear. Rapid strong action by armed mobile police patrols proved most effective, and when attacked, these relatively small crowds generally melted into sidestreets and reappeared elsewhere. It was not until 10 a.m. that a crowd estimated at 2,000 to 3,000 had assembled in Telok Ayer Street in China Town. This crowd remained in the area for the next three hours or so, throwing stones and bottles at the police, turning over and burning vehicles. The army joined the police in attacking it, and by 1 p.m. it had been broken up without the need to open fire. It split into crowds of not more than 500, one of which moved off towards the Katong area.

KEEPING THE CROWDS DOWN TO MANAGEABLE SIZE

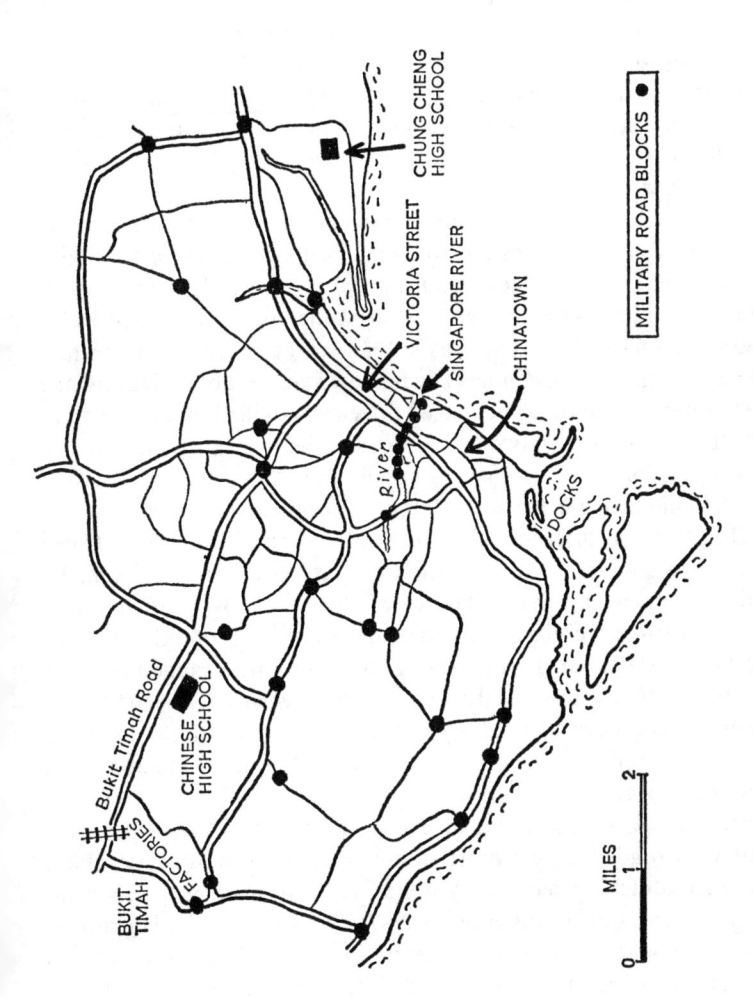

Figure 11 Singapore, Main Roads into the City

The military roadblocks were not attacked, but they served their purpose, and at no time did the crowds in China Town, Victoria Street and Katong link up to form dangerous mobs of 20,000 to 25,000. If crowds of that size had made concerted attacks against key points, they could only have been cleared by drastic action to induce mass panic and flight. It is this kind of action which dramatizes the situation, creates public martyrs and builds up bitterness between the crowds and the police, which was the most important Communist aim at this stage. The police and the army defeated it by keeping the crowds apart.

Nevertheless, during the morning and afternoon, violence by relatively small crowds of 200 to 500 built up. Six more of the police radio vehicles were attacked during the morning. In one of these attacks, an eleven-year-old boy amongst the crowd was killed by an overshot, and another man was killed by a blow from a baton in a police charge on the China Town crowd at 12 noon. During the next two hours, another boy, aged fifteen, was killed by an overshot, and three more rioters were shot dead whilst charging small police patrols of four or five men in roads and alleys around Victoria Street. This brought the total death roll thus far to seven.

This, the early afternoon, was the peak period of violence. Between 12 noon and 4 p.m. there were thirty-four attacks on persons, vehicles and government property, thirteen of them by crowds of over 100. Observed from roving helicopters, harried by promptly directed patrols and diverted by roadblocks, many began to range back into the outlying areas. 200 students stoning vehicles on the Bukit Timah Road were spotted by a helicopter which itself dispersed them by dropping tear gas grenades and at the same time drenching them with dye.

At about 2.30 p.m. a crowd of about 1,000 had built up on the main crossroads by the airport, about six miles from the city centre, and were attacking vehicles. A police patrol of three men saw a car carrying four Europeans heading for this crossroads and, realizing that this would lead to trouble, set off in pursuit. When they arrived the car was being attacked. The three policemen, led by a Chinese inspector, went in, and the mob turned its attention to them. Armed only with revolvers the three policemen stood their ground until the car had extricated itself. Charged by the crowd, they fired seventeen revolver shots, killing one and wounding one, before they withdrew.

The rioters in fact only killed one civilian. This was at 3.30 p.m.

in Victoria Street, when they attacked a City Council vehicle. The driver, a Malay, tried to defend himself with his starting handle, and was pursued by the Chinese crowd into a sidestreet and battered to death. The racial implications of the incident created a wave of anxiety, and appeals by leaders of the Malay community for calm and restraint were broadcast by Radio Singapore at frequent intervals throughout the rest of the day. The 1964 riots were later to demonstrate how explosive such an incident might have been.

At 3.15 p.m. the curfew was reimposed, and promulgated by public address vehicles and by low-flying aircraft with loudspeakers. There was no appreciable decrease in the number of incidents, but more of them were in rural areas.

By the evening of 26 October, the first five of the six battalions extracted from the jungle on the mainland had crossed the causeway into Singapore, and the military outnumbered the police on the ground. There was some discussion as to whether the GOC or the CP should have overall responsibility. The traditional practice laid down in the manuals was that, once the army had been called out the military commander should assume responsibility, which he would discharge mainly with the use of his soldiers, with the police in a supporting role. In the Singapore riots, however, the police and soldiers were all widely dispersed and operating in small parties each under radio control through its own channels. Sensibly, therefore, it was decided not to disrupt these chains of command. Though the Governor authorized the GOC to assume full responsibility, the police retained independent powers under the CP, whose own powers remained unimpaired.[9] Thanks to having a joint HQ from the start, a joint plan, and excellent liaison built up over the riots of the previous years, this worked well, though in different circumstances or with different personalities it might have been unsound.

Between dusk (about 6.30 p.m.) and 8 p.m. two more people were killed, one in China Town, where a police patrol used a pistol when they were charged by a crowd of 200, and the other at the Naval Base fifteen miles out of the city, by a Royal Naval patrol which fired in support of police who were stoned when they attempted to remove a barricade.

Thereafter during the first part of the night, the number of incidents actually increased, though they were perpetrated by smaller crowds. Between 8 p.m. and midnight, twelve barricades were erected. After midnight, there were only a handful of incidents by small gangs of curfew breakers, who attacked vehicles and erected one more barricade. Apart from this the night was generally quiet.

So, at least, it seemed to be on the surface. Behind the scenes, however, the night of 26/27 October was the most active – and the most decisive – of the year.

The Special Branch Swoop

Special Branch cover of the Middle Road Unions and Schools was excellent. This was partly because the MCP in Singapore was operating almost entirely through Open Front activities at this stage. At any rate, Special Branch knew who the leaders were, and where and when they met.

On the night of 26/27 October, the leaders of all the main branches of the SFSWU and of the other Middle Road Unions met together for a Conference at the headquarters in Middle Road. Seventy-four were present, including Lim Chin Siong.

At the same time, 343 of the factory members and students were meeting at the SFSWU 4th Branch HQ in Bukit Timah Road. There were meetings at two other SFSWU Branches, at the Hock Lee Branch of the Singapore Bus Workers Union and at the Singapore Farmers Association in Jurong.

These six meetings, widely distributed over the island, were all raided by Special Branch during the early hours of the morning, with the approval of the Council of Ministers. The raid on the Middle Road HQ went smoothly, so smoothly, in fact, that Alan Blades (then Head of Special Branch), looking back, wondered whether it wasn't part of Lim Chin Siong's 'martyr' policy. He obviously expected it, as he had withdrawn and salted away all the Unions' funds, which were considerable.[10] All the seventy-four present were detained, including Lim Chin Siong, who was to remain in detention for the next three years.

The 4th Branch HQ on the Bukit Timah Road, however, was strongly defended. There was a barricade of bicycles over which entry was resisted by men with iron bars, sticks and bottles of acid. Eventually the police broke down the door after using tear gas and firing some shots, wounding three rioters. Inside, they found blackboards marked up with the current riot situation, stacks of food, medical supplies, and other signs that the building was prepared for use as a strong point. The 343 occupants (who included many Chinese High School students) were screened and 70 detained.

The other four branches were also raided. In all, 618 people were found inside the six headquarters, of whom 234 were detained. At the same time, the police found and detained 82 known Secret Society members who were 'believed to be connected with the riots'.[11]

The Riots Subside

As news of the arrests spread on the morning of 27 October there was a revival of public confidence. On the other side, with the simultaneous removal of the entire top level of the Open Front leadership, and of a large number of its subordinate leaders and activists, there was a marked lack of organized activity. Though eleven people had been killed or mortally wounded on 26 October there were no 'martyrs' funerals' or other organized demonstrations on 27 October.

Sporadic incidents did, however, continue during the day, though on a much smaller scale. The curfew was lifted at 6 a.m. and by 8.30 a.m. crowds of 200 had collected both in Victoria Street and China Town, erecting barricades and attacking vehicles, and just before 10 a.m. there was another attack on a police radio van by a crowd of 500. Generally, however, the crowds were dispersed even more quickly than on the previous day, partly due to an additional technique in which the army, the R.A.F. and the police all took part. A network of rooftop observation posts was manned by parties of soldiers, each accompanied by a police constable. These overlooked the main riot areas of China Town and Victoria Street. As soon as a crowd formed, they would either descend and deal with it themselves, or notify a helicopter, which would swoop on the crowd with tear gas and dye grenades.

There was only one fatal incident during the day – the last of the riots. The crew of a police radio car were attempting to remove a barricade when they were charged by a crowd of 300. They opened fire and killed a seventeen-year-old boy who was leading the charge.

At 4.30 p.m. the curfew was reimposed until 8 a.m. on 28 October. Thereafter there were minor incidents only. The curfew was kept on for three more nights. Of the six infantry battalions brought into Singapore from the mainland, two returned to the jungle war on

1 November, and the other four the next day. They had to play little direct part in the riots (indeed only one was deployed at all) but their rapid appearance in such strength (they amounted in fact to 30 per cent of the infantry deployed in Malaya) undoubtedly played a part in the rapid subsidence of the riots. Alan Blades, the Head of Special Branch, states that:

> 'It was Lee Kuan Yew's opinion, later on, that it was the sight of tanks and military force, rather than the arrest of the ring-leaders, that caused the trouble to subside and he, and Goh Keng Swee in particular, were all for the earliest show of bayonets etc. when they took over responsibility for internal security after June 1959.'[12]

Summary of Events

These riots had the greatest significance and effect of any in the history of Singapore, and indeed had the makings of being the bloodiest. In the event, they were over very quickly, with relatively little bloodshed and damage. This was due to some extent to bad timing and control by the rioters' leaders, but predominantly to good planning and bold and rapid action by the military and the police.

There were in all thirteen deaths – only one inflicted by the rioters. No policemen or soldiers were killed, though five were detained in hospital, as were forty-two of the rioters. Chief credit for the relatively low casualties must go to the strict prohibition at pain of death of unauthorized possession of arms and ammunition, which had been enforced under the Emergency Regulations for the previous eight years. Throughout the riots, there were no cases of the rioters using firearms.

Because the rioters were unarmed, the police and soldiers could afford to use their weapons with restraint. They opened fire 114 times, firing 761 rounds – an average of less than 7 rounds per incident. Most of the occasions when the police fired (108) were when radio cars or small patrols fired in self-defence, and they caused 11 deaths, 3 of them by overshots amongst the bystanders. A naval patrol fired once killing one man. The army fired 5 times; twice in support of police against rioters throwing bottles from houses, and 3 times when isolated vehicles were attacked whilst carrying despatches at night. In all, the soldiers fired only 14 rounds and killed no one – a really astonishing record considering their widespread deployment and the number of incidents.

31 vehicles were burned, and another 101 damaged. Three buildings were burned, and two others damaged. Of the total of 150 events classed by the police as 'incidents' the great majority were on 26 October. Most of them (79) consisted of attacks on persons and property, chiefly private cars. 32 were against individual police and military vehicles. 107 of them were concentrated within the two areas, each about one square mile, of China Town and Victoria Street (Fig. 10). These were the main housing areas of the poorer urban Chinese – dock labourers, street traders etc. It is significant that on no occasion were the crowds able to converge into the vast open space of the padang facing the City Hall and other main public buildings. Had they done so they would have presented the traditional pattern of a huge unmanageable assembly threatening a key point and faced by a line of soldiers, who would have eventually had no recourse but to open fire and shed blood in full view of a highly charged audience. Yet the City Hall and the padang were located between China Town and Victoria Street and within a mile of the main rioting areas on either side, and were the declared target of the demonstration marches. That they never attacked it was because the joint police/military plan was especially designed to prevent the crowds from converging, by means of its combination of roadblocks, patrol cars and mobile riot squads, served by helicopters and, later, by rooftop patrols.

The Performance of the Government Forces

Helicopters were used in these riots for the first time on record and proved an outstanding success. The five helicopters flew 136 sorties in all, totalling 90 flying hours. They were able to keep a continuous watch on the worst areas, usually carrying a senior police officer on board, and in direct radio contact with a combined police/army headquarters. They provided a platform, immune from retaliation, from which tear gas, dye grenades and leaflets could be launched, and they were often able to spot and disperse crowds and prevent them from reforming without calling other forces at all. They thereby established an awesome respect for the ubiquity of the Security Forces. At the same time they cooperated with rooftop patrols in directing police and army radio vehicles to deal quickly with other assemblies.

The pilots of the three reinforcing helicopters were at some disadvantage in lacking intimate knowledge of the city, but this was partly overcome by the inclusion of police officers in the crew.[13]

The rooftop patrols introduced on the second day also proved most successful. They were concentrated on the areas where most of the potential rioters lived, and where there were many of the foci (such as the Middle Road HQ and the Hokkien Association) where crowds collected. They were able to watch the crowds forming up, especially in the narrow alleys, and either take action to disperse them themselves, or notify their Company HQ who could call in helicopters, patrol cars or riot squads by radio. The rooftop patrols, being a last-minute improvisation, were not equipped with radio. They used yellow flags to signal for action. Often the helicopter crew saw and acted on these signals. If not, the headquarters of the infantry company providing the patrols could see and interpret their signals, and call for action by radio.

The success of the forty police radio cars and of the riot squads has already been described. The key was to be on the scene quickly and act boldly – once again creating an image of ubiquity and strength. Considerable gallantry was shown by small numbers of policemen facing large crowds, of which a few examples only have been quoted.

Apart from providing eyes and ears, the main function of the army was to provide a framework within which the police could operate freely and flexibly – a reversal of normal practice. On this occasion it was the police who provided the striking force – and who did most of the shooting. With an *armed* police force, this has many advantages, for they are the best judges of how demonstrators and hooligans react, and the use of police against crowds is less emotive than the use of soldiers. Had members of the crowd been armed, or the police unarmed, their small patrols could not have done what they did. In the face of the MCP 'armed struggle', the arming of the police throughout Malaya was essential. In more normal times, the fact of a police force being unarmed contributes so much better to law and order that it should be armed only with reluctance.[14] There is, therefore, a risk of drawing false lessons from this departure from the normal British police and military roles, though it proved right in Singapore in 1956.

The main elements of the army's framework were the twenty-nine roadblocks, and the road patrols in outlying areas. One of the army's functions was to relieve as many policemen as possible from

THE PERFORMANCE OF THE GOVERNMENT FORCES

duty at night, so as to leave them fresh for the main battles of the day.

The army, for example, took on the great majority of the curfew patrols – which, though the task was a routine chore, were responsible for nearly half the arrests (1,034 out of 2,346). They moved in vehicles, slowly, concentrating on minor roads, and dismounting to investigate the narrow alleys on foot. To keep down the number of arrests, and to maintain good relations with ordinary citizens, they were instructed to apply the rules sensibly, accepting that many people had not heard the announcement of the curfew, or that they might be out on reasonable errands such as seeking medical aid. Each army curfew patrol was accompanied by a policeman, who did the questioning of curfew breakers.

The good communications between headquarters, patrols and helicopters gave the police and army a tremendous advantage over the rioters. Now that cheap 'walkie-talkies' are available to anyone, this advantage may be reduced in future riots.

Government handling of public relations was also excellent. The Police Secretary acted as spokesman for all services, and the radio was used most effectively. Conducted tours were provided for correspondents, who were well and frankly briefed, and photo cover was extensive. The result was a favourable local press.[15]

This led in turn to a favourable reaction by the public. Attendance at work remained throughout at a high level despite transport difficulties, and after the riots there was a marked swing away from the Middle Road Unions to the TUC. This was another example of a city people, faced with violence and the threat of chaos, rallying to the side which gave the best promise of restoring law and order.

The really decisive stroke, however, was the series of raids by Special Branch on the night of 26/27 October, which scooped up almost the entire open front leadership. Whether or not Lim Chin Siong again deliberately allowed it to happen as part of his 'martyr' policy, this was a dramatic manifestation of the intelligence cover enjoyed by the police, which in fact enabled them to hold the initiative throughout the whole campaign, from the original action against the SCMSSU in September, through to the restoration of tranquility in the city at the end of October.

In the long run these arrests also proved to be of major advantage to Lee Kuan Yew and the moderate wing of the PAP, who were able during the next three years to build up the party to a position of political dominance (which it holds to this day) with themselves as unchallenged leaders, unmolested by manoeuvres by Lim Chin Siong and his 'first eleven'. In 1957, an unsuccessful bid to capture the leadership of the PAP by the Communist 'second eleven' led to them too joining Lim and the others in detention. Lee Kuan Yew was to play this advantage with great skill, retaining the support of Lim's followers by making their release a condition of his taking office in 1959, but watching that the 1959 election ordinance was so drafted that the ex-detainees could not themselves stand for election. The ex-detainees did thereafter make an attempt to capture power (in 1961–2) but Lee Kuan Yew was by then just secure enough to defeat the challenge. If it had not been for the October 1956 riots and these resulting arrests, the story might have been different. So in this respect too the riots proved to be a critical point in the history of Singapore.[16]

The Performance of the Revolutionaries

The riots were intensely disappointing to the Communists. The achievements of their Open Front leadership over the previous two years had been impressive. They controlled an important sector of the trade unions, and a majority of the students at the Chinese schools. They had developed an issue – Chinese education, and particularly the helping of younger students by older ones in their academic work – which evoked widespread sympathy amongst the predominantly Chinese population, who could be rallied under the banner of the Civil Rights Convention in patriotic protest against the 'oppression' of the Chinese speaking community by a Colonial Governor and a Council of Ministers who were virtually all English-educated and by a predominantly Malay Police Force, and Malay, Gurkha and British soldiers.

The Communists had an excellent open and semi-secret chain of command and control: to every bus garage, to most taxi-drivers and trishaw riders, to most dockworkers, to a large number of factory branches and small farmers and to virtually every class in every Chinese High School – both for boys and for girls; also to many of their parents through the Parents' Friendly Association, and through many other Front organizations. As Lee Kuan Yew recorded later, by working and manifestly appearing to work selflessly and ceaselessly ....' the Communists, although they had only a few hundred active cadres, could muster and rally thousands of people in the Unions, cultural organizations and student societies.'[17]

Their secret cell structure was weak, but this was probably not a factor in the failure of the riots, because even a strong secret structure would not have had the channels to take over the open leadership in time to maintain the momentum after Lim Chin Siong and his colleagues were arrested. Nor indeed should party cell members have exposed themselves in attempting to do so. A better secret structure might, however, have enabled the MCP in Singapore to have recovered from the setback in the longer term which, to this day, it has failed to do.

The real failure must inevitably lie with the Open Front leadership, and particularly with Lim Chin Siong himself, who G. G. Thomson considers to have failed primarily as a tactician. He had come to the top at school as an organizer rather than as a thinker. His organization provided him with a *locus vivendi* and an opportunity in classical Leninist style, but these proved to be of no avail as he misread the tactical signs, which were more skilfully read by Lee Kuan Yew, who kept out of trouble in the riots and later outmanoeuvred the Communists at their own game.[18] On the other hand, Lee Kuan Yew retained the highest regard for Lim's capabilities and did not write him off as a long-term threat.[19]

Lim himself subsequently admitted to Douglas Hyde, in the course of their long discussions in Lim's cell in Changi gaol in the middle 1960s, that he had completely misread the mood of the Chinese workers in 1954-6. During his speeches they had cheered his references to sympathetic issues, such as his calling for an end to Colonialism, referring with pride to mainland China, or calling on them to strike for better conditions. But, he said, they were cheering the issues in themselves and not their ideological implications, to which he thought they were committed when in fact they were not. They were pro-Chinese rather than pro-Communist.[20]

Along with uncertain leadership, the Communists' tactics were weak. The crowds were launched with high passion by the Civil Rights Committee, but the aim seemed only to be to provoke violence, and (apart from a plan to present a protest to the Minister of Education) they had no clear targets, such as the threatening or seizure of key points. No particular individual clashes were planned.

Leaders and agents did not seem to be charged with specific tasks. It was assumed that their training in ABL, Hsueh Hsih and sympathizer cells would provide sufficient guidance for them to exploit opportunities as they arose.

A Comparison with the Hong Kong Riots of 1967

It is interesting to contrast these riots with the riots in Hong Kong in 1967, which continued with varying intensity for eight months. There were some similarities in the settings: Singapore and Hong Kong were both island colonies, predominantly Chinese, and Communist Middle Schools play an open and important part in Hong Kong's education system. The trade unions in both cases were fairly evenly split between a Communist Federation and a TUC. The Communist Party in Hong Kong operates openly and legally, with the gigantic moral support of China on the frontier a few miles away.

From May to December 1967 Hong Kong was torn by serious and well organized riots, both inside the cities of Victoria and Kowloon, and by mobs crossing the frontier from Communist China. This confrontation was clearly a by-product of the Cultural Revolution in China, though there was subsequent evidence that it was initiated without the approval of Mao Tse Tung or of his Foreign Minister,[21] and ended in a complete climb-down by the Communists, the 'five demands' which they made publicly and militantly at the start being ignored and then quietly forgotten.

Hong Kong had a population of about four million, roughly half of whom were refugees from Communist China who had entered during the seventeen years since Mao Tse Tung seized power. Though the Colony had achieved miracles in housing and creating employment for these refugees, there were obvious difficulties in both fields.

The immediate excuse for the outbreak of rioting was an industrial dispute in an artificial flower factory. During the next eight months about fifty people were killed in riots and in bomb explosions. There were, in all, over 1,500 bombs which either exploded or were neutralized by the army and the police.

The four million people in Hong Kong lived mainly in the two principal cities, Victoria (on Hong Kong Island) and Kowloon (on the mainland), which have amongst the highest population

A COMPARISON WITH THE HONG KONG RIOTS OF 1967

densities in the world. The Colony Boundary runs through what is now the middle of Kowloon, and there is a hinterland of 365 square miles, the New Territories, which are leased to Britain until 1997. There is a twenty-two mile frontier between the New Territories and Communist China, and under the Treaty people are free to cross both ways at authorized points to cultivate land on the other side of the frontier. Much agricultural produce is also wheeled (or driven on the hoof) across the one main road bridge from China at Man Kam To for sale in the Colony, and there is also much traffic across the one railway bridge at Lo Wu. These two points were the scenes of much of the frontier rioting, and so was the fishing village of Sha Tau Kok which is split by the frontier – the market again being on the British side.

The Communist Party in Hong Kong is legal, and has its headquarters in the Bank of China Building, which is built like a fortress. As in Singapore, some of the trade unions (63) were affiliated to the Communist Federation of Trade Unions (FTU), and about the same number (62) to the TUC, with 115 unattached. The FTU controlled Public Utilities and the dockyard.[22]

The Communist Party in Hong Kong also runs a number of Middle Schools which play a large part in secondary education in the Colony.[23]

The Communist techniques used in the Hong Kong Riots were more militant than those used in Singapore. Strikes were encouraged, despite the strong government warning that striking public utility workers would lose their jobs. The FTU paid strike pay of $HK 500 per month.[24] When the man lost his job he was asked to 'earn' his $500 by painting slogans and sticking up posters. The Communists photographed him doing this, and then showed him the photograph, saying that it had been 'filched from the police'. They used this to persuade him to go underground, reduced his pay till he was desperate, and then forced him to earn his keep by violence – including the planting of bombs.[25] There was a standard rate for planting bombs – $40 for a hoax, $200 for a live one, $300 if it exploded, $400 if it killed someone, and $500 if the perpetrator went to prison. Some militant Communists were contemptuous of this mercenary technique as 'killing the spirit of revolution', as 'capitalist enterprise' and as 'attracting money-grubbers, not militants'.[26]

The riots were organized on similar lines. Police observers amongst the crowds estimated that stone-throwers earned 50p to £1 per day, a reasonable Hong Kong wage. Histrionic collapses by 'injured' rioters were carefully rehearsed, with 'blood' smeared on their faces (from chickens or ketchup bottles). Bandages were held ready for spurious application – with more 'blood'. Above all, trained leaders were switched from one area to another during the riots.[27]

The organization and execution were first-class, and yet these riots failed in their object as dismally as those in Singapore. The reason, again, was good police work, coupled with rapid but not unnecessarily aggressive military action. The Communists were taken aback by the astonishing and immediate popular reaction against rioting. Public meetings were held to support firmer counter-action. The police suddenly became the colony's heroes, and a fund for improved educational opportunities for policemen's children had risen to £62,000 within ten days of the outbreak of violence. Television coverage of the riots caused public disgust, and the dislocation of vital examinations did not help the Communist cause amongst an education-conscious Chinese community.[28] A series of highly aggressive attacks were then made from Communist China on the frontier police posts, but these too stood firm with army support. Violence continued in the form of bomb incidents. Between May and September the Bank of China spent $HK 1 million on rewards to bombers, but at this stage they stopped further payment.[29] A significant and paradoxical factor here was a quarrel between the Anti-Persecution Struggle Committee, representing the workers, and the official representatives of the Peking Government, which was concerned to keep up the foreign exchange earnings from Hong Kong, backed by the Chinese Communist business men in Hong Kong, who did not wish to see their volume of business curtailed by continuous strikes.[30] By the end of 1967 the entire campaign had subsided, and the militant and unusually specific demands which had been supported by Communist China were quietly abandoned unfulfilled.

The riots in Hong Kong in 1967 were far better led than those in Singapore in 1956, but both failed because the leaders underestimated the peoples' instinctive desire for law and order, which caused them to rally to the government the moment it became clear that the security forces were standing firm without the use of undue violence.

If the government had given way in Hong Kong, the result (as demonstrated in Macao) is not hard to guess. In Singapore the

A COMPARISON WITH THE HONG KONG RIOTS OF 1967

1956 riots gave each of the four sides (the British, Lim Yew Hock's government, Lee Kuan Yew's moderate wing of the PAP, and the Communists) and the public an idea of where each of them stood and how far each was prepared to go. Above all, the success and consequent prestige of the police kept the battle off the streets for the next seven years, enabling Lee Kuan Yew to establish his political position and conduct the political struggle with his rivals in the Assembly, in Party Committees and in private meetings, without coercion by mob violence.

The riots of 1955 and 1956, however, had left their mark. The Communists realized that unless they had reasonable scope for conducting subversion and intimidation in the schools and trade unions and could weaken the power and decisiveness of the security forces in dealing with violence on the streets, they could not hope to oust the existing government. The Singapore government, on their side, recognized that a solid internal security structure, not too vulnerable to passing political whims, was essential if they were to persuade the British to allow them to progress to full independence, and the Malayans to accept them into the Federation. As a result, the burning issue throughout the political struggle of the next seven years was to be internal security.

Chapter 8 The Struggle for Political Control

Constitutional Conference in London 1957

If the effect of the 1956 riots was to convince the Singapore Government that it must maintain internal security in order to gain independence from Britain and admission into the Federation, their effect in London and Kuala Lumpur was the natural complement – a more cautious approach by the British Government towards independence, and hostility in the Federation Government towards any kind of merger with Singapore.[1]

In March 1957 while the Federation was in the final stages of preparing for complete independence (due on 31 August 1957), an all-party delegation from Singapore was invited to London for a conference on a Constitution which was still to give no more than limited self-government and which was not to be brought into force until 'a date after 1st January 1958'.[2] All the same, because of the prestige he had gained in London as a result of the riots in October 1956, Lim Yew Hock was able to negotiate a more favourable Constitution than many would have expected – or, indeed, than many thought desirable at the time. Even this might never have been granted if there had seemed to be any serious likelihood of the PAP being elected to form the first government under the Constitution (remembering that at this time they had only three out of the twenty-five selected members in the Assembly). Indeed, Lee Kuan Yew himself and his fellow 'moderates'[3] in the PAP were regarded with considerable apprehension, both in London and in Kuala Lumpur, because of the willingness of the PAP to accept people whom Special Branch knew were Communists. Past experience suggested that once a political party accepted Communists in its ranks, they were virtually certain to take control of it in the end.[4] Some thought that Lee Kuan Yew himself was watching which way the cat was going to jump, and would be ready to go along with the Communists if they prevailed, just as Castro was to do four years later in Cuba. The fact that merger with the Federation was a major plank in the PAP platform[5] was itself regarded in Kuala Lumpur with deep suspicion, not only because it would land them with a Chinese majority,[6] but also because, just when the Malayans were snuffing out their own Communist Party in the jungle and attaining independence, they did not want to import another, urban based revolutionary party and start all over again.[7]

Nevertheless, Lee Kuan Yew was one of Lim Yew Hock's delegation of five Assemblymen who went to London in March 1957, and Lee played a dominating part in the negotiation[8] of the constitutional proposals, which were signed on 11 April. The main features of these proposals were that

(a) *Ex officio* and nominated members of the Legislative Assembly should be abolished, and its elected Membership increased to fifty-one. The Chief Minister would become Prime Minister, and would preside at meetings of the Council of Ministers, in which the three *ex officio* would be replaced by elected Ministers.[9]

(b) The British Governor would be replaced by a Malayan-born head of state, to be appointed by the Queen on the advice of the British Governor in consultation with the Singapore Government.[10]

(c) The British Government would be represented by a U.K. Commissioner, who would not attend the meetings of the Council of Ministers, but would receive copies of their Agenda and would have the right to see papers which he considered liable to affect the U.K. responsibility for external affairs and defence.[11]

(d) There would be an Internal Security Council composed of three British, three Singaporean and one Federation member – the latter to have the casting vote (see below).

(e) The British Government reserved the right to suspend the Constitution 'if in their opinion the internal situation in Singapore had so far deteriorated as to threaten their ability to carry out their responsibilities for external affairs or defence or if the Singapore Government had acted in contravention of the Constitution'. In this event the U.K. Commissioner would assume the government of Singapore.[12]

The most controversial argument in the Constitutional proposals was on the provisions for maintaining Internal Security (IS). The British Government insisted that 'persons known to have been engaged in subversive activity should not be eligible for election to the first Legislative Assembly of the new State of Singapore', though it was accepted that future policy in this respect would be a matter for the Singapore Legislature to decide after the first elections. The disagreement of the Singapore Delegation was recorded in the Report as follows:

'The Singapore Delegation expressed their opposition to this departure from normal democratic practice and protested at the unilateral imposition of this condition. They made it clear that they could not accept Her Majesty's Government's proposal. For Her Majesty's Government it was stated that this was a condition precedent to the new Constitution which they would have to impose. It was the view of Her Majesty's Government that some temporary restriction of this kind was essential to safeguard the orderly development of democratic government in Singapore against the danger of Communist subversion. Future policy in this respect would be a matter for the Singapore Legislature to decide after the first elections. In the circumstances the Singapore Delegation took note with regret of the intention of Her Majesty's Government.'[13]

It is probable that the majority of the Singapore Delegation in fact welcomed this provision, but it was better for their anti-colonial image in Singapore if they were seen publicly to contest it. They might therefore have been somewhat embarrassed if the British Government had not insisted upon it as a precondition of the Constitution, and the British Government will have been well aware of this.[14]

Responsibility for Internal Security

The key feature of the provision for IS was the Internal Security Council (ISC). It was agreed by all sides that this would consist of

Three Singaporeans (the Prime Minister and two others)
Three British (the U.K. Commissioner and two others)
One Minister from the Federation of Malaya.

The U.K. Commissioner was to be Chairman but in the event of a disagreement between the three Singapore and three U.K. members, the Minister from the Federation would have the casting vote. To avoid snap votes, it was laid down that, when a vote was to be taken, all members or their duly authorized alternates would attend the meeting and vote.[15]

The Constitution was attacked by David Marshall, the ex-Chief Minister, who criticized both Lim Yew Hock and the PAP for agreeing to it. In the Assembly on 26 April he issued a challenge to fight any member on the issue in a by-election in that member's own constituency. Lee Kuan Yew at once accepted the challenge,[16] and both he and Marshall resigned their seats on the 30th. Lee defended the Constitution on the grounds that Singapore, as an important British military base in a predominantly Chinese island, was most unlikely to be granted independence from Britain as a separate state, so that the overriding object of the Singapore people must be a merger with the Federation; and that this would never come about unless the Federation Government had the means to ensure that the MCP was not being allowed to establish a base in Singapore.[17]

Amongst the other internal security measures accepted by the Singapore Delegation in London in April 1957 were that the three senior police officers, i.e. the Commissioner of Police, his Deputy, and the Director of the Special Branch, would be appointed on the recommendation of the Singapore Public Service Commission – a body formed in 1955 of community leaders without political commitment. The Internal Security Council would be informed and could challenge these recommendations once, but thereafter, if confirmed by the Public Service Commission, they would stand.[18]

It was also agreed that British troops might have to be used to aid the civil power in dealing with internal disorder. The decision to request such aid would rest with the Singapore Minister.[19] (It must be remembered, however, that the U.K. Commissioner retained the right *in extremis* to suspend the Constitution and govern himself, thereafter reserving the right to call in British troops if he thought it necessary.)

The PAP Executive Committee Changes Hands

Lee Kuan Yew was duly returned in his by-election, Mr. Marshall having decided after all not to contest it and to 'retire from politics'.[20] Lee, however, was now having trouble with the left wing of his own party. In August 1957 supporters of the imprisoned Lim Chin Siong managed to secure six of the twelve seats on the Central Executive of the PAP at the annual Party Conference. Lee accused them of rigging the vote by bringing non-members into the Conference,[21] and he and his fellow 'moderates' refused to take office. For a short while, Lee lost control of the party, but a few days later the police arrested five out of the six left-wing Committee members for subversive activity in the Trade Union Congress.[22] Lee resumed the PAP Chairmanship, and acted quickly to prevent a recurrence. To quote his own account:

> 'After this experience we amended our Party Constitution to make sure that the Party cannot be so easily captured. We instituted two classes of members – ordinary members and cadre members. Ordinary membership is open to all and secret penetration by Communists into this group is easy if they send in their people who are not yet well known. But only those who have proved over a period of time that they are sincerely and honestly with the Party can become cadre members. An election of the Central Executive Committee is only by cadre members.'[23]

This incident was, however, of considerable embarrassment to Lee Kuan Yew in the Assembly. where Lim Yew Hock naturally claimed to have saved the PAP from itself by these arrests. On 23 August the Government tabled a White Paper[24] giving details of MCP aims and activities in Singapore, quoting in detail from recently seized documents dated between April and June. Reaffirming the fundamental aim of the MCP as the establishment of a Communist State, using revolutionary violence if necessary, the White Paper said that, as a preliminary step, or where violence had failed, the Party aimed to join, influence and finally control organizations or groups whose legitimate aims provided a cover for their activities. Party workers infiltrating such legitimate organizations took the greatest care to hide their connection with the MCP. Being trained Communists they did not require frequent directions from the Party, but were able to interpret events and any published statements made by the Party. The organizations often had no idea that they were being penetrated, nor that they were being subconsciously indoctrinated with Communist ideas.[25]

The White Paper described the MCP campaign of 1954–6, culminating in the arrest of its leaders in the riots of October 1956.

It then quoted from a document seized in a Singapore MCP cell, dated April 1957:

'It is only after the people's strength is comparatively superior, while the rulers are weakened, especially when their armed strength is facing disintegration, that a riot can be expected to achieve victory,'

and declared that current policy was to remain under cover, conserve strength, consolidate the United Front, and win over groups or individuals to their cause.[26]

A June 1957 document was also quoted, giving details of the technique for gaining control of a farmers' union in a rural area of Singapore. It said that:

'There must not be deliberate competition for the offices of Chairman and Treasurer at the outset, so as to avoid arousing suspicion'

but it added that the Party aim was still to work quietly towards getting their men in eventually as Chairman, Treasurer and General Affairs Officer, which in fact in the case quoted they did.[27]

Recalling the dissolution of the SFSWU in October 1956, the White Paper recorded that the Singapore General Employees Union (SGEU) was now operating from the same Middle Road premises, and had revived the Singapore Trade Union Working Committee (STUWC) which had in 1956 claimed to represent ninety-five Trade Unions, and now claimed thirty-two. They had already revived sufficiently to test their strength against the TUC group of unions in a rival May Day demonstration, and on 18 July they had held a meeting at Middle Road to discuss tactics for gaining control of the TUC.[28]

The White Paper described in detail the Communist penetration of the PAP, and particularly of its Cultural and Education Committees, through which it ran picnics and other functions which were used to promulgate Communist propaganda. The White Paper quoted another MCP document dated June 1957 which had described the Party's relationship with the PAP, and had discouraged any idea of splitting the PAP, whose basic policy was correct, even if some of its methods and theories were not. The document had added:

'We are sure that some of the PAP inclinations can be changed.'[29]

The White Paper recorded that, despite the arrest in October 1956 of fourteen office bearers and other important members of the PAP, a number of known members of the secret Communist organization still held various offices in the PAP and others remained as ordinary members.[30]

In the Assembly debate on this White Paper, Lee admitted that his party was not impervious to Communist penetration, but denied that this was confined to the PAP. 'The MCP is denied political existence, and must resort to clandestine methods to enter the constitutional political arena', he said, adding that the dissemination of propaganda foreign to the PAP's aims was the work of a few individuals and that 'the Party leadership . . . had consistently stamped out such activities, and that they had been consistently firm and resolute in their non-Communist stand'. He challenged the assertion in the White Paper that 'from past experience it is quite clear that there is no prospect at all that these legal organizations will be able to purge themselves of Communist influence' and claimed that the PAP, unlike the TUC, was quite capable of looking after itself.[31] Few people then believed him.

The Communists Send a Plenipotentiary

In March 1958, according to a later account by Lee Kuan Yew, the MCP tried a bold new tactic with him. They sent a plenipotentiary – known by Lee Kuan Yew, and hereafter, as the PLEN – to make secret contact with him.[32] At this time, the secret element of the Singapore Communist Party was based in the Rhios islands – a rash of tiny islands about twelve miles from Singapore which are part of Indonesia. A great many small boats regularly crossed these waters in the process of fishing or carrying merchandise, and with forged identity documents it was not difficult for individuals to pass to and fro. Since these islands were remote from Jakarta and therefore only loosely administered by the Indonesians, they formed a secure sanctuary for the very small secret element of the Party.

The approach was made to Lee Kuan Yew by an intermediary whom he knew to be connected with the Communist organization, and Lee agreed to meet the PLEN in Singapore, and to respect his confidence.

Lee first decided to test the PLEN's credentials by checking whether he really did have control over the Open Front cadres still operating in the Singapore unions and political parties, and asked him to prove his good faith by ordering one Chang Yuen Tong to resign from the City Council and from the Executive Committee of the Workers Party formed by David Marshall since his resignation. Sure enough, a few weeks later, Chang did indeed resign from both bodies, and Lee was satisfied.

The first of their clandestine meetings took place just before Lee left for the London Constitutional talks in March 1958, and there were three more between then and the elections in June 1959. The PLEN'S main concern was to find out whether the PAP was really willing to work with the Communists in a united anti-colonial front. Lee drew attention to the errors which Lim Chin Siong had made in 1956, which had resulted in him and others being detained, and to the attempts which the Communists had made to seize the leadership of PAP in August 1957. The PLEN explained that these errors were the result of difficulty in communicating instructions to Lim Chin Siong and the other Open Front leaders in time; that now, however, Lee was dealing with the top, with the men who decided the policy and gave the orders, and that they would keep their word on any agreement made with him. Lee, however, declined to commit the PAP.[33]

Lee Kuan Yew's actions and attitudes at this time must be judged in the light of three things

(a) As a shrewd politician, he was aware of a quite remarkable swing of public opinion in his favour, and he was confident that the PAP would gain a majority at the next election. There had been a clear pointer to this in the City Council elections in December 1957 when the PAP won fourteen of the fifteen seats – a very quick recovery after the troubles of August 1957. (This recovery was led by Ong Eng Guan, who became the City's first and only Mayor, but who broke with Lee Kuan Yew in 1960.)
(b) Lee was prepared to go quite a long way in risking the 'stooge' label in order to ensure that the Communists did not get control of his Party.
(c) He was determined to achieve independence through merger with the Federation as he knew that he could not deal effectively with the MCP without at least the *threat* of superior force behind him.

His campaign to reassure the Federation Government and people continued throughout 1958. For example, the PAP Journal *Petir*, in an article on 'The Socialist Revolution', said that the Alliance

Party was anti-merger because

(a) They feared a Chinese majority in their electorate (the Chinese amounted to 70 per cent of Singapore's population and would have added 18 per cent more Chinese to the Federation's population).
(b) They feared leftists with Chinese support, and did not differentiate between Socialists and Communists. *Petir* said that the PAP must allay these fears.[34]

At the end of 1958, the government passed new citizenship regulations which extended the franchise to virtually the whole adult population, irrespective of race. This presented little problem in Singapore where (unlike the Federation) one race, the Chinese, was predominant both in political and economic strength. The universal franchise did, however, mean that the 1959 elections gave great power and authority to the new government and to the Constitution under which it was elected.[35]

The 1959 Elections

By the beginning of 1959, it was becoming clear to everyone, including Special Branch[36] (which was still in effect under British control) and to the Communists, that the PAP was heading for victory in the forthcoming elections, and Lee Kuan Yew became more confident in his renunciation of the Communists as partners. For example, in an election speech on 26 May 1959 he said

'In this fight the ultimate contestants will be the PAP and the MCP – the PAP for a democratic, non-Communist, socialist Malaya, and the MCP for a Soviet Republic of Malaya. It is a battle that cannot be won by just bayonets and bullets. It is a battle of ideals and ideas. And the side that recruits more ability and talent will be the side that wins.'[37]

The election in June 1959 was an even greater landslide than expected. Though the PAP got only 53 per cent of the votes cast, they won 43 of the 51 seats. Lim Yew Hock, who had gathered the remnants of the Labour Front and others into a new Singapore Peoples' Alliance (SPA) won only 4, the United Malay National Organization (UMNO) 3, with 1 Independent.[38]

This was not as good as it looked for Lee Kuan Yew, however, as there was still a strong Communist element within his own Party.

He had cooperated with them to rout the right wing. The battle with the left – already forecast in his election speeches – lay ahead.

Lim Chin Siong Released

His first act on attaining power was to honour his promise to release Lim Chin Siong and the other five[39] left-wing PAP leaders arrested during the 1956 riots. They had not, of course, been able to stand in the elections themselves, so they could not sit in the Assembly, but he did appoint some of them as political secretaries in his various ministries – Lim Chin Siong to the Ministry of Finance and Fong Swee Suan to the Ministry of Labour and Law.[40]

To many British and Malayan observers at the time this seemed two-faced in the light of Lee Kuan Yew's pre-election speeches such as that quoted above and those he made in the Assembly. It seemed that his public speeches were designed to lull the British into granting him full independence, and the Federation into accepting merger, whilst in private he was bringing the Communists back into the fold of his party.

These criticisms do not hold water. Apart from the political necessity of making their release a part of his election platform in order to win left-wing votes, Lee Kuan Yew had from the start insisted that the best way to handle the Communists was to provide them with a political forum and demolish their case in public debate. He had already taken firm action to prevent them from taking over the Executive Committee of the PAP as described earlier in this chapter. Throughout the detention of the six left-wing leaders in Changi gaol, he had visited them regularly and tried to talk them round. During these talks, Lim Chin Siong had offered to go away to Indonesia to 'study' (presumably with the PLEN in the Rhios islands) if this would lessen the PAP fears, but Lee Kuan Yew answered that the MCP would merely appoint another open front leader if Lim were not in Singapore.[41] Before they were released he persuaded all of them except Lim Chin Siong to sign a document declaring that there was no justification whatever for the continuance of the armed insurrection by the MCP. Even Lim signed a document acknowledging that the insurrection had been defeated because the MCP had failed to establish itself as a nationally based movement. Neither of these documents, however, specifically rejected Communism for Singapore, and the most that Lee Kuan Yew could get, even from the other five, was a 'solemn declaration' to him that in the event of conflict they would fight with the PAP against the MCP. Because of Lim's refusal to sign the first document or to make this latter declaration, Lee Kuan Yew told the PAP executive committee, in the presence of all six, that, while he was prepared to accept the good faith of the other five, he could not vouch for Lim Chin Siong's sincerity and wanted him to prove it. It is significant that none of the six were allowed to become cadre members of the party (see above), and they were therefore barred from voting in the election of the Central Executive Committee of the PAP.[42]

A fair summary of the situation is that Lee Kuan Yew believed that he could handle these people out in the open, and was in any case politically committed to releasing them if he were elected. He did his best, with only partial success, to convert them to his way of thinking, and meanwhile made sure that their powers were limited, but at no time did he change his own attitude to the problem of dealing with Communism. His public statements in the Assembly and elsewhere remained consistent on this point.

For the first year of the PAP government, Lim Chin Siong showed 'sweet reasonableness', no doubt hoping to be accepted back on to the Executive Committee, but Lee Kuan Yew knew after nine months (by March 1960) that Lim was working against him within the unions and the rank and file of the workers, and that Fong Swee Suan in the Ministry of Labour was doing the same.[43]

The Hong Lim By-Election

Meanwhile, Lee Kuan Yew was having trouble from another direction. His Minister for National Development, Ong Eng Guan, who had gained notoriety in 1957 by making sensational anti-British gestures as Mayor of the City Council, began in June 1960 to criticize the PAP leadership and demand a 'return to the Revolutionary Manifesto of 1954'. He was expelled from the PAP in July 1960, and took two other Assemblymen with him into opposition to form the United Peoples' Party (UPP), thereby reducing the PAP strength to forty out of fifty-one. In December 1960 Ong resigned to fight a by-election in his own constituency of Hong Lim, which he had won for the PAP with the largest majority of any candidate in the 1959 elections.[44]

The Hong Lim by-election was fought in April 1961, and Ong Eng

Guan was returned in triumph with two-and-a-half times more votes than any other candidate. He achieved this, surprisingly, without the overt support of Lim Chin Siong, or of any of the PAP Assemblymen who were to defect and form the Barisan Sosialis party only a few months later.[45] Nevertheless, Lee Kuan Yew was bitterly hurt by this defeat, which he later put down to discontent over housing, social welfare, and the over-strict control of immigration and of the grant of citizenship. Moreover, he was prepared to fight the election with his hands tied to some extent by the need not to prejudice his long-term aspiration for merger with the Federation and for the attraction of overseas investment into Singapore.[46] In one of his election speeches, for example, he said 'we are not playing to a Singapore audience but we have to play to a pan-Malayan audience'.[47]

The Plenipotentiary Identified

In March 1961, just before the Hong Lim by-election, the PLEN made a further approach through a courier to Lee Kuan Yew. Lee says that by this time he knew PLEN's identity, having seen his photograph in a Special Branch file marked 'To be arrested on sight' soon after he took over as Prime Minister, in October 1959. He did not tell the Special Branch of his meetings with the PLEN, but he did note the PLEN's true name – Fang Chuang Pi. He did not reveal his name publicly until 1963,[48] but in March 1961 he did indirectly indicate to the PLEN that he knew who he was: the PLEN had from the start operated under the *nom de plume* of Lee Yek Han (i.e. incorporating Lee's surname) so, when Lee Kuan Yew was asked in March to provide a *nom de plume* for himself, he in turn incorporated the PLEN's surname and called himself Fang Ping An. At their next meeting on 11 May the PLEN, in true cloak and dagger style, acknowledged Lee's discovery of his identity (and also thereby to some extent his trust) by thanking him for some help he had given to one of his (the PLEN's) relatives.[49]

At this meeting (11 May) the PLEN urged Lee to insist on the abolition of the Internal Security Council as a target for the 1963 Constitutional talks. Three weeks later, Lim Chin Siong and five others came out with an identical demand, further convincing Lee that they were getting secret instructions from the Communist underground.[50] This public statement by Lim Chin Siong on 2 June

1961 was the first overt sign of a break between him and Lee Kuan Yew.[51]

The Formation of the Barisan Sosialis

The break was starkly confirmed at another by-election in the Anson constituency in July 1961, in which David Marshall had decided to reverse his retirement from politics and stand as a candidate for a new party of his own which he called the Workers Party. Lim Chin Siong stated that he would only support the PAP candidate against Marshall if the party agreed to seek the abolition of the Internal Security Council. Lee – with his eyes firmly on merger – refused to do this and, on 11 July, announced that the PAP was prepared to break with its own dissidents if necessary. Two days later, he demanded the resignation of Lim Chin Siong, S. Woodhull and Fong Swee Suan as Political Secretaries.[52] On 15 July, with Lim Chin Siong's support, David Marshall was narrowly returned with a majority of 546 in an electorate of 9,000, of whom 1,500 abstained.[53]

Five days later (20 July) Lee Kuan Yew called for a vote of confidence in the Assembly. Eight PAP members crossed the floor and another five abstained. On 26 July these thirteen formed the Barisan Sosialis (Socialist Front) Party. Thus, the complexion of the Assembly was radically changed. The PAP now had only 26 out of 51 seats. They were opposed by 16 to their left (13 Barisan, 2 UPP and David Marshall, who, though previously regarded as being to the right of the PAP, had won his seat with left-wing support) and 8 to their right (4 SPA, 3 UMNO and one independent).[54]

'The British Plot'

At this crucial debate on 20 July, Lee Kuan Yew drew attention to the fact that Lim Chin Siong and his friends had been in conference with the U.K. High Commissioner, Lord Selkirk. He later described these meetings as a cunning British plot to lull Lim Chin Siong into believing that the British would make no difficulties if he and his friends were to attain power by constitutional means. This would encourage them to become more militant, and in turn force the PAP government to curb and contain their subversive activities. This would suit the British, and also do much to reassure the Federation Government, who were reluctant to accept a common market or merger with Singapore so long as they feared that the PAP was giving shelter to the Communists. Lee Kuan Yew said that the British, who had great experience in dealing with such delicate situations, had no comment when he described these meetings with Lim and his interpretation of their meaning.

Given the British green light, he said, the Communists blundered in June into their conflict with the PAP. Following Lim's statement about the ISC on 2 June, they made an angry statement on 12 June demanding the immediate release of detainees, reunification of the trade unions and various relaxations of citizenship and censorship regulations designed to facilitate the revolutionary struggle.[55] This, and the challenge in the Anson by-election, led on to the open breach and the crossing of Lim's supporters in the Assembly over to the opposition in July.

Lee Kuan Yew said that their plan was not to bring about another general election, but to persuade at least twenty-six Assemblymen to continue under their leadership still using the PAP label. Dr. Lee Siew Choh would become Prime Minister and Dr. Sheng his Deputy Prime Minister. Both of these men, he said, were politically naïve and believed that there was more political future for them if they cooperated with the Communists.[56]

Lim Chin Siong's attempt to suborn a majority of Assemblymen to his side appeared on the face of it to fall short by only one seat, since the government could only muster 26 out of 51. In theory, since the 25 non-PAP members included 4 SPA and 3 UMNO, who were to the right of both the PAP and the Barisan Sosialis, Lee Kuan Yew should have been able to rely on their voting with him against the Barisan on a decisive issue. In practice, however, some of the right-wing members would have gone to great lengths to bring Lee Kuan Yew down, even at risk of landing Singapore with a Communist government – or, perhaps more realistically, of landing the British with the problem of sorting out the mess if Lee Kuan Yew were to fall. Lim Chin Siong, for his part, devoted many hours during the next few weeks trying to persuade a number of other PAP members to cross the floor, but without success.[57]

The Proposal for Merger

On 27 May 1961 the Malaysian Prime Minister, Tunku Abdul Rahman, first publicly mooted the possibility of merger in a speech to foreign journalists in Singapore. This statement probably did much to provoke Lim Chin Siong's demand for the abolition of the ISC on 2 June, and the Barisan Sosialis eruption in July. Lee Kuan Yew himself states that the fight began when the PAP announced their programme on 9 June that in the 1963 Constitutional talks they would seek independence through merger, either with or without the Borneo territories.[58]

The proposal had been under active discussion between the Federation, Singapore and British governments for some time, and there had been a number of meetings between Ministers of the three governments and other senior officers from the territories concerned since January 1961.[59] Lee Kuan Yew realized that some form of merger was essential to his political survival and that he had to carry the Malayans and the British governments with him. In the event they backed him to the full and, in parallel with his own activities within Singapore, there were three Constitutional Conferences in November 1961, July 1962 and July 1963 in which the terms of the merger were worked out.

Nevertheless, as late as 4 May 1961 the Tunku had displayed considerable reservations, when he said that Singapore could not be accommodated within the Federation until its people had proved that they were loyal to Malaya as a whole.[60] Lee was therefore probably being quite honest when he told the PLEN on 11 May that there was no immediate likelihood of the Tunku agreeing to a merger, though the PLEN no doubt thought he had been deliberately deceived when the Tunku made his announcement on 27 May.[61]

Ong Eng Guan's sweeping victory in the Hong Lim by-election in April 1961 may well have been a major factor in bringing the Tunku round to the idea of merger. Though his initial reaction was expressed in his statement of 4 May, he was probably persuaded thereafter by Lee that the economic problems which caused the by-election defeat could only be cured by merger – or at the least by the formation of a common market, and by 27 May he was presumably convinced that, rather than face the risk of the people of Singapore rallying to the leadership of extremists, he would do better to make a positive public move of support for Lee Kuan Yew.[62]

After the split in the Singapore Assembly on 20 July, Lee Kuan Yew and the Tunku pushed on fast with plans for merger. On 24 August they announced agreement in principle under which Singapore would retain control of education and labour in exchange for accepting fewer seats in the Federal Parliament than would be justified by her population. The Central Government would control external affairs, defence and security.[63] In terms of population, Singapore should have had 24 seats in the Federal Parliament. In fact they agreed to accept only 15, to be occupied by members of the Singapore Legislative Assembly in proportion to the parties therein. At this time the 15 comprised 12 PAP and 3 Barisan Sosialis.

On 21 September Dr. Goh Keng Swee (the Singapore Minister of Finance) said that there should be a referendum for the people of Singapore to decide whether to accept or reject merger. The Barisan Sosialis opposed this, saying that the issue should be decided by a general election. Lee Kuan Yew interpreted this as a stalling tactic, based on the hope that in a general election no party would gain a clear mandate.[64] It was over this period that he gave his series of twelve broadcasts over Radio Malaya (from 13 September to 9 October) subsequently published in his pamphlet, *The Battle for Merger*,[65] giving his detailed account (frequently quoted above) of his political battle with the Communists and of his meetings with the PLEN.

Opposition members accused Lee Kuan Yew of using the radio with a pro-government bias, and both this and his alleged restriction of freedom of the press have been criticized by the Associated Press.[66] Whether or not there was any justification for these complaints, there was probably an element of pique, because Lee Kuan Yew was undoubtedly a more effective radio speaker than his opponents. Complete freedom to criticize the government is in any case unusual in countries whose political institutions are in the early stage of development, and there was probably greater freedom of speech in Singapore than in most of the new democracies – and than in many older ones. As well as time on radio, the opposition were given full rein in the Assembly, whose debates were public, and were published promptly in full in Hansard and freely in the Press.

The Referendum on Merger

In November 1961 the Tunku and Lee Kuan Yew published their Heads of Agreement for merger,[67] and it was announced that the Referendum would take place in 1962. In a debate in the Assembly on 20 November it became clear that all major parties (including the Barisan Sosialis) now accepted the necessity of some kind of merger,[68] but there was argument over the terms, particularly of citizenship.

In a further debate on 16 March[69] the Assembly voted that, since all parties agreed on merger, the choice in the referendum should not include the option of rejection, but simply a choice of three sets of terms which were finally decided in later debates (in June and July) as follows:

A. Merger based on the Heads of Agreement
B. Merger with the same terms for Singapore as for the ex-British Colonial States of Penang and Malacca
C. Merger on terms no less favourable than for the Borneo States.[70]

B was the Barisan proposal, and C a choice proposed by the ex-Chief Minister Lim Yew Hock, on behalf of the SPA. The significance of the choices was complex, and was concerned with issues, such as citizenship, which are not relevant to this study. Their importance lay in their future effect on the balance of parties in the Assembly, because the government at the last minute incorporated a proviso that a blank voting paper would be counted as a vote in favour of the PAP proposal (A). This was because the Barisan had announced that they would canvas for blank papers. Had they had the acumen to conceal this intention until the bill had been passed, it would have been humiliating for the PAP to have passed an amendment adding this clause.[71] Nevertheless the proposal resulted in the defection of a fourteenth PAP member, Mrs. Hoe Puay Choo, who resigned from the Party, later joining the Barisan Sosialis. This left the government with only 25 out of the 51 seats. Nevertheless, with the support of SPA and UMNO members it was able to pass a Bill authorizing the referendum on 6 July.[72]

The referendum took place on 1 September 1962. Of 624,000 eligible voters, 561,000 cast ballots. Of these 397,000 (71 per cent) were for the PAP's alternative A, with less than 2 per cent each for B and C. 144,077 (25 per cent) were blank. Even excluding the blanks, however, the 397,000 positive votes for alternative A amounted to well over half the total eligible electorate of 624,000, so the PAP could fairly claim a victory on any count.[73] Their proviso over the blank votes, in fact, had proved unnecessary.

Indonesian Confrontation and the Renewed Detention of Lim Chin Siong

The proposal for merger was strongly opposed by the Government of Indonesia, who objected to the inclusion of the Borneo territories.

In this President Sukarno was strongly influenced by the powerful Indonesian Communist Party (PKI), who spearheaded the policy of Confrontation against Malaysia.[74]

In December 1962 there was a sudden revolt against the government of the Sultan of Brunei – the smallest and richest of the three Borneo states. This was quelled in a few days by British troops flown in from Singapore. The Brunei revolt (which was a rather pathetically amateurish performance by an underprivileged group with some genuine grievances) was undoubtedly encouraged if not actually sponsored by Indonesia. The PKI had recruited a force in readiness to attack Malaysia before the revolt under the cover name 'West Irian Volunteers', and out of the next revolt grew the Confrontation with Malaysia which continued with armed raids and insurgencies on the mainland and in Borneo until after Sukarno's collapse in 1966. By early 1963, consorting with the Indonesians was treated in Kuala Lumpur as treachery.

In their New Year messages, the Barisan Sosialis leaders made statements denouncing the way in which Malaysia was being formed, and referring to the Brunei revolt as a sign of 'the people's will to freedom'.[75] On 2 February 1963, 111 persons were detained by Special Branch in 'Operation Cold Store' covering both Malaya and Singapore. Those detained included Lim Chin Siong,[76] S. Woodhull, James Puthucheary and his younger brother Dominic. Four days before the Brunei revolt its leader, Azahari, had been in Singapore, where he was in the constant company of Lim Chin Siong.[77] In all, 24 of those arrested in Singapore were members of the Barisan Sosialis, and 7 of the parties associated with it. 11 more were connected with Nanyang University, which was becoming a growing centre of subversion.[79]

These 111 detentions were decided upon by a meeting of the Internal Security Council which was held in Kuala Lumpur, and was attended by Lee Kuan Yew. He himself claimed that he would have preferred to leave these arrests until after merger[80] (which was timed to take place on the sixth anniversary of the Federation's Independence in August 1963).

The climax was now approaching in the Singapore Legislature, when the finely balanced Assembly would be taking its final vote for independence through merger, and there would be a new general election. This political activity was somewhat hampered for the opposition when, on 22 April, Dr. Lee Siew Choh led a march on the Prime Minister's office to protest against the detentions of Lim Chin Siong and the others. 5 were arrested on the spot and 7 more later. They were not tried until 29 August, when 8 were convicted on a charge of rioting, the other 4 (including Dr. Lee) being acquitted. Though some had been released on bail while awaiting trial, committal proceedings and the preparation of their cases had considerably harassed the Barisan leaders during this critical electoral period.[81]

Independence and the 1963 Elections

Meanwhile, on 1 August, the Assembly voted for Lee Kuan Yew's plan for merger, now slightly revised to increase its attraction as regards citizenship,[82] and was adjourned *sine die*.

Intensive delaying action by Indonesia in the United Nations had resulted in the merger being put off until 16 September. A general election was held in Singapore (now part of the new Federation of Malaysia and wholly independent of the U.K.) on 21 September. The PAP term of office could in fact have run until June 1964, but Lee Kuan Yew announced a snap election, at the minimum notice, in the first week of September 1963. This was a shrewd political move because he was able to exploit his success in the referendum, and gain a clear mandate quickly before opposition had time to develop in the event of merger working out unfavourably for Singapore.[83]

This was the first election in Singapore in which television had been available for use by the political leaders. Lee Kuan Yew, already a successful radio speaker, proved to have a flair for television, and emerged as a clear winner. The composition of the new Assembly was: PAP 37 seats (47 per cent of the vote), Barisan Sosialis 13 (33 per cent). The other parties were totally eliminated except for the UPP, Ong Eng Guan retaining Hong Lim, though with a greatly reduced majority. UPP candidates in all polled 7 per cent of the total popular vote, while the Alliance Party (incorporating UMNO) polled 8 per cent without winning a single seat. It is significant that Malay PAP candidates captured all the seats previously held by the UMNO for the Alliance Party in predominantly Malay constituencies. The PAP enjoyed sweet revenge at Anson, where David Marshall (this time standing as an Independent) polled only 416 out of 8,436 votes,[84] the PAP candidate winning the seat in a fairly close battle with the Barisan candidate. It is significant that the Barisan Sosialis successes were largely confined to rural areas, where the PAP had done less to improve the people's lot than in the urban areas, in which PAP won all but 3 seats.

Alan Blades explains the comparatively high strength of Communist supporters in the rural areas of Singapore as follows: first, because opposition to the Japanese had been easier in rural areas, where Communist leadership and sentiment had survived the occupation; secondly, because during the Emergency, many Chinese peasants moved from the Federation to Singapore to evade resettlement – some of them specifically to organize supplies for the guerrillas; thirdly because most peasants were China-born and Chinese educated, and therefore more influenced by propaganda from China than were the locally born Chinese in urban areas. Chinese rural villages in Singapore retained the feeling of 'living in China'; and fourthly because in the city there were many other influences, including money-making and rubbing shoulders with a wide variety of people. Even in the intensely Chinese China Town area of the city, the Secret Societies were very strongly entrenched, and regarded the Communist Party as a hated rival.

The End of the Merger, and Lee Kuan Yew's Consolidation

Immediately after the elections, on 26 September, twenty preventive arrests were made at Nanyang University and those arrested included graduates who had stood as Barisan candidates in the election. An abortive general strike on 8 October was followed by the arrest of the strike leaders of the Barisan-dominated Singapore Association of Trade Unions (SATU). The arrested included three Barisan Assembly members. All this was made easier for Lee Kuan Yew by the fact that the arrests were made by the Federal Government which had now assumed responsibility for internal security in Singapore under the Malaysia agreement.[85]

Subsequent events are covered in Part III but will be outlined briefly here to put the period described into perspective. There were serious riots in 1964, with some loss of life, but these resulted from racial conflict between Malays and Chinese, caused by a rift between the PAP and racially extremist Malays in the Federation, and were not part of a revolutionary process in the sense of trying to seize political power by illegal means.[86] They no doubt contributed to the deteriorating relations between the predominantly Chinese government of Singapore and the predominantly Malay central government in Kuala Lumpur. The break between them, however, resulted more directly from a bid by Lee Kuan Yew to get a wider political foothold for the PAP by putting up PAP candidates in nine of the constituencies on the mainland of Malaya in the 1964 elections. Although the attempt was a failure in that only one PAP candidate was returned,[87] many Malay politicians interpreted it as a bid by Lee Kuan Yew for eventual premiership in Kuala Lumpur. After months of vituperation, Singapore was expelled from the Federation in August 1965, and became a wholly independent state. Sukarno was overthrown soon afterwards and Confrontation ended in August 1966. Through all this, Lee Kuan Yew's political strength and popularity grew in Singapore, as his efficient administration (especially in the fields of housing and education) bore fruit. Alan Blades regards this as the biggest factor in the PAP success against Communism, i.e. the

'... tremendous drive of Lee Kuan Yew and his chief associates to provide an honest administration and the huge housing, education and industrial opportunities needed so quickly in order to show the people, even including many of his wealthy right-wing opponents, where success lay. Success has followed success, which happens more markedly with the Chinese than it does everywhere else and, most important of all, he has been able to do this, or at least to get it under way patent for all to see, before the end of his period of dangerous flirtation with the Communists within his own party. In this process he has had reason to be grateful to the Tunku both as a longstop and as a contrast.'[88]

G. G. Thomson comments in similar vein:

'While the Communists were acting and organizing the political process was developing, and it is only in relation to that process that the Communists can be set in a perspective of contingency rather than in the perspective of inevitability of success in which they are often set. The success of Communism is always someone else's failure to find an alternative solution to the problems to which any body politic is heir.'[89]

In March 1968 Lee Kuan Yew called another general election and Dr. Lee Siew Choh announced that no Barisan Socialis candidates would stand as the election was 'a fraud'. The Communist threat in Singapore is now in almost total abeyance. Singapore's economy grows apace, with the PAP supreme (though some effective opposition might be better for their political health) and Lee Kuan Yew has emerged as one of the Commonwealth's leading statesmen – a development by no means unknown in the lives of other leaders who have been regarded as dangerous firebrands during their countries' advance to independence.

Having worked in partnership with the Communists, however, and having narrowly outwitted their attempt to take over not only his party but the Government of Singapore, Lee Kuan Yew has no illusions about their resilience, dedication and ability to exploit any conflict or dissent in society to revive their fortunes. There is still substantial opposition to the PAP in Singapore and, thanks to parliamentary elections in which voting is compulsory, the strength of this opposition (20-25 per cent) has been regularly quantified and demonstrated over the past 25 years. Because it is fragmented the opposition has won only one seat (in 1981); and it is demoralized by the realization of its rejection by an unassailable popular majority. It has no credible prospect of power – at least so long as Lee Kuan Yew continues to lead the PAP.

Yet the Government still retains what are by liberal democratic standards very strong powers for internal security and to combat crime; not so much because it seriously fears subversion in the 1980s but because it is conscious that Singapore's economic and social success owes a lot to effective curbs on industrial disruption, the secret societies, the pushing of drugs and other forms of crime. It is therefore reluctant to give up these powers – and the majority of the population seem to accept them and continue to vote for the PAP. Liberals may ask at what point 'majority rule' becomes 'the tyranny of the majority', but the PAP's answer is that it works and that it has brought security, public order and prosperity to the people of Singapore.

Part III of this book (Chapters 19 and 20) examines these powers more fully; how they have been used in the 20 years since Lee Kuan Yew was firmly established in power in 1963; and how far they are still necessary and justified, with particular reference to his projected retirement in 1988.

Part II RURAL GUERRILLA REVOLUTION – THE EMERGENCY IN MALAYA

Chapter 9 The First Years of the Emergency

Launching the Armed Struggle

We now revert to the situation described at the end of Chapter 2, when Chin Peng decided to switch the emphasis from the cities to the rural areas and launch the armed struggle. This decision followed the return of MCP delegates from a Communist Youth Conference in Calcutta in February 1948,[1] which may have had some influence, though the decision was primarily the result of frustration of the attempt at an urban revolution.

The call to mobilize was made in March. Of the 10,000 ex-MPAJA members on the books, only 3,000 took to the jungle in the next three months, calling themselves 'The Malayan People's Anti-British Army' (MPABA). The police and the army, who knew a lot about the camps the guerrillas planned to use, launched an operation against them in April, and captured documents which proved that they had an organized military structure.[2] The general headquarters was in the jungle about twelve miles south of Kuala Lumpur.

While the MPABA went through the administrative processes of mobilizing and training in the jungle, the PMFTU, which controlled over half the Trade Union Members in the Federation,[3] planned a series of militant strikes aimed to convince the British that there was no stable future for their industries.[4] One source suggests that they planned to declare a Communist Republic in Malaya in August 1948, by which time it was hoped that the British would have decided to write off their losses and abandon the country.[5]

Incidents in the rubber estates and tin mines from May until mid June took on a new and more violent character.[6] From 17 May to 7 June there was a wave of arson and destruction of machinery, most of it (though not all) tied to plausible labour disputes. 12 managers and foremen (11 of them Asians and only 1 European) were murdered. During the same period the police killed 7 and injured 23 more in fights with strikers.[7]

On 12 June the new Trade Union Ordinance (see Chapter 2) became law. The PMFTU became illegal and its unions in the Federation disintegrated. The leaders of the PMFTU, who included a number of experienced ex-MPAJA commanders, took to the jungle.

Up till now, it appeared that the MPABA, busy with its mobilization, had played little part in the violence in the estates and mines, but on 16 June there were 5 more murders, 4 of them (in the Sungei Siput district of Perak) being later ascribed to the killer squad of the 5th Regiment MPABA.[8] Three of the victims this time were British planters – which Chin Peng later admitted to have been a mistake as it aroused many of the British officials who had until then been rather complacent.[9]

A State of Emergency

On 19 June after several more murders, the High Commissioner (Sir Edward Gent) declared a State of Emergency in the Federation, and Singapore followed suit on 23 June.[10]

This was the first step in the development of a comprehensive system of Emergency Regulations which have now become a model for controlling the population in the face of a widespread and organized revolutionary movement which uses violence and the threat of violence as well as propaganda. These Regulations were amended and improved and by 1953, after eight years of urban and guerrilla insurgency, they had reached a peak of effectiveness.[11] They speak for themselves, but they have also been fully analysed in two excellent monographs.[12]

Sir Robert Thompson, who had much to do with the development and enforcement of the Emergency Regulations in Malaya and thereafter tried vainly for four years to persuade the Government in South Vietnam to introduce similar measures, stresses the importance of emergency legislation being wide enough and strict enough to ensure that police, soldiers and all other government officials can do what they need to do to maintain or restore order without having to act outside the law. The public, he says, will accept remarkably tough measures provided that they are taken under a law of the land that has been duly and publicly enacted, and warns that a government whose officials and security forces act outside its own laws cannot hope in the long run to earn the willing support and respect of its people.[13]

GUERRILLA STRATEGY AND TACTICS 1948

The most urgent and effective Emergency Regulations were those giving power to arrest and detain without trial – an unavoidable suspension of liberty when the functioning of the normal processes of law is deliberately made unworkable by the repeated intimidation of witnesses.[14] The police at once arrested nearly 1,000 known Communist Party Members or sympathizers, though many others had already taken to the jungle. By the end of 1948, 1,779 were held in detention and another 637 (together with 3,148 families) deported.[15] During the next nine years (i.e. until the Federation became independent) 33,992 were detained for varying periods, and another 14,907 deported. Each detention was subject to review every six months.

Even more important, in the long term, were the regulations requiring the registration of the entire adult population (over twelve years), and other measures such as Tenants Registration, to enable the police to spot strangers in a village. Every person over twelve was photographed, thumbprinted and issued with a National Registration and Identity Card (NRIC). This massive process began in July 1948 and was completed in eight months. The MCP reacted violently, killing photographers, destroying NRICs and killing or maiming those who concealed them from the guerrillas.[16]

Other regulations, mainly introduced later, gave the government and their security forces the power to remove squatters from land to which they had no title and to resettle them in villages in which they could be protected and controlled.

Another fundamental measure was the strict control of firearms, ammunition or explosives, unauthorized possession of which was punishable by death. This contrasts with Vietnam where it was estimated that there were a million weapons at large and unaccounted for by 1965.[17] Other regulations gave the police the power of search and seizure, the enforcement of curfews and the dispersal of assemblies.[18] The MCP itself was declared illegal on 23 July.

On 29 June the High Commissioner, Sir Edward Gent, was recalled to London for consultation and was killed four days later in an air crash. In September Sir Henry Gurney was appointed to succeed him.[19]

Guerrilla Strategy and Tactics 1948

The MPABA, inheriting the heroic image of the MPAJA from the

Japanese war, enjoyed wide popular support amongst the rural Chinese and especially amongst the squatters. Their plan followed Mao's strategy of working inwards – to seize selected areas adjacent to the jungle, while estates and mines were seized by strikers, these later being linked and expanded as 'liberated areas'. They were, however, surprised by the quick and determined reaction of the police and the army. They were able to seize very few populated areas, and even from these they were driven out within a few hours.[20]

The MPABA initially mobilized eight regiments, later increasing to ten. Generally, in 1948–9, they lived in large camps of up to 300 guerrillas, with parade grounds and lecture huts concealed under the canopy of giant trees. About 3,000 guerrillas in all lived in these jungle units, and some 7,000 to 8,000 more lived in the open, serving as part-time guerrillas in an organization known as the Self Protection Corps. During 1949 they also built up a political organization of State, District and Branch Committees, partly in the jungle and partly outside, whose chain of command was separate from that of the regiments (Fig. 12).[21]

The underground masses' organization outside the jungle (the *Min Yuen*) was at this time rather informal and undeveloped. The MCP assumed that the Chinese rural population would rise spontaneously in support of the guerrillas.

Guerrilla operations, mainly carried out by units of 50 or so, were aimed at terrorizing waverers and informers amongst the villagers, and paralysing the economy by slashing rubber trees so that they bled to death, smashing mine machinery, and ambushing buses, trucks and trains. From June until October 1948 they killed 223 civilians of whom the great majority were Chinese (only 17 being European) but in doing so they lost 343 guerrillas,[22] and while they undoubtedly had the moral support of much of the Chinese rural population, there was no sign of the widespread popular rising against the government for which they had hoped.

Meanwhile, the MCP had been at work on a comprehensive Directive, which was completed in December 1948. This recognized that a quick decision was now out of the question, and that they must settle down to a protracted war, for which permanent jungle bases would be required. Two-thirds of the MPABA were to withdraw into the deep jungle, uninhabited except by a handful of aborigines, to train and reorganize. The remaining third were to remain as independent companies in camps on the jungle fringe,

MALAYAN COMMUNIST PARTY ORGANIZATION

BEFORE 1949

```
CENTRAL COMMITTEE
SECRETARY GENERAL
POLITBURO | MILITARY HIGH COMMAND
```

- STATE COMMITTEE
  - DISTRICT COMMITTEE
  - BRANCH COMMITTEE
  - MASSES ORGANIZATION

} not fully developed until November 1949

- REGIMENTS
  - COMPANIES
  - PLATOONS

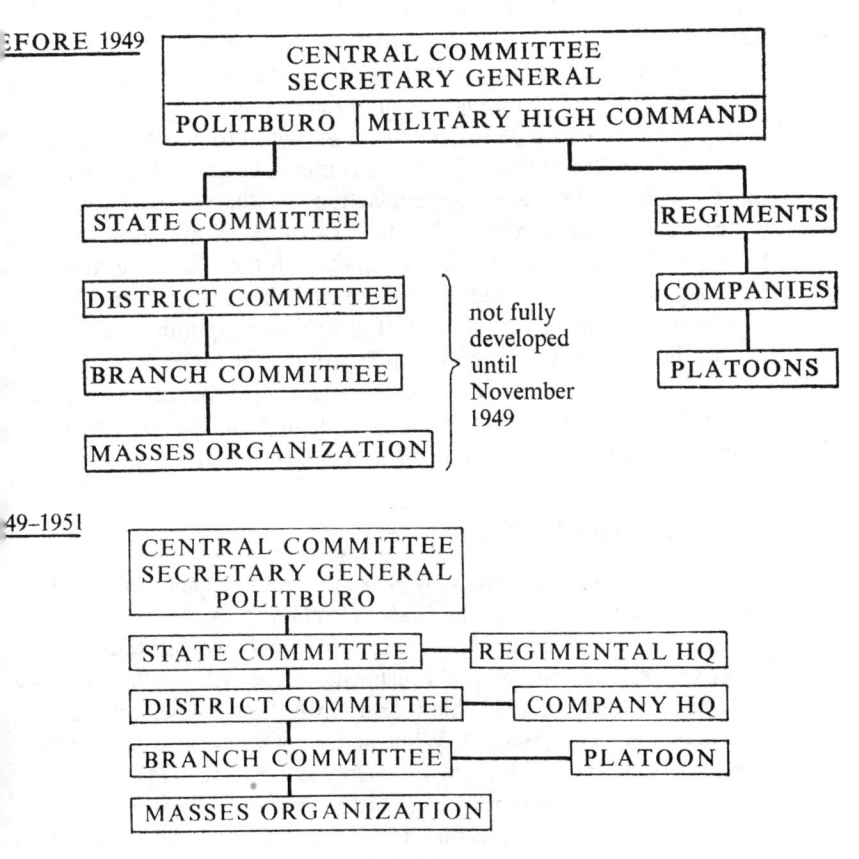

1949–1951

- CENTRAL COMMITTEE SECRETARY GENERAL POLITBURO
  - STATE COMMITTEE —— REGIMENTAL HQ
  - DISTRICT COMMITTEE —— COMPANY HQ
  - BRANCH COMMITTEE —— PLATOON
  - MASSES ORGANIZATION

Figure 12

continuing reduced operations amongst the squatters and in the rubber estates and tin mines. The MPABA was renamed the 'Malayan Races Liberation Army' (MRLA).

At the same time, there was a reorganization and integration of the political organization with that of the regiments. Instead of having separate chains of command, each MCP Branch Committee was to be given control of a platoon of the MRLA as its striking force. The headquarters of the company to whom these platoons belonged was to be responsible to the District Committee which controlled the Branches, and the Regimental Headquarters to the State Committee.[23] This organization is shown in the second part of Figure 12.

In April 1949 this new Directive was put into force. Terrorist incidents fell to less than half. In the meantime, however, the Government had also been taking urgent action. By the end of 1949, the police force had been expanded from 9,000 to 43,000 and the 10 army battalions increased to 18. This, coupled with the sudden decline in terrorist incidents, gave the impression that the first crisis had been weathered, and there was a wave of government optimism. Though this optimism proved somewhat premature, the MCP had missed what may have been one of its best chances of victory, and it never regained the initiative, nor did it ever again have the spontaneous support of such a large part of the Chinese rural population.

Controversy in the MCP

At this time a violent controversy broke out in the higher ranks of the MCP, between Siew Lau, the State Secretary of Malacca, and the Politburo. It was conducted in a series of strongly worded theses and directives, reminiscent of the Bolshevik–Menshevik conflict in the early 1900s. Early in 1949, Siew Lau wrote three theses criticizing the December 1948 Directive. While accepting that armed revolution was the only way of dislodging an enemy as powerful as the British, he said that the first objective must be the outlying villages where the British were weakest. Nevertheless, he felt that it would be fatal to pursue this struggle until multi-racial support had been created. Malay support must be attracted, since without it success was an 'idle dream'. Since 70 per cent of the population worked on the land, support must be founded on the economic interests of the land workers, whose outstanding demand was to own the piece of land on which they worked.[24] Thus, Malaya could not become a Socialist

State until after the revolution which must be a gradual process, in which the big capitalists and landlords were dispossessed, and production begun by individuals owning their own land and small enterprises, which should then be expanded into medium-sized estates and light industries and eventually be nationalized.

The Politburo replied with a furious directive, distributed throughout the Party, denouncing Siew Lau as a 'deviationist'. He was accused of a fatal error in categorizing rubber workers as 'agricultural', and thereby deducing that they were entitled to equal shares of the rubber estates. From the social and economic standpoints, rubber and tin must be regarded as industries, and the party must nationalize the big estates from the start in the interests of the people.

The controversy continued, and Siew Lau wrote more letters and pamphlets, criticizing the stealing of identity cards and the slashing of rubber trees and the aggressive use of guerrillas at the expense of the people, and describing the Party Executive as 'Buffalo Communists'.

Many of Siew Lau's ideas were later to be incorporated in the MCP Directive of October 1951, but he paid the inevitable price of being premature. In August 1949 he was demoted, and expelled from the Party in November. In May 1950 he and his wife were executed by an MCP killer squad.[25]

A few weeks later, on 27 June 1950, another leading Communist came out of the jungle to surrender, Lam Swee, who had been Secretary-General of the Pan-Malayan Federation of Trade Unions before taking to the jungle on 16 June 1948. Like Siew Lau he was under a cloud for criticizing party policy, but he wisely did not wait for events to take their course. Some months after his surrender he published his ideas in a pamphlet, *My Accusation*. These ideas, which represent a trade unionist's views, have been well set out by Alex Josey in his 'Trade Unionism in Malaya'.

Despite its sharp treatment of dissenters, the MCP had realized by the end of 1949 that it was losing ground, and issued a fresh directive, though it did not at this stage reflect the views of Siew Lau and Lam Swee. On the contrary, it was more militant in its attitude to the rural population. For reasons of face-saving and confidence, the new directive (dated 12 November 1949) was described as 'Supplementary Views' on the previous directive, which, it claimed, had after a year's experience been proved correct but suffered from lack of detail. Even deep jungle bases were precarious, it said, as government troops from Kuala Lumpur could get almost anywhere within a day. There was practically no such thing as an isolated spot in Malaya. 'Relative dispersion' was therefore necessary. The guerrillas must operate on the jungle fringe, in smaller units, since heavy concentrations were disadvantageous for withdrawal.

The directive then analysed the government's strength. Since there were no weak links in the administrative system it would be hard to wipe out, but it derided British troops and air attacks in particular which, it said, had killed only one guerrilla in one and a half years.[26]

The directive admitted that it had been a mistake to abandon the major part of the peasant organization after the Japanese war. The development of the strength of the masses, it said, was never spontaneous, but required organization, indoctrination and mobilization. The masses still lacked the determination to sacrifice their jobs, homes, families and personal safety.

It declared that the 1948 Directive was wrong in saying that protracted war could not be conducted without permanent bases. It was true that it would eventually be necessary to form permanent bases, since without them it would not be possible to develop People's Governments, or to drive the British out of Malaya. For the time being, however, temporary bases would suffice, and the essential feature of the new plan was to turn the squatter areas into temporary bases, in which the Masses Organization (*Min Yuen*) would operate along the lines of a governing body. As each area was abandoned by the security forces, the *Min Yuen* would assume governmental powers, leading to the establishment of permanent bases in which the guerrillas could reform into 'Guerrilla Army Corps' to engage and defeat the government forces.[27]

Sir Harold Briggs

Meanwhile the government had begun to realize that, even if they could contain the guerrillas by military action, they could never eliminate them without a better intelligence organization. The CID, geared for normal crime, was quite inadequate to cope with a large-scale rebellion supported by an organized underground movement.

On 6 September 1949 the government announced generous surrender terms which in effect amounted to an amnesty for all except those found guilty of murder. 116 guerrillas surrendered within four months, and 'Surrendered Enemy Personnel' (SEP) began to play a major part in intelligence operations.[28]

These 116, however, were mostly waverers and the surrender rate quickly fell away. At the end of 1949 the MCP offensive was resumed with greater ferocity and greater skill. Concerned with the deteriorating situation, the British government in April 1950 appointed a Director of Operations (a retired General, Sir Harold Briggs) with wide powers of coordination over the police, the army and the civilian departments concerned with the Emergency. Up till this time the army had been called out in aid of the civil power for what had been regarded as a temporary disturbance and, though it had operated under its own officers it did so under the overall direction of the Commissioner of Police (CP). Because the CP had neither the experience nor the staff to control the widespread military operations which had developed, there was a good deal of inefficiency and friction.

Briggs's first act was therefore to set up a Federal War Council and War Executive Committees at State and District levels (generally known by their abbreviated titles of SWECs and DWECs). In these committees, the responsible civilian official was Chairman, with the local police and army commanders taking joint decisions with him.

Resettlement

Briggs next set about resettlement of the Chinese squatters on the jungle fringe. Originally driven to fend for themselves by unemployment during the 1932 slump, the squatters' numbers had been swelled by others escaping from Japanese ruthlessness in the villages in 1942–3, when their only help, leadership and indoctrination had come from the Communist guerrillas, to whom they remained solidly loyal. Owing nothing to the government, independent, scattered, unprotected and uncontrolled, they provided an ideal base for the guerrillas.[29]

Various unsuccessful attempts had previously been made to resettle some of them, and Briggs implemented the recommendations of a committee which had been formed in December 1948. In June 1950 with terrorist incidents at five times their 1949 level, and with over 100 civilians (mainly Chinese) being murdered every month, a crash programme of resettlement was begun. By 1952, 423,000 Chinese squatters had been resettled in 410 New Villages at a cost of

$41 million. Counting other existing villages into which some squatters were absorbed, and labour lines concentrated under government orders on the estates, 740,000 rural Chinese (almost all of them, in fact) were gathered into wired and defended perimeters (Fig. 13).[30]

Despite inflammatory efforts by the MCP, there was surprisingly little opposition to this programme, or even evasion, and very little violence used against the government officials responsible for its execution. Very few of the Resettlement Officers – either British or Chinese – were murdered, though they lived in the New Villages. An important factor here was that they were not charged with 'unpopular' duties such as collecting taxes, registering young men for conscription or making overt reports of people's movements. For the villagers, they provided the only source of alleviation of their hardships, and the guerrillas knew that their murder would be unpopular. This situation contrasted with Vietnam, where Village Chiefs were required to do all these things, were often murdered and in fact seldom dared to sleep in their villages.[31]

Another reason was that resettlement in Malaya was carried out by soldiers in frightening strength but with a consideration which contrasted with the ruthlessness of both the Japanese and the Communist guerrillas; squatters were given Temporary Occupation Licences both for their houses and agricultural smallholdings which greatly increased their feeling of security, bearing in mind that they had previously had no legal title whatever to their land;[32] there was also an unprecedented opportunity for work for the displaced squatters on the rubber estates due to the demands for rubber arising from the Korean war;[33] and the MCP could not in any case have accepted any large influx of squatters into the jungle due to shortage of weapons and supplies.[34]

Protection was a vital element of resettlement. The squatters were not moved into a New Village until a police post could be provided. This again contrasts with Vietnam, where there were no police located in the villages at night, and the locally enlisted auxiliary army units, where provided, generally lived in separate defended compounds outside the villages.

Tenants Registration was also introduced, whereby the householder maintained a list of all occupants, duplicated in the Police Post, and was obliged by law to notify any arrivals and departures within a day.[35] Food was also controlled, and this was effective since

RESETTLEMENT

RESETTLEMENT AND REGROUPMENT

SIZE OF NEW VILLAGES

Size (people)	Number of Villages	Total in these villages	Percentage of villages of this size	Percentage of people in these villages
Under 100	12	769	3	1
100–500	169	51,874	35	9
500–1,000	116	79,886	24	14
1,000–5,000	169	340,710	35	59
5,000–10,000	10	73,405	2	13
Over 10,000	2	26,273	1	4
Unknown	2	—	—	—
Total	480	572,917 (say 573,000)	100	100

PERCENTAGE BY RACE IN NEW VILLAGES

86% Chinese	9% Malay	4% Indian	1% Others
(493,000)	(52,000)	(23,000)	(5,000)

DEGREE TO WHICH NEW VILLAGES WERE NEW

On new and isolated sites	32%
'New Suburbs' (separate, but near towns)	16%
Built around existing small villages	24%
Unclassified	28%

LABOUR REGROUPMENT
1951–3

	Population	% Chinese	% Malay	% Indian	% Others
Estates*	510,000	29·0	16·0	50·0	5·0
Mines	80,000	68·7	17·6	13·6	0·1
Others	60,000	71·8	14·0	14·0	0·2
Total	650,000	246,000	104,000	274,000	26,000

* Mainly Rubber, Pineapple and Oil Palm

Based on Sandhu, pp. 164–174.

Figure 13

most Malayan acreage is devoted to inedible commodities such as rubber and tin, and the guerrillas could only get rice through their contacts with the people. Because large units were difficult to feed, they split into smaller ones, and these were more within the power of the village police posts to hold off until help came. Starvation became a spectre, and an increasing amount of the guerrillas' efforts were devoted to acquiring food. Since rice was the staple diet without which their health and morale would quickly collapse, they were prepared to take great risks to get it, and it was this which was to provide the police with their greatest opportunity for intelligence projects.

Special Branch

In May 1950, a month after his arrival, Briggs had appointed a study group to investigate the Intelligence Services, as it was evident that the CID, designed for the detection of crime, was not staffed or trained to cope with the flood of tactical intelligence which could be acquired from the people in the New Villages. In August 1950 a separate Special Branch of the police was formed with responsibility for all tactical intelligence and counter-subversion, and the CID hereafter dealt only with the investigation of crime.

Briggs realized, also, that it was essential to have a single intelligence organization. Rival intelligence services tend to spy on each other, and to conceal information from each other. A single informer will, if he can, collect rewards from several intelligence organizations for the same information, which may well be unreliable but will appear at the centre to be 'confirmed' by several sources as happened in Vietnam.[36]

Much of the work of compiling the guerrillas' Orders of Battle was done by Military Intelligence Officers (MIO), but they were all placed under command of the Head of Special Branch (HSB) in each State, and of the Circle[37] Special Branch Officer (CSBO) where operations were in progress. Intelligence information from all sources was fed into Special Branch, and all agents and informers were handled by them. MIOs collated and disseminated tactical intelligence in a form in which army units could use it, but they could only disseminate such information as the HSB or CSBO authorized. In particular the identity of agents and informers was known to the minimum possible number of people.

The CSBO was normally a Deputy Superintendent of Police (DSP) equating in rank roughly to an Army Major. At District level was an Assistant Superintendent of Police (ASP) with about two Inspectors who equated roughly to Army Warrant Officers. In 1950–1 most of the DSPs and ASPs were still British, though from 1955 onwards they were gradually replaced by Asians. The Inspectors were almost invariably Chinese or Indian, and handled most of the agents.

At the bottom level, there were one or two detectives (Chinese) in most New Villages. They lived in the security of the Village Police Post compound, and worked in civilian clothes. They were known by sight to most of the villagers, though, like their Communist opposite numbers, they made much use of cut-outs (e.g. shopkeepers, taxi-drivers etc.) to avoid compromising their informers. Though they seldom handled delicate intelligence projects, their presence gave confidence to favourably inclined villagers, and made it easier for them to give casual information, for which rewards were paid.

Sources of information included agents, informers, reports from patrols, air reconnaissance, captured documents, dead bodies, and captured and surrendered enemy personnel (CEP and SEP). On occasions, *Min Yuen* executives were identified by informers in the villages in which they had worked. Such informers were particularly hated, and were killed without mercy if suspected by the *Min Yuen*. Anonymous questionnaires were also used, but with limited results.[38] Both of these methods were subject to abuse by malicious villagers who wished to settle old scores.

From the start, the aim of Special Branch was to penetrate the MCP organization, but this was seldom achieved on any substantial scale until later in the Emergency, as will be described in Chapters 11 and 12. Penetration was easiest in urban areas, and especially in small towns. This, together with the relative ease of shadowing suspected individuals, was a partial explanation of the failure of the Communists to provide more effective support for the guerrillas from the towns – particularly food supplies. Otherwise, this would have been very hard to stop due to the virtual impossibility of wiring and patrolling a long city perimeter, and of preventing the smuggling of food in the profusion of lorries, taxis and cars which emerged from it every day.

At the other end of the scale, the smallest villages, though expensive in manpower to defend, were the easiest for Special Branch activities, because people knew each other and strangers were easier to spot.

The Malay constables could provide little intelligence as they had neither friends not relations amongst the Chinese villagers. The Chinese Home Guards, however, were most valuable to Special Branch, both because of their local relationships and also because of the fact that government officials and police could speak to them in the course of duty without arousing suspicion.

The most difficult for Special Branch – and consequently the best Communist bases – were the larger villages, such as Yong Peng (6,000), in Central Johore which is described in Chapter 10; also Kulai, in South Johore, and Sungei Siput in Perak. All of these maintained powerful MCP branches which were among the last to crack (see also Chapters 10 and 14).

The MCP courier systems were particularly vulnerable, especially in 1950–2, when many messages between jungle units were carried by 'open' *Min Yuen* couriers using public transport. Special Branch, in fact, often knew the contents of MCP orders and reports before the guerrilla units to whom they were addressed.

The best casual informers were often the shopkeepers, who could tell the Special Branch detectives the names of people who had bought extra food. The Army could then ambush the rubber lots in which these people worked, often with success.

Rewards

For casual information of value, the police were authorized to pay fairly small rewards – perhaps $50 to $100 (two weeks' or a month's earnings) – enough to encourage more, but not enough to make the risks of wholesale fraud worthwhile.

If, however, the information led directly to the killing or capture of a guerrilla on the wanted list the rewards were very generous indeed.

In 1951, the scale of rewards was as follows:

Secretary General (Chin Peng)	$60,000
State or Town Committee Secretary	30,000
„ „ „ „ Member	20,000
District Committee Secretary	14,000
District Committee Member or MRLA Company Commander	10,000
MRLA Platoon Commander	6,000

District Committee Member or	
MRLA Section Commander	5,000
Cell Leader	3,000
Others	2,000

Later, these figures were doubled, and for some of the higher ranks quadrupled,[39] and a 30 per cent bonus added if the quarry was taken alive.

Guarding against corruption in the payment of these huge rewards engaged much attention from senior Special Branch officers. The dealings between an agent and the Special Branch inspector handling him were necessarily secret, undocumented and known to as few other officers as possible. The actual disbursement of rewards was done by State and Circle Special Branch Officers (at this time almost 100 per cent British) but there was considerable opportunity for private deals to be done between the inspector and the recipient of the reward. If there were such cases, none came to light, and the successful prevention of this dangerous form of corruption was a creditable achievement.

The rationale for these fantastic rewards lay, of course, in the risk. In the early years, agents who took the risk were often moved to new districts or even new countries where they had to start a new life under a new name. Surprisingly, however, many who had received this blood money subsequently came back to their own area with impunity, and later on they often did not even bother to move.[40]

Surrendered Enemy Personnel (SEPs)

No less surprising was the behaviour of the Surrendered Enemy Personnel (SEPs). They were almost invariably ready to give information, and would often lead out an army patrol at once, and help to kill the men who had been their comrades in adversity for months or years, within hours of deserting them.[41] Some, showing courage as well as treachery, would reassure the night sentry by giving the password and advance as a friend, silently disable him, and then creep into the sleeping camp with an army or police patrol, pick out the leader and kill him as he slept before the turmoil of capturing or killing the rest began.

The treachery was sometimes compounded or delayed. In 1954, for example, a guerrilla was wounded and captured. As he lay dying in hospital a SEP, who had been out for a year, questioned him and pinpointed the deep jungle camp of a Regional Committee Member (Ah Kwang) in the deep jungle. The SEP, who had previously been Ah Kwang's bodyguard, led out a patrol just before dusk, and surrounded the camp. The patrol killed Ah Kwang and his five companions as they sat eating a meal, for they had taken a chance on the assumption that army patrols were almost always setting up camp for the night at this time, and they had put out no sentries.

More often, however, the SEPs would carry out their treachery within hours or days of surrender. British soldiers were constantly amazed by their coldblooded and savage duplicity. One explanation, undoubtedly, was a powerful capacity for pique. Whilst he was with the MCP guerrillas during the Japanese occupation, Spencer Chapman observed that a Chinese would do anything, even at the expense of his own life, to get his own back on someone who had humiliated him.[42] The SEP realized that he would lose much face amongst his family and neighbours by having to admit his error in joining the Communists. During the months in which he was brooding on the question of whether to make the break, this prospect would engender a bitter hatred of the Party that had trapped him into this unbearable situation. This hatred would be focused on his immediate Communist boss – fanned by the awareness that this boss would show him no mercy if for one moment he suspected his thoughts of desertion.

At the same time, he perhaps feared that, so long as any of the men in his gang remained alive, a chance encounter in a back alley, even in ten or twenty years' time, could prove more than embarrassing. He would sleep more soundly if they were dead.

Then, for a man faced with frighteningly uncertain prospects of employment in his new life outside, the reward was a real lure. An SEP qualified for only half rates, but nevertheless, if he were instrumental in the death or capture of his leader (say, a Branch Committee Secretary) and four or five others, might expect a reward of up to $15,000 – that is, more than twelve years' normal working wage.

Another factor, pointed out by Alan Blades, is a positive need in the Chinese character to participate in secret activities.[43]

It usually took a potential SEP many months of heart searching before he made up his mind. Even those who had joined hesitantly and had soon felt doubts took an average of more than a year to decide to surrender. The weakest characters, i.e. those who had been most reluctant to join or coerced into joining, were, not surprisingly, the quickest to decide to surrender but, having made the decision, the most hesitant in carrying it out.

Not all SEPs were traitors. Some simply surrendered and returned to civil life, after a period of rehabilitation, having betrayed no one. Others – especially senior ones late in the Emergency – came out realizing that the war was lost and with the humane intention of bringing their scattered commands out of the jungle with the minimum loss of life. Some cooperated with Special Branch over a period of several months, keeping their own defection strictly secret, and going out to lead in their branches and platoons, one by one. They found them by appearing in full uniform at their courier meeting point on the appropriate day (which only they and the courier knew) and getting the courier to lead them to the guerrillas, whom they then persuaded to come out with them. They faced considerable risks, which increased with each unit they visited, but they earned huge rewards (see Chapter 14).[44]

Surrenders were sometimes induced or negotiated. In Perak, for example, Special Branch identified and contacted an open courier and through him sent a message to a Branch Committee Member to meet a senior Communist at a rendezvous. The BCM came, and was captured, with two couriers. The two couriers were sent back to fetch a DCM, who surrendered and told of a forthcoming meeting due with two others. Special Branch awaited these two in due course, and, in all, four ranking Committee members and ten other guerrillas were captured or surrendered.

As with agents, fears of retribution – even of those who had helped to kill their ex-comrades – proved unfounded. Many SEPs live openly and without fear in Malaya to this day. One, for example, earned nearly $250,000 in rewards and is a prosperous businessman. Another, earning $50,000, used it to buy a small rubber estate, on which his four employees are also SEPs. None seem to be sensitive about their past, and they live happily with their families in houses on the estate.

Another New Communist Directive – October 1951

It was in the latter part of 1950 that government fortunes began to turn, as resettlement got into its stride and the intelligence activities of the new Special Branch began to take effect. Government tactics also changed. From October 1950 all operations were directed towards the security of the villages and of the places where the people worked. The task of the police was to protect the population and break up the Communist cadres amongst them (the Masses Executive of the *Min Yuen*). The army was to dominate the jungle fringe, and not to be drawn away into operations in the deep jungle.

The effect of these measures is shown in Figure 14. During 1950 and 1951 fighting on and around the jungle fringe reached the peak of its violence but, while the Security Force casualties remained much the same, their monthly rate of contact with the guerrillas was doubled between mid 1950 and early 1951, and the number of guerrillas killed each month was doubled too. By August 1951 the previously gloomy tone of government assessments of the situation had been replaced by much greater confidence, and a growing number of guerrillas were being killed on the jungle fringe and in the estates as a result of information from the people.

Discouraged by their waning popular support and alarmed by their casualties, the MCP Central Committee issued a Directive in October 1951 which radically changed the focus of their campaign. They realized what Siew Lau had pointed out two years earlier – that terror and economic disruption were alienating the people, whose support was essential if they were to win the war. They therefore ordered members to stop destroying rubber trees, tin mines, factories, reservoirs and other public services, derailing civilian trains and burning New Villages. Certain people should still be killed, such as reactionaries, traitors, unpopular non-Communist Trade Union leaders, senior civil servants, police officers, any captured British or Gurkha soldiers, and British officials and managers (but not British health officers or engineers). They were, however, to beware of injuring the masses with grenades and stray bullets and to avoid all violent actions of a kind which antagonized peasants and workers.[45]

Because of disruption of the MCP courier system, this directive took many months – in some cases up to a year – to reach the outlying branches on the jungle fringe[46]. It was ironical that on 6 October 1951, within a week of its being issued, the MRLA achieved its greatest triumph – the ambushing and killing of the British High Commissioner, Sir Henry Gurney. The fact that he was the victim was almost certainly fortuitous.[47]

The ambush had a double irony. It gave the impression of a peak of guerrilla aggressiveness just as the MCP had decided to abandon terror as its prime weapon (though a senior government official

Figure 14 Monthly Statistics

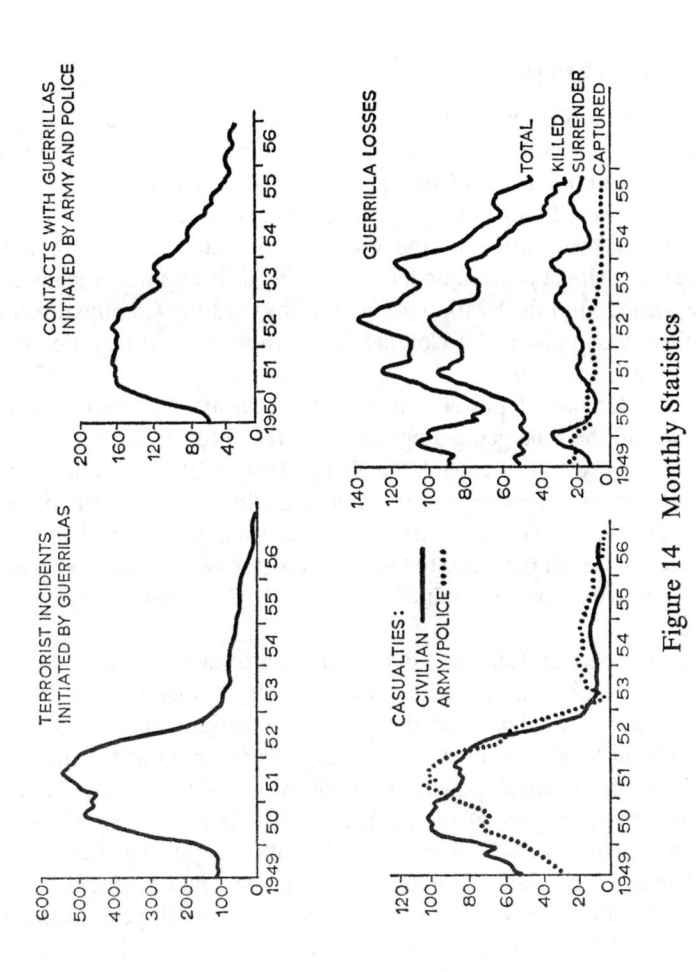

remained fair game even under the new Directive). It also accelerated the Party's defeat by jerking both the Federation and British governments into taking more drastic action, and shocked the public, including the rural Chinese, into accepting such action as inevitable.[48]

Sir Gerald Templer

The British Government's answer – in February 1952 – was to despatch General Sir Gerald Templer as combined High Commissioner, Commander-in-Chief and Director of Operations, with far wider powers than those granted to Gurney or Briggs. For the first time, the prosecution of the war and the running of the country became a single process under a single head. Briggs had already left, exhausted, and died within a few months, and the Commissioner of Police was replaced by Colonel A. E. (now Sir Arthur) Young as Templer took over.

Templer had full powers and used them. He also had the machinery to amend the Emergency Regulations if they proved inadequate.[49] In fact, however, he accepted the Briggs Plan as it stood and implemented it with fresh vigour and determination. During his two years of office (1952–4) two-thirds of the guerrillas were wiped out, the incident rate fell from 500 to less than 100 per month, and the civilian and security force casualties from 200 to less than 40 (Figs. 14 and 15).

This aspect of Templer's dynamism and leadership is well known and well reported. His other achievements, however, were no less important – notably a major advance in self-government at every level from Kuala Lumpur down to the villages, and outstanding progress in rural development, both of which played a big part in winning the support of the people. By the time Templer left, most villages had elected Village Councils, and the strong multi-racial Alliance Party under Tunku Abdul Rahman had emerged as the leading political party, with a firm guarantee of self-government to come. In 1955 the Tunku was to be elected to power with a majority of 51 out of 52 seats, and was subsequently re-elected three times. Though the Federation has had and may still have its share of political and racial troubles, it has in fact been one of the most stable countries in South East Asia in the fifteen years since the Tunku was elected.[50]

Village Government

In Malaya, unlike Vietnam, there had been a fabric of government from the centre to the villages for a very long time. This had been ruefully admitted by the MCP in its first directive in December 1948:

> 'The British have already created a totalitarian, complete, penetrating system of administration, from the Federal Government down to small towns and Malay Kampongs ... We have nothing like Federal provincialism to exploit ... nor is there any weak link in the enemy's administrative system for us to exploit ... Our hope of wiping out the enemy's rule in a certain region and thereby setting up a permanent base still faces many objective difficulties and obstacles.'[51]

By contrast, Sir Robert Thompson, speaking in 1966 on Vietnam, said

> 'The real problem with South Vietnam has been to have a Government at all, whether democratic or not. It does not matter to me very much what the political top is. If there is no machinery underneath it to carry out a single instruction of the government, a government is not going to get very far, whatever aims and high ideals it may have.'[52]

There had been no such fabric of government amongst the 400,000 Chinese squatters in 1948–9. After resettlement in 1950/51, Village Committees were appointed by the British District Officer (DO) in consultation with community leaders. After Templer's arrival, the government passed the Local Council Ordinance (1952), under which, when the DO was satisfied that they were ready, Council Areas were gazetted in which villages elected their own Village Councils by adult suffrage. These Councils collected rates and licence fees, supplemented by government grants, for specific facilities such as dispensaries, schools and community halls.[53] They collected no general taxes, and enlightened DOs ensured that they were seen to achieve a fair number of successes on the people's behalf. As a result, few were murdered, as the MCP realized that this would react against them. This again contrasts with Vietnam, where underpaid local officials had to collect taxes and register men for drafting, and were often suspected of corruption, so their assassination by the Vietcong was frequent and often popular.[54]

CASUALTIES IN THE EMERGENCY 1948-60

	1948	1949	1950	1951	1952	1953	1954	1955	1956	1957	1958	1959	1960	Total
GUERRILLAS ELIMINATED:														
Killed	374	619	648	1079	1155	959	723	420	307	240	153	21	13	6711
Captured	263	337	147	121	123	73	51	54	52	32	22	8	6	1289
Surrendered	56	251	147	201	257	372	211	249	134	209	502	86	29	2704
Total	693	1207	942	1401	1535	1404	985	723	493	481	677	115	48	10704
SECURITY FORCES ELIMINATED (i):														
Police	89	164	314	380	207	58	53	47	25	5	3	1	—	1346
Soldiers	60	65	79	124	56	34	34	32	22	6	7	—	—	519
Total	149	229	393	504	263	92	87	79	47	11	10	1	—	1865
RATIO OF ELIMINATIONS — GUERRILLAS/ SECURITY FORCES	4	5	2½	3	6	15	11	9	10	44	68	115	—	5·7

CASUALTIES IN THE EMERGENCY

CIVILIANS KILLED AND MISSING:												
Killed	315	334	646	533	343	85	97	62	30	22	3	3	—	2473
Missing	90	160	106	135	131	43	57	57	26	2	—	3	—	810
Total	405	494	752	668	474	128	154	119	56	24	3	6	—	3283
TOTAL POLICE, SOLDIERS AND CIVILIANS KILLED AND MISSING	554	723	1145	1172	737	220	241	198	103	35	13	7	—	5148
WOUNDED (ii):												
Police	119	170	321	454	278	53	89	60	32	11	6	8	—	1601
Soldiers	92	77	175	237	123	64	65	43	47	22	13	1	—	959
Civilians	149	200	409	356	158	15	31	24	36	7	—	—	—	1385
Total	360	447	905	1047	559	132	185	127	115	40	19	9	—	3945

Notes (1) No police or soldiers are listed as 'captured' or 'missing'. Any who were were assumed killed.
(2) Estimates of guerrillas wounded are not shown as they are unreliable. The total recorded was 2,819.

Figure 15

The first Village Councils were elected in May 1952 and by March 1953 one-third of the Chinese New Villages had elected Councils.[55]

In the competition for 'The hearts and minds of the people', crystallized in the MCP October 1951 Directive and Templer's campaign in the villages, the government had one overwhelming advantage: they were able to offer engineering improvements such as roads, water and electricity which the guerrillas could never match.[56] In a White Paper, Templer said that:

> 'The foundations of a better life in the New Villages will be not only freedom from fear but also water supplies and sanitation, schools and dispensaries, the growth of civic sensibility and pride in communal as well as individual achievements.'[57]

A government official was reported as saying 'The degree of co-operation we get from a village is in almost exact proportion to what we have put into it.'[58]

Psychological Warfare and the Information Services

The battle for the hearts and minds of the people was won by Templer and his successors, and by Tunku Abdul Rahman, not so much by propaganda as by visible progress in security and development, which led to confidence and contentment in the prospect of a government victory and of the end of strife. Most important was security inside the villages by night which depended on the integrity of the village police post, and the patrolling of the village streets by the policemen while the people slept. Coupled with this security was development,[59] the development of opportunities for education and higher earnings, of housing, water supply and electricity, and of a village government to further these things and to redress grievances. Templer's achievement was all the greater because the price of rubber – inflated by the Korean War during the critical years of resettlement – fell from an average of 169 cents per lb. in 1951 to 67 cents in 1953.[60]

Nevertheless, development alone would not have succeeded without good Information Services to tell the public what was happening, and by a good Psychological Warfare Service to tell the guerrillas too, and to undermine their morale.

These two activities were divided for most of the Malayan Emergency, but initially a service to cover both functions was formed in

PSYCHOLOGICAL WARFARE AND THE INFORMATION SERVICES

June 1950 under Hugh Carleton Greene, who was later to become Director-General of the BBC. Initially it was part of the staff of the newly created Director of Operations, but in October 1952, as part of Templer's policy of integrating the war with the routine functioning of the government, it was placed under the Director-General of Information Services. In March 1954 the Psychological Warfare Section was separated, under that title, and transferred back to the Director of Operations Staff, which was located at Federal Police Headquarters. Here it remained until the end of the Emergency. From 1954 onwards, therefore, Psychological Warfare was conducted in close collaboration with the police Special Branch.

When Templer had arrived, he had underlined the links between the attitude of the soldiers and police ('Operation Service'), propaganda and rural development. Unless the government forces acted decently and within the law, 'civic action' was 'eyewash'. As later expressed by Sir Robert Thompson, one of the strongest government cards was to draw attention to the contrast between the Communists' 'Illegality, Destruction and Promises' and the Government's 'Legality, Construction and Results'.[61]

In September 1952, Templer brought citizenship rights to 1,200,000 Chinese and 180,000 Indians by legislation to confer federal citizenship on anyone born in the Federation.[62]

This, coupled with the concentration of money on providing amenities for the Chinese New Villages,[63] led to accusations that Templer was pro-Chinese.[64] Some of the Malays, and British officials who supported them, complained that priority for development was being given to ex-squatters who had been supporting a vicious rebellion, whereas the Malay Kampong dwellers who had loyally supported the government were left to struggle on at subsistence level. There was, of course, much truth in this allegation, but such a policy was essential if the war was to be won quickly, which in the long run was the most important of all things to the Malays.[65]

Other communities also felt that they had reason for complaint against the impact of the Emergency on their communities. The dilemma of Chinese businessmen, smallholders and shopkeepers, subject to extortion of protection money, death if they refused to pay it and imprisonment if they did, was a difficult one. The Indian community had religious problems: rubber planters and tin-miners had views about curfew times. In order to explain and discuss these problems and, where possible, to resolve them and secure better cooperation, community leaders were invited to become unofficial members of the SWECs and DWECs – up to a maximum of six on each SWEC and normally three on each DWEC. The State and District Information Officers also attended.[66] These 'unofficials' and the Information Officer attended only the full SWEC and DWEC meetings, i.e. once every week or fortnight, and not the day-to-day 'Operations SWEC/DWEC' and they were not given access to the more secret papers and directives, but their participation in the full meetings undoubtedly did much to improve cooperation by the public.[67]

In addition to this participation of community leaders in policy-making, they were regularly briefed on the progress of the war and so were Village Council and Committee Members, local politicians, planters, miners, selected trade union leaders and headmen.

Good Citizens' Committees were formed, which held public rallies to denounce Communism and even – on occasions – led the entire population of villages to the jungle fringe to shout 'surrender' to the supposed guerrillas inside.

This probably had little effect on the guerrillas or on their hardcore supporters, but it did have an influence on public opinion as a whole.

The methods of propagation of information were developed as the Emergency progressed, and are described in more detail in Chapter 12, which also gives examples of the 'Talking Points' which were found by experience to be effective for use by Information Officers in discussions with New Villagers.

The government recognized that polemics and exaggerated reports of successes did not pay. It was essential for the Government Information Service to establish a reputation for truth. It was better not to conceal mistakes, but to admit them and announce the remedy. The government also took care not to promote hatred – especially between the Malay police and the Chinese villagers. They realized that it would be necessary to live with the after-effects of their propaganda.[68]

As the Emergency progressed, the Press was taken more and more into the confidence of the government. For example, Harry Miller, of the *Straits Times*, was kept fully briefed by the Director of Operations, and by the Police in Kuala Lumpur, and was also given every facility in visiting Special Branch Officers and troops on the ground. Later, the editors of all newspapers were briefed regularly on major operations, with time embargoes, or requests to respect their secrecy for an indefinite period. This policy proved itself in some very delicate Special Branch projects with far-reaching results, when the editors of all leading papers in all languages were taken into the government's confidence for several months, and the secret was never betrayed (see Chapter 13).[69]

Within a few months of its formation, Carleton Greene's Emergency Information Service was joined by a senior Communist defector, Lam Swee, as described earlier in this chapter. Shortly afterwards (in February 1951), a brilliant young Chinese graduate of Raffles College, C. C. Too, was appointed to the staff as Chinese Assistant. He later became head of the Psychological Warfare Section, and remained so until his retirement in 1983.

From these early months onwards, psychological warfare leaflets, broadcasts, etc., were composed by Chinese who had either been in the jungle themselves or had worked closely with others who had. The propaganda was practical rather than ideological. General promises of good treatment after surrender proved less effective than accounts by SEPs of what had actually happened to them. These were where possible given personally in public in villages where the SEP was known by the *Min Yuen*, or printed in the SEP's handwriting on leaflets bearing his photograph. These included recent photographs of SEPs who had surrendered some time ago, to show that they had not been maltreated or killed.

Sir Robert Thompson has suggested that surrendered or captured guerrillas should be treated according to a categorization. Some were harmless but useless and should be sent home. Others were of immediate use to Special Branch. Of those captured unwillingly, some would be worth attempting to rehabilitate, while others were recalcitrant and (if they had been captured and not surrendered) should be tried for their crimes.[70]

The Psychological Warfare Section had to decide which of those still in the jungle were worth trying to suborn, and which were to be discredited by 'smearing'. Black propaganda, i.e. statements purporting to come from MCP leaders, and which were calculated to rebound against them, was also used.

C. C. Too and his staff worked very closely with Special Branch. They spent many hours studying captured documents and letters, which both guided their propaganda and gave valuable intelligence clues.

The success of the Psychological Warfare campaign can be judged by the fact that the MCP later imposed a death penalty for reading government leaflets.[71]

White Areas

In the Autumn of 1953 Templer tried a bold experiment in Malacca, where Special Branch were satisfied that the MRLA was ineffective and the MCP organization had been disrupted over a number of districts. These districts were declared a 'White Area', and virtually all Emergency Restrictions were lifted other than the continued registration of the population. A generous rice ration was allowed and shops remained open day and night. The tappers could take a midday meal with them to work. There were no curfews, and there was free movement of people and goods.[72]

The people were warned that the restrictions would be reinforced at once if there were a resumption of Communist activity or terror in the area. Templer calculated, however, that the public relief at the end of restrictions was so great that he could be sure that any attempt by the *Min Yuen* to reactivate their organization would quickly be betrayed to Special Branch.

This was a considerable risk, and each time a new White Area was proposed there were powerful voices – often including Special Branch – warning against it, lest the *Min Yuen* organization that had taken years to root out might revive and regain its grip of the people within a few months. It was argued that the guerrillas would only need a very few loyal supporters to provide their essential needs and that the bulk of the population would be able to give no information because they had no contact.

In the event, however, Templer proved right. No White Area ever in fact had to revert to black.[73] The competition for the hearts and minds of the people was well on the way to being won by the government in 1954.

Chapter 10 Organization for Survival

The MCP Reorganization, 1952–3

In the two years of Templer's rule (1952–4) two-thirds of the guerrilla force was eliminated. Since the *raison d'être* of the MCP jungle organization was to organize and indoctrinate the people (and, unlike some guerrilla armies, they never lost sight of this fact) the bulk of these losses had to be borne by the MRLA – the fighting units – which were milked to keep the political and supply organization adequately manned.

They continued to lose heavily. During the period 1951–7, their total casualties (9,000) far outnumbered their recruits (3,000) and their strength fell from 8,000 to 2,000. Yet still they kept their branch and district organization largely intact, except in the white areas. The number employed in it remained much the same though the proportion was much higher, and the MRLA strength fell very low (Fig. 16).

The reorganization carried out after the issue of the MCP Directive of October 1951 was designed for survival and political manoeuvre, not for offensive military action. Despite the dwindling of the fighting force, the political and supply organization did survive more or less intact and fully active until 1957, and was not completely eradicated until 1960. Even then a nucleus remained, and still remains, in the Thai border area, where it runs a thriving organization to train new young guerrillas and cadres in preparation for renewing the war when the time is ripe. As an example of tenacity, this, in a smaller way, parallels the achievement of Mao Tse Tung after the Long March.[1] The MCP organization from 1952 to 1958 is shown in Figure 17.[2]

In 1953, to escape harassment, Chin Peng moved his Central Committee from Pahang (Central Malaya) northwards across the border to a secure base in south Thailand where there was a strong Chinese minority of 30,000, which had not been resettled into villages where it could be protected or controlled, and was unrestricted by

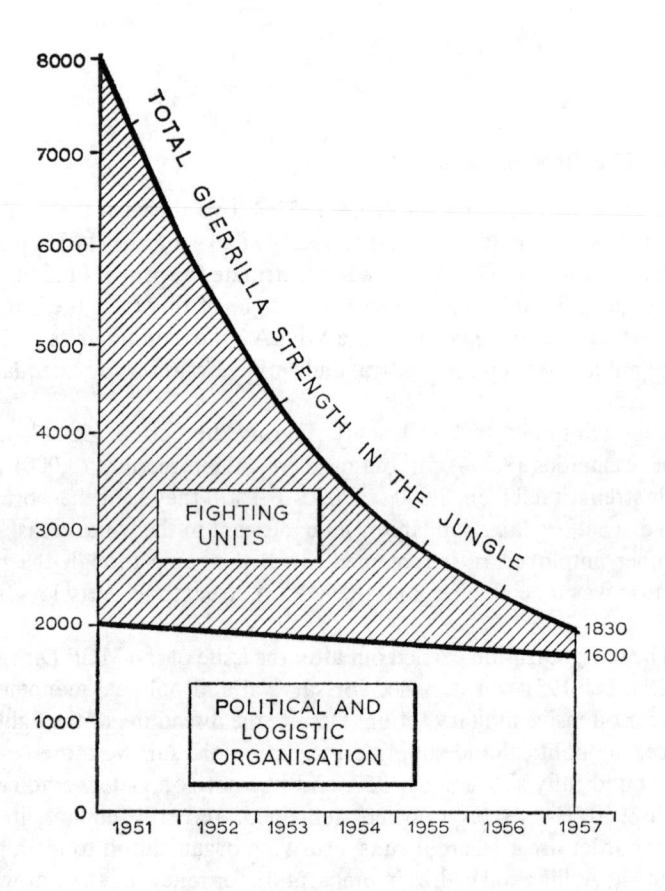

Figure 16 MCP Political and Logistic Organization and Fighting Units 1951–7

MALAYAN COMMUNIST PARTY ORGANIZATION 1952-58

```
                    ┌─────────────────────────┐
                    │   CENTRAL COMMITTEE     │
                    │   SECRETARY GENERAL     │
                    │      (Chin Peng)        │
                    │      POLITBURO          │
                    └─────────────────────────┘
                               │
                               │
                    ┌─────────────────────────┐
                    │  SOUTH MALAYA BUREAU    │
                    │  Yeong Kwo until 1956   │
                    │  Hor Lung 1956–8        │
                    └─────────────────────────┘
```

Central Committee dealt directly with Northern States / Southern States

Northern States:—
Kedah
Penang
Perak
Kelantan
Trengganu

STATE OR REGIONAL COMMITTEES
Secretary (SCS/RCS)
Members (SCM/RCM)

Southern States:—
Selangor
Pahang
Negri Sembilan

Regions
Johore-Malacca Border
North Johore
South Johore

ARMED WORK FORCE — often combined — ARMED WORK CELL

DISTRICT COMMITTEES
Secretary (DCS)
Members (DCM)

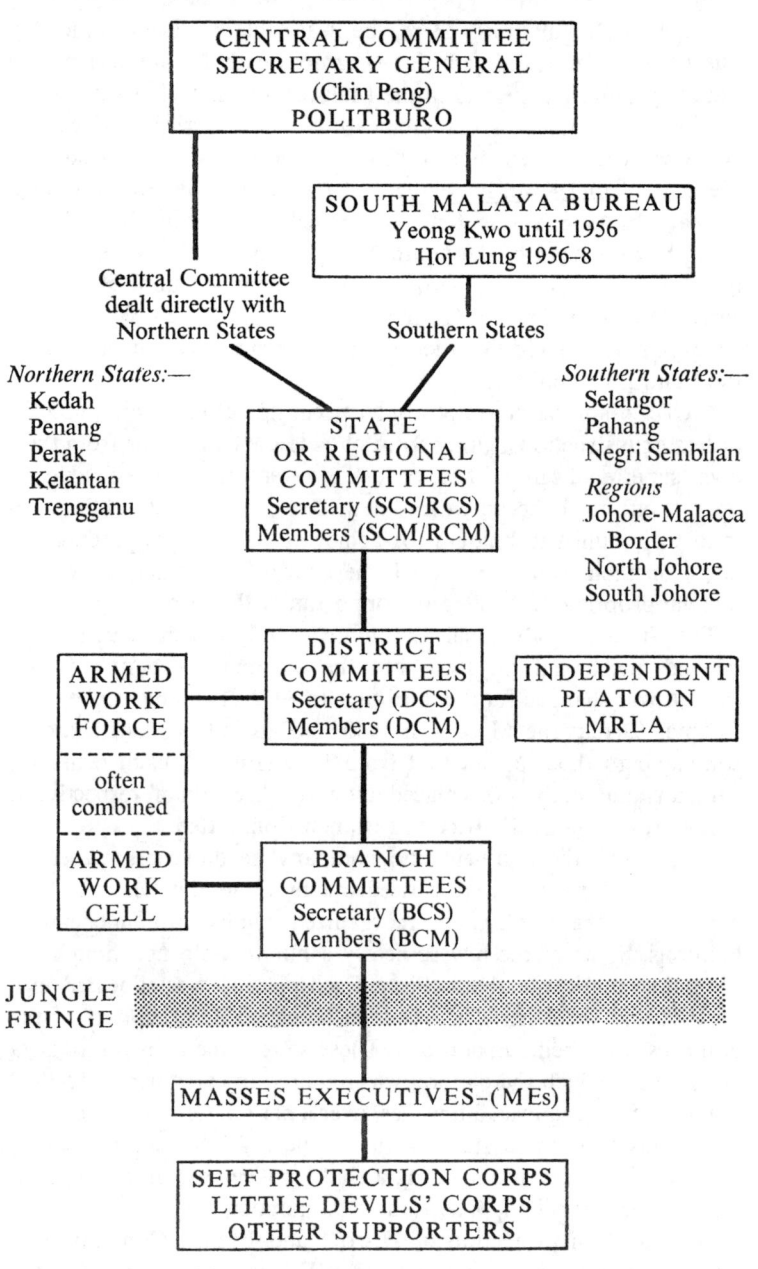

INDEPENDENT PLATOON MRLA

BRANCH COMMITTEES
Secretary (BCS)
Members (BCM)

JUNGLE FRINGE

MASSES EXECUTIVES–(MEs)

SELF PROTECTION CORPS
LITTLE DEVILS' CORPS
OTHER SUPPORTERS

Figure 17

Emergency Regulations. Here, he was able to keep some 400 guerrillas under training in large camps, with lecture rooms and parade grounds, as he had in the Malayan jungle in 1948-9.

This meant that his communications with southern States and Regions became even more difficult, so he left his Vice Secretary-General, Yeong Kwo, in Selangor at the head of the South Malaya Bureau. In 1956 Yeong Kwo was killed in an ambush, and Hor Lung became head of the South Malaya Bureau, thereafter located near the Johore/Pahang border, were it remained until Hor Lung surrendered in May 1958. During these two years (1956-8) Hor Lung states that he received no orders or communications of any kind from the Central Committee.

MCP Committees did not in fact need, nor often receive, specific orders or instructions, either from outside the country or from their own superior headquarters, but they were nevertheless able to operate effectively because they knew their aim, understood the well-tried Communist techniques for achieving it and were prepared to apply on their own initiative whichever of these techniques seemed most appropriate to exploit any opportunity that arose.

The State and Regional Committees and branch structure remained unchanged till 1957, but the command structure of the MRLA was changed for the third time in 1952. It will be recalled (see Chapter 9) that the MRLA in 1948 had an independent chain of command to the top, but that from 1949 (Fig. 12) each regiment, company and platoon was placed under the direction of, respectively, a State (or Region), District and Branch Committee.

From 1952 the regiment and company headquarters ceased to exist. Their functions were carried out by State and District Committees and the MRLA was reorganized wholly into Independent Platoons. Some of these were nearly a hundred strong, though the normal strength was about thirty. Each platoon was allocated to a District and the District Committee launched it in support of the branches for specific operations. These were sometimes on a quota basis, under which the platoon was required to carry out a specified number of, say, railway ambushes, over a period. On other occasions operations were requested by the branch, for such purposes as acquiring weapons, intimidating a shaky police post or home guard platoon, or disciplining a section of the population.

For the local protection of District and Branch Committees, a number of Armed Work Forces (AWFs) and Armed Work Cells

(AWCs) were formed from 1950 onwards. They were a development partly from the original killer squads, and partly from the assimilation into the jungle of members of the Self Protection Corps (SPC – the part-time village guerrillas) for whom life in the villages had become too insecure. The AWFs and AWCs normally worked in civilian clothing, and took on much of the work of sabotage and elimination of government informers. As the guerrilla strength dwindled, they were gradually absorbed into the branches, and the Branch Committee and the AWF or AWC became indistinguishable.[3]

The Parallel Hierarchy

With their new organization, despite their losses, the MCP succeeded in maintaining a viable hierarchy of secret government, paralleling the Federation Government, with its SWECs, DWECs and Village Councils, right through until 1958 (Fig. 18).[4]

Outside the jungle the activities of the people were increasingly focused around the trusted Masses Executives (MEs), who were generally the only ones who had direct contact with the guerrillas. Fewer and fewer people were involved, and the MEs often dealt entirely with relatives who they knew would not betray them. Many of the MEs were themselves related to the guerrillas in their branches – a further example of the strength of Chinese family ties, and of their reliance on them in times of stress.

The Self Protection Corps continued to function, consisting mainly of boys and girls between eighteen and twenty years old. In Yong Peng (Johore) for example, they continued to report for jungle training once a week until 1953. Thereafter their duties, like those of the majority of their comrades in the jungle, became mainly logistic. They bought or collected the rice and smuggled it out of the gates in order to protect the MEs from the risk of being compromised at the gatecheck. The MEs picked it up from pre-arranged dumps outside, and took it on to dumps or meeting places where it was collected by the branch guerrillas.

In villages where popular sentiment still supported the guerrillas (especially in Perak and Johore) the children still ran errands and formed an intelligence screen as members of the 'Little Devils' Corps'.

A branch might be responsible for some five to ten villages and labour lines, containing up to 10,000 people. Figure 19 shows in diagrammatic form some typical functions of the various elements in

ORGANIZATION FOR SURVIVAL

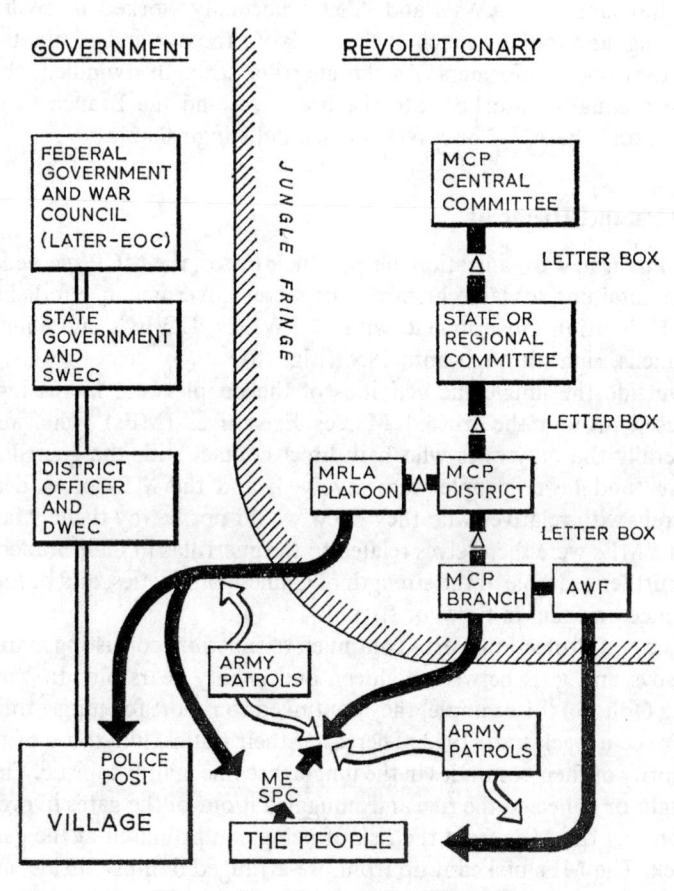

Figure 18 The Parallel Hierarchy

THE PARALLEL HIERARCHY

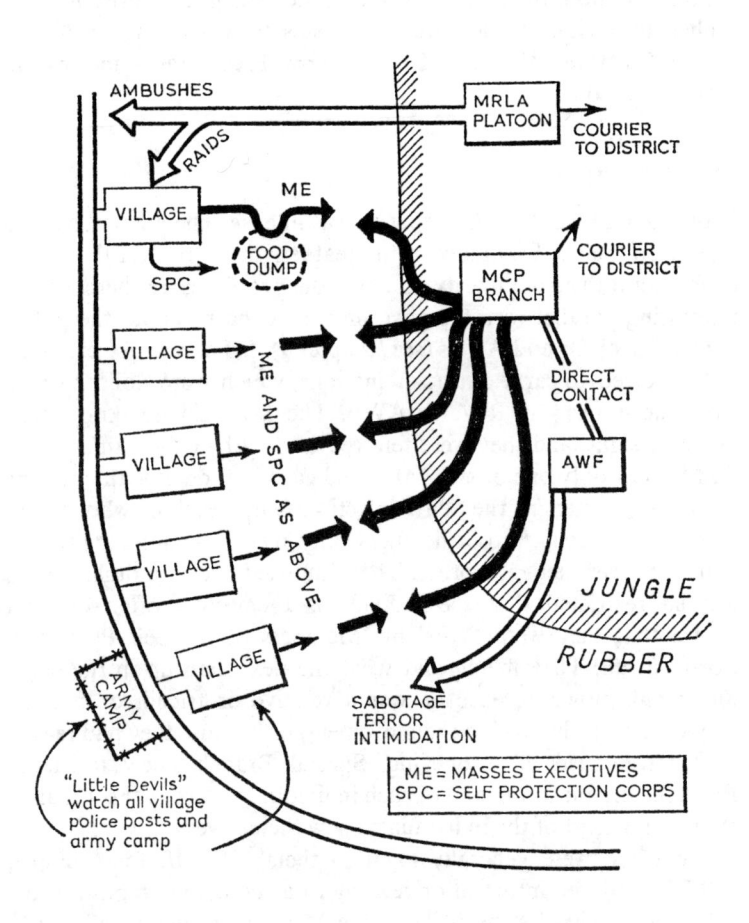

Figure 19 MCP Branch Organization

the MCP structure around some of these villages and one of the estates in which their inhabitants worked. In the jungle are the MRLA platoon, the AWF and the branch, with its courier links to higher authority. Outside are the Masses Executives, the Self Protection Corps and the Little Devils' Corps. Precise tasks and organizations varied.

MCP Security

From 1954 onwards, MCP security was intense. The guerrillas relied utterly on their MEs, and went to great lengths to protect them, and to maintain their popularity amongst the people. Here there was an interesting parallel with the government's concern about the public image of its ROs and AROs (see Chapter 9). MEs were, for example, not expected to carry out assassinations, which were done by men from the jungle – MRLA or AWF. The MEs did not know each other by sight, and they were referred to only by code names. Each BCM knew only one or two MEs, and each ME dealt with only one or two supporters in the Self Protection Corps each of whom dealt with a small cell, whose members only met him individually and seldom if ever met each other. Their knowledge of the organization was so restricted that the individuals themselves often did not realize that they were 'MEs' or 'Members of the Self Protection Corps' at all. They merely did what the next man up in the chain told them, either because he was a relative or friend, or because they were vaguely loyal to the movement, or because they had reason to be frightened of disobeying. Special Branch knew far more about the organization, and of each individual's place in this organization, than most of the individuals knew themselves.

The MCP were generally loyal to their MEs. If, for example, an ME had given information leading to a successful ambush of the police or soldiers by the MRLA, the ME was normally called into the jungle to avoid risk of capture, and his family was cared for.

One penalty of the very tight security was that, if an ME was arrested, his part of the organization often melted away because no one else knew the supporters with whom he dealt, and they were usually glad enough to be off the hook.

This inability to reconstitute an interrupted cell system contrasts with the effective arrangements for doing so in Singapore (see Chapter 3). This was partly because of deteriorating morale in rural areas and partly because, at this time, security in the rural organization had to be more strict than in Singapore for a number of reasons. First, because contacts had to be far more frequent: every pound of rice, every pair of shoes or trousers, every torch battery, pencil or bottle of aspirin for the jungle had to be smuggled by the organization, whereas the urban revolutionary could buy his requirements in a shop. Secondly, whereas an underground worker in the city risked only detention, an ME who organized food collection faced the death penalty if he were caught.[5]

Security of courier communication was also tightened up. There would be one jungle letter box in use between the district and each of its branches, known to the courier from the branch and the courier from the district. They would call there on pre-arranged days of the week, or every other week, to drop and pick up messages. The two couriers called on different days, and neither normally knew the days on which the other one called. There was an alternative letter box for each branch/district link, known to both couriers, which was put into use immediately either suspected that the Security Forces might have detected the original one. Later in the Emergency the alternative was sometimes known only to the District Committee Secretary until he decided that the time had come for a change. This security was effective, but at a heavy cost in delay and dislocation if a courier defected, or was shadowed by the soldiers or by Special Branch or killed. Once broken, the link was often never re-opened, as the district and the branch never found each other in the jungle again.[6]

The pattern of life in the Chinese villages reflected the growing concern of the MCP over security as Special Branch methods became more effective. In one typical rubber growing area, for example, the local MCP branch was responsible for 200 families comprising a little under 900 people. About 60 of these worked on a 1,000 acre European-owned rubber estate and the remainder worked on a number of smallholdings each of 8 to 10 acres. In 1950 about 90 per cent of these families had paid subscriptions to the branch. On every rubber estate, one or more cells, each of four or five members, organized the collection of subscriptions and other activities. The branch committee guerrillas had moved freely amongst them, dressed as rubber tappers and carrying only pistols. Indoctrination meetings had been held regularly, sometimes in the rubber plantations and sometimes in people's houses. Security was lax because virtually everyone was involved, and everyone knew everyone else – as was the case in some of the Catholic slums in Belfast in 1972.

By 1953 the picture was very different. The guerrillas of the branch committee no longer dared to make direct contact with the people for fear of betrayal. The branch was supported by an AWC of five or six men, who camped just inside the jungle fringe and carried rifles, but wore civilian clothes. The AWC also avoided direct contact with the tappers, and worked through five Masses Executive Committees on the estates, and each of these in turn had a cell system under it. There were thus three levels of cut-off from the branch to the tappers – the AWC, the MEs and the cells. The branch was not only responsible for feeding itself, its AWC and the local MRLA platoon, but also had to provide part of the food for the district and higher committees deeper in the jungle. It thus had to gather enough for fifty or sixty men each day, and it was this constant activity which gave Special Branch its opportunities for penetration of the system.

In some areas, all the tappers lived in compounds (or *kongsis*) on the estate. One such estate of 4,000 acres had 180 workers, all Chinese, living in two *kongsis*. In 1949 they had given the guerrillas 100 per cent support and had contributed 50 cents per head per month. No formal organization had been necessary. The guerrillas had gathered the tappers together for mass meetings on the estate during the slack period of the day between tapping the trees in the morning and collecting the latex in the afternoon. Food was at that time unrationed, so the people had simply brought out what the guerrillas needed and handed it over at the meetings.

In 1950 security had to be tightened. The people instead took the food to dumps (known to all) on the jungle fringe. The branch guerrillas then transferred it to branch dumps known only to themselves and the MRLA platoon. The platoon then sent men to take the food from branch dumps to its own platoon dumps whose location the branch did not know. Dumps were moved about every three months, or whenever footprints began to make them too easy to find.

In 1951 a further cut-off was added in the form of seven MEs, who were thereafter the only people who went to the jungle fringe at all. By 1953 the number of MEs had fallen to three and they only had contact with about 20 per cent of the people. They were most apprehensive of betrayal within the *kongsis*, and whenever possible bought the food in the big towns and smuggled it in by bus or concealed in the loads of lorries, rather than risk being seen buying more than usual in the *kongsi* shops.

Methods, of course, varied. Another example is taken from a branch which was responsible for a larger area with a population of 3,000 – mainly Chinese, of whom about 1,000 were involved in supporting the guerrillas by 1953. This support was again organized through a cut-off system of AWCs and MEs, and in this case there were over 100 MEs on the estates, working in Committees on the bigger estates and as individuals on the smaller ones. Each individual ME was responsible for about ten people with whom he alone dealt for everything – food, money, clothing, medicines etc. This branch again had about 50 guerrilla mouths to feed which, at 5 lb. of rice per head, involved smuggling out some 250 lb. of rice per week. Each ME built up his own small cache of rice (in a tin or jar) somewhere amongst the rubber trees he tapped, along with any clothing, medicines, stationery etc. he had been instructed by the AWC to procure. AWC men would emerge from the jungle fringe and the ME would lead them to his cache. This, of course, gave ideal opportunities for ambush if Special Branch could identify an ME and persuade him (tempted by the huge rewards) to become an agent. This was typical of the intelligence techniques developed from 1954 onwards and described in the next chapter.

Money was as important as food and the amounts involved were quite large. This particular branch raised some $3,000 a month in 1953, of which about $1,000 came from a $1 subscription by about 1,000 of the tappers. About thirty smallholders and shopkeepers had to subscribe $50 per month as the price of being allowed to continue in business, and a few bigger business owners had to subscribe more.

Those described above were all rubber-growing areas. In the tin mines the workers had less contact with the MCP. They were perhaps unduly cautious, because the mines (which are all open-cast) were usually worked throughout the night and it was not difficult for the miners to hand over supplies by prior arrangement in the dark. In fact this seldom happened – possibly because the miner was not so personally vulnerable to coercion as the tapper working in isolation in his rubber lot. The Chinese mine owners, however, were much more vulnerable to pressure. The MCP normally demanded from them a 'tax' of 2 per cent to 5 per cent of the output, and even a small mine could produce $50,000 worth of tin per month, therefore yielding $1,000 to $2,500 to the MCP. If the owner refused he faced the threat of having his mine machinery destroyed, if not a worse fate.

Target for 1954–6 – A Typical MCP District (Yong Peng)

As the Emergency progressed, the MCP District Committee became the most important guerrilla grouping. With its own MRLA platoon, it became the lowest formation to possess independent striking power. Having several branches it could survive the loss of, or the loss of contacts with, any one of them – or even of all but one.

One of the most militant hardcore MCP Districts was Yong Peng. In 1952 this district contained about 200 of the 1,000 guerrillas in Johore, and held out against continuous pressure until ordered to surrender by Hor Lung after his defection with the South Malaya Bureau in 1958. The remarkable tenacity of the guerrillas in this district, and their success in maintaining a strong measure of popular support to the last, makes it worthy of particular study (Fig. 20).

When North Johore was finally declared a White Area in August 1958, the Defence Minister of the newly independent Federation of Malaya, Dato Abdul Razak, visited Yong Peng to make the announcement. Only 100 of the 6,300 villagers turned out to hear it. Razak said 'Although we are making this place White, it is not because of any help from you'. The *Straits Times*' headline recording these events must have given some grim satisfaction to Communist die-hards – 'NO THANKS TO YOU – DATO RAZAK LASHES OUT AT YONG PENG'.[7] Such was the character of the guerrillas and their supporters in what had been regarded by the Japanese, by Templer and now by Razak as one of the toughest Communist districts in Malaya.

Yong Peng MCP District contained over 40,000 people, and included the large town and coastal port of Batu Pahat in its extreme south-west corner. This town was set in a Malay hinterland and its Communist organization had been smashed in 1950.

Of the 27,000 who lived in the rural areas of the district, about 11,500 were Chinese. Many of the estates had Indian labourers, and the south and west of the district was largely Malay.

There was a sharp contrast between the pattern of housing in the

TARGET FOR 1954-56 – A TYPICAL MCP DISTRICT

BRANCH ORGANIZATION – YONG PENG MCP DISTRICT

Branch	Strength incl AWF	Masses Executives	Areas of Operation	Villages which served these areas	Population* Chinese	Total
Chaah	25	30-40	Jahore Labis Oil Palm Estate	Chaah NV Jahore Labis	1970 2017	5069 5020
Lam Lee	20	20-30	Union and Lam Lee Estates	Union Est Lines Lam Lee Est Lines	78 248	211 547
Yong Peng	15	20-30	Estates N and NW of Yong Peng	Yong Peng NV (some worked on estates under other branches)	2943	6287
Sam Kongsi	15	20	Yong Peng River Estate	Yong Peng River Estate Lines (plus many more from Yong Peng NV)	94	258
Batu Pahat North	20	20	Sri Medan Iron Mine and Estates South of it	Sri Medan Iron Mine Tongkang Pechah	500 1017	500 1208
Kangkar Bahru	20	20-30	Yong Peng Estate	Kangkar Bahru NV Yong Peng Est A Div Yong Peng Est B Div Yong Peng Est C Div Labis Kongsi	389 375 277 329 81	916 813 733 855 262
Chia Chu Kang	25	20-30	Estates SE of Yong Peng	Kg Haji Ghafar NV (plus many more from Yong Peng NV)	108	234

* MCP supporters were organized by the Masses Executives in the Estates on which they worked rather than the villages in which they lived.

Figure 20

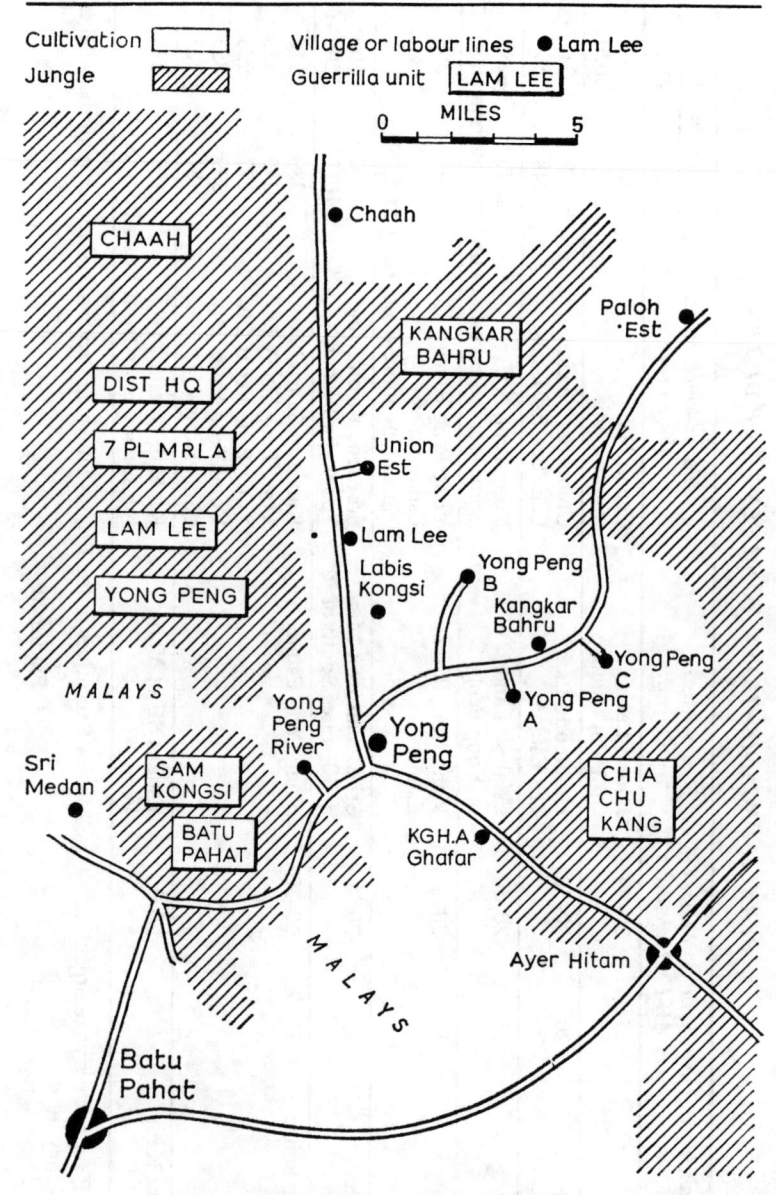

Figure 21 Map of Yong Peng District

TARGET FOR 1954-56 – A TYPICAL MCP DISTRICT

rubber estates north and east of the town of Yong Peng, and in the Malay areas to the south and west of the town, in which there had been no resettlement. The individual Malay houses were spread along the tracks and irrigation ditches, about fifteen in every cultivated kilometre square. At an average of 5.7 per Malay household,[8] this worked out at eighty-five men, women and children in each kilometre square of the map, evenly distributed and unprotected.

By contrast, in the rubber estates north and east of Yong Peng, there were about 122 kilometre squares under cultivation. The total population listed in police records for these areas (including Yong Peng itself) was 10,682. This gave a very similar average – eighty-eight per cultivated square kilometre. But in this case they were concentrated in nine villages, each of which was defended.

Apart from Batu Pahat and the Malay areas in the south and west, Yong Peng MCP District contained two main cultivated and resettled areas – around Chaah and Yong Peng. The Chaah area consisted of a concentrated oil palm estate of about 120 square kilometres, with a population recorded as 10,089 of whom 3,987 were Chinese.

The central area near Yong Peng contained 7,552 Chinese, of whom just over 2,000 lived in wired villages within the Malay areas. Apart from one Iron Mine at Sri Medan (about twelve kilometres west of Yong Peng), and individual peasant smallholdings, all the cultivated land was planted with rubber.

To organize this district, the MCP had approximately 200 guerrillas in 1952-3. They were split as follows (Fig. 21):

District HQ	10
No. 7 Independent MRLA Platoon	40
Branches (including AWFs):	
Chaah	25
Lam Lee	20
Yong Peng	15
Sam Kongsi	25
Batu Pahat Rural	20
Kangkar Bahru	20
Chia Chu Kang	25
	200

The branches and their AWFs/AWCs worked as single entities. Their combined strength accounted for 150 of the 200 guerrillas in the district.

The branch organizations are shown in Figure 20, showing also the number of Masses Executives, who numbered 150–200.

Chaah Branch was weakest in relation to the population. This was because the Johore Labis Oil Palm Estate was highly developed, with a network of long straight roads which made patrolling by the Security Forces much easier.

Lam Lee Branch served a small population on two estates, where it had strong support. The branch sometimes lived in the hills to the east of the estates.

Yong Peng Branch ran the estates astride the main north–south road, three to four miles north of Yong Peng. All the labourers lived in Yong Peng New Village. The guerrillas usually lived in the jungle to the west, but sometimes camped in the tongue of marshy jungle which cuts across the road immediately north of Yong Peng. This branch was in close touch with the District Headquarters, which also camped north-west of Yong Peng.

The Sam Kongsi Branch was another very strong one, with solid support from the tappers on the Yong Peng River Estate, some of whom lived in the small labour lines on the estate (known as Sam Kongsi), but most of whom came to work from Yong Peng.

The Batu Pahat Rural Branch drew support from the Sri Medan Iron Mines and from the workers on the Chingiap Plantation and Chee Hock Huat Estate, who lived in Tongkang Pechah.

North-east of Yong Peng, the Kangkar Bahru Branch operated on the large Yong Peng Estate whose workers lived in five villages and lines as shown in Figures 20 and 21.

Finally, the Chia Chu Kang Branch, another strong one, drew support from the Chinese who worked south-east of Yong Peng, all of whom lived in the town except for 108 in the small New Village of Kampong Haji Ghafar.

Yong Peng was one of the real hard core of Communist-supporting districts, rivalled only by Kulai in South Johore and Sungei Siput in Perak. All had been strongly Communist during the Japanese occupation and had survived numerous 'drives' by the British. They were among the three last districts to succumb. Yong Peng can therefore be regarded as typical of the kind of target which forced the British to evolve the technique of the federal priority operation using food denial as an aid to intelligence. The evolution of this technique is described in the next two chapters.

Chapter 11 The Development of a Successful Technique

A Difficult Target

During 1953 the guerrillas were at their least aggressive, and continued to kill less than a fifth of the number of civilians and Security Forces that they had in 1951. Their own losses, however, remained very high indeed. The Security Forces were killing or capturing six guerrillas for every man they lost.

During 1954, however, the guerrillas became very much harder to find. It was estimated that a soldier might expect to do 1,000 hours on patrol or 300 hours in ambush before he encountered a guerrilla. The type of intelligence which had sufficed until then had been more or less the conventional brand of police and military battle intelligence. The soldiers on patrol would follow up tracks and footprints, check the passes of tappers who acted suspiciously or who were away from their accustomed beats, and try to formulate the pattern of movement of the guerrillas and of their meetings with the people. The police Special Branch would watch who talked to whom, discover who was related to whom, and thereby pick on people who knew something. They had also developed the exploitation of SEPs to a fine art. Most of the Special Branch information came from these SEPs and from informers (i.e. people who could tell them what had happened already, thereby building up the pattern).

The agent, i.e. the man who knew future Communist movements and was prepared to betray them in advance, was at this stage a fairly rare bird.

From 1954 onwards, with the guerrillas thin on the ground, doing their best to lie low and evade contact, and confiding their secrets only to a chosen few instead of to a mass of friendly villagers, the recruiting of agents became a vital element in the government campaign. Killing guerrillas was dependent on this, and went hand in hand with the main task of digging out the Communist roots in the villages. This was to take another six years. During these six years, both the Communist techniques for survival and the government techniques for acquiring and using intelligence reached a degree of refinement which has probably never been equalled in any other insurgency.

Food Denial Operations – Early Attempts

The method of acquiring and using agents was to spy on the guerrillas' contacts with the people, identify those who were in touch with them, persuade a number of these to turn traitor, and so disrupt the rest of the organization that the guerrillas were fairly sure to go on relying on at least some of these people who would in the end betray them by giving 'advance precise information'.

Known in intelligence jargon as 'turning', this process of suborning people already working for the Communists proved far more effective than attempting to insert police agents from the outside. The latter was sometimes achieved, but it had become less easy than in the earlier days of the Emergency, because the MCP now recruited its guerrillas and supporters with greater care, and imposed long probationary periods, in which they were tested and proved before being entrusted with delicate secrets. In any case, newcomers into the system were suspect, since – especially in the later years of the Emergency – few people gave active support to the Communists without good reasons – for example because they were relatives of guerrillas, or because the MCP had some kind of a hold whereby they could be blackmailed.

To select a field for recruitment of agents, Special Branch had to look into the purposes for which the guerrillas needed to make contact with the people. In the first years of the Emergency they had dealt with the Chinese rural population in mass, at public propaganda meetings in the rubber estates etc., with no precautions other than the posting of sentries. After 1952 the activities of Special Branch compelled them to confine their contacts to those whose direct support they needed. This support was described in the previous chapter, and took the form of information, readiness to distribute propaganda, and, above all, supply of food, money, medical equipment, pencils and paper, radios, torches, batteries, clothing etc. And the most vital item of all was rice.

Passive denial of food supplies was not in itself sufficient to bring

FOOD DENIAL OPERATIONS – EARLY ATTEMPTS

about a collapse. Its value was as a means of creating intelligence. The technique, evolved over the period 1952–5, was to build up on the general intelligence picture by so restricting and controlling the flow of supplies – especially of rice – that the suppliers could be identified. Some could then be 'turned' and persuaded to give 'advance, precise information' such as would enable police and army patrols to be in ambush at, or on the route to, some specific guerrilla rendezvous or pick-up point at the right moment.

The restriction of supplies as an operational aid was not itself a new idea. It had been tried as early as July 1949, in Operation SNOW WHITE astride the Pahang–Johore border, when rice was rationed and stocks limited in the shops. The hope at that time was not so much to recruit agents, but to supplement normal intelligence by helping the security forces to detect the habits (even if not the identity) of suppliers, so that patrols and ambushes could be better fitted to the likely pattern of their movements. Rationing helped because it gave the timid or reluctant supplier an alibi for not producing anything, so that the hard core had to take greater risks to provide more, and were therefore more likely to be spotted. This particular operation failed because rationing only lasted for a month and the guerrillas never really felt the pinch. Nevertheless, even at this stage, a number of battalions had begun to appreciate the opportunity offered by the logistic weaknesses of the guerrillas and to base their operations on an intelligent assessment of how they, if they were the guerrillas, would move, eat and camp. Those who did this were the most successful – notably the Suffolk Regiment.[1]

The pattern of deployment of troops and police which evolved was to allocate most of them to a framework of battalions – mainly split into companies (of about 100 soldiers). Each company was responsible for supporting the police and eliminating the guerrillas in the district in which it lived. Periodically, troops were taken away from their framework operations to take part in larger operations designed to destroy a particular guerrilla gang. Up till 1952, however, these big operations had been based on general rather than specific information and had met with little success.[2]

The first attempt at a major operation based on the large scale arrest of Communist food suppliers was Operation HIVE in the Seremban District of Negri Sembilan, in the second half of 1952.

It was to some extent fortuitous, in that the newly posted commander of 63 Gurkha Infantry Brigade (Brigadier M. C. A. Henniker) was told that he was to receive a large and temporary reinforcement of troops for two months, and so he and his State War Executive Committee set about deciding how best to use them.

There was at this time a general reaction against big operations in the jungle, and a feeling that it was better to stick to framework operations.[3] This was a healthy reaction, because troops were generally most effective if left to make steady and unspectacular progress in eliminating guerrillas by ambushes and patrols in their own districts where they had got to know the country and the people. Interruption and relaxation of this framework pressure simply allowed the guerrillas to make up their losses and reorganize their strained and disrupted supply system, and this had happened all too often when troops were taken away to be thrown into vast sweeps and encirclement operations in the jungle, which killed very few guerrillas and did nothing at all to reduce their hold on the people. Indeed, the guerrillas were presented with a propaganda point, by being able to claim that the government could not beat them even when it turned thousands of troops onto them – the familiar 'Paper Tiger' argument.[4]

This was appreciated from the start by Briggs, who expressed the view in October 1950 that a strong section was a match for any bandit gang, especially if it also used 'sting and disappear' tactics. It was seldom that anyone except the first few men got the chance to fire, and small patrols were more controllable, adaptable, less noisy and hence less vulnerable. They were also more mobile and capable of surprise.[5]

Briggs, as he gained experience as Director of Operations, had begun to get an inkling of the true value of food denial. In his earliest directive, in May 1950, he had spoken of forcing the guerrillas to attack the Security Forces on their own ground. This had proved to be a false hope because the guerrillas could, and did, lie low for days or weeks on end, provided that they had food dumps in the jungle.[6] In October 1950, therefore, Briggs urged the army to be patient in interdicting the guerrilla supply lines, since their dumps must run out before long, and they could then not exist without support from the *Min Yuen*. This necessitated movement, he said, and it was movement which made them vulnerable to ambush.

It was these two tactics: to force the guerrillas to make contact with their suppliers and to expose themselves by moving in generally predictable areas, which were at the centre of the plan made by

Brigadier Henniker and the Negri Sembilan SWEC to make use of the extra troops they were offered. Operation HIVE was only partially successful, but it did mark a major advance in thought over the conventional military response to the allocation of a temporary reinforcement, and it taught several important lessons.

This was the first operation to aim, not only to destroy the armed guerrilla units in the jungle, but also to disrupt the infrastructure of Masses Executives and cells amongst the people in the villages and estates.

The Seremban MCP District, roughly twenty-five miles square, was at this time estimated by Special Branch to contain eighty-six guerrillas of whom thirty-one were in No. 3 Independent MRLA Platoon, and fifty-five in the District and Branch Organization.[7]

The reinforcement quadrupled the number of troops in the district – raising it from the normal framework of three companies to three battalions.[8]

To deceive the enemy during the preparatory stages, a fictitious operation (WHIPCORD) was planned around Bahau, some forty miles away, for which maps were issued, and a ramp was ordered to be built at Bahau railway station in readiness to unload a large consignment of extra vehicles.[9]

Planning for Operation HIVE began in June 1952. Certain areas in the Seremban District were selected as killing grounds, where the army and police patrols and ambushes would concentrate their efforts. There was some discussion as to whether to arrest all known suppliers in the district, or only those outside the killing grounds, in the hope that the guerrillas would be drawn into the areas where the ambushes awaited them. Eventually, it was decided to arrest all known suppliers which, it was hoped, would force the guerrillas to recruit new suppliers in a hurry, and whom it would be easier for Special Branch to detect and 'turn'.[10]

Stage I of the plan was to establish an outer ring of ambushes to prevent an exodus from the killing ground. Stage II was to ask the normal police informers to advise in which areas the guerrillas were operating. Stage III was the arrest of all known suppliers, with the dual aims of obtaining more information and forcing the guerrillas to consume their reserve dumps of food in the jungle. This would be followed by a pause, Stage IV, in which troops would be rotated for rest while the guerrillas were expected to lie low, eating away their dumps. Stage V – the killing stage – would come when their stocks were running low so that they would have to come out of the jungle to seek new sources of food from the villages.

The operation began on 20 August, when one Gurkha battalion with two squadrons of the Special Air Service Regiment (SAS)[11] manned the outer ring of ambushes in the jungle. Intensive searches by patrols discovered five or six camps, three of which were big enough for thirty to fifty men.[12]

At the same time, all known suppliers were arrested, 107 of them, including 50 Masses Executives. Those arrested also included the ones who were already giving information to the police, as they would otherwise have come under suspicion. As a result, all information dried up, and one battalion was pulled out to rest.[13]

On 4 September, the first two guerrillas were killed. Soon afterwards a courier was killed carrying documents, and information began to come in from other guerrillas who surrendered. In the second month of the operation, as expected, the kill rate rose, and by the time the two months were up and the reinforcing battalions were withdrawn (21 October) a total of twenty-five guerrillas had been eliminated – over a quarter of the guerrilla strength in the district.[14]

These were, by any standards, two highly successful months, considering that less than 100 men were being hunted in 600 square miles of jungle. The operation was too short, however, to complete the destruction of the district organization, which was soon able to recover. It was the solution to this last problem – the destruction of the district organization beyond recovery – that was to elude the government for two or three more years.

The operation revealed some loopholes in food control. A good deal of rice was grown in the area, and there had not been the tight control of the harvest that was to be imposed in later operations. Rice dealers were allowed 5 per cent for wastage – 'enough to feed 86 men for a lifetime', and the searching of rubber tappers going out of the village gates to work was not strict enough to prevent the very small leakage required by the Communists.[15]

The Malay Special Constables and civilian searchers on these gatechecks were later to be supplemented by British soldiers (see Chapters 12 and 13).[16]

Another important lesson from this operation was that, no matter how great the pressure, the guerrilla political and logistic organizations (Branch committees, armed work cells etc.) did not leave their own areas; first because they dared not abandon their painfully built-up food supply lines; and secondly because they were forbidden to do so since their job was to organize and lead the 'masses' in their particular area.[17] They could not afford to break the secret and personal links with their masses executives in the villages – which no one else would be able to take up. Indeed, once 'off the hook', most of the supporters used to take good care not to let anyone get them involved again.

Operation HIVE was a significant pioneering effort but its intelligence was still largely obtained from informers who knew only of past events and patterns. The operation was not long enough to enable Special Branch to 'turn' suppliers into agents, who could give 'advance, precise information'.

The Latimer Report

This weakness was analysed in a brilliant debriefing report on Operation HIVE, by a young Military Intelligence Officer attached to Special Branch, Captain H. S. Latimer. This report proposed a pattern of operations which proved in the end, with only minor improvements, to be the battle-winning pattern for the remaining seven years of the Emergency. Some of its proposals, however, such as the central cooking of rice in the villages, were not to be introduced for another three years.

Latimer proposed that operations should be in two phases. In Phase I, to last two to three months,[18] Special Branch would make a detailed research and analysis of the records of movements and habits of the guerrillas and of their supporters over the past two years. There would also be a thorough topographical study, and an intense intelligence effort to build up details of the personalities and organization of the guerrillas and their supporters. As the picture took shape, the District War Executive Committee would plan the operations which were to comprise Phase II.

Phase II would begin with a curfew and supply denial scheme, with rationing, restriction of stocks and strict searching of people going out to work. At the same time, food suppliers would be arrested, and, using the mass of information they had built up in Phase I, Special Branch would try to 'turn' some of them into agents.

Hereafter, Latimer proposed tactics which were designed to lead the guerrillas into killing grounds, which were, in fact, the areas of rubber etc. in which prospective agents worked. Everything possible was to be done to drive the guerrillas away from the areas outside these killing grounds, by tightening food control and saturating them with patrols and ambushes. Conversely, inside the killing grounds, there was to be judicious relaxation of food control and other regulations, and troops were to be kept out of them. The guerrillas would thus be able to move freely and to acquire confidence in the suppliers who operated in the killing grounds, including the ones who had been 'turned'. This would lead to 'advance, precise information' on which individual ambushes could be laid.

Latimer's ideas were not fully understood or applied for some years, but to him must go the greatest credit for the solution of the problem of 'digging out the roots'.[19]

Improving the Pattern

Meanwhile, as Operation HIVE concluded, another operation – HAMMER – was launched on similar lines in the State of Selangor. Various improvements were made, and forty-four guerrillas were eliminated – over half of them being SEPs. The District, however, contained five branches, of which only two were attacked. Though disrupted, they were not destroyed. The operations proved that it was of little permanent use to attack anything less than a complete district in this way, since the District Committee was able to survive on the support of the branches which had been left intact, under whose cover it could rebuild the others by calling members of the Masses Organization into the jungle to become guerrillas. This is precisely what happened within a few months after Operation HAMMER.

Another conclusion was that, since the guerrillas normally stockpiled at least one month's food, operations would have to last for at least three months if food denial was to be really effective. (It was later found that even three months was not long enough.)

The post-mortem on Operation HAMMER also underlined importance of civil police and military cooperation, and concluded that the army must be prepared to go for weeks without a contact by operating in areas where there was no information simply to keep the guerrillas out of them so they would make touch with their supporters in other areas where Special Branch wanted them.

Following the experience of Operations HIVE and HAMMER

and of three other concurrent operations in the state of Pahang, a controversy developed amongst the hierarchy in Kuala Lumpur. The traditional school of thought was that it was the elimination of the higher echelons of leadership that mattered; that penetration at the level of the food suppliers in the villages would give leads only into the MCP Branches, or with luck into the District Committees, but certainly not into the Regional, State and Central Committees which, if left intact, could rebuild any District or Branch Committees which were disrupted. The other school of thought, led by more progressive members of Special Branch influenced by the Latimer Report, was that if the MCP Branch and village supply systems were eliminated the more senior ranks would have to make contact with the villages direct, and that this would make them more vulnerable.

In retrospect, it was proved by later operations that, though the second school got nearer the truth, neither was wholly correct. The real lead into the higher guerrilla headquarters and MRLA platoons came not so much through their having to collect their own food as through betrayal by surrendered guerrillas from the Districts and Branches who had been responsible for obtaining their supplies from the people and passing them back into the jungle, and by couriers who knew the way to the State, District and MRLA camps. In the operations described, the troops had found it a waste of time to lie in ambush for these tiny HQs and platoons in the deep jungle, using only guess-work and without 'advance precise information'. There was little hope of getting such information from the arrested village suppliers, simply because they never met the higher HQs and MRLA units. Special Branch HQs in Kuala Lumpur was therefore beginning to think in terms of an exploitation Phase – a Phase III – in which some of the more senior SEPs who had come in during Phase II would give 'advance precise information' about the movements of the higher HQs and MRLA platoons.

This hope was realized with devastating effect between 1953 and 1955 in a series of highly successful operations in Pahang, which eliminated 80 per cent of the guerrillas in the State, enabling Emergency restrictions to be lifted over a large part of it, which was declared a White Area (see Chapter 9).

It was during these years that the pattern conceived by Latimer was refined and proved.

Chapter 12   The Final Pattern

Selection of the Target

In June 1954, eighteen months after Latimer's report, the technique for the 'federal priority operation' was promulgated as a policy for universal application whenever it was decided to concentrate a mass of police, troops, food controllers, information and psychological warfare teams with the aim of destroying both the guerrillas and the infrastructure in a single MCP District, such as the Yong Peng District described in Chapter 10. During the next two years this technique was further refined and by 1956 it had reached its peak of efficiency. Thereafter it was to be applied, in a series of overwhelming blows, district by district, to destroy the entire MCP organization within the borders of the Federation by 1960.

The policy instructions stressed the importance of careful selection and definition of the target. It must be a district in which the MCP had contact with the masses so that Special Branch penetration could lead back to the guerrillas. The target district should also be one whose destruction should provide a lead towards another important target.

Leads into neighbouring districts in fact became easier as the pressure on the MCP increased, and towards the end of the Emergency these leads were sometimes so well developed that it became necessary to incorporate several districts into the target. As a district or branch found its sources of supply eroded by successful framework operations it began to seek fresh sources from adjacent districts or even to amalgamate with them. Alternatively, if a guerrilla branch were seriously weakened or wiped out, the *Min Yuen* in its area would sometimes be approached and led by a neighbouring branch. In 1956, for example, in the Yong Peng District (see Chapter 10 and Figure 21) the Kangkar Bahru Branch, which had until then dealt solely with the Yong Peng Rubber Estate to the south-west of it, took over responsibility for the Paloh Estate in the next

PHASE I – ACQUIRING AGENTS

district to the north-east, where the guerrilla branch had been wiped out but the supporting infrastructure amongst the tappers was intact. Since the Yong Peng District was run by an able and determined leader, he would have kept his district supplied from Paloh and other places if Yong Peng alone had been the target for attack. When the final operation against Yong Peng was mounted in 1957 (Operation SHOE) it therefore had to incorporate two other districts into the target.

Wherever possible, however, a single MCP district was the target.

Outline of Phases

The Federal Priority Operation as defined in 1956 was divided into three phases:

Phase I: A preliminary period of one to three months in which intelligence was built up. (In practice this was more often four to six months.)

Phase II: The beginning of the operation itself, with an intensification of food control and Security Force (SF) pressure.

Phase III: The exploitation of the enemy's loss of morale and increased flow of intelligence by SF ambushes, patrolling and attacks on camps. Food control, however, was not relaxed.

Phase I – Acquiring Agents

The SB plan began with an area survey. The first part listed the estates, inhabited localities, village populations (broken down into races) communications and topographical features. The second part listed the record of MCP activity, with all available data about guerrilla units, camp sites, habits, contacts with the people and terrorist incidents over the past year.

This was followed by a list of all guerrilla personalities and a study of their relatives and friends. A special search was made for any avenues which might provide the basis for an intelligence project against an individual, e.g. particular tastes in tobacco or drugs or links with girl friends.

A similar study was made of the Masses Organization, looking for clues as to the pattern of the cells, their contacts and their responsibilities. Leads to individuals were again particularly sought. Sources of the materials needed by the guerrillas were also analysed, e.g. food, medicine, stationery, clothing, radios, watches and – oddly important – DOM Benedictine, which was very popular in the jungle.

During this phase, the Security Forces had the task of provoking intelligence where SB knowledge and intelligence were inadequate. Their operations were generally designed to force the guerrillas to resort to areas in which SB hoped to acquire agents. At the same time, the troops patrolled other areas intensively (often with no hope of contacts) to help to ensure that the guerrillas used the areas which Special Branch wanted them to use. Thrusting military commanders, seeking more fruitful action to boost the morale of their soldiers, were firmly restrained from precipitate action.

As the pattern of study and patrolling gave indications of promise, SB made a number of selective arrests of persons with suspected Communist connections, in fairly small numbers to no apparent pattern. Some of those arrested were quickly 'turned' and released; others, who could not be turned, were kept in detention.

In some cases, a suspect who could not be arrested because of insufficient evidence was 'blackened' instead. This was done by frequent overt enquiries about him by the detectives in the village. This had the effect either of making the guerrillas or MEs frightened of using him, or making them so suspicious of him that he had to flee the area.

Victims for arrest were selected on two main considerations: evidence that they were in touch with the guerrillas, and evidence of their vulnerability to persuasion. The evidence of involvement was often gained only after the hard core MEs had been detained or compromised, so that the guerrillas were forced to rely on their weaker supporters, often having to coerce them to take risks which they were reluctant to take. Many of the best leads came through relatives, some of whom could be persuaded that the best way of getting their sons or nieces or cousins off the hook was to put them into the hands of the SB Inspector who could promise that if all went well there would be a big reward, whereas to continue to be mixed up with the guerrillas could lead only to imprisonment or death in the end. Another useful lead was for the SB detective in the village to make friends with the shopkeepers to see which families bought extra food. While rice was rationed, some of the more perishable cereals (such as biscuits or Quaker Oats) were not, and the family might be passing its rice into the jungle and living on the more perishable substitutes at home.

The process of 'turning' was usually a mixture of persuasion and drawing attention to the rewards (though some of those arrested were so relieved at the prospect of getting off the hook that they needed little persuasion). The likeliest victims were those 'in a spot' – for example those who had embezzled party subscriptions or were in love with a girl whose father was a guerrilla.[1]

As a result of all this activity the SB Appreciation classified the various estates and villages in two respects: first, the degree of activity of the Masses Organization – very active, little activity or no activity; and secondly the degree of SB cover – sources in direct contact with SB (i.e. agents), other sources (i.e. informers) or no sources. On the basis of this assessment they would apply varying tactics in the operation of food denial. At one end of the scale those offering no sources of information but with much food supply activity would be subjected to the strictest possible food control, with central cooking and intensive searches to prevent food being smuggled out to the guerrillas. By these measures it was hoped to force the guerrillas to rely on a few really trusted suppliers, who would thus be forced to take risks, spotted by Special Branch and then, if possible, 'turned'; if they could not be 'turned' they would be held in detention so that the guerrillas would have to rely on others who were less determined or less trustworthy. At the other end of the scale were the areas in which there was much activity and also agents in direct contact with SB. These areas were potential killing grounds and food denial was manipulated to exploit them – in other words, food control would be tight generally but would be discreetly relaxed to allow the 'sources' to make contact.

Towards the end of Phase I SB made a detailed appreciation of the guerrilla and Masses Organization and finally selected the killing grounds. They then confirmed the plans for Phase II, including details of the mass arrests to be made on D Day.

D Day

As D Day for Phase II approached, extra troops and police reinforcements began to move into the area, and there was noticeable activity in the repair of village perimeter fences, the installation of perimeter lighting and clearance of undergrowth around villages and along the sides of roads. Though wherever possible only preparatory work was done before D Day, some increase in activity was inevitable and could not fail to be noticed, so a deception plan was essential to confuse the guerrillas and their supporters as to the timing, the geographical focus and the extent of the forthcoming operation.[2]

On D Day the first event, usually before dawn, was the simultaneous arrest by SB of all known members of the Masses Organization in every village serving the target MCP District – excluding only those who had already been established as agents, and certain others who did not know that they were suspected but whom SB believed might become agents if they were left on the ground. Deprived of the majority of their working supporters, the guerrillas would eventually come to rely more and more on these agents or potential agents as suppliers or be forced to recruit new ones, many of whom would be reluctant and unreliable. Some were arrested for 'turning', others for interrogation and release with a view to 'turning' later if they resumed contact with the guerrillas, others released and 'blackened' and others held for prolonged detention – just as has already been described during Phase I.

At the same time, strict food denial was imposed on the whole area except for specific and discreet relaxations required by SB. Every house was searched for surplus stocks, and the stocks in food shops reduced to the permitted level. The rice ration was reduced to the bare minimum, normally 3 or $3\frac{1}{2}$ katties (5 lb.) per week per adult male and less for women and children Alternatively, in some villages, no rice was allowed at all except that cooked in communal kitchens. This was perishable and the people could therefore buy as much as they liked, so central cooking eventually became quite popular.[3]

Reinforced search parties were placed on every village gate. In Operation SHOE (Yong Peng, Labis, Paloh Districts), for example, some 1,500 police (including 200 women) manned about 100 gates in 50 villages – an average of 12 to 18 per gate They operated at full strength in the early mornings and afternoons when the people went out to work and came back, and on a shift system of 2 or 3 men in between.

On D Day, or within a few days afterwards, every village was visited by an Information Services Team, to announce the operation, explain about food rationing and other restrictions, and to urge cooperation in order to complete the operation as soon as possible.

PHASE II

In one operation, for example, where there was a rural population of 125,000, 2 Information Officers and 6 mobile loudspeaker vans were allocated for the operation as a whole, but 26 additional mobile vans were allocated for the first week of Phase II. In addition, there was widespread use of leaflets, posters, film shows, SEP tours, drama troops and prominent speakers.

Visiting speakers and information officers were given talking points, which were also used in the form of scripts for the loudspeaker vans. These scripts outlined the purpose of food denial, and stressed that it would continue until the MCP in the district was destroyed; promised immunity from prosecution for those who gave information quickly; explained how to give information discreetly and listed the rewards for doing so. After Malaya became self-governing (1955) and then independent (1957) the scripts stressed that the MCP was now fighting a government elected by the people, and gave convincing proof of the general hopelessness of the Communist cause – a telling point with the pragmatic Chinese.[4]

Psychological warfare was also stepped up, in cooperation with SB. Leaflets were dropped in the jungle, and voice aircraft flew over it broadcasting personal messages from SEPs, and from the relatives of guerrillas. People were persuaded to forward letters to friends and relations in the jungle, guaranteeing good treatment, and giving details (with photographs) of the freedom and prosperity of others who had surrendered. Care was taken not to boast of successes which had not yet been achieved.

Phase II

For about two months after D Day, SB could expect a lull in information. Realizing that the operation had begun, the guerrillas would lie low, living on their dumped stocks of food. Meanwhile, they tried to find out all they could about the pattern of food denial, where it was strictest, and which of their suppliers had been arrested. During this period, the Security Forces concentrated mainly on supporting food control, frequently reinforcing the morning gate checks, establishing road blocks and patrolling outside village perimeters at night. Patrolling was concentrated away from the killing grounds, and in particular in areas where SB cover was poor, to ensure that the guerrillas were prevented from replenishing their food stocks from these areas.

As their stocks were consumed, they had to renew their contacts with the *Min Yuen*. Ambushes were laid in the killing grounds on advance precise information. Hungry and harassed, guerrillas began to surrender. The SEPs produced more information and the cracks in the MCP Branch and Masses Organizations began to spread.

There were no big battles, and eliminations were generally in twos and threes:

> 'The battles, even in the killing stage, were still not spectacular – nothing like the set-piece affairs in North Vietnam in the 1950s, or South Vietnam in the 1960s with whole battalions lying in wait for each other. If we had lost the battles of 1950 and 1951, this is what our war would have been like; but we did not lose them. Although 250 guerrillas might be in the district of a major operation, we seldom met them after 1952 in parties of more than 30; most often, they numbered a dozen or less . . . A major operation was, in fact, a host of minor operations.'[5]

Phase III

Phase II merged into Phase III as the branch organization ceased to function. The MRLA units and the higher HQs in the deep jungle began to become desperate for food. Sometimes they came to the jungle fringe and fell into the clutches of agents. Once their pattern of communications was known, their destruction was fairly quick (see also Chapter 14).

Provided that there was little risk of reactivation by neighbouring MCP District or Branch Committees, the area could then be declared White and the troops, police reinforcements, food denial and information staffs moved on to fresh fields, leaving only the normal police and home guards, together with one or two trusted agents, ex-MEs or even ex-guerrillas, to let Special Branch know if the *Min Yuen* showed signs of revival.

A Strategy to Finish the War

Until 1955, *faute de mieux*, the government strategy had been to roll up the Communists from the south, starting with Johore. This had a certain logic, as the Federation's only land frontier was with Thailand at the northern end of the peninsula. Chin Peng had used this same logic in 1953 when he had moved his Central Committee from Pahang across the Thai border.

The strategy of rolling up from the south, however, never began to work, as the state of Johore (along with Perak which adjoined the Thai frontier) had historically one of the two strongest Communist organizations in the country, which proved to be the last to crack, and the MCP's popular support remained until their men had finally come out of the jungle – as was vividly shown at the time Yong Peng was declared a White Area (see Chapter 10).

By 1955, the spectacular successes in Pahang, and the achievement of self-government by the Federation, with the imminent promise of full independence, had convinced Chin Peng that he must seek a political solution.

In June 1955, by means of a letter signed with a pseudonym (Ng Heng), the MCP suggested truce talks, and Chin Peng met the Chief Ministers of the Federation and Singapore (Tunku Abdul Rahman and David Marshall) at Baling, near the frontier of Thailand. Chin Peng offered to lay down his arms in exchange for political recognition of the MCP. This was firmly refused by the Tunku, and Chin Peng returned to the jungle. He sent out the word to concentrate on subversion in the large towns. This, of course, was already in hand, and the MCP campaign in Singapore was to reach its peak on the streets in the following year (see Chapters 5 to 7). Meanwhile, the battle for survival of the guerrillas in the jungle and of the Masses Organization in the villages continued. It was still to take more than four more years to dig out the roots of it.

General Bourne had in 1954 succeeded Templer as Director of Operations (though there was once more a civilian High Commissioner, Sir Donald McGillivray, over him). In January 1956 he issued a fresh review of the situation and a fresh strategy. Exploiting the success in Pahang, priority was to be given to driving a White Area belt right across the Federation from coast to coast and then to extend the breach northwards into Perak or southwards into Johore.

This strategy followed the principle of dealing with the weakest areas first and working outwards to the strongest. This was logical because in a target adjacent to a White Area, the people would be aware of the good fortune of their neighbours and be looking forward to similar relaxations themselves. Moreover, as the target MCP district was weakened, it could expect no help from the flank where the organization had been smashed. And, most important of

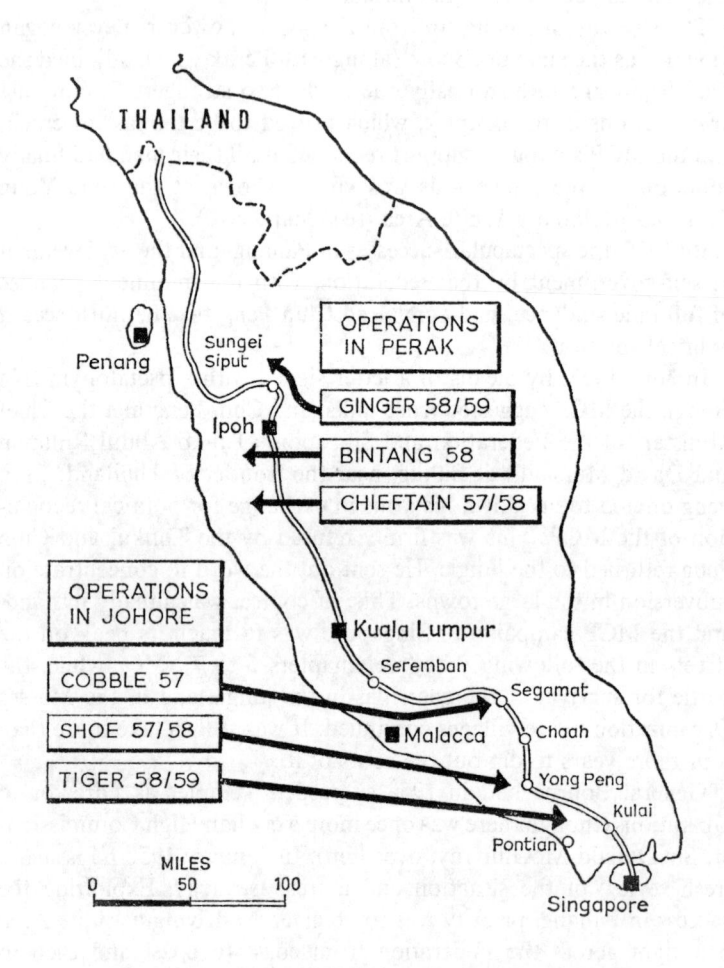

Figure 22 Federal Priority Operations, 1957–8

all, as it became possible to withdraw troops and police from the weaker areas, the government was able to concentrate greater and greater strength, until, in the end, overwhelming force could be (and was) concentrated on the hard nuts to be cracked in Perak and Johore.[6]

Early in 1956, operations in Selangor and Negri Sembilan were making good progress, and planning began on Phase I of Operation LAUNCH, later renamed COBBLE, in the Segamat District of North Johore, the first of a series of major operations including SHOE in the Yong Peng District of Central Johore and TIGER in the Kulai and Pontian Districts of South Johore, which was to clear the Federation Southwards to the causeway across the Straits to Singapore by the end of 1958. At the same time, a similar series was being planned to work northwards through Perak to the Thai Frontier (Fig. 22). The timing of the Johore Operations was built around Merdeka (Independence Day 31st August 1957).

July 1956	Op COBBLE – Phase I (Segamat)
January 1957	Op COBBLE – Phase II
January 1957	Op SHOE – Phase I (Yong Peng/Labis)
June 1957	Op SHOE – Phase II
December 1957	Op TIGER – Phase I (Kulai/Pontian)
April 1958	Op TIGER – Phase II

At this point, April 1958, there was a dramatic development when Hor Lung, head of the MCP South Malaya Bureau, came in to surrender. His surrender, which will be described in Chapter 14, was followed by a rapid crumbling of most of the remaining guerrilla units and Masses Organizations in Johore. Thus, the targets of Operations SHOE and TIGER disintegrated before the operations had run their normal course, and a study of them could therefore be misleading.

Operation COBBLE, however, was all over before this except for Phase III, of which Hor Lung's surrender was the decisive dividend – though a somewhat delayed one. Phases I and II of Operation COBBLE can therefore be studied as a model of the process of digging out the roots of a hard core district in the latter stages of the Emergency. Segamat MCP District enjoyed strong traditional support from the people. Its situation in 1956, however, differed from that described for Yong Peng in 1953 (Chapter 10), in that the total number of guerrillas to be fed in the jungle had become considerably smaller. Nevertheless, although the MRLA strength was very low, one at least of the branches in Operation COBBLE in 1957/57 was still of roughly the same size (15–20) as those around Yong Peng in 1952/53.

Chapter 13 Operation Cobble – 1956–7 – An Example of a Federal Priority Operation Based on Food Denial

Operation COBBLE – The Setting

The Target of Operation COBBLE was the single MCP District of Segamat, which contained some twenty predominantly Chinese villages and estate labour lines. The total population of the District was about 37,000 of whom just over half (21,000) were Chinese. About 8,000 lived in the thirty-four Malay Kampongs in the district, and these were largely unaffected by the operations. 18,000 (12,000 Chinese) lived in Segamat Town. The real battle ground, however, was around those twenty villages and labour lines, whose population of some 11,000 contained about 9,000 Chinese (Fig. 23).

The guerrillas were organized into a District Headquarters, three branches and an independent platoon. The branches were very small. The Selumpur branch ran its 'parallel hierarchy' amongst 4,800 Chinese who worked mainly on smallholdings in the western part of the district and consisted of 20 guerrillas.[1] The other two branches were much smaller. The Bukit Siput Branch (8 guerrillas) worked amongst the rubber tappers on the large estates in the centre of the district, while the Tenang Branch (2 guerrillas) worked amongst the many loggers in the Forest Reserve in the north-east corner, though it too had some rubber tappers in its area. The 32nd Independent Platoon MRLA had one section detached to a neighbouring district; the remainder, under its commander Kin Fai shared its operations between the Selumpur and Bukit Siput Branches.

The Selumpur Branch

The Selumpur Branch (Fig. 24) had an almost ideal area for working. The Branch Committee was in dense jungle some 10 miles north of Segamat Town. Between the jungle and the town lay 100 square miles of smallholdings (mainly rubber and coffee) interspersed with tongues and corridors of swamp and abandoned holdings now over-

OPERATION COBBLE – 1956-7

OPERATION COBBLE – VILLAGES AND POLICE POSTS

Place	No. of Gates	Police on Gates	Total Police	Chinese	Ind.	Mal.	Total
SEGAMAT TOWN	10	85	93	12355	1930	3437	17722
SELUMPUR							
TAMBANG 7th Mile	2	10	16	405	—	148	553
MAUR RIVER Est Div 2	2	10	17	84	92	91	267
,, ,, Div 1	1	5	20	59	91	84	234
BULOH KASAP NV	4	20	28	2627	54	106	2787
BULOH KASAP Est Div 1	2	10	29	14	154	—	168
,, ,, Div 3	2	10	32	70	160	3	233
PEKAN JABI NV	2	10	13	613	5	8	626
KAMPONG TENGAH NV	1	5	10	932	—	—	932
TOTAL *SELUMPUR*	16	80	165	4804	556	440	5800
(plus 31 kampongs)					(7000)		(7000)
							(estimated pop.)

232

THE SELUMPUR BRANCH

BUKIT SIPUT/TENANG						
SEGAMAT Estate SIDING Div	2	10	14	63	77	—	140
BUKIT SIPUT NV	2	10	19	2144	3	—	2147
BUKIT SIPUT Est	3	18	26	74	93	13	180
LABIS BAHRU Est	3	15	36	140	224	6	370
SEGAMAT Est GENUANG Div	2	10	39	13	240	15	268
POGOH Est	3	15	27	142	56	27	225
CHUAN MOH SAN Est	3	15	21	214	63	27	304
VOULES Est RUSSELL Div	3	15	22	66	4	5	75
SEGAMAT Est TENANG Div	2	10	15	69	116	18	203
VOULES Est MAIN Div	3	15	34	577	237	94	908
VOULES Est, C Div	2	10	16	374	222	163	759
TOTAL *BUKIT SIPUT/TENANG*	28	143	269	3876	1335	368	5579
(plus 3 kampongs)						(1000)	(1000)
TOTAL *SELUMPUR/BUKIT SIPUT/ TENANG* excluding SEGAMAT TOWN and kampongs	44	223	434	8680	1891	808	11379
GRAND TOTAL including SEGAMAT TOWN and kampongs	54	308	527	21035	3821	4245	37101

Figure 23 Operation COBBLE, Villages and Police Posts

OPERATION COBBLE – 1956-7

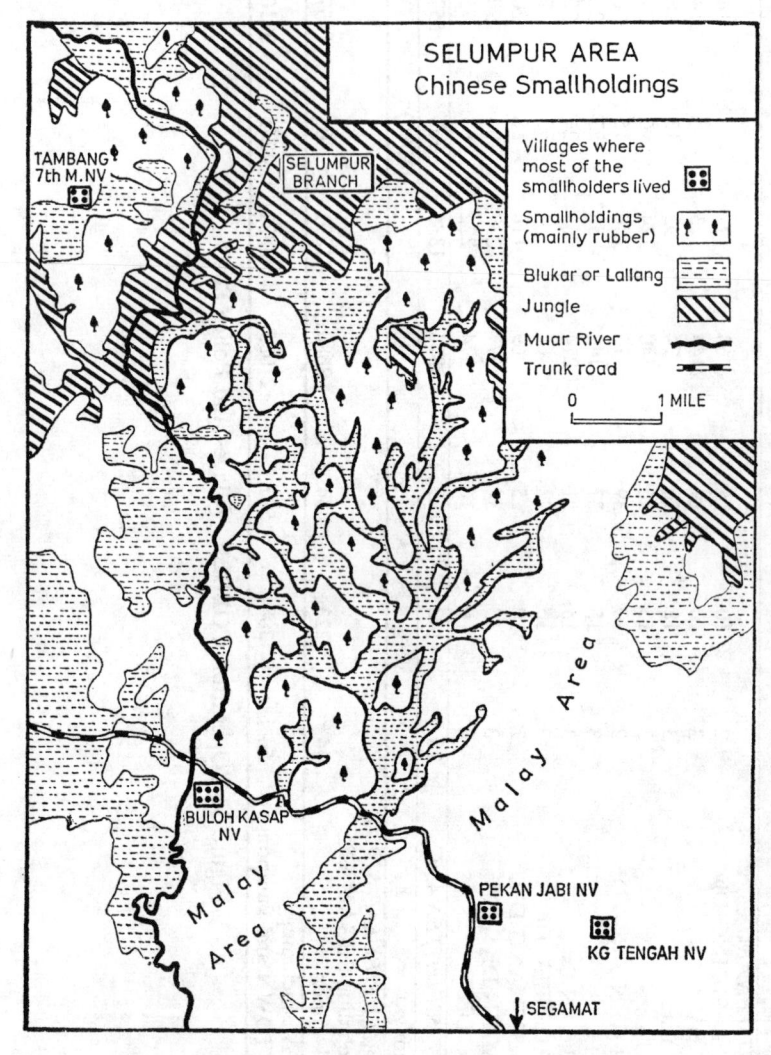

Figure 24 Selumpur Area, Chinese Smallholdings

grown with head-high *lalling* and *blukar* (secondary jungle), which offered perfect cover for moving and lying in wait for the people when they came to work on their land.

There were no less than 1,500 of these smallholdings, worked by the 4,800 Chinese men, women and children in the area, which made the task of government administration very difficult – far more difficult than on the big estates, since there was no central authority which could be ordered to operate curfews for its workers, or to clear undergrowth at pain of a fine. Each family was generally self-employed and aggressively independent. The incoming troops found them hostile and sullen, even the children. They had, for the past eight years, been subjected to a series of 'operations' by hundreds of soldiers, all of which had left their local guerrilla branch intact. Its tough and wily leader, Ming Lee, was credited by many with supernatural power.[2]

The smallholders lived mainly in four New Villages (NV), one of which (Tambang 7th Mile) was the other side of Muar River which marked the boundary of the government administrative district of Segamat (Fig. 25). These four villages were:

Buloh Kasap – containing the largest number, 2,627 Chinese.
Tambang 7th Mile – 405 Chinese, who came across the river to work, and also carried supplies from another village (Batu Anam NV – 1,168 Chinese) outside the district.
Pekan Jabi – with the best Communist organization, supported by the majority of its 613 Chinese.
Kampong Tengah – where the majority of the 932 Chinese also supported the guerrillas. (It was here that Hor Lung eventually surrendered.)

In addition, supplies were delivered from Segamat Town by supporters in pirate taxis, who dropped them or handed them to smallholders at the roadside in the Kampong Kawah area.

The tasks of the Selumpur Branch were: first, to indoctrinate the people with Communism, preaching faith in ultimate victory, and obtaining recruits for the Masses Organization or for the jungle army; secondly, to collect intelligence, supplies and money for the branch, for 32nd Independent Platoon and for the District and higher HQs; and thirdly, to provide targets, guides and a launching base for terrorist raids by 32 Platoon.[3]

Its leader, Ming Lee, acted more confidently than was normal at

OPERATION COBBLE – 1956–7

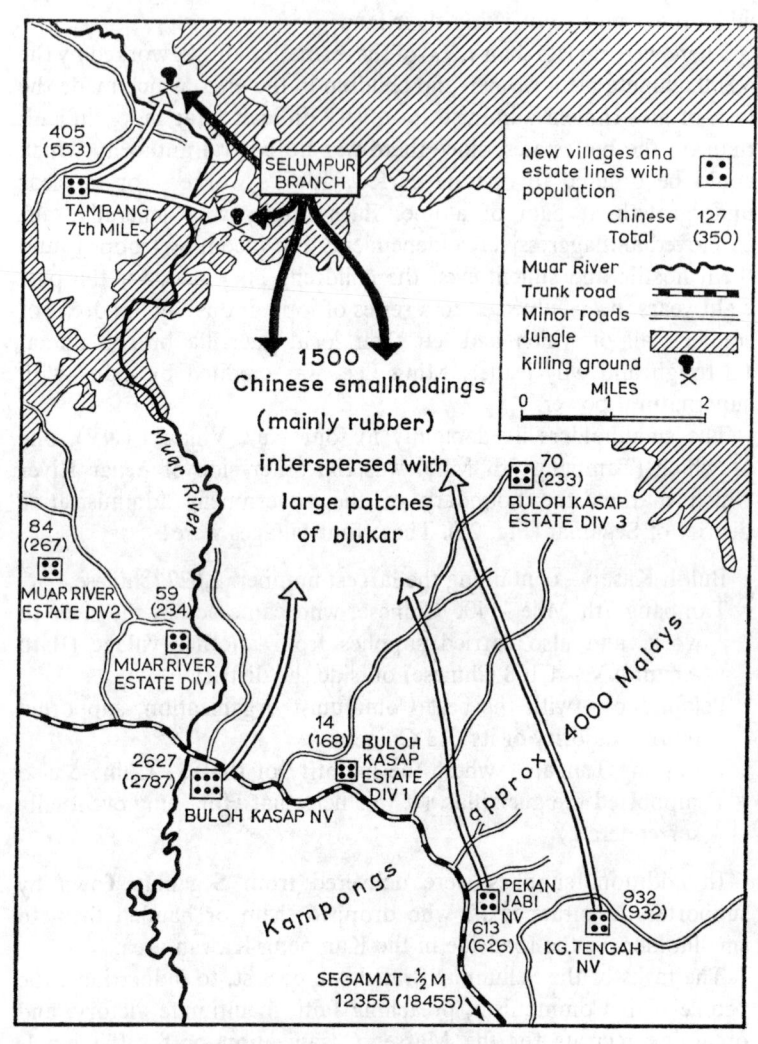

Figure 25 Selumpur Branch

this stage of the emergency, as is borne out by the police log of his activities in a typical period of three weeks early in 1956:

18 February   Ming Lee, with three others, distributed propaganda pamphlets to the workers on the Hup Heng Estate, and ordered them to provide $500 within a week.

21 February   Ming Lee, with two others, gave a lecture to the workers on the Chuang Nam Estate, urging them to join the organization and drive the British out of Malaya. He took away 3 bags of fresh fruit.

27 February   Ming Lee, with 14 others, came out of the jungle on to the Field 33 Estate, and summoned all the workers together. He told them to smuggle food out of their villages and dump it in a certain spot near the jungle fringe next day. He warned them not to inform the police.

8 March   Two guerrillas, one believed to be Ming Lee, visited the Ban Joo Sin Estate, and warned the owner that no rubber collection would be allowed until he had paid $400 arrears in his subscriptions.

11 March   A strong party with Bren guns and other weapons, led by Ming Lee, distributed copies of *The People's Awakening News,* and conducted a preliminary inquiry into the killing of a guerrilla by the Security Forces during the previous week.[4]

It was relatively rare for guerrilla leaders to make personal contact at meetings of workers in the estates in 1956, when most of them were protected by two echelons of cut-out men (armed work forces and Masses Executives) from the risk of betrayal by individual members of the public. Ming Lee was clearly confident that his support amongst the rural Chinese was still so strong that such individuals would not dare to betray him.

The Bukit Siput and Tenang Branches

The Bukit Siput Branch, which at the start of Phase I of Operation COBBLE was seven or eight strong, was well known and held in much respect by the population. Its terrain was very different from that of the Selumpur Branch, though more typical of Malaya. For the ten miles south of Segamat, the main Kuala Lumpur/Singapore road passed through European-owned rubber estates, which butted onto the jungle only one or two miles away on the north-east side of the road, and three to five miles away on the south-west. The Bukit Siput Branch was thus able to live in relative security only two or three miles north-east of the road, within a mile of the clearly defined jungle fringe, from which they could quickly spot the tappers in the tidy rows of trees which were characteristic of European-owned estates (Fig. 26).

Bukit Siput New Village, on the main road about three miles east of Segamat, contained a very strong Communist organization. All but three of its 2,147 inhabitants were Chinese. The other main source of support was the small labour lines of the Siding Division of the Segamat Estate, containing 63 Chinese and 77 Indians, about a mile North of Bukit Siput village. There was also considerable support amongst the tappers on the Chuan Moh San Estate, on the south side of the road, and specialist commodities were smuggled out along the main road by individuals from Segamat Town.

The Tenang Branch, by the time Operation COBBLE began, was down to only two guerrillas, who worked jointly with the Bukit Siput Branch and were combined with them later in the operation. Their geographical situation was similar to that of the Bukit Siput Branch (rubber estates astride the road). They received bulk deliveries by vehicle along the main road from Segamat, about eight miles away, which were smuggled to the jungle fringe by workers on the Pogoh Estate. The main task of the branch, however, was to collect subscriptions from the loggers who worked in the jungle which butted onto the Pogoh Estate, and which was a Forest Reserve. A number of timber tracks penetrated into this jungle, and the Tenang guerrillas took a toll of $80 to $100 a month from each timber lorry. In all, from lorry tolls and loggers' subscriptions, these two guerrillas collected about $35,000 a quarter, most of which went to the higher HQ of the North Johore Regional Committee and the South Malaya Bureau.

In all, the population in the combined areas of the Bukit Siput and Tenang Branches was under 7,000, of whom 3,876 were Chinese.[5] Their contribution to the Communist cause (especially the money collected by the Tenang Branch) is a striking example of what a very small underground organization can achieve in a fairly prosperous rural area of South East Asia.

THE BUKIT SIPUT AND TENANG BRANCHES

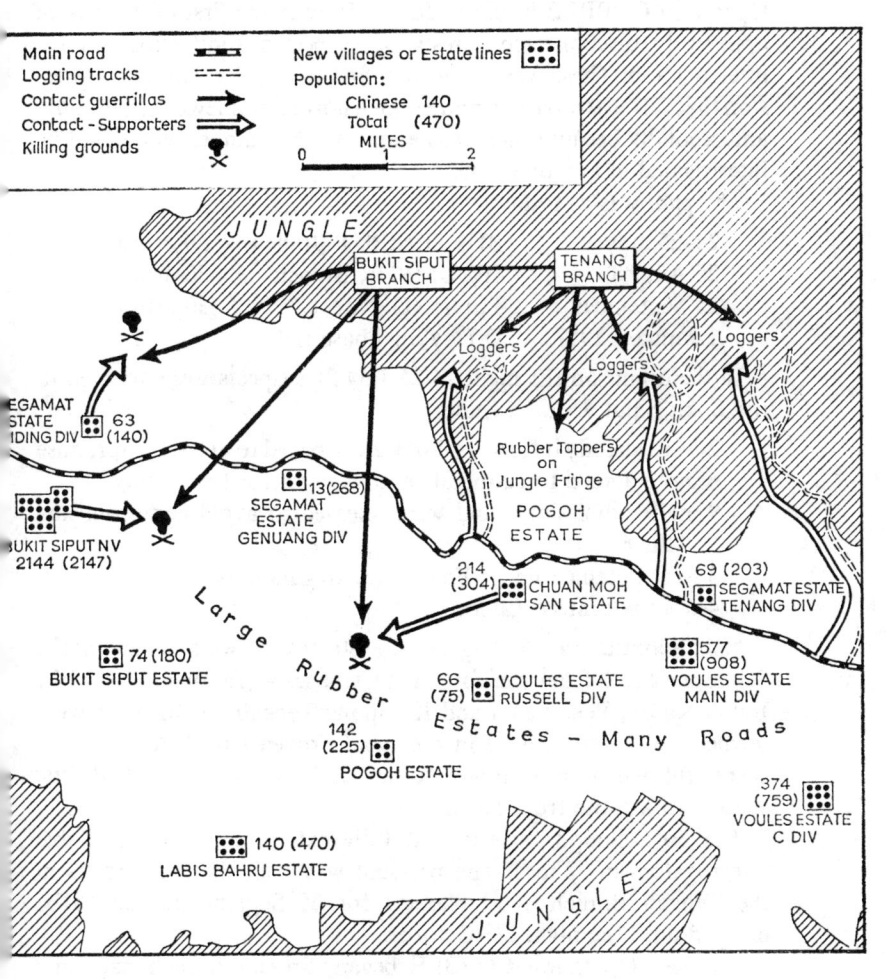

Figure 26 Bukit Siput and Tenang Branches

Operation COBBLE Phase I – Intelligence Activity

After some months of preliminary study and planning, Phase I of Operation COBBLE began in July 1956 with the first of a series of apparently disconnected arrests of suspected food suppliers for interrogation. These were staggered, first to avoid giving the impression that this was anything more than a normal framework operation, and secondly because there was a limit to the number who could be interrogated at any one time.

The plan was as follows.

24–25 July	BUKIT SIPUT Branch	30 arrests
25 August	SELUMPUR Branch	30 arrests
25 September	TENANG Branch	30 arrests
1 January 1957	D Day for Phase II	

In the event, on the night 24/25 July 24 suspects were arrested in the Bukit Siput area. Of these

- 2 were already informers, but were arrested to avoid compromise
- 6 more agreed to cooperate and were released as 'turned'
- 9 made admissions, and were released to avoid compromising the 6
- 3 were detained under Emergency Regulations
- 4 were not interrogated.

Next month, on 25 August, the 30 arrests were made in the Selumpur area, from the four main villages – Tambang 7th Mile, Buloh Kasap, Pekan Jabi and Kampong Tengah. Of these 11 were 'turned', of whom only 7 in the event proved useful. Most of the successful ones were in Buloh Kasap, and Special Branch had little success with those from Pekan Jabi.

The 30 Selumpur arrests had fully extended all the available interrogators in Johore. The pressure was such that the arrests in the Tengah Branch area, planned for 25 September, had to be delayed until the night 2/3 October.

Before Operation COBBLE began, Special Branch had only 4 registered agents in the District. As a result of the interrogations, 11 were recruited, bringing the total to 15. Altogether, the intelligence dividends from Phase I were as follows:

New agents able to give advance precise information	11
New informers for secondhand or historical information	13
New casual informers	7

PHASE I – OPERATIONS IN SUPPORT OF SPECIAL BRANCH

Phase I – Operations in Support of Special Branch

Meanwhile, additional troops were being moved into Segamat District. The framework battalion already there was a Gurkha battalion, which in Phase II was to concentrate on the Bukit Siput Branch. Another battalion, the Rhodesian African Rifles, was already in a neighbouring district, from which it could operate in Segamat. In July, a third battalion, the 1st South Wales Borderers (1 SWB), moved up from South Johore and established its HQ and one company in Segamat itself, with three other companies in operational camps close to (but not inside) three of the hard core New Villages: Buloh Kasap, Pekan Jabi and Kampong Tengah.

The eventual target of 1 SWB was to be the Selumpur Branch. Initially, however, presumably to give the impression that it had come as a routine relief for the Gurkha framework battalion, it operated in the Bukit Siput area as well until the start of Phase II.

Before the Phase I arrests were made, the troops patrolled the cultivated areas, to deny contact (so that the guerrillas would be less likely to be told of the arrests) and to put the suppliers in the right frame of mind to talk. Once the suppliers had been released after interrogation, the troops were kept out of the cultivated areas, in order to encourage the guerrillas to re-establish contact.

Thus, throughout the month of August, 1 SWB were allowed to patrol the estates and smallholdings in the Selumpur area, in order to promote intelligence, soften up the less determined suppliers and to enable the soldiers to learn their way around the maze of trails, cultivation and secondary jungle.[6]

The regimental officers and soldiers were naturally keen to get into areas in which they were likely to meet guerrillas, but Special Branch were insistent that they should not go into Phase II prematurely and 'blow the gaff'. There was also much donkey work to be done in preparing the detailed plans for food denial, estimating and obtaining the funds to strengthen fences etc.

Nevertheless, a close understanding was built up between the Commanding Officer of 1 SWB (Lt. Col. Miers), the District Officer and the Special Branch Officer. During August, when the interrogation of Bukit Siput suppliers was well under way the Special Branch officer decided that it would be worth the risk to 'blow' one of his agents before Phase II began. This would be quite consistent with a framework operation, and might aid deception by using the battalion destined for the main target (the Selumpur Branch) in the Bukit Siput area.

This agent, whom Colonel Miers nicknamed 'Henry' in his book,[7] was a regular supplier of the Bukit Siput Branch. The Special Branch officer brought 'Henry' into his house after dark and there, in armchairs behind drawn curtains, the Colonel was invited to come and meet him. The three of them discussed their plans with remarkable frankness, the Special Branch officer being confident that 'Henry' would not double-cross them at this stage, first because he had already given away more than the Communists would forgive, and secondly because there was a large reward at stake.

'Henry' told them that the guerrillas never gave him advanced warning of what they wanted him to do, but normally waylaid him on his way to work in the rubber. Alternatively, they would send another tapper to fetch him, and he would be led to meet them on the jungle fringe, approaching across open ground which they could watch to ensure that he was not followed. Sometimes they sent him straight away into the villages to buy small items, such as medicine or an electric torch. More commonly, however, he would be asked to bring out a larger consignment of food (presumably thrown over the village fence at night and picked up later, or smuggled out of Segamat in a lorry) in a sack on his bicycle and dump it in a patch of undergrowth in the rubber estate whence the guerrillas would come and collect it at night.

'Henry' reluctantly accompanied a moonlit night patrol, dressed as a soldier with an oversized jungle hat flopping over his face, and showed them this dumping area. It was clearly unsuitable for a successful ambush, particularly at night.

To reach this dump from the jungle fringe however, the guerrillas had to pass over a belt of swamp, crossed by only two causeways. 'Henry' agreed to telephone the battalion next time he put food in the dump, saying – as a simple code – that there was a good picture on at the cinema that night, and asking the soldier who answered the telephone to come and see it. This seems both dangerous and naïve, but it was certainly safer for a Chinese to invite a 'British Tommy' to come to the cinema than to send a message to the police.

In due course the message came. Ambushes were mounted on both the marsh crossings with electrically operated flares in the trees. The best shots in the battalion, intensively trained to shoot at night, manned the ambushes. Four guerrillas came and three were killed.[8]

PHASE I – OPERATIONS IN SUPPORT OF SPECIAL BRANCH

'Henry' collected his reward. The three dead guerrillas included a District Committee Member ($12,000 reward) and two others ($4,000 each) – total $20,000 (about £2,300). This represented about 17 years' pay at the average rubber tapper's earnings of $100 a month, and there are now many owners of small businesses or estates in Malaya who bought them with rewards obtained in this way.

Though this successful ambush could plausibly be represented as framework, the Special Branch Officer nevertheless decided that he must deter other potential agents from blowing their information too soon. He had a promising collaborator in the Siding Division who looked likely to be able to give another lead into the Bukit Siput Branch, and he decided to conserve him. He had no cover at all, however, in Bukit Siput New Village itself, from which regular food lifts were still being made by the guerrillas themselves. He therefore decided to make some further arrests in September 1956, some of them by means of clandestine pick-ups.

Meanwhile 1 SWB were concentrating their patrols in the Selumpur area again, and in the final month of Phase I (on 1 December) they killed two guerrillas – the first to be eliminated in the Selumpur Branch for twelve months. This was the result not of 'advance precise information', but of deduction by Special Branch after the detailed study of the pattern of Ming Lee's movements over a long period. At a remote part of a rubber estate was a store for liquid latex. Supplies would be hidden in this shed, and Ming Lee would leave a concealed 'shopping list' for his local Masses Executive to pick up when he collected the supplies. Ming Lee gave no warning of these visits, but Special Branch deduced that such a visit was due in the first seven days of December. The battalion mounted an ambush in the only available cover, some bushes about five yards from the shed, and only a few feet from trees which were regularly worked by tappers. Thus, perfect concealment and absolute stillness were essential, and the five men in the ambush party had to eat, drink and perform bodily functions where they lay, throughout tapping hours – ten hours on end from 6 a.m. to 4 p.m. Since the ambush was planned to be in position for ten days if necessary, the party was to be relieved each night during the silent hours of the curfew.

In the event they did not have to wait long. At 11.30 on the first morning, the ambush commander, Major Gwynne Jones[9] saw tappers converging on the shed, at the door of which they were received by two guerrillas in smart uniforms with Red Star caps. Neither of them was Ming Lee, who Gwynne Jones still hoped would come, so he held his fire. The meeting lasted an hour, after which the guerrillas were clearly preparing to leave, so Gwynne Jones sprang to his feet and shot the leader dead. The second guerrilla dodged into the trees but was pursued and shot down by the soldiers. He was not quite dead when Gwynne Jones came up on him, and he tried unsuccessfully to hide some documents under the grass. He used his last breath to spit in Gwynne Jones' face.

It transpired that Ming Lee had intended to come to the meeting himself, but had injured his foot, and the two dead guerrillas were members of his bodyguard.[10]

Meanwhile, two more guerrillas from the Bukit Siput and Tenang Branches had been eliminated, bringing the combined strength of the two branches, which were then amalgamated, to five men. Thus in all, during Phase I, seven of the forty or so guerrillas believed to be in the District had been eliminated. Several food dumps had been discovered, though the guerrillas were still judged to have some three months' supply in stock. Above all, the Special Branch had greatly increased their coverage of agents and informers.

Based on the prospects offered by these agents, Special Branch in December selected their killing grounds (Figs. 25 and 26). These were based on agents in

Tambang 7th Mile NV	(Selumpur Branch)
Bukit Siput NV	
Siding Div Labour Lines	Bukit Siput and
Chuan Moh San Estate Labour Lines	Tenang Branch

In the Selumpur Branch the aim was to plan ambushes on advance precise information in the smallholdings, into which the Tambang people crossed the river to work. In the other cases, the aim was to draw the guerrillas in as close as possible to the villages themselves to be ambushed on the perimeter.

Operation COBBLE Phase II

Phase II began on 1 January 1957 with the simultaneous arrest of 60 more suspected suppliers (92 had been planned, but 32 of these had been frightened out of the area during Phase I).

At the same time, strict rationing was imposed. Villages in turn were cordoned at dawn and searched for hidden food in the houses. Food inspectors checked stocks in shops and removed surpluses. Tighter curfews were imposed. All the logging areas in the Tenang area were closed for six months from 1 January. Police, reinforced by women searchers and troops, manned fifty-four gates through which villagers went out to work from Segamat Town and from the twenty villages and labour lines which contained a significant proportion of Chinese.

This required considerable reinforcement of police. The number of police required to man the gates is shown on Figure 23. In all, 308 of the 527 police in the District were on gate checks at peak periods. These figures do not include 6 platoons of Chinese Home Guards in the three main villages in the Selumpur area, nor the Malay Home Guards in 15 of the 34 Malay Kampongs.

In relation to the small number of guerrillas (believed to be 33 at this stage, but in fact nearer 25),[11] and bearing in mind that there were also three battalions in the district, the ratio of Security Forces to guerrillas was extremely high. On the other hand, the police were not employed against the guerrillas at all, but in controlling the population. In the villages about which the operation was conducted, there was an average of about one policeman or home guard to every fifty people. Even these figures, however, do underline the immense effort which had to be concentrated to dig out the Communist roots in hard core areas.

The peak periods for searching at the village gates were when the bulk of the rubber tappers went out to work (6.0 to 7.0 a.m.) and when they returned (1.30 to 2.30 p.m.). It was not possible in these periods to search every tapper meticulously, and the aim was to search 20 per cent thoroughly each morning. British troops helped in these searches, and became adept at sensing whom to search. The smallholders, in particular, were smuggling out rice in small quantities – concealed at intimate places on their bodies, in the tubular frames of bicycles, in bicycle pumps, in tins concealed in night soil buckets, and in the hollow bamboo poles which the villagers used as yokes to carry these buckets.

The rice ration was severe. Adult males received 3 katties (that is, about 4 lb.) per week, while females and children under 12 had only $2\frac{1}{2}$. No individual was allowed to hold more than one week's ration, and no retailer more than two weeks'. On 31 estate labour lines[12] all rice was cooked in central kitchens, and the people were not allowed to hold any dry rice at all, but they could buy as much cooked rice as they liked at meal times.

In all, 17 types of food were restricted, including salt and all dried and tinned foods. On the other hand fresh meat, fresh fruit, live poultry, vegetables and root tapioca were not restricted, provided that the possessor could, if called upon, satisfy a magistrate's court that he was holding them for lawful purposes.

There were very severe restrictions on what a person could take out of the gate to work: one bottle of tea, coffee or rice gruel, and an ice cream or beverage containing not more than 15 per cent sugar. Except for those from labour lines with central kitchens, the tappers would start the day hungry from their tightly rationed daily diet, and in a long day's work in the field they suffered real hardship. But this harshness achieved its object, for large numbers of workers were able to claim the alibi that it was impossible to smuggle out food, and there was growing evidence that the guerrillas were suffering from a severe shortage of nutrition.[13] And, of course, the narrowing number of suppliers was a major factor in helping Special Branch to recruit and exploit agents.

Other restricted articles (clothing, stationery, medicines, etc.) were as described in Chapter 12.

Preventing smuggling in vehicles was a different problem as the main road cut through the centre of the district, and passed through many towns and villages with strong Communist organizations – notably Segamat. Vehicles carrying restricted articles had to be covered by tarpaulins securely laced down, and to carry a written manifest of their contents. They were forbidden to leave the main road without a police escort, or to move between dusk and dawn. Nevertheless, a single sack of rice, dropped into the ditch for later collection on a quiet stretch of road could feed the Selumpur branch guerrillas for a fortnight, and no doubt often did.

Apart from police and military road blocks, searches etc., food control was enforced by 2 food inspectors, each accompanied by 2 policemen and 2 soldiers, who inspected dealers' stocks, and checked their books against ration cards.

Curfew times were as follows:

4.15 p.m. Rubber curfew – all to be out of rubber estates
7.00 p.m. Perimeter curfew – all to be inside their villages

OPERATION COBBLE PHASE II

11.00 p.m. House curfew – no one on the streets (except in Segamat)
5.00 a.m. House curfew lifted
6.15 a.m. Other curfews lifted

The life of a rubber tapping family in the New Villages ran to a pattern governed by these curfews. From 4 a.m. onwards, they would be up, feeding babies and cooking a fair-sized meal of rice and fish, or perhaps an egg from the chickens scrabbling in the yard. This meal had to last most of the day.

By 5 a.m. many of the tappers, impatient to be out in the cool of the day when the latex flows best, would be queuing at the search barriers. In some villages, when it was practicable and safe to hold a 'cushion' of people between the search barriers and the village gates, the search would begin soon after 5 a.m. under floodlights. Generally, however, searching was concentrated between 6 and 7 a.m.

Complete families would go out into the rubber: father and mother and the older children with bicycles, carrying the younger children on the handlebars, with latex tins and tapping knives strapped on the back. (Latex tins with false bottoms were a common device for smuggling rice.) Only the babies and the very old grand-parents would be left at home to keep each other company. Even a six-year-old child was useful in the rubber: he would go ahead of his father or his older sister, darting from tree to tree stripping off the congealed latex from the previous cut. By these means, each adult or teenager could tap some 500 trees a day and, if the latex flowed well, could hope to earn $100 to $120 a month. If a family could bring in four or five such incomes, life became reasonable for them, and they could spare some of their older children, especially the boys, to go to be educated at the High School in Segamat. It was hard to connect these boys, in their spotless white shorts and shirts and polished bicycles, with the parents in their dusty black cotton trousers, stained with latex, as they all waited together to be searched by the Malay constables and the British soldiers at the village gates.

They usually waited with patient resignation, but sometimes the teenage girls would giggle and try to provoke the Malay constables and occasionally, with several hundred Chinese pressing at the barriers, the atmosphere would become uglier. The constables – scarcely more than boys, and fresh from their kampongs with only a few weeks' training – would be sorely tempted to skimp the search and release the pressure, and it was here that the moral support of a British corporal with half a dozen men could be decisive.

By the middle of the day the latex would have ceased to flow, and the tappers would complete the round of emptying the cups into their tins and taking them to the weighing sheds. This is where they would often be contacted by the Masses Executives or by the guerrillas themselves, and, if the guerrillas were confident, they would hold propaganda meetings and call for public votes of solidarity. In a district like Segamat it was not easy to swim against the stream, so the high police rewards for informers were really necessary.

By 4.15 p.m. the rubber estates had to be clear. This was to allow patrols and ambushes to get into position before dark, near suspected dumps, or on guerrilla approach tracks through the rubber or the jungle fringe.

During the afternoon and evening, schoolteachers would run primary school classes in the villages for the children back from tapping, and parents would do their shopping if this had not already been done by 'granny' during the morning.

By 7 p.m. all were inside the perimeter fence, on which the floodlights played, and which was patrolled throughout the night. If a guerrilla raid or food lift was expected, an army ambush would just have time to get into position outside the fence before the last of the light had gone.

7 to 11 p.m. were the sociable hours of the day. The families would eat their main meal, and would call on each other. The coffee shops would be busy, and the Mah Jong pieces would clatter on the tables as the men gambled with their earnings. Some would seek comfort in opium. This was the time when the Masses Executives did much of their work and the Special Branch detective and his agents would be on the prowl, watching from the shadows to see who talked to whom, and who called at whose house.

By 11 p.m. all were confined to their homes. Police and home guards would patrol the streets to guard against the man with the knife creeping around to deal with 'traitors to the people'.[14]

There were, however, inevitably a few loopholes in the house curfew. Most houses, for example, had outside privies between the house and the perimeter fence. These provided an alibi for villagers who were seen moving outside, possibly hoping to toss bags of rice over the fence into patches of long grass for collection later, or to signal to raiders outside, or to cut gaps for them to come in. Even a small village, with a population of 1,000 or so, would have a perimeter over a mile long, and it was not easy for patrols inside or outside them to make them 100 per cent watertight.[15]

By 4 a.m. the village would come alive, with many lights bobbing down to the privies, and the daily cycle would begin again.

Operation COBBLE – The End of Phase II

The story of the final destruction of the Selumpur in Phase II is well told in Miers' book.[16] When it began it was quickly over.

First, an agent led Miers and Gwynne Jones to a camp containing five guerrillas. In daylight it was not possible for them to get close enough to shoot effectively, and the Colonel and his company commander watched fascinated as the five guerrillas played a child's game of 'tag' for exercise. That night the camp was raided. Three happened to be away from it, one more escaped and one was killed. Later, two others came in to surrender.

The next guerrilla was killed in the ambush of a small rice dump – a big glass acid jar, buried beside a track so that the only thing above the ground (and concealed by loose leaves) was the neck, into which the tappers poured their contributions of rice as they passed. His condition left no doubt that the guerrillas were very short of food. Another was shot in an ambush of a shed regularly used as a pick-up point. Two Chinese police inspectors dressed as coffee plantation workers acted as a decoy to lure in a guerrilla known to be separated from his gang and desperate to get food. Two more were killed in an ambush based on clever deduction from the now very detailed information of the pattern of guerrilla movement, and another surrendered in the same ambush. Then Ming Lee himself walked into two ambushes, in one of which one of his companions was killed, but he escaped both times. This brought the number of eliminations in the Selumpur Branch to 11 – 2 in Phase I and 9 so far in Phase II.

Ming Lee himself seemed indestructable, and Special Branch charts showed 7 others at large with him.

The day after his second narrow escape, however, Ming Lee had had enough, and asked an ancient Indian rubber tapper to lead him to the police station. The old Indian was so flabbergasted with his reward that he fainted. Like most surrendered guerrillas Ming Lee was ready to cooperate to the full, and talked freely. He said that his greatest problem was food. As dumps ran low, and his trusted suppliers were detained or, worse still, became informers, he had to take more and more risks to get food, and casualties mounted in a vicious circle. He had asked the MCP District Committee for permission to move temporarily to a new area, but was told to stay. Finally, he realized that the battle was lost. Special Branch were pleasantly surprised to hear that, of the seven they thought remained, one had died of wounds, one had been killed by a buffalo, and two others had disappeared in the jungle without trace. This left only three. Ming Lee agreed at once to go out with a patrol to try to lure these three survivors into an ambush, but they did not come. Nevertheless, the Selumpur Branch was finished as an effective force and never revived. Ming Lee, after a brief spell in the Rehabilitation Centre, became groundsman at the Segamat Cricket Club.[17]

The end of the Bukit Siput/Tenang Branch was more sudden and spectacular. Special Branch at last got a good agent in Bukit Siput New Village, who said that the gang, bold to the last, were coming at night to a certain spot on the village perimeter to pick up sacks of food passed over the fence by the villagers. The Gurkhas laid an ambush and shot well. All the five remaining members of the branch were killed outright.

The cross fire cracked through the village and some of the bullets penetrated the thin walls of the tappers' houses, but no one stirred. When dawn came, the police went round to check for casualties, and to question the people in the houses which had been hit. All said that they had heard nothing – even some who had been sleeping in beds beside which the wall was peppered with bullet holes.

Meanwhile, the police had laid down the five bodies outside the police post. The people filed past. As they counted the bodies and recognized their faces, their attitude changed. Every guerrilla was dead, and the threat was gone – and they knew which was the winning side. They began to talk freely, and all that remained of the Bukit Siput Masses Organization was quickly rounded up.

Remnants of the Segamat MCP District HQ, however, still existed, and there was evidence that Hor Lung and the South Malaya Bureau were still receiving supplies from the Masses Organization in the Selumpur area.[18] It was therefore still not safe to declare this a White Area, and Operation COBBLE moved into what proved to be a prolonged Phase III, the final dividends of which are described in Chapter 14.

Chapter 14 The Crumble and the Hard Core

A Successful Framework Operation

Through 1957 and 1958, the cavalcade of federal priority operations moved northwards and southwards from the centre, demolishing on the average two or three hard core MCP districts every six months. There were, however, some thirty other MCP Districts, still not White, in which framework operations continued. The guerrilla organization in these districts was often just as strong as that described in Yong Peng and Segamat, but the *Min Yuen* was weaker so it was possible to break them without such a concentration of effort.

When the Selumpur and Bukit Siput Branches collapsed under the pressure of three battalions and a thousand police and home guards in September 1957, two companies of the Rifle Brigade were starting a framework operation against 50 guerrillas to the south-west of Segamat – the survivors of the one-time 200-strong Johore Malacca Border Committee's command.

One of the two company commanders, Major Frank Kitson, had a genius for intelligence, which he had already revealed two years previously against the Mau Mau in Kenya.[1]

Finding on his arrival that there was no intelligence cover in the district, he turned his whole company on to creating it. He divided intelligence in his own mind into 'background information' about the guerrilla gangs and their habits, and 'contact information', which enabled soldiers to find or ambush the guerrillas. There was no federal priority operation in the area, and Kitson was convinced that he would never get enough contact information unless he created it himself. He therefore set about developing the background information first. He distributed his men in twos and threes around the rubber and logging tracks to watch the faces of the people going to work until they could recognize any strangers who appeared. After a few weeks they had provided enough background information, in conjunction with that he received in the normal way from Special Branch, to deduce the area of jungle in which one of the gangs (the Kebun Bahru Branch) was living, and that they were likely to visit one of two or three villages on one of two or three nights.

These villages were on the opposite side of the road from the guerrilla camp, and a careful study of the ground revealed that there were only six of the many tracks debouching from the road into the adjacent rubber estate which led right through into the jungle where the camp was. He therefore ambushed these six tracks until the gang came – which eventually they did. By good fortune and good shooting his ambush party killed the leader – the District Committee Secretary. This disconcerted another of the gang so much that he surrendered next day and led Kitson's men to the camp. It was empty when they arrived, but the soldiers ambushed it and killed another when the gang returned. This led to another surrender, and the gang got really jittery. A fifth man tried to surrender and killed a sixth who tried to stop him. At this the branch disintegrated completely and the remnants fled to other gangs.

Kitson then turned his attention to another gang, the Grisek Branch. Starting once more by building up background information, his men contacted the branch three times in three weeks and killed four of them. Two more then surrendered, and, after a night of interrogation they were persuaded to join a patrol the next day. To show his confidence Kitson armed them and placed them in the ambush party. More kills and more surrenders led to mounting pressure, and the Grisek branch and the other branches and districts collapsed one by one. Soon only the Regional Committee Secretary (RCS) remained, with his staff of seven and with no districts, branches or *Min Yuen* with whom to maintain contact with the people in the villages. In January 1958, six months after the operation began, they too came in to surrender.[2]

Hor Lung and the Collapse in Johore

By April 1958 despite the pressure of priority operations in Johore, only the coastal districts occupied mainly by Malay fishermen and the Johore/Malacca Border Region cleared by Kitson's framework operation had become White Areas.[3] The remainder of Johore, together with most of the adjacent state of Negri Sembilan, was still black. Even the Segamat District, where operation COBBLE had virtually destroyed the branch organization, was still black, because Hor Lung and his South Malaya Bureau HQ were intact and believed to be living in the deep jungles north of Segamat. Intensive Phase III operations had found camp sites and evidence that food was still coming from the Masses in the Segamat District, and from a small supply group operating further north into Negri Sembilan.[4]

In February 1958, four guerrillas from this supply group surrendered and, on their information, the chase became hotter. On 5 April 1958, quite unexpectedly, Hor Lung himself, alone and having discarded his uniform, walked into the enquiry office of the Police Post at Kampong Tengah, two miles from Segamat.

He did not at once announce his identity, but did so a few hours later in the seclusion of the Special Branch office in Segamat. It was quickly checked from police photographs.[5]

In a signed statement in his own handwriting, later published in facsimile in the press, he declared his reasons. He recognized that Malaya's independence, granted on 31 August 1957, was a 'glorious page' in her history, even though it fell short of what the MCP regarded as ideal and that the Alliance Government, though its policy differed from that of the MCP, was legally elected and recognized. He accepted that the people wanted peace to improve their living conditions.

'We therefore determined to consult the government on this matter and as a result of this we accepted the reasonable terms laid down by the government.'[6]

During the next four months, working in the strictest secrecy and living in the houses of a number of Special Branch officers in turn, Hor Lung went back into the jungle in uniform, contacted the various couriers on their appointed days at the letter boxes, and got them to lead him back to their units, one by one. There he set himself the task of persuading them to come out. He is reticent about how he did it, but it is clear from his published statement that he still regarded himself as a Communist, and had not renounced his ideals. He presumably based his persuasion on the proposition that his comrades could better achieve these ideals from outside the jungle rather than from inside. He gave a further hint of this in his statement:

'Starting from the end of May up to the present moment, all the comrades in North Johore and in other States in South Malaya who could be contacted have accepted these terms and left the jungle one after another to come out and live a life of peace. For the past two or three months the government has firmly carried on its promises and accorded us fair, equitable and reasonable treatment.'[7]

He probably varied his line to suit what he knew of the character of the particular leader of the branch or platoon concerned. No doubt they all realized, as he did, that the armed struggle was lost in any case, and were glad of a chance to get out with their lives and with the approval of their commander.

He brought out 160 guerrillas in all, and qualified for a huge reward, even at the half rates due to an SEP. In all, $469,000 was paid out,[8] of which Hor Lung's share was $247,000. He now lives prosperously and in no apparent fear of retribution.

Amongst those he brought out was 'Kim Cheng', who had run Yong Peng District with such success for the past ten years (see Chapter 10). 'Kim Cheng' in turn brought out the militant No. 7 Platoon MRLA, which Hor Lung said would not accept his order to surrender. 'Kim Cheng' donned his uniform and went alone into their camp, at considerable personal risk, with a Police Special Branch officer hovering in the jungle nearby. The Platoon agreed to accompany him on condition that they marched out fully armed and thereafter negotiated their own terms with weapons in hand. The police officers agreed, and the twenty armed uniformed guerrillas sat down in the home of the British Special Branch Officer and argued it out. They demanded, among other things, that the government should provide $2,500 which was due in arrears of pay to the Masses Executives for their work. Special Branch agreed, on condition that each ME came forward with detailed evidence of the activities for which payment was due! There were, of course, no takers, but No. 7 Platoon had made their point and, honour satisfied, they handed in their arms.

For his part in this bizarre and hazardous negotiation, 'Kim Cheng' earned a reward of $50,000. He and his wife (who had also been in the jungle since 1948) used it to buy a small rubber estate, on which he employs a staff of four, all SEPs, including an ex-member of the Selumpur Branch Committee (see Chapter 13). 'Kim Cheng', who now has five young children, lives a happy and comfortable life, in close friendship with one of his ex-enemies from Special Branch. He is a man of great natural charm and dignity, and is proving as successful as a small capitalist as he did as a Communist.

Not all of Hor Lung's 160 SEPs elected to settle in the new Malaya. Some chose instead to accept the government's alternative offer of free repatriation to China, without interrogation.[9] Amongst these was Ah Chiau, the District Committee Secretary of Pontian MCP District, who appeared much earlier in this story in connection with the subversive activities amongst the Chinese school children of Ayer Baloi (Chapter 4). In the latter stages of the Emergency she ran a district as hard to crack as Yong Peng, with only 5 surviving guerrillas and 400 active supporters. She was still only thirty-five when she decided to accept the surrender terms and carry her Communist convictions back to China. She, too, impressed Special Branch with her dignity and charm. She would have been a good leader in any sphere.

By September 1958, there were still 1,000 guerrillas left in the Federation, mainly in Perak and across the Thai Border, but only 70 of them now remained in Johore, and these were all eliminated by early 1959.

Perak

The final battle in the other hard core state, Perak, was a tougher one, but was also successfully concluded in 1959. As it happened, although it took longer, the crumble in Perak started earlier than in Johore, and also began with a 'Super SEP' – though he was not quite as senior as Hor Lung.

He was a Regional Political Commissar, and he surrendered in October 1957. An exceptionally shrewd young British Special Branch officer conceived the plan for him to do precisely as has already been described for Hor Lung – and indeed, this operation was the model on which Hor Lung's was based. The Political Commissar, over the next six months, brought out 118 guerrillas – virtually the entire organization of South Perak.[10] There were a few of these who he was convinced would not answer his call, and these were ambushed and killed instead. They were the toughest of them all, who, unlike Ah Chiau, would not trust the government to honour its promise to repatriate them without brainwashing, and fought to the death.[11]

In both of these operations, the principals (the Political Commissar in 1957 and Hor Lung in 1958) lived in great secrecy. So, for a time, did the guerrillas they brought out. As the number grew, however, it became more and more difficult to prevent something leaking out, yet the smallest hint would have alerted that tiny core of dedicated Communists who would have gone to any lengths to trap the 'traitor', and would have in any case nullified his activities by applying a complete emergency change of courier routes and jungle letter boxes. At an early stage, therefore, the Director of Operations advised the Prime Minister to allow the editors of the leading newspapers to be given the outline of the operations, and to ask them to quell unwitting initiative by their reporters. This confidence was fully respected and no hint whatever leaked out until the news was released – of the 118 in Perak in June 1958, and of Hor Lung and his 160, as already described, in August.[12] The Press was publicly thanked for its discretion by the Prime Minister when he gave his Press Conference.[13]

The hard core in Perak was in the north, in the tin mines, around Ipoh, and in the tapioca fields and rubber estates in the Sungei Siput District, which had been Chin Peng's stamping ground in the Japanese occupation, and where the Emergency had begun in 1948 (see Chapter 9).

In January 1958, there were still 170 guerrillas in these two districts of whom about 20 were in the single surviving MRLA Unit (No. 13/15 Platoon), and 160 were in the district and branch organization, which was almost as strong as it had ever been. During the previous four years only 83 guerrillas had been eliminated, of whom at least 42 had been from the MRLA platoons. The pattern was similar to that described in the Yong Peng District of Johore (see Chapter 10). Excluding the city of Ipoh (150,000), the population in the small towns and villages numbered 125,000. The vast majority of the Chinese in the area supported the MCP. They operated an elaborate intelligence system, and it was almost impossible for Security Forces to enter the area without the guerrillas being informed. This was particularly effective in the tapioca areas, in which the crop stands roughly chest high, enabling the Communist supporters to watch unobserved, and then, when necessary, to stand up and 'adjust' their highly coloured head-scarves with a flourish, as a signal to the guerrillas overlooking the fields from the jungle covered hillsides. Most of the cultivated areas north of Ipoh were planted with tapioca. This type of terrain was unusual in Malaya but was common in the Philippines and Vietnam, where the guerrillas used a similar system of signalling.[14]

15 January 1958 was D Day for Phase II of Operation GINGER directed against these 170 guerrillas and their *Min yuen*. It was the last federal priority operation of the Emergency, and followed the pattern described in Chapter 12. Since all the weaker areas had by then already been cleared, it was possible to raise the four battalions in the district to seven and to strengthen the police and Home Guard as well. Phase II lasted fifteen months (i.e. until April 1959) by which time the 170 guerrillas had been almost entirely wiped out. The great majority (112) surrendered, 50 were killed and the remaining 8 escaped across the Thai Border to join Chin Peng. Thus the last MCP stronghold on Federation soil was destroyed. The judgement that it was the strongest proved correct as it was here that the MCP first reappeared when it revived its guerrilla activities in 1971.

Kedah – A Different Approach

Before considering the Thai Border situation, it is worth examining an entirely different approach – neither framework nor priority operation – which was used to neutralize the guerrillas on the Malayan side of the Border in the northern state of Kedah.

This was a typical watershed frontier; it had only two road crossings, one at each end, with a 100-mile strip of mountainous jungle, twenty miles deep, between them. It was to Baling, on the southern of these two roads, that Chin Peng crossed for the abortive truce talks in 1955.

Between these crossings there were only two minor road systems, splitting into fingers and petering out altogether as they reached the jungle about twenty miles from the frontier.

In this strip of jungle there were a number of tiny but fertile valleys, cultivated by families or small communities of a semi-nomadic mixed Thai-Malay breed known as Sam-Sams. They were wholly non-political, and knew nothing of Malaya, or Thailand, or Communism, or democracy, or indeed of government of any kind. They lived at subsistence level, growing *padi* in the flooded fields beside the streams, which also provided their fish. To get to a market, or to a doctor or a school, meant a fifteen- or forty-mile walk along a jungle trail, and they did not find this worthwhile. Nor did the government find it practicable to bring any of these services to them – until 1957.

Meanwhile, however, the guerrillas found them most useful. The branches and platoons whose main work lay amongst the rubber estates in the cultivated plains of Kedah lived in these jungles, and obtained ample food from the Sam-Sams, for which they paid in full from the funds they gathered from their Chinese supporters on the estates. They provided the Sam-Sams with tools for building their houses and for tilling their land, with medical supplies and clothing, all of which they brought in from the plains. They also gave them and their children a certain amount of education.

In such circumstances the standard food denial operation – or framework based on food denial – would have been useless. This was more so because the plains of Kedah contain large rice-growing areas. Though grown by Malays, this rice was in such profusion that it could not be wholly denied to the guerrillas. This pattern applied over much of Vietnam, where food denial was also ineffective. The Sam-Sams were not amenable to resettlement in a strange environment and when previous attempts had been made to resettle them they had melted away again into their jungle valleys.

The solution was to link up the existing fingers of road with a sixty-four-mile arc of new road embracing the Sam-Sam communities. This was done by military engineers (Malayan, British and Gurkha) concurrently with the major operations in Perak and Johore from 1957 to 1959. Trucks thereafter plied regularly along this road to take produce to market and to bring in agricultural equipment and fertilizer. Schools and clinics were established, doctors paid visits and ambulances took the sick and injured to hospital. The Sam-Sams at last had a stake in government, and helped the police and army in ousting the guerrillas from their valleys.

The *Min Yuen* in the plains of Kedah was not as strong as in Perak or Johore, and, deprived of their sanctuary among the Sam-Sams, the guerrillas either succumbed to framework operations or crossed into Thailand.[15]

The Aborigines

A similar approach had been made to the problems of deep jungle bases for the guerrillas amongst the even more remote aborigine areas in the mountain spine of Malaya. The aborigines were averse to normal village life and, if resettled, melted away to resume their semi-nomadic life of 'shifting cultivation' in the jungle, usually several days' walk away from civilization. The solution was the establishment of jungle forts – really little more than defended camps occupied by between thirty and a hundred men of the police Field Force – in areas attractive to aborigines. These forts became trading posts, offering air-transported tools, clothing etc. to the aborigines in exchange for their jungle-grown rice and tapioca, and as wages in kind for work or for service with jungle patrols. They were also medical posts, with a weekly visit from the doctor, and provided primary education. Drawn by the availability of these advantages, without the need to change their way of life, the aborigines shifted their cultivations to these areas, and, cooperated with the police in eliminating the guerrilla bases.[16]

The Thai Border

There remained – and still remains – Chin Peng's active sanctuary across the Thai Border, where on 1 September 1957 it was estimated that he had 450 to 500 guerrillas, mainly living in large training camps in the 1948–9 style.

Chin Peng's decision in 1953 to move his Central Committee and Training Base from Pahang to South Thailand has already been described (see Chapter 10). The population in South Thailand included some 30,000 Chinese, mainly working in rubber, and living dispersed, each family close by the rubber lot on which it earned its living. There had been no resettlement, so they were subject to neither protection nor control. Food was unrationed, and there were no other restrictions like those in Malaya. Most of these Chinese probably had little objection, and in any case no alternative, to providing the very small support in terms of food, money and information that was needed to maintain 450 to 500 of their fellow Chinese as guerrillas in the neighbouring jungles. As early as April 1954, Special Branch in Kuala Lumpur had realized that this guerrilla community was unlikely to be eliminated.

The situation remained the same for the next three years, and more. In August 1957 the author of this book wrote a forecast of the MCP collapse (which was, in the event, to begin a month later with the defection of the Regional Political Commissar in Perak and then of Hor Lung in Johore) but added:

'There would still remain, however, several hundred [guerrillas] firmly established in the undeveloped country astride and beyond the Thai Border. It would be wrong to divert much effort to this area until the main inhabited areas [of Malaya] are cleared. Even then, successful operations would depend on the enforcement of unpopular civil measures, such as resettlement and food denial. The Thai Government is unlikely to be politically strong enough to enforce really effective Emergency Regulations or to mount major military operations in South Thailand. We should, therefore, base our future strategic thought on the assumption that Chin Peng will retain an army of at least 500 in South Thailand, and may well draw in more from the Federation. This Army will be able to live in relative security, to train and to expand and to wait, as the Communists waited in China, in the hope that political and racial difficulties and the progress of subversion will create the conditions suitable for renewal of their intervention in the Federation or Singapore. The best guarantee against this will be growing prosperity and a strong, efficient and enlightened Government. These will best be ensured by losing no time in shaking off the load of the Emergency from the wealth producing areas and by weakening the Communist potential for subversion in the villages and the towns.'

A quarter of a century later (1983) this threat remained in much the same form though Chin Peng's guerrilla strength North of the Thai Border grew from 500 to 1,500 with about 300 more in relatively small groups in the deep jungle in the Northern half of the Malayan Peninsula. This increase consisted almost entirely of new blood since the old guerrilla organization in Perak and Johore completely disintegrated in 1958–59 as described earlier in this chapter. During the 1960s and 1970s, Chin Peng used his hard core in Thailand as a training organization, recruiting disaffected young Chinese from villages in Kedah, Perak and Pahang. These recruits, many in their teens, were trained in both guerrilla and *Min Yuen* techniques, some remaining with Chin Peng and others returning to their villages as 'sleepers'. In the late 1960s they were ready to reactivate the guerrilla and cadre organizations in much the same form as in the 1950s though on a reduced scale. Their resurgence will be examined more fully in Part III.

PART III THE AFTERMATH AND
          THE PROSPECTS FOR
          MALAYSIA AND
          SINGAPORE

Chapter 15 The Balance Sheet in 1963

A Year of Decision

1963 was a historic year for the two nations of Malaya and Singapore. Tunku Abdul Rahman's Alliance Party and Lee Kuan Yew's PAP were both firmly established and both were destined to remain in power without a break for the subsequent 20 years. Singapore achieved its independence from British rule in that year and merged with the already independent Malaya as part of The Federation of Malaysia. Although Singapore was to leave the Federation two years later, both Malaysia and Singapore have prospered, with two of the world's highest economic growth rates. Despite their ethnic mixtures there have been many fewer people killed in communal disturbances than in other countries with similar racial, tribal or religious mixtures.

There are a number of reasons for these two success stories. In both countries historical accident and the pressure of events had thrown up a leader to match the hour; and both countries had endured and defeated a determined and highly professional attempt to impose on them a totalitarian communist system at birth.

For both of these things Britain can fairly claim a share of the credit. As in almost all her colonies she had consciously built up cadres of able political leaders and administrative officials, giving them the education, the responsibility and the experience, shrewdly accepting that their popular support and thence the stability of their countries would depend upon their being seen to struggle for their independence and to win.

Successive British Governments, both Labour and Conservative, had shown both resilience and finesse in defeating the Communist challenge which had led to most South East Asian countries having authoritarian governments of the right or left. Only Singapore and Malaya remain as genuine parliamentary democracies and it is no coincidence that they are both the most stable and the most successful in the region.

These twenty years 1963–83 have not been without incident or without challenge: Confrontation with Indonesia (leading to the collapse of Sukarno, not of the Tunku); the collapse of the merger; the racial riots of 1964 (Singapore) and 1969 (Kuala Lumpur); the resurgence of the Communist guerrilla organization in Malaysia; the collapse of Vietnam, Laos and Cambodia and instability and disturbance in Indonesia, Burma, Thailand and The Philippines; and a world recession. The final chapters of this book will review these years but, since they represent a totally new era, it will be appropriate first, in this chapter, to gather together some of the lessons from the years of insurgency which ended with lifting of the Emergency Regulations in Malaya in 1960 and the triumph of Lee Kuan Yew in the struggle for power with the left wing faction of his own party in 1963.

Urban and Rural Revolution

The progress of events in Singapore and Malaya underlined the contrast between the techniques of urban and rural revolution. In Singapore the revolution was run by a very small cadre of party members, with a larger proportion of the people openly involved, but with very small loss of life. In the cities of the Federation, although most contained an overwhelming majority of Chinese, the revolution failed to get any appreciable hold at all, but in the Chinese villages and in the jungles around them there was a far bigger Party organization, with many fewer of the public openly involved, though with far more of them being killed than in Singapore.

This reflects the contrasting fears and aspirations of city and rural people mentioned in Chapter 1. City people fear a collapse of order, of being without work, wages, food, water and other public utilities, and tend to rally to the government in face of excessive violence or disruption unless that government is manifestly less likely to be able to restore order than the revolutionaries – a stage never approached in Singapore.

By contrast, the isolated rural Chinese such as the squatters and the rubber tappers at work had little answer and little hope of protection against the threat of murder, abduction and looting of their food stocks. To acquire support, therefore, the revolutionaries made these threats very real by killing those who resisted them. At the peak of the Emergency they killed many more civilians than soldiers, and of the civilians killed the overwhelming majority were Chinese.

Although they remained separate until 1963, Singapore and the Federation would probably have stood or fallen together. Neither the British nor the Communists could for long have governed one without the other. The revolutionary efforts in both therefore proceeded concurrently, though with varying intensity and success.

These variations were not laid down in any MCP Master Plan. The Communists in all areas worked towards standard aims as opportunity arose. Where they succeeded, like ants seeking a way over a belt of puddles, they exploited their success. Their members and supporters were less often motivated by specific instructions emanating from the Central Committee (whose communications were appallingly difficult and slow) as by the study of dogma which made up the greater part of the work of the cells, and which told them how best to act in any given situation.

The MCP did, however, influence the priority of effort in city and countryside by switching more of its best members from one to the other, notably in 1945 and 1948. It must be asked whether this paid them and which field gave greater promise.

The first change, in 1945, was probably wrong. Had the MCP maintained its thriving anti-Japanese guerrilla army, with its loyal rural Chinese support, faced by weak and discredited Malay local administrations the British would have found it remarkably difficult to have revived the tin and rubber industries and, had they failed, they would have probably been glad to abandon the Federation and Singapore. The factors which guided the MCP away from this choice were their lack of thought and preparation resulting from the sudden surprise ending of the war by the atomic bombs; the British 'penetration' of their jungle army which they had accepted to help them fight the Japanese (though they could quickly have liquidated the men of Force 136 if they had planned to do so); the obvious delight of the great majority of the people of all races at the defeat of the Japanese and the end of the war, which was reflected in a joyful welcome for the British, with the hope they offered of a return to a better life; and the predominance in Communist theory at this time (before Mao Tse Tung's success) of the urban revolutionary strategy.

With the re-establishment of British authority and of the British-managed tin and rubber industry, it may be that the MCP's cause was already lost by 1948. They had by that time been effectively blocked in Singapore. Had they kept their rural organization intact from the war, and had they concentrated from 1945 to 1948 on weakening the tin and rubber industries and strengthening their hold on the workers in these industries instead of putting their effort into Singapore, the rural rebellion might have succeeded – particularly in view of the mistakes in military tactics made by the British up till 1952, and the initial weakness of the police intelligence service.

The MCP Organization in Singapore

The MCP in Singapore certainly put its money on a Leninist type of organization. More modern revolutionaries, particularly in Europe, have a great deal to learn from it, for their organizations in 1968 proved greatly inferior to that of the Singapore Communists from 1947 to 1956. Patrick Seale and Maureen McConville in *French Revolution 1968* (London, Penguin 1968) give a remarkable picture of the chaotic lack of organization and of the ineffectiveness of the many amateurish revolutionary movements attempting to rally popular support and provoke confrontation with the police in Paris in 1968. The end of that story – the rally of the mass of the people to the government – speaks for itself.

The control of about half the trade unions by the SFTU, with its open and legal link with the MCP, was a strong start towards a parallel hierarchy, or Trotsky's 'dual power'. So was the emergence of the SFSWU (for the unions) and the SCMSSU (for the students) in 1955–6.

The revolutionary organization in the trade unions in 1947 was a model of how such things should be run. The three prongs: the open leaders and members of the legal Communist Party; the Party Groups of secret Communist members holding key posts in legal trade union committees; and the wholly secret party cell system, fostering and exploiting grievances on the shop floor, were screened from each other but were all controlled by the Town Committee. Strikes, as a result, were well timed and well co-ordinated with each other and with the political situation.[1]

The organization for growth of the cell system downwards was also greatly strengthened and made more secure by the intermediate level of the Anti-British League. The sympathizer cells, which carried out the function of screening potential recruits, were always liable to contain turncoats or agents planted (or turned) by Special Branch. The Party cells themselves, however, were fully insulated from betrayal by these people because of the intermediate cells of ABL members who had proved their reliability by previous service in sympathizer cells.

The student organization in the Chinese-language schools, as well as incorporating the ABL and sympathizer cell structure, also had an open structure greatly superior to that of most contemporary student organizations. In the open, there was a central and legal Committee in secret touch with a Party representative outside the school. This was the School Committee which, through its Standard Committee for each age group, ensured that boys sympathetic to its ideas were elected to most of the Class Monitor posts. At the grass roots, the open and seemingly laudable Tuition Cells fed promising boys across to be exposed to more direct indoctrination in the secret Hsueh Hsih cells, which in turn formed a source of members for sympathizers and ABL cells, which in turn had their link with the Party outside.

The MCP in the Chinese-language schools had one great advantage not enjoyed by the schools and universities in the USA, Latin America, Europe and Japan – nor indeed by the present schools and universities in Singapore: because of the emotional appeal of Chinese culture, the starvation of Chinese-language schools in comparison with English-language schools, and the bias in favour of the English-educated in searching for jobs, the SCMSSU enjoyed the support of the great majority of the students in its schools, and those who did not want to support it had little option but to do so in face of this weight of public opinion, which took an aggressive form.

This favourable public opinion, however, was created and developed by the organization as well as supporting it.

The ability of the Party and its supporting organizations to attract and foster genuine idealism, particularly amongst the young, should not be underrated, and this was publicly conceded by Lee Kuan Yew at the crucial moment of his fight against Communism. A most convincing example of this idealism was the work of 'Hong', the Communist teacher at Ayer Baloi described in Chapter 4.

The weakness of the organization lay in its own extremely tight security. Shortcomings were concealed from higher authority in order to safeguard reputations, and from subordinate cells in order to maintain confidence. In addition the information reaching members was scanty and slow due to the complex system of couriers and cut-out men. This resulted in members working in great obscurity and was a major cause, for example, of the fatal tactical errors made in the October 1956 riots and the events leading up to them. These contrast with the tactical successes of the government, the police and the army, whose officers were fully informed of what was happening.

Achievements and Failures of the MCP in Singapore

The aim of the MCP in Singapore up till 1955 was to oust the British colonial government and substitute a Communist one, in conjunction with a similar aim in the Federation of Malaya. During the transition stage to independence (1955–63) when the British were clearly on the way out, their aim became to capture control of the elected Singapore government, either by constitutional or revolutionary means.

Both of those aims were perfectly feasible. The most promising years for the first were 1945–7; for the second, they were 1956–7 (to coincide with Malayan independence) and 1962 (to coincide with the end of British responsibility and of reserve powers of intervention).

The Party failed in both aims, and achieved little in the way even of erosion of authority; so far from accelerating the British withdrawal and the final attainment of independence, it almost certainly retarded them.

Its achievements were therefore no more than those of a football team which trains for a number of championship matches but loses every one. Yet that team might come within a single goal of winning, and the achievement of their preparation can be assessed by whether they can keep within striking range of victory, whether they can seize the chance of the vital goal if it comes, and whether they can hold the championship after they have won it.

On this assessment the MCP organization in the trade unions in 1947 and 1956 and in the Chinese schools in 1955–6 were of championship standard. The political organization was probably not, even when it seemed to be within a single vote of capturing power in 1962.

But the MCP lost. It is therefore fair to ask whether they might have done better with wholly different training and tactics – and in particular whether they could have succeeded with the now more fashionable urban guerrilla philosophy of bringing about a popular rising by continuous demonstration, violence and dislocation, without the delays involved in building up an organization and fostering a revolutionary situation. In theory, such violence and dislocation, leading to bloody confrontation with foreign soldiers and foreign-officered police, could have resulted in such chaos that neither the Port of Singapore nor the British Military Base could have functioned, An intermediate stage might have been the granting of concessions to strikers, leading to a growing attraction of new members to the MCP-controlled union federations – the GLU, the SFTU and the SFSWU in turn – which would have enabled the Party to withhold labour wholly and at will from the Port and the Base. In their other overseas bases, once such facilities had ceased to be able to fulfil their function economically, the British had shewn realism in getting out – as they had in 1948 from Palestine, and in 1954 from the Suez canal – both times abandoning huge assets and supposedly vital strategic advantages. Had there been an abandonment of Singapore to the Communists in the 1940s or the 1950s, this would have carried with it a British abandonment of Malaya.

The evidence suggests, however, that confrontation without organization would not have brought things to this stage in Singapore. First, because the army and the police were very strong, with ample reinforcements quickly available from the Federation (as was proved in the riots in October 1956, when six battalions were withdrawn from the Malayan jungle and appeared in Singapore within two days); secondly because neither the army nor the police could be penetrated or disaffected, since they were mainly manned by British, Gurkhas and Malays, none of whom had any reason to support a Chinese Communist revolution; thirdly because, with so much at stake in Malaya and in the port and military base in Singapore, the British would have fought far harder than they had fought in the Middle East, where many of the assets (notably the oil installations) were largely unaffected by the withdrawals; and fourthly because the majority of the Singapore Chinese, sensing all these things, and not wishing to throw away either British capital or law and order, would have rallied to the government rather than to the MCP in the face of a real threat of chaos, because the government always appeared the likelier of the two to be able to restore order. Premature violence and confrontation would have accelerated the arrest of the leaders and, without its organization behind it, the Party would have passed beyond hope of recovery.[2] Returning to the football analogy, instead of losing 3–2 they would have lost 10–nil.

The Singapore Government's Handling of Violence and Coercion

The government's most cost-effective and its most decisive weapon was its intelligence arm, the Police Special Branch. Its arrests in 1932 and its (supposed) planting of Lai Tek in 1934 weakened and poisoned the MCP almost from its birth. The arrest of the complete Singapore Town Committee in 1950 made the urban end of the revolution ineffective during the critical years of the guerrilla conflict in Malaya, and for some time afterwards. The intelligence cover in the Chinese schools in 1955 proved to be an adequate counter to a dangerous and powerfully united organization with tremendous potential for sympathetic confrontation. And the Special Branch swoop on the SFSWU was the decisive stroke in defeating the rioters in October 1956.

The government's choice and timing of counter revolutionary legislation were also sensible. The 1948 Trade Union Ordinance, the State of Emergency in 1948 and the action against the SCMSSU and the SFSWU in 1955–6 were all good examples of this.

Police organization and techniques, after their failures in the 1950 Hertogh riots, provided a model that has been studied by many other police forces.[3] The far-sighted contingency planning in 1956 for 'Operation PHOTO' ('Failure of Talks Operation') paid big dividends, and in the execution of the Operation the joint police/army control, the police radio car system, the timely deployment of military roadblocks and roof top observation posts, the use of helicopters and the handling of Public Relations were all excellent. Many of these techniques developed in the Singapore riots of 1956 were clearly recognizable in the British Army's handling of the initial disturbances in Northern Ireland in 1969–70.

The image of the soldiers as peacekeepers rather than as killers was remarkable in the circumstances but it was founded on fact. The deployment of the army in the Hertogh riots in 1950 quickly ended the bloodshed. Thereafter, the army did not kill or lose a single man (though the navy killed one) in Singapore. Their appearance on the streets in October 1956 was undoubtedly greeted with relief by the majority of the population.

The government's timing in the riot situations themselves was also good. A notable example was the dispersal of the crowd outside the Chinese High School on the night of 25 October and the clearance of the schools without an audience at dawn next day.

With such a high standard of play on the day the government deserved to win, but this excellence has perhaps undeservedly overshadowed the performance of the MCP.

Lee Kuan Yew

Lee Kuan Yew has a place in history as one of the only politicians who marched to power arm in arm with Communists, and managed to discard them. He also inherited the British peacekeeping (or, some would say, suppressive) apparatus and techniques and continued to use them to good effect. Since he has had independent power, there has been no country in South East Asia with such a proportionately low rate of death and damage in riots and disturbances. He consolidated his position and his prospects with an equally high record of administrative achievement, in housing, education and economic development. Though there were some stirrings amongst his intellectuals, there is no doubt that the majority of Singaporeans were with him in heart and mind.

The Communists' Balance Sheet in the Village War in Malaya

Like their comrades in Singapore, the guerrillas and their supporters in the jungles and the villages of the Federation were defeated, though they salvaged a good deal from their defeat – enough to revive their campaign if circumstances became propitious. They would not be the first remnant of a beaten army to survive and come back to win.

About their dedication and faith in final victory there can be no doubt. The fortitude of the tiny bands of guerrillas, such as those in Yong Peng (Chapter 10) and Segamat (Chapter 13) which held out for six or twelve months against the concentrated efforts of twenty or even sixty times their strength of soldiers, when to all appearances the war was lost, must rank high in the annals of human endurance.

The biggest achievement of the MCP in the Federation, therefore, was their refinement of the art of survival in the latter years of the Emergency, 1954–60. Though they were much inspired by the example of Mao Tse Tung, who had recovered from the agonies of 1934 to rule China in 1949, their circumstances were very different. After the long march, Mao's republic in Yenan was well populated but out of range of effective interference by the Kuomintang forces. The MCP guerrillas, on the other hand, were in virtually unpopulated jungle, but within a few miles of strong government forces. In China the armies on both sides and all the population were Chinese. In Malaya there was a strong interracial flavour and, though this helped the MCP to rally the Chinese population against the British, Gurkha and Malay security forces, it did deny them the chance of penetrating and suborning the army and the police – as was done so effectively in China, and as it was earlier in Russia and later in Cuba.

Chin Peng's guerrillas, having at first tried to apply Mao's theories too rigidly to their very different environment, later devised their own techniques for survival. They made best use of the dense jungle to remain intact within easy walking range of their supporters, and developed the most intensive security discipline to avoid detection and betrayal.

After 1954 they showed a rare understanding of the real function of the guerrilla revolutionary which was to indoctrinate the people and organize their support, and they judged this to be more important than destroying the government forces – the reverse of Debray's philosophy. As their jungle strength was eroded, the combat units were milked to keep the political organization up to strength.

Unlike their comrades in Vietnam, the MCP guerrillas had no 'active sanctuary' on their borders – such as China provided for the Vietminh and North Vietnam for the Vietcong. The Thai Border offered reasonable immunity for Chin Peng's command and training base, but it was not a practical channel for weapons and supplies. Nor (because of the distance from China) was coastal shipping. The MCP had therefore to rely on local sources: captured weapons from the army and police and supplies from the villagers. This, in fact, was a blessing in disguise, because there were always plenty of guns, with ammunition to fit, within range of their raiding parties, and because the people who were persuaded to give them food and other supplies were committed and involved. It is significant that, until the North Vietnamese Army entered South Vietnam in force in 1965, the Vietcong relied on similar sources for 90 per cent of their equipment.[4]

Did the MCP miss a chance of victory in 1948? Perhaps they did. They had certainly missed one in 1945–6 when they weakened their rural organization to concentrate on the cities. In 1948 they belatedly attempted to disrupt the rubber and tin industries, but they paid the price paid by so many revolutionaries before them of having an inadequate organization for popular support. The popular rising they hoped for never came.

Perhaps they could have driven out the British by other means. Their violence was directed against Chinese 'collaborators' rather than against the British themselves: from June till October 1948 almost all the 223 civilians they killed were Chinese, and only 17 were Europeans. They no doubt calculated that widespread murders of British rubber planters and tin miners would have provoked more violent British reaction and reinforcement. They may well have been right, but it is doubtful whether the rubber and tin industries could have survived unrestricted attacks on its British managers, the nature of whose work made them extremely vulnerable. With the managers decimated or unable to supervise their industries, the financial losses might have been so great that the companies, and then the British government, might have decided that Malaya would never again provide a sound economic investment, and that some kind of political solution leading to a withdrawal would be wise.

   This is by no means certain. The British have historically been stubborn in the face of this kind of personal violence; more so than against other tactics such as sabotage or withdrawal of labour – which the MCP could have organized successfully in the tin and rubber industries in 1945–6 had they tried to do so. Having failed to do this, they may have missed their only other chance of outright victory by their forbearance from wholesale murder of Europeans in 1948. By 1949 the six-fold crash expansion of the police and the pouring of more British troops into Malaya had taken away this last chance, however slender, of quick success.

   The wholesale murder of Chinese, however, did not show any similar promise of victory, and the MCP were wise to turn away from it in October 1951. Though they never looked like building up the support they needed from the public except by violence, their relative forbearance probably helped them to survive without inflicting scars on the rural Chinese which would have been held against them in the 1960s and 1970s and beyond. If, one day, Malaya, including Singapore, becomes a Communist-oriented Chinese dominated country, history may credit Chin Peng's success in surviving on the borders of Malaya, leaving little bitterness behind him in the Chinese villages, as a decisive factor.

The Government's Response

The government's achievements in the Federation are easier to perceive since they defeated their enemy and drove him right out of the country, even if they did not leave him quite dead; and they did this with astonishingly little loss of life and little damage to the country.

One of their most important contributions to the art of counter-insurgency is recorded in the comprehensive 150-page system of Emergency Regulations, as finally amended in 1953. This book contains the essence of the legal provisions which five years of experience had proved necessary in order to prevent the guerrillas from obtaining effective support from the people in the villages – a bible of population control. The regulations for registering the village population and the resettlement of the squatters were of special importance and were implemented with determination, sense and skill.

Through the public acceptance of resettlement was greatly assisted by the boom in the price of rubber arising from the Korean War, a more important factor was the decision not to move the settlers into any New Village until enough constables had been trained to man a police post inside the village, day and night. This was not done in Vietnam, where in many villages people who actively helped the government had no protection from the Vietcong's 'man with a knife' at night, with obvious results.

Village security was the firm base on which the government campaign was built in Malaya. It depended upon the integrity of each small police post, which was in turn dependent on the army to ensure that it was not attacked with overwhelming force.

Also dependent on this security was the establishment and integrity of the elected village government and rural and community development. Village security and village development were vital planks in the propaganda platform which eventually convinced the rural Chinese that the government could win, and that it was in their interest for it to do so.

Also worthy of note is the system of command and control which the government developed in 1950. After nearly two years of weak and divided command, General Briggs arrived as Director of Operations and introduced the State and District War Executive Committees, on which the responsible civil official, police and military commanders conducted operations jointly under the chairmanship of the civilian. It was a further two years before the Director of Operations (in the person of General Templer) was given full power over all these resources at the top. In the later stages, after Independence, a British Director of Operations and a British Army Commander worked under the direction of the elected Malayan ministers.

If the decisive defensive element was village security, the decisive offensive element was intelligence. The Police Special Branch was British led but employed Chinese officers to handle Chinese agents, and was probably the most efficient of its kind in the world. By the mid 1950s, the great majority of guerrillas were known by name, and Special Branch had acquired photographs of most of them from others who had been captured, or from their relatives in the villages. The handling of agents and surrendered guerrillas was outstandingly successful. The offer of very large rewards – paid only for information which led to the death or capture of a wanted man – was an important factor here, but equally important was the psychological treatment of the Chinese defectors (whether guerrillas or their supporters) which successfully induced them to betray their comrades.

The government technique for acquiring intelligence reached a degree of complexity and refinement which offers a useful example for future governments trying to dig out the roots of a guerrilla insurgency, though it must be viewed in the context of the particular circumstances prevailing in Malaya. Important amongst these were the proximity of the jungle to the tin mines and rubber estates, the fact that the rural economy was mainly based on cash crops and not on food, and that such rice as grew locally was almost entirely grown by Malays, who were hostile to the rebellion.

This technique, which depended on exploiting the reliance of the guerrillas on rice which had to be smuggled out of the Chinese villages and turning a proportion of the smugglers into police agents, was described in Chapters 11, 12 and 13. A significant point was the very small number of food smugglers who needed to be turned into agents to bring success. For example, in the Segamat District before Operation COBBLE, there were only 4 registered Special Branch agents who were able to betray the guerrillas by giving advanced information about them. The process of arresting and turning food supplies yielded another 11, bringing the total to only 15. And this was in a district containing some 37,000 people of whom 21,000 were Chinese, in which over 500 police and 1,200 soldiers were concentrated in an attempt to root out about 30 guerrillas in a federal priority operation.

Such federal priority operations were like sledge-hammers cracking nuts – but they did crack them. Nevertheless, some nuts were cracked by less ponderous weapons in 'framework operations' like the one described in Chapter 14. In these too, however, the decisive factor was intelligence.

Praise is also due to the government's strategy of dealing first with the areas in which the MCP were weakest, so that these could then be lightly policed while overwhelming strength could be concentrated on the really hard nuts at the end. Coupled with this was the 'White Area' policy, under which risks were taken in lifting restrictions from areas which had been dealt with so that the population felt that they were rewarded for their cooperation, and trusted; also so that the people of neighbouring districts, envying their freedom, were encouraged to emulate them.

But the real key to the government's success was that it concentrated its attention on the people in the villages rather than on the guerrillas, whom they regarded as clandestine political organizers rather than fighters. This is just how the MCP regarded them, as do most Communist parties – but not all governments.

Leninism or the New Left?

As in Singapore, the Communist guerrillas in Malaya lost their battle. Would they have done better if they had followed the guerrilla philosophy of Regis Debray? If instead of tying themselves to a support organization based on particular villages, the guerrillas had operated as mobile *focos;* buzzing like bees, cohesive around the swarm but with the swarm moving to evade the swipes of soldiers; hoping that the other insects (i.e. the rural Chinese) would have been inspired by the activity of the bees to buzz spontaneously around the *foco*, wherever it moved? And would the government and its soldiers and police have been stung to death?

As in Singapore, all the evidence suggests otherwise. Whenever a guerrilla branch under intense military pressure shifted from its area and broke its links with its known supporters in the villages, Communist support in that area never revived. The faithful lost heart, and the reluctant were thankful to be off the hook. If the guerrillas came back, one of these people would usually betray them. If they tried to create links with other villages they got little response, became hungry and dispirited, and eventually dispersed – the weaker ones to surrender (if not forestalled by execution) and the stronger ones to join other branches. Had the MCP followed the theories of the New Left, they would not have won, nor would they have held on for twelve years.

How far is evidence from Malaya valid in general? Probably considerably more so than that from Cuba (the sole success on which Debray's theories are based) and certainly more so than that put forward by other theorists who can claim no basis of success at all. The MCP were not badly placed in 1948. The government forces were weak and ill prepared, with little previous experience of fighting against guerrillas in the jungle. The Malays, though hostile to a Chinese takeover, were weakly organized and shamed by the Japanese occupation. The MCP had three years of wartime experience, and tremendous prestige. The rural Chinese were generally prepared to support them, and many of them dedicated to doing so. The Chinese are a tough and brave people. It would be hard to find better material for a popular rising, but they failed to rise in 1948 because the MCP had allowed their rural organization to lapse.

Debray's claim that the Cuban people rose spontaneously to Castro's tiny *foco* in the Sierra Maestra without any cadre organization amongst them is itself suspect. They did not give effective support to Castro until the morale of the government officials and soldiers in the provinces was withering on the vine as a result of the rotting of its roots in Havana. The people responded to Castro's leadership when they acquired a sense of impunity, when their fears and dislike of the officials and soldiers had turned into contempt. But the rotting of the roots of Batista's regime was primarily due, not to Castro's rural guerrillas, but to a combined Communist and radical liberal movement in Havana.

Though the MCP failed both in Singapore and in the Federation of Malaya, the conclusion is that their excellent organization brought them nearer to victory than if they had tried to operate without it, by violence and confrontation in the cities and with mobile guerrilla *focos*, not linked to villages, in the jungle.

Their relatively narrow defeat was due more to the skill of the governments and their forces than to MCP shortcomings. The Party has continued to function, mainly on orthodox lines, both in West and East Malaysia and in a lower key through front organizations in Singapore but with very little success, so the aftermath of the conflicts of the 1940s and 1950s brought relative peace and prosperity to both countries. This aftermath, and the prospects for the future, are the subject of Part III of this book.

Chapter 16 Malaysia and her Neighbours

Confrontation

The Emergency in Malaya formally ended on 31 July 1960 with the lifting of Emergency Regulations from all the eleven states in the Federation. The proposal for a merger of these eleven states of the Malayan Peninsula and Singapore and the British colonies in Borneo was first mooted publicly in May 1961. The progress of this proposal and its eventual realization on 16 September 1963 were crucial in Lee Kuan Yew's struggle for power and were therefore described in that context on pages 155-161.

The merger, however, led to the damaging period of Confrontation with Indonesia in 1962-66 which resulted in the fall of President Sukarno and did much to consolidate the new Federation of Malaysia.

Kuala Lumpur had always feared a merger between Malaya and Singapore alone because this would have made the Chinese the dominant community. By 1961, however, it was clear that Britain's colonies in Borneo (Sarawak and North Borneo, later renamed Sabah) were ripe for independence but would not be viable on their own. By incorporating Malaya ('West Malaysia'), Singapore and the two Borneo territories ('East Malaysia'), the new Federation of Malaysia would comprise 42 per cent Chinese, 39 per cent Malays, 9 per cent Indians and 10 per cent indigenous Borneo peoples. Although the Chinese would still be the largest community, the Malays felt that they would be sufficiently diffused. This suited Lee Kuan Yew very well because he had long wanted to merge with Malaya and knew that, without the counter weight of the Borneo peoples, this would be politically impossible. He also welcomed the opportunities for trade and development in Borneo as part of Malaysia.

The Sultan of Brunei, whose small territory lay between Sarawak and Sabah and was rich in oil, did not wish to join. There was, however, active and, as it transpired, violent opposition to the formation of Malaysia from two quarters: President Sukarno of Indonesia and a radical Muslim movement in Brunei led by A.M. Azahari.

Azahari's ambition was to bring about an Islamic revolution, ousting the ruling hierarchy (the *pengirans*) around the Sultan and to absorb Sarawak and Sabah into a Greater Brunei. He was encouraged by The Philippines, which had designs on Sabah, and by Indonesia, which hoped to absorb all three Borneo territories into the rest of their Island of Kalimantan. Both, no doubt, thought that it would be easier to take them from an unstable 'Greater Brunei' than from Britain or Malaysia. Of more immediate concern to the British, however, was that Azahari had been seen regularly in the company of Lim Chin Siong in Singapore and this might indicate links with the Clandestine Communist Organization (CCO) in Sarawak. In early December 1962 a British security sweep in Brunei and Sawarak was widely believed to be imminent.[1]

In the early hours of 8 December Azahari's supporters suddenly rebelled and occupied every town in Brunei, including the Shell complex at Seria and two border towns in Sabah and Sarawak. The Sultan called for assistance under his Defence Treaty with Britain. The British reacted very quickly, flying troops from Singapore by the evening of 8 December and within a few days the revolt was crushed. Azahari himself had flown to Manila on 7 December, where he issued a 'Declaration of Independence' which was roundly condemned by all the Governments which were to constitute the Federation of Malaysia.

While crushing the Brunei revolt, the British also arrested known members of the CCO in Sarawak – presumably as already planned in their security sweep. This, in the event, proved counter productive because some 1,500 young Chinese, mainly members of the CCO, fled across the border into Kalimantan where the Indonesians promptly put them under training to cooperate in the invasion which was to be the first step in their Confrontation with Malaysia.[2]

This invasion began in April 1963, when Indonesian troops crossed the border and seized the police station at Tebedu, uncomfortably close to Kuching, the capital of Sarawak. Other incursions followed.

The process of merger continued, however, and on 16 September 1963, The Federation of Malaysia was formed. Sarawak and Sabah (North Borneo) ceased to be British territory but, at the request of the Malaysians, British and other Commonwealth troops remained and a British General – Sir Walter Walker – continued as Director of Operations of all troops, including Malaysians, who were defending the Borneo territories against Indonesian attacks. He was operationally responsible, not to any British authority, but to the National Operations Council (NOC) of elected Malaysian Ministers headed by the Prime Minister and the Defence Minister. The British, of course, had the power to withdraw their General, or even their troops, if the Malaysians had insisted on their doing anything unacceptable to the British Government but, so long as they remained (as they did), all the troops, from five countries, operated under a single General, himself responsible to the elected Government of the territory in which they were operating. This was in marked contrast to the US and other troops operating in South Vietnam in the same period.

This command structure and the skill and experience of the troops gained in the 12 years of the Malayan Emergency resulted, during the next three years, in one of the most remarkable military campaigns in British, Commonwealth and Malaysian history. At the start there were only three battalions, later reinforced to 12, to defend a 1,000 mile frontier against a large Indonesian regular army, itself well trained and battle-experienced from its own war of independence from the Dutch ending with the acquisition of West Irian in 1963.

Three of the 12 battalions were Malay, mainly in Sabah, the other nine being British, Gurkha, Australian and New Zealand. Their success rested mainly on intelligence, which was initially supplied by 1,500 Border Scouts recruited from the indigenous tribes which straddled the wild jungle-covered mountain border, supplemented by reports from agents recruited in the villages.

For the first year, however, the Indonesians held the initiative because their troops were regularly sent across the frontier into Borneo while the British and Malaysians were scrupulous about observing international law because no state of war had ever been declared. After the formation of Malaysia on 16 September 1963 and the transfer of responsibility for Borneo from London to Kuala Lumpur the Indonesians stepped up their incursions into Borneo and also launched raids (albeit abortive) on Peninsular Malaysia. The Malaysian Government decided that they could no longer tolerate Indonesian army units forming up in Kalimantan, raiding police and army posts in Sabah and Sarawak and then withdrawing into an 'active sanctuary' behind the frontier. They therefore authorised discreet cross-border operations, initially to a depth of 5,000 yards, later extended to 10,000 and occasionally 20,000 yards. These were usually targeted as a result of clandestine reconnaissance by the British SAS. The main function of the operation was to acquire intelligence and to harrass the army camps from which the Indonesians mounted their incursions so that they would withdraw them and this, in the roadless jungle country of the border, would give more time (and intelligence) to enable the Malaysians and British to be ready for them and to ambush them.[3]

This tactic was wholly successful, and the Indonesians, who had no effective intelligence on the Borneo side of the border, were almost invariably ambushed and suffered heavy casualties. In all it is estimated that some 2,000 Indonesians were killed at the cost of 59 British and Gurkha dead.[4]

The Chinese-run CCO in Sarawak constituted a more serious threat. They operated on similar lines to the MCP in Malaya, with a well established village cadre organization supporting guerrillas who had been trained across the border in Indonesian Kalimantan, with a total membership (guerrillas and supporters) of 24,000.[5]

During 1965, serious internal troubles broke out in Indonesia. On 30 September, an attempted coup ascribed to the Indonesian Communist Party (PKI) was thwarted by the army and was followed by a furious massacre of Communists by Muslims, the estimates of those killed ranging from 80,000 to 1,000,000. The PKI was virtually destroyed and with it one of the chief pillars of Sukarno's power. By March 1966 he was forced to delegate most of his power to the army Chief of Staff, General Suharto, who quickly opened negotiations with Kuala Lumpur and a peace treaty was signed on 11 August 1966. As a face-saver for Indonesia it was agreed that the people of Sabah and Sarawak would be given the chance, as soon as was practicable, to reaffirm their choice to remain part of Malaysia. Sukarno was later placed under house arrest and Suharto formally installed as President.

The rebellion of the CCO in Sarawak, however, was by no means over. The Chinese constituted 31 per cent of the Sarawak population, compared with 17 per cent Malay, 32 per cent Sea Dyak (Iban) and 20 per cent others. Many of the Chinese and Dyaks resented the Malay-dominated Kuala Lumpur Government taking over, arguing that at least the British would one-day go away whereas the Malay 'colonists' intended to stay for ever. The CCO's aim was to form Sarawak, Sabah and Brunei into a 'People's Republic of North Kalimantan', with Indonesian support but, when this support was withdrawn after Sukarno's collapse in 1966, they found themselves deprived of their 'active sanctuary' across the border and had to reorganize. By 1971 their strength had reached about 1,000 activists with perhaps 30,000 supporters amongst the 240,000 Chinese in Sarawak. Their most spectacular operation was an ambush in 1972 near Sibu in which 15 Malaysian Rangers were killed.[6]

Meanwhile, however, Special Branch were having considerable success both in 'turning' CCO supporters in the Chinese villages and in attracting SEPs willing to cooperate in bringing out their comrades, using the techniques developed in Malaya in the 1950s (e.g. see pages 180–83 and 212). In September 1973 two senior SEP's paved the way for a letter, a month later, to the Chief Minister from the CCO's guerrilla leader, Bong Kee Chok, proposing peace talks. These were conducted with commendable good faith by the Sarawak Government, and led to a Memorandum of Understanding whereby surrendered guerrillas were given a pardon and would be free to take part in politics but the Communist Party would remain proscribed. By the time this was publicly announced on 4 March 1974, nearly 500 had surrendered by negotiation[7] and this was the beginning of the end of CCO activities, though a hard core of about 200 have remained at large, confining their operations to hit and run raids.[8]

The End of the Merger

Reverting to 1965: Confrontation had cemented Kuala Lumpur's relationship with the Governments of Sarawak and Sabah but in the meantime relations between Kuala Lumpur and Singapore had deteriorated. The trouble had begun within a few weeks of the merger, when Tunku Abdul Rahman's ruling Alliance Party (UMNO, MCA and MIC) joined forces with a number of small parties in Singapore to form a new grouping, the SPA, to oppose the PAP in the Singapore elections in September 1963. (These were described in Chapter 8). The Tunku's reason, presumably, was a very real fear that a PAP landslide might later encourage Malayan Chinese voters on the mainland to jump onto the bandwagon, enabling the

PAP to supplant the MCA as the Chinese party in the Alliance in the Federation.

The SPA failed to win a single seat in the 1963 elections, but its intervention had precisely the effect it aimed to avert. Six months later Lee Kuan Yew decided, contrary to his earlier intentions, to field PAP candidates in constituencies in the mainland states in their elections on 25 April 1964. He did indeed claim to be the best representative for Chinese voters in the Alliance; he may also have feared that disillusioned MCA voters might defect to the left wing Socialist Front, which was widely regarded as a Communist front, so he hoped that they might instead defect to the PAP. In the event only one constituency fell to a PAP candidate, Devan Nair, an Indian trade union leader who took the seat from a Chinese independent, not from the MCA. Nevertheless, the Alliance was alarmed at the PAP's intervention, interpreting it as a clear indication that Lee Kuan Yew saw the supplanting of the MCA in the Alliance as a route to Premiership of Malaysia – the whole of Malaysia.[9]

A few weeks later, in July 1964, serious communal rioting broke out in Singapore, largely arising from Lee Kuan Yew's refusal to grant Malays in Singapore the same privileged status as they enjoyed in the mainland states. These riots, which will be examined more fully in Chapter 19, were the only serious communal riots to have occurred in Singapore since the Hertogh riots in 1950[10] and caused Lee Kuan Yew and the Tunku to consult to find ways of reducing racial tensions.

Chinese resentment of discrimination in favour of Malays, however, remained and in May 1965 Lee Kuan Yew gathered four opposition parties in Malaya and Sarawak to join the PAP in the Malaysian Solidarity Convention standing for a 'Malaysian Malaysia' instead of a 'Malay Malaysia'. Again this alarmed the Alliance, and especially the more militant Malays in UMNO (the 'ultras') who saw this as another manifestation of Lee's ambition to become Premier – this time by attracting not only the Chinese communities but the poor and discontented of every race to follow his leadership. Their anxiety was increased by the growing international prestige which Lee Kuan Yew was acquiring as a statesman on the international scene.[11]

In June 1965 the Tunku left to attend the Commonwealth Prime Ministers' Conference in London and, while he was there, fell ill and remained in UK for medical treatment, so Tun Razak acted as

Deputy Prime Minister for two critical months. Razak had talks with Lee Kuan Yew and later with his Finance Minister Dr. Goh Keng Swee in an attempt to defuse the situation but it became clear that there were no solutions other than for either Lee Kuan Yew to cease to be Premier of Singapore or for Singapore to leave the Federation.[12] The ultras, and the Malay press, were in full cry and the Tunku saw only one possible course; he 'shot the fox'.[13] He expelled Singapore from the Federation, despite urgent appeals from Lee Kuan Yew. Razak and Goh Keng Swee had worked out terms for the split in time for the Tunku's return on 6 August. Lee Kuan Yew saw the Tunku in a last attempt to avert the split but to no avail and, in an emotional broadcast on 9 August, he announced that Singapore was an independent state.

The split was, in the circumstances, remarkably amicable and statesmanlike. The two countries made firm commitments for economic and defence cooperation including the continued use by the Federation of military bases (including the naval base) and other facilities on the island – all of which were vital for the continuing Confrontation with Indonesia.[14]

ASEAN

This cooperation continued and has continued until this day. In August 1967 Malaysia, Singapore, Indonesia, The Philippines and Thailand formed The Association of Southeast Asian Nations (ASEAN) for economic, social and cultural cooperation and for maintaining stability in the area. ASEAN was remarkably successful in all its fields during the subsequent 15 years, notably in eradicating restrictions on free trade. All its constituent countries maintained average economic growth rates of between 5 and 10 per cent – at least up till 1982 when the world recession pulled them down but they still remained amongst the highest in the world, vying with Japan. Singapore, with its free port status, its talented and disciplined workforce and its liberal incentives to attract overseas investment, led the field (see Chapter 19).

The Resurgence of Guerrilla Warfare in Malaysia

In the following year (1968) Chin Peng's Communist Party of Malaya (CPM – as the MCP became known after that time), whose survival and retraining in Thailand was referred to on pages 259–60, felt ready to resume its campaign in Malaysia. It had been building up its strength from its original 500 survivors by attracting recruits from amongst the 30,000 Thai Chinese (and some Muslims) in South Thailand; it also attracted about half its new recruits from amongst the Malaysian Chinese in the border states of Kedah and Perak, and especially from the original hardcore villages North of Ipoh. Many of the latter underwent courses of training as guerrillas or cadres and then returned to their villages to lie low until the time came for action.

The Thai police and intelligence were less efficient than those of the Malaysians and the CPM were able to train in large, permanent and well found camps with little interference. One such camp was discovered late in 1966 (hastily abandoned) by a joint Thai-Malay patrol, scarcely 100 yards in from the jungle fringe. In it, the patrol picked up a roll of film which recorded the events of a recent 'Open Day'. Over 90 armed guerrillas in uniform had marched past a row of senior officers, in Moscow May Day style, on an impressive balcony (found intact) under a huge Hammer and Sickle. There were pictures of propaganda plays, showing mock-up tanks and guns ('Paper Tigers'); of singing, dancing and games; of a large audience of civilians, mainly young, attending a lecture; and of a festive children's tea party.

On 1 June 1968 the CPM broadcast over Radio Peking an announcement of its intention to resume the armed struggle and on 17 June a police patrol was ambushed close to the frontier, killing 17 police officers. The race riots in Kuala Lumpur in May 1969 (see next chapter) gave a boost to their recruiting and later in that year there were a number of CPM terrorist murders (e.g. of an ex SEP in Sintok in Kedah), ambushes and sabotage attacks.

By 1971, guerrilla strength was estimated to be 1,200[15] though the number trained and sent back to their villages probably exceeded 3,000.[16] They had resumed contact with their traditional villages and were operating in a very similar pattern to that of the 1950s. One of their suppliers, arrested by the police in 1971, commented that there was no need for them to organize propaganda work because the majority of the villagers were already staunch supporters.[17]

Between 1970 and 1974 a series of splits, some of them bloody, occurred within the CPM. Believing that it was being penetrated by government agents amongst the recruits coming across the frontier for training, the CPM launched a purge and about 200 members were executed. At this time the CPM was organized in three regiments – the 8th in the West facing North Kedah, the 12th in the Betong Salient facing the Kedah/Perak Border and the 10th (Malay) Regiment facing North Kelantan. In February 1970 the 8th Regiment refused to carry out the executions ordered and broke away to form the Communist Party of Malaya (Revolutionary Faction) – CPM (RF). The leadership of the Second District of the 12th Regiment also raised objection to the purge and a long drawn out ideological struggle ensued. Eventually Chin Peng ruled that the liquidations were correct and the Second District also broke away and formed its own Communist Party of Malaya (Marxist-Leninist) – CPM (M-L) – just Northwest of the Betong Salient, leaving the mainstream CPM with the remainder of the 12th Regiment in the Betong Salient itself, the 10th facing Kelantan and a number of smaller 'Special Districts' elsewhere. Thus by 1974 there were – and still remain – three independent movements – the CPM (RF), then 260 strong, the CPM (M-L), 150 strong and the orthodox CPM, 970 strong in Thailand with about another 200 operating in Malaya – just under 1,600 in all.[18]

This split did not reduce the scale of violence, since the three factions vied with each other to prove their virility and to attract recruits. The CPM (RF) and CPM (M-L) were the least effective, relying more on the 'foco' tactics ascribed by Regis Debray to Che Guevara rather than on the patient Maoist build up of village cadres coupled with terrorist attacks on government officials, police and informers, as practised by the orthodox CPM. The terrorist incident rate in 1974–75 rose to its highest peak since 1958. Two senior police officers were shot down in the streets of Kuala Lumpur and Ipoh and 50 other policemen and soldiers were killed in the worst four month period of 1975.[19]

From 1976, however, government operations began to prevail, based on the familiar Special Branch techniques against the *Min Yuen* cadre organization. By 1977 the CPM organization was so much eroded that it became increasingly difficult for the guerrillas to operate in the Federation and the incident rate declined to a level below that before the resurgence began in 1968.

By 1982, however, there were still some 2,000 guerrillas in South Thailand (See Figure 27), about half of them Thai and half Malay-

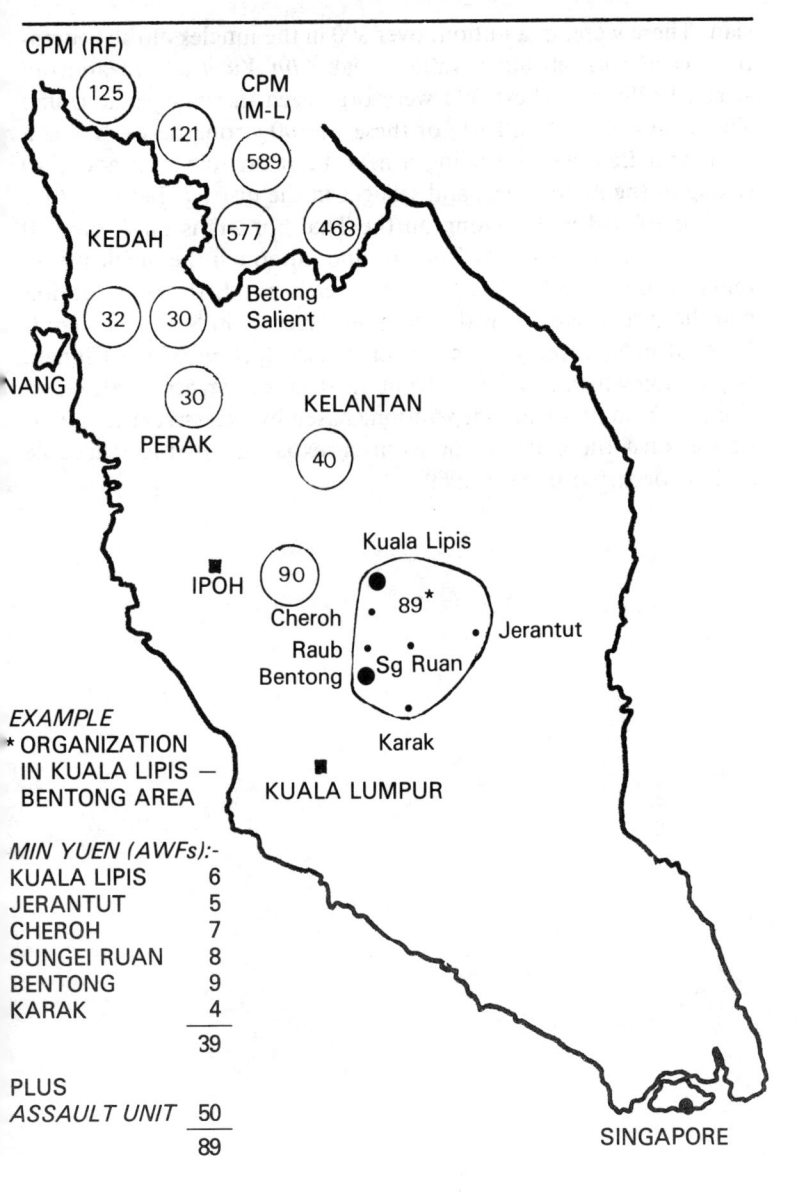

THE RESURGENCE OF GUERRILLA WARFARE IN MALAYSIA

CPM (RF) — 125
121
CPM (M-L) — 589
577
468
KEDAH
Betong Salient
32
30

NANG

30
PERAK
KELANTAN
40

IPOH
90
Kuala Lipis
Cheroh • 89*
Raub • • Jerantut
Bentong ● Sg Ruan
Karak
KUALA LUMPUR

EXAMPLE
ORGANIZATION IN KUALA LIPIS — BENTONG AREA

MIN YUEN (AWFs):-

KUALA LIPIS	6
JERANTUT	5
CHEROH	7
SUNGEI RUAN	8
BENTONG	9
KARAK	4
	39

PLUS
ASSAULT UNIT 50
89

SINGAPORE

MILES
0 — 50

Figure 27   Charted Strength of CPM Guerrillas in 1982

sian. There were, in addition, over 300 in the jungles of the Federation, each with an albeit rather weak *Min Yuen* organization in selected villages. These 300 were organized in six Assault Units. The biggest most Southerly of these was 90 strong between Kuala Lipis and Bentong, including a *Min Yuen* organization about 40 strong in the main towns and villages in the district. Bentong (not to be confused with Betong on the Thai border) is only some 30 miles Northeast of Kuala Lumpur and, although the incident rate remains low, and Special Branch cover is good, the organization and the threat remain, with numerous reserves in South Thailand. It could grow rapidly in the event of disaffection of the Chinese population which could arise from the strains of an economic recession, or from political exasperation caused by excessive discrimination against the Chinese, or from an explosion of racial trouble such as occurred in May 1969.

Chapter 17 The 1969 Riots in Kuala Lumpur

Race and Politics in Peninsular Malaysia

The riots in Kuala Lumpur in May 1969 had a drastic and lasting effect on Malaysian politics and in particular in mainland West Malaysia, the 11 states of Peninsular Malaysia. In the entire 12 year Emergency (1948-60) less than 12,000 people died including guerrillas, soldiers, police and civilians (see pages 188-9). In 1951 a total of 668 civilians and 504 soldiers and police were killed – the worst *year*. By contrast, within a *few days* in May 1969, it is probable that about 1,000 people died. Many people believed that the true figure was nearer 2,000.[1]

Even more surprising, however, is that this has been the only serious racial rioting since 1945. The racial mixture in Peninsular Malaysia must be one of the most explosive in the world – Malays just under 50 per cent, Chinese 37 per cent, Indians 11 per cent and others 2 per cent.[2] Two other factors made it especially explosive: first, the easy-going Malays had held onto most of the political power while the more industrious Chinese and Indians had thus far held the lion's share of both wealth and incomes; and secondly there have, ever since 1948, been constitutional special rights for Malays, not only to safeguard their political position but also to give them specific economic advantages to enable them to catch up with the more successful 'immigrant' races. These special rights, though generally accepted by the richer Chinese and Indian middle class for the sake of peace, were resented by the poorer ones who felt unfairly handicapped against Malays who seemed not prepared to work as hard as they did or to acquire the skills.

The historical basis for these special rights lies in understandings between the British and the Malay Sultans when the tin and rubber industries were rapidly expanded to meet the demands of Europe during the late 19th century. The tin industry had long been dominated by Chinese miners, and Malays had always preferred their traditional life of agriculture and fishing. The Chinese and Indians imported in large numbers by the British for the expanding plantations and mines earned much more money than the Kampong Malays so land reservations were established for the Malays to prevent them from being bought out. Later, the Malays were further compensated by being given preference for jobs in Government service. There were also restrictions on citizenship (since many Chinese and Indians intended one day to return home). When the 1957 Independence Constitution was being negotiated, these citizenship restrictions were relaxed in exchange for a continuation of the special rights for Malays.

Under Article 153 of the 1957 Constitution the King (in practice on the advice of his Government) can reserve for Malays such proportion as he may think reasonable of (a) positions in public service, (b) scholarships and training privileges or facilities and (c) permits or licences required for certain trades or businesses. Article 89 preserves existing Malay land reservations.[3] These provisions of the Constitution are entrenched against change. All remained in force in 1969 and, as a result of the riots, were greatly extended in favour of the Malays in 1971 as will be described.

Another source of racial resentment on both sides has been the issue of the national language and the medium of instruction in the schools. In 1957 the Constitution recognised Malay and English as the National Languages, to be reviewed after 10 years. The National Language Act of 1967 made Malay the only official language but laid down that English might be used 'where deemed necessary in the public interest' – e.g. in matters of law.[4] This did not go far enough for the more extreme Malays who saw any retention of English as giving an advantage to the 'immigrant races'. In July 1969 the Government announced its intention to enforce the use of Malay as the medium of instruction in all schools, one year at a time starting with the lowest primary forms and working through to the Universities by 1982. This was one more step in the constant erosion of the use of their own languages and of English in education which caused much discontent amongst Chinese and Indians, many of whom, as a result of the 1967 National Language Act, had already turned to more radical parties at the expense of the Alliance Government.[5]

The special rights and privileges for Malays, however, though on the face of it inequitable, have probably been a major factor in avoiding bloodshed because the Malays, while normally peaceful, polite and self effacing, can explode into a frenzy of violence like no other race, and it is significant that the word 'amok' is one of the only Malay words in worldwide use.

The Alliance

The principle credit for the remarkably low scale of communal violence from 1957–69 must go to Tunku Abdul Rahman for his vision and political skill in uniting the great majority of Malay, Chinese and Indian voters behind the Alliance Party. In the Municipal Election of 1952 (the first stage in the advance to Independence) he forged an electoral alliance between the United Malay National Organization (UMNO) and the Malayan Chinese Association (MCA) which was in 1954 joined also by the Malayan Indian Congress (MIC). Under their electoral agreement, for example, the Alliance would put up MCA candidates in constituencies with a predominance of Chinese voters and UMNO would encourage Malay voters to vote for the MCA and vice versa in Malay constituencies. By these means the Alliance gained a massive 51 out of 52 seats in their first General Election in 1955. The Alliance, later widened to include additional parties in the Barisan Nasional (BN), has held power without a break ever since, both in the Federal Parliament and, with rare exceptions, in every State Assembly. This has been crucially important because the Alliance Government has given the highest priority to averting grounds for racial strife; also because the UMNO/MCA/MIC electoral pact has meant that, in the main, electoral voting has not been on racial or religious lines.[6] The only major exception to this was in the 1969 elections with murderous results. Indeed, such racial strife as did occur before 1969 was generally unconnected with elections of any kind.

When Malaya became independent in 1957, the Tunku and his fellow Alliance politicians – and indeed the British policemen, soldiers, officials and businessmen who stayed on in the country – were less concerned about the jungle war, which had by then declined to a very low tempo, than by the prospect of an explosion of racial violence. There were fears that Chinese mobs, believing that with the coming of Independence the British army would no longer intervene, might try to overwhelm Malay police posts or intimidate Malay people to drive them out of their villages or urban housing areas;[7] or that the Malays, believing the police and the army to be on their side, might similarly try to drive out the Chinese and Indians. Since virtually all the armed uniformed constables and (apart from the British) virtually all infantry soldiers were of Malay race, this potentially had all the makings of a bloodbath. In January 1957 there had been an ugly incident in Penang, arising from a Chinese procession, in which four people were killed and 48 injured.[8] Over the Merdeka period in the latter part of 1957, however, the Chinese generally kept a low profile, the Malays celebrated with restraint and there was no trouble.

For the next 10 years, apart from minor clashes between small gangs of Malay and Chinese youths, in which only one or two of each side were killed in all, there was no lethal rioting with a racial flavour at all. There was, however, a taste of things to come in November 1967 in Penang when political demonstrations led to violence which spread to the neighbouring states of Perak and Kedah, and about 25 were killed and many hundreds injured.[9]

The predominance of the Alliance and the non-racial mould of Malayan politics survived until 1968. Up to then, parliamentary opposition to the Alliance had come from only two parties, The People's Progressive Party (PPP) effective only in Perak and the Pan Malayan Islamic Party (PMIP or PAS) whose strength lay in the predominantly Malay states of Kelantan, Trengganu and Kedah. The PPP, founded by the two Seenivasagam brothers (of Ceylon Tamil extraction) was socialist rather than racial but the PAS was avowedly Malay and Islamic attacking the Alliance for 'selling out' the Malay inheritance by sharing it with the Chinese and Indians.[10] The only other parties which had members elected to the Federal Parliament before 1969 were the Socialist Front (SF) - a coalition of the *Party Ra'ayat* (PR) and the Labour Party of Malaya (LPM); the PAP (see pages 282-283); and the United Democratic Party (UDP - formed by Dr. Lim Chong Eu, previously Chairman of the MCA). None ever got more than one (or occasionally two) seats or as much as 4 per cent of the vote except for the PAS which gained 9 seats in 1964 with 21 per cent of the vote.

The 1969 Elections

After Singapore left Malaysia in 1965 the PAP in Peninsular Malaysia renamed itself the Democratic Action Party (DAP) and cut its links with the PAP (the DAP has since drifted a long way from the PAP and from Lee Kuan Yew). The DAP in 1969 still stood for a 'Malaysian Malaysia' and, though it attracted few Malays, it drew a substantial number of Chinese and Indians from the Alliance, especially in Kuala Lumpur. Its main thrust was against the MCA, whom it accused of letting down the Chinese, not least in passing the National Language Act of 1967 and especially in accepting the enforcement of the use of Malay as the sole medium of instruction in the schools. Another new centre party which drew Chinese and Indian votes from the Alliance was the *Gerakan Ra'ayat Malaysia* (Malaysian Peoples Movement – hereafter 'Gerakan'), formed in 1968. This was inspired chiefly by two respected Chinese politicians, Dr. Tan Chee Khoon who had left the Labour Party and Dr. Lim Chong Eu, formerly of the MCA and UDP. Both felt strongly that the special rights for Malays and the language laws in the schools were inequitable for the other races. The richer Chinese businessmen stuck to the MCA and the Alliance because they saw this as the best guard against racial strife and a collapse of order but many of the smaller Chinese merchants were drawn to the DAP and Gerakan.

In the 1969 General Election there was thus a party or group of parties on either side of the main racial divide – the PAS telling Malays to abandon UMNO because it was 'selling them out to the immigrant races' and the DAP and Gerakan telling the Chinese that the MCA and MIC were 'selling *them* out to the Malay hierarchy'. Racial issues therefore became a major factor in the election for the first time.

Polling day was 10 May and the result was dramatic. Not only did the racial issues attract many Malays and Chinese to the two wings; they also undermined the whole basis of the UMNO/MCA/MIC electoral pact. In some constituencies with a Malay majority the UMNO candidate was defeated by a DAP or Gerakan Chinese candidate because the Malay vote was split between UMNO and the PAS. In the Selangor state election, for example, in the constituency of Ampang in Kuala Lumpur, UMNO (6,601) and PAS (3,560) polled 10,261 votes between them but the DAP candidate won with 7,634.[11] Worst hit of all was the MCA which lost heavily to DAP and Gerakan, causing great resentment amongst its UMNO partners who had mobilized the Malays to vote for the MCA to no avail. Similarly, UMNO lost seats to the PAS because the MCA failed to deliver the necessary Chinese voters to support the UMNO candidate due to the intervention of a DAP or Gerakan candidate.

The comparative figures for the 1964 and 1969 Federal Elections are shown in Figure 28.

Figure 28. General Elections, Peninsular Malaysia, 1964 and 1969

Political Party		1964	1969	Change
Alliance	UMNO	59	51	−8
	MCA	27	13	−14
	MIC	3	2	−1
PAS		9	12	+3
PPP		2	4	+2
DAP (PAP in 1964)		1	13	+12
Gerakan		—	8	+8
SF		2	—	−2
UDP		1	—	−1
Vacant		—	(1)*	
Total Alliance		89	66	−23
Total non-Alliance		15	37*	+22
Grand Total		104	103*	

* One candidate died during the election campaign so the election in his constituency was deferred. This seat is not included in the totals for 1969.

This result did not threaten the Alliance's ability to form a Government – in fact even less than it appears because unofficial candidates supporting the Alliance in the forthcoming elections in East Malaysia ensured a still greater majority in the Federal Parliament. Far more serious for the Alliance, however, were some of the simultaneous elections for State Assemblies. The Alliance had already lost the Kelantan State Assembly to the PAS some years earlier – the only State before 1969 without an Alliance Government. In May 1969 the Alliance just held Trengganu and Kedah but with majorities of only 2 and 4 respectively. Much more serious, however, were the Alliance losses to 'immigrant' parties in Penang, Perak and Selangor.

In Penang, Gerakan captured power with a landslide, winning 16 of the 24 seats but, since the result was unambiguous and there was in any case a Chinese majority on Penang Island, this gave rise to little racial tension. In Perak, the Alliance just failed to get a majority (19 out of 40) but, even if the PPP (12), DAP (6) and Gerakan (2) had joined forces it was most unlikely that the single PAS member would side with the 'immigrant' parties; but the Alliance did appear on the face of it to have lost its overall power and this led to celebrations, demonstrations and reactions with some loss of life – though on nothing like the scale of that in Kuala Lumpur.

In Selangor, then the capital state, the Alliance won exactly half the seats, and tensions rose dramatically during the next two days. The incumbent State Chief Minister, Dato Harun bin Idris, had comfortably retained his own seat and he at once approached Dr. Tan Chee Khoon, who had won both a state and a federal seat, to ask Gerakan to form a coalition with the Alliance. Dr. Tan declined, saying 'I have said many times that I will not sleep with Alliance Partners. Now, more than ever when they are castrated, how can I do so?'[14]

The humiliation of the MCA was intense, both in the federal and state elections and their leader, Tan Siew Sin, announced at a press conference on 13 May that the MCA, having been rejected by the Chinese voters in a democratic vote, would not participate in either Federal or State Governments. This was a tactical move to induce Chinese voters to reflect on the disadvantages of having no Chinese representation in government, in the hope that they would return to the MCA in the next election.[15] The announcement, however, caused further alarm and resentment amongst the Malays many of whom felt that the MCA had already let the Alliance down and was now trying to torpedo it. Some may even have seen the spectre of a total split with all Chinese and Indian members (including those elected

Table 29. Election Results in Three States, 1964 and 1969[13]

POLITICAL PARTY		PENANG 1964	PENANG 1969	PENANG Change	PERAK 1964	PERAK 1969	PERAK Change	SELANGOR 1964	SELANGOR 1969	SELANGOR Change
Alliance	UMNO	10	4	−6	22	18	−4	13	12	−1
	MCA	6	—	−6	12	1	−11	8	1	−7
	MIC	2	—	−2	1	—	−1	3	1	−2
PAS		—	—	—	—	1	+1	—	—	—
PPP		—	—	—	5	12	+7	—	—	—
DAP		—	3	+3	—	6	+6	—	9	+9
GERAKAN		—	16	+16	—	2	+2	—	4	+4
SF/PR		2	1	−1	—	—	—	4	—	−4
UDP		4	—	−4	—	—	—	—	—	—
Independent		—	—	—	—	—	—	—	1	+1
Total Alliance		18	4	−14	35	19	−16	24	14	−10
Total non-Alliance		6	20	+14	5	21	+16	4	14	+10

with UMNO support) joining the opposition, though there was at no time any actual risk of that. At all events, there was acute concern amongst both federal and state ministers that racial rivalries and resentments could explode into violence which could rapidly spread across the whole nation.

Dr. Lim Chong Eu, who had already been nominated by Gerakan to be Chief Minister of Penang, clearly felt the same and, after consultation with Tun Abdul Razak, was instrumental in a decision by Gerakan not to support any anti-Alliance coalition in either Perak or Selangor. This decision, which could have done much to defuse the situation, was unfortunately not announced by the Gerakan Secretary-General until the early evening of 13 May by which time the rioting in Kuala Lumpur was already beyond control.[16]

The Riots of 13 May 1969

The atmosphere in Kuala Lumpur was tense even before the election because, on the eve of polling day there had been a huge Chinese funeral procession for the burial of a young Chinese, allegedly Communist, who had been killed in a clash with police on 4 May in Kepong, a suburb Northwest of Kuala Lumpur. This procession, on 9 May, was originally restricted by the police to 1,000 people and to a route clear of sensitive areas, but left the agreed route and turned into a massive Communist-led demonstration of 10,000, which sang provocative songs outside such places as UMNO headquarters. The police had great difficulty in restraining retaliation by young Malays.

So feelings were already running high in Kuala Lumpur when the first election results began to come through on 11 May. As the pattern emerged, the Malays became increasingly bitter and resentful against all around them – the PAS for splitting the Malay vote (as at Ampang), the MCA for letting them down and the DAP and Gerakan for leading an 'immigrant' attack on the special rights of the Malays. Above all, they faced with alarm the possibility that the domination of Government by the Malay half of the population would collapse.

This was precisely how the jubilant Chinese and Indians who had voted for DAP and Gerakan saw it too. The Chinese and Indians made up a clear majority of the population in Kuala Lumpur. On the evening of 11 May there were spontaneous 'victory celebrations' by groups of young DAP and Gerakan supporters who toured the streets, and particularly through and on the fringes of Malay districts of the city and suburbs. They shouted taunts and insults at the Malays such as 'Malays go back to your Kampong', 'Aborigines go back to the jungle', 'why should the Malays rule our country', 'We'll thrash you now, we have the power' and 'Kuala Lumpur now belongs to the Chinese'. Some of them aimed gestures and insults at the women which were calculatedly offensive to Muslims.[17]

Meanwhile Dr. Tan Chee Khoon obtained formal police permission for an organized Gerakan demonstration on the evening of 12 May. The permit limited it to 1,000 but about 4,000 took part including Dr. Tan and other elected candidates. Smaller groups of exuberant demonstrators, however, broke away and continued the taunting of the Malays as on the previous day. One such group broke into the grounds of the Dato Harun's residence on the Northern outskirts of Kuala Lumpur and demanded that he move out of the house as he was no longer Chief Minister. (he was not in fact at home at the time).[18]

By this time, Dato Harun was under strong pressure from Community leaders to approve an UMNO counter demonstration for the next evening (Tuesday 13). Harun felt unable to refuse, as the Gerakan demonstration had been allowed. He was also an extremely popular politician, particularly with the young Malays, and he felt that he was best placed to control it. He therefore specified that it must be treated as a happy celebration since, despite the taunts, the Alliance did in fact still have the plurality, both federally and in the State. It was announced that the demonstration would start from his house at 7.30 p.m. on 13 May.[19] (see Figure 30)

The tension was such that throughout the 13th, many young Malays (especially the fanatical 'Corps of Rugged Youths') and young Chinese (led by the secret societies) had been arming themselves with *parangs*,[20] daggers, axes, iron bars etc., and hooligans of both races were filtering into Kuala Lumpur.

Serious violence began at about 6 p.m. A group of about 100 Malays were walking from the Malay suburb of Gombak in the North en route for the Chief Minister's residence to join the UMNO demonstration, and they passed through the district of Setapak, where many of the previous evening's demonstrations had begun. The Malays were carrying banners and shouting slogans and fights broke out on the streets between them and Chinese and

THE RIOTS OF 13 MAY 1969

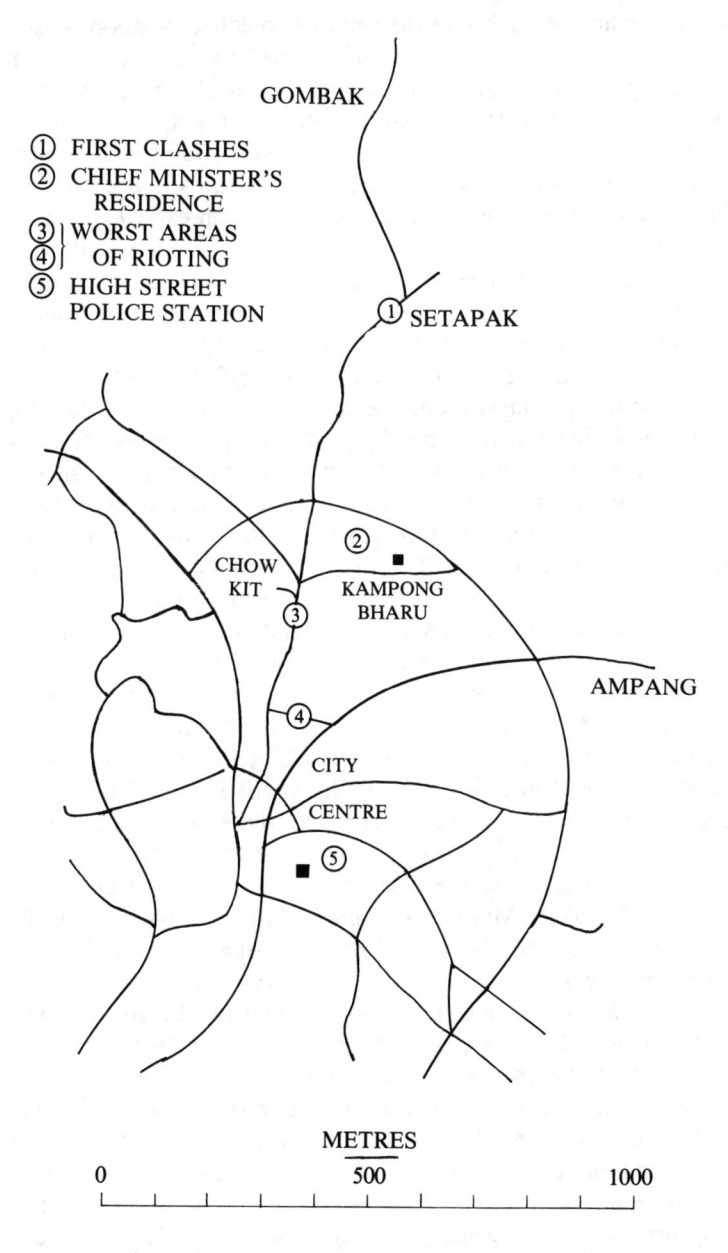

① FIRST CLASHES
② CHIEF MINISTER'S RESIDENCE
③ ⎫ WORST AREAS
④ ⎬ OF RIOTING
⑤ HIGH STREET POLICE STATION

Figure 30   Kuala Lumpur Riots 13 May 1969

Indians, who ran back into their homes to collect weapons – iron pipes, sticks and *parangs*. The Malays tried to get weapons from local shopkeepers who promptly closed their steel shutters. Most of the Malays returned to Gombak for their own weapons but a few cut through the crowd, some on motor cycles, to join the Malay demonstrators forming up outside Dato Harun's house, already numbering four or five thousand, many of them carrying *parangs* and other weapons wrapped in newspaper. Wild stories of what was happening in Setapak spread through the crowd, and grew with the telling. Taunts from a passing busload of Chinese and Indians set them off and the Malays ran amok. By 6.40 p.m. the first three Chinese lay dead beside the road, pulled off their vehicles and hacked to death. Malay mobs wielding their *parangs* were heading off to the Chinese districts nearby. Dato Harun, hearing the commotion, ran out of his house, jumped on top of a bus and tried to restrain the crowd but to no avail. At about 7 p.m. he went back inside and telephoned Tun Razak, who at once drove to the Prime Minister's Residency where he found the Tunku being briefed by a senior police officer. Though facts as yet were scarce, it was clear that the rioting was communal, with already some fatal casualties, and with the Malays in the main taking the initiative. Most of the rioting was thus far confined to the Northern districts of Kuala Lumpur around Setapak and Harun's residence but it was spreading fast, particularly to the principal Malay district of Kampong Bharu and the Chinese areas across the roads from it. The Tunku and Razak both wanted to go at once into these riot areas but were dissuaded by the police. Instead, they and some other ministers went to the High Street Police Station in the City Centre. At 7.20 p.m. Razak, as Minister of Home Affairs, ordered an immediate curfew throughout the state of Selangor. At 8 p.m. he authorized troops to be engaged.[21]

In all, 2,000 soldiers and 3,600 police were deployed. By this time, both Malay and Chinese districts were becoming fortresses with barricades at the entrances. The Chinese and Indians remained largely on the defensive at their barricades apart from a few secret society gangs. Groups of young Malays, however, ran wild, killing, looting and burning in the Chinese areas. For the Malays the curfew was difficult to enforce because many thousands of them had come into town from outlying villages for the procession and had nowhere to go. The police and army tried to cordon off Kampong Bharu as one large curfew area, with Malays milling about in the streets. In the Chow Kit Road and some other Chinese areas, however, people were confined to their houses and this gave rise to one of the accusations that the Malay soldiers were not impartial, for many Chinese houses were set on fire and their occupants were shot dead by troops as 'curfew breakers' when they ran out into the street.[22]

All the troops initially deployed were from the Malay Regiment which is 100 per cent Malay (though later some of them were replaced by the multiracial Federation Regiment). There is little doubt that some of the Malay soldiers and policemen were more than ready to shoot Chinese and Indians, and less than ready to restrain or fire upon the rampaging Malays. In mitigation it must be said that much of the taunting during the 11th and 12th had been directed at the police, but the Malay predominance in the ranks of the police and the infantry is a factor which must be borne in mind, and is always in the minds of the Indians and Chinese.

The worst of the rioting burned itself out during that first night, 13/14 May. By that time Kuala Lumpur was under *de facto* martial law,[23] and the number of dead had probably run into four figures, the great majority of them Chinese.

Parliamentary Government Suspended

On 14 May a State of Emergency was declared. Though sporadic violence continued for some days in Kuala Lumpur and spread into Perak and a number of other states, none of it approached the scale of that on the night of the 13/14. Nevertheless tension remained high in Perak and Penang and to a lesser extent in Malacca and other states where the Alliance had suffered heavy losses, and, of course, also in Selangor. Indeed, in a majority of State Assemblies the Alliance had fallen from predominance to at best a precarious balance. There was a deep feeling of insecurity amongst the Malay population and Kuala Lumpur had shown how easily they could be provoked into running amok. The Federal Ministers were still extremely worried that the whole country could explode into civil war.

After two days of agonised discussion they decided to declare a new emergency and to suspend parliamentary government indefinitely, a contingency for which the Constitution had always allowed. Federal and State Assemblies and Executive Councils were suspended on 16 May and a National Operations Council (NOC) set up to rule the country by decree until further notice.

The Tunku appointed Tun Razak as Director of Operations to preside over the NOC, declining the position himself. Its members included the MCA and MIC leaders (Tun Tan Siew Sin and Tun Sambanthan) and two other Malay ministers, with the Chief of Staff of the Armed Forces, the Inspector General of the Police and two senior civil servants. Suggestions by Dr. Tan Chee Khoon of Gerakan and other Opposition leaders that it should be an all party venture were rejected.[24] At the same time, members were nominated for State Operations Councils to govern the states in place of the suspended State Executive Councils.[25]

The NOC had much of the flavour of a military government and the daily assessments and requests of its police and military members were nearly always accepted.[26] In practice Tun Razak exercised almost dictatoral powers for the next 1½ years as Director of Operations through a structure of National, State and District Operations Councils reminiscent of the State and District War Executive Committees (SWECs and DWECs) during the 1948–60 Emergency. The curfew was lifted in mid June (though it remained in force in the border areas because of the resurgency of Communist guerrilla activity described in the previous chapter). There was one more serious outbreak of violence in Kuala Lumpur between Malays and Indians on 28 June in which five people were killed,[27] but generally the NOC managed to keep the peace until it judged it safe to restore parliamentary government in 1971.

Chapter 18 Malaysia's New Economic Policy and Future Prospects

The Creation of a National Front

In January 1970, Tun Razak set up a National Consultative Council of 66 members drawn from all parties except the DAP (which put up a candidate who was in detention and refused to participate when he was rejected). Its task was to seek ways of strengthening racial harmony to provide a secure base for restoring parliamentary democracy. In August 1970, with the Council's approval, the NOC decreed a strengthening of the Sedition Act of 1948 to prohibit the discussion of sensitive issues by making it an offence to attack or challenge certain fundamentals of the Constitution in public; e.g. to advocate the suspension, alteration or abolition of the laws relating to the powers of the Sultans, citizenship, the national language (Article 152 of the Constitution), or the special rights enjoyed by Malays (Article 153).[1] The effect of this was to separate these sensitive issues from the electoral process so that opposition parties like the DAP were legally barred from raising them and the 'ultras' and the PAS were deprived of the need to defend them.

On 21 September 1970 Tunku Abdul Rahman retired as Prime Minister, exhausted and depressed by the collapse of the racial harmony which had been the primary aim of his political life. At the same time he published a book saying that he had passed from being the happiest to the unhappiest Prime Minister in the world. For the riots, he blamed the opposition parties of both wings (DAP, Gerakan and PAS) and the Communist Party (perhaps exaggerating the effect of their funeral march the day before polling day) concluding that 'May 13 is a lasting reminder to us all how dangerous it can be to disregard the Constitution and to play about with the sensitivities, traditions and customs of the various races, especially in our highly mixed society of so many races and creeds'.[2]

Tun Razak succeeded him as Prime Minister and Parliament reassembled on 23 February 1971, 21 months after its suspension.

Razak defused the political situation further by widening the Alliance coalition. He began, with great political acumen, by arranging for the Alliance to join as junior partner in a coalition with the Gerakan Party's overall majority in the State Assembly in Penang. He followed this a few months later by joining a coalition with the PPP in Perak. In September he achieved an even more significant success by reaching an agreement with the PAS to operate a coalition in both Federal and State Parliaments, including the Kelantan State Assembly where PAS were in the majority. He was criticised for applying pressure through control of the distribution of Federal development funds for use in the PAS - controlled State of Kelantan but thereafter the Alliance had a share in that Government and now, with its coalition in Perak and Pahang, in every State Government. On 1 January 1973 the PAS leader, Dato Mohammed Asri, joined the Federal Cabinet as Minister for Land Development.[3] The fruits of this political bargaining were that UMNO entered the 1974 Elections as senior partner in a new grouping consisting of 6 political parties in the National Front (*Barisan Nasional* - BN)

Figure 31. General Elections Peninsular Malaysia, 1969 and 1974[4]

Party		1969	1974	Change
BN:	UMNO	51	61	+10
	MCA	13	19	+6
	MIC	2	4	+2
	PAS	12	14	+2
	PPP	4	1	−3
	Gerakan	8	5	−3
Total Alliance*/BN		66*	104	*UMNO, MCA, MIC
Opposition:	DAP	13	9	−5
	Pekamas	—	1	+1
Total Opposition		37†	10	†including PAS, PPP and Gerakan
Grand Total		103	114	

which swept the board. In Peninsular Malaya the number of Federal seats had been raised to 114 of which the BN won 104 (compared with the Alliance's 66 in 1969). The only opposition members elected were 9 for the DAP and 1 for *Pekemas*, a breakaway Party from Gerakan led by Dr. Tan Chee Khoon.

This new coalition affected the fortunes of the parties within the BN; PPP and Gerakan lost ground whereas UMNO, MCA and MIC all regained it. Of the 40 seats in East Malaysia (Sabah and Sarawak) the BN parties won 31, giving them an overwhelming majority of 135 to 19 in the Malaysian Federal Assembly and they retained control of all the State Assemblies. They won every seat in Kelantan, Pahang and Perlis and better than two thirds majorities in all the others.[5] This new multiracial coalition left the opposition weak and divided with the UMNO-dominated BN in a position as powerful as that of Tunku Abdul Rahman's Alliance in the 1950s and 1960s.

In 1976, in the wake of this astounding triumph of political cobbling, Tun Razak died quite unexpectedly and Dato Hussein Onn became Prime Minister. In a surprise move he invited Dr. Mahathir bin Mohamad, generally regarded as an 'ultra', to become his Deputy Prime Minister.

On 16 December 1977, following a factional struggle in Kelantan and growing friction between PAS and UMNO, the PAS left the BN and went back into opposition. Despite this, however, the BN retained a majority of 131 to 23 in the 1978 elections, the PAS retaining only 5 seats, with 15.5 per cent of the vote. The DAP share rose to 16 seats with 19.2 per cent of the vote, but the BN, with 57.5 per cent of the vote held 85 per cent of the seats.[6]

The New Economic Policy

In parallel with his successful restoration of Malay dominance in politics, Tun Razak embarked upon a far-reaching transference of economic power to the Malays or to Government-controlled Malay institutions with his New Economic Policy (NEP).

The Constitutional special position of the Malays had not led to much material prosperity. The Chinese and Indians were still twice as well off as the Malays and the 1970 Census Report revealed that the mean monthly income of Malay households was 179 Malaysian dollars compared with 387 for the Chinese and 310 for the Indians.

This was because nearly 70 per cent of those Malays officially classed as gainfully employed earned their living from some form of agriculture, usually in uneconomic small holdings, using traditional methods, short of capital and often in debt to Chinese and Indian moneylenders. Moreover 90 per cent of all households where the income was below 100 dollars per month were in rural areas where the majority of the population was Malay.[7]

As part of the NEP, Razak introduced the concept of the *Bumiputras* (literally 'sons of the soil' incorporating both the Malays and other indigenous peoples but excluding 'immigrant races'). In 1970, the Malays owned less than 2 per cent of the limited companies in Peninsular Malaysia.[8] Taking the Malaysian economy as a whole, the *Bumiputras* controlled 3 per cent of the corporate sector, Chinese and Indians 37 per cent and foreigners 60 per cent.[9] The foreign share was particularly dominant in rubber, oil palm and tin-mining.

Tun Razak launched his NEP in 1971 with the ambitious target of bringing about *Bumiputra* ownership of 30 per cent of the share capital of all private enterprises by 1990, a further 40 per cent to be held by other Malaysians of any race and 30 per cent by foreign investors.[10] It was envisaged that these percentages would be achieved over the years out of economic growth and not by disinvestments. The Government had no wish to frighten away foreign investors.

Since there was clearly no question of Malay farmers or fishermen or civil servants or even the relatively few Malay millionaires raising this vast amount of capital, the bulk of it was initially found from a central bank, the Bank Bumiputra, which raised its capital in the normal way by borrowing and by attracting investment including government investment. Other government agencies were MARA (the successor to the Rural and Industrial Development Agency) and PERNAS (*Perbadanam Nasional*), a state trading organization which now controls a long list of enterprises. Both of these were established in the 1960s, but have been greatly expanded since 1971. More recently a very large Government-owned unit trust was set up, *Permodalan Nasional Berhad* (not to be confused with PERNAS above) in which Malays, who had traditionally preferred to invest in land and property, were encouraged to invest indirectly in equity shares.

In 1975 the MCA set up a Chinese central organization, the Multipurpose Holdings Berhad (MHB) which was able to acquire major shareholdings or control of foreign companies and also to provide managerial, technical and financial resources to make small Chinese businesses more modern and competitive. Most Chinese firms have traditionally been small sole-proprietorships or partnerships, many of them family based.[11]

One of the earliest aims of the Government was to 'repatriate' the foreign-owned rubber and oil-palm plantations, by first acquiring a substantial shareholding with representation on the Board and then acquiring a majority shareholding. A good example of this was the take-over of Guthries, in which they had by 1980 acquired a 25 per cent share. In 1981, Guthries' sold their trading arm, Guthrie Berhad, to the MHB and *Permodalan* began negotiations with some of the larger institutional shareholders (including two Singapore banks and the M and G unit trust group). In a four hour 'dawn raid' in the London Stock Exchange on a Monday (7 September 1981) they acquired these shares plus enough others (mainly from small blocks held by Malaysians) to give them the requisite majority holding.[12] Then in June 1982, having already 'repatriated' the estates of Dunlop and Barlow's, they acquired a majority holding in the last of the major British plantations, Harrisons and Crosfield. A year later, in June 1983, the *Bumiputras* (including government institutions holding shares on their behalf) had raised their share of the equity in companies incorporated in Malaysia to 15 per cent (halfway to their target), the Chinese and Indian share having also climbed slightly to 37 per cent and the foreign share falling to 45 per cent.[13]

Another means of gaining managerial control, if not financial ownership, was by the practice of the Government taking 'management shares' in foreign companies. When oil and natural gas were discovered in territorial waters, a monopoly state-owned corporation, PETRONAS, was set up in 1974, with sole right (other than for foreign firms granted direct permission from the Prime Minister) to the refining, processing and manufacturing of petroleum and petro-chemical products. In 1975 all companies *marketing* such products (including existing subsidiaries of the multinational oil companies) were required to issue 'management shares' to PETRONAS representing one per cent of the firms paid-up capital but each management share carried the equivalent voting rights of 500 ordinary shares. PETRONAS thus gained effective control with very little investment. Razak's declared aim was to force the companies to give Malays a greater share in the profitable retailing of petrol.[14]

In a more general setting, new foreign firms can sometimes only obtain business licences if a stated proportion of the capital is owned by a Malaysian institution and this normally means a *Bumiputra* institution. In practice, what firms often do is to 'lend' up to 70 per cent of their capital to a *Bumiputra* institution or to a Malay individual or corporation, the loan to be repaid with interest in the form of 'work' provided by Malay directors and others on the company's payroll so that the loan is gradually converted over the years to Malay ownership.

This may also overcome another restriction often applied to the granting of a new licence. Under the Industrial Coordination Act of 1975, every enterprise engaged in manufacturing of any kind requires a licence from the appropriate ministry and the Minister can attach any conditions he considers to be in the national interest. These conditions may require that the work force must contain at least 30 per cent *Bumiputras* – or sometimes the percentage proportional to the population (e.g. 50 per cent in West Malaysia) – at every level including managerial levels. Moreover, the licence can be revoked at any time if these conditions are not fully met. The primary targets for this Act were established foreign or Chinese firms which had in the past failed to give Malays an increased share either in total employment or in the better paid jobs.[15]

Another condition which has affected the Chinese businessman for many years is that licences to start a new business in certain fields may be granted only to *Bumiputras* (e.g. operating a taxi firm) and in others the ministry will insist on at least a stated proportion of those licences going to *Bumiputras*.

These two provisions led to an abuse which bedevilled and to some extent still bedevils Malaysian society – the 'Ali-Baba' system, whereby a Chinese ('Baba') who wants to start a business will find a Malay ('Ali') who is willing for it to be registered in his name in exchange for a lump sum or salary but leaves the Chinese to run the business. This can be extended to larger businesses in which the required proportion of the directors are 'Alis', receiving a salary for doing no work. Some retired politicians or officials, for example, may have as many as 20 directorships, with salaries which they do nothing to earn.

Chinese and Indian businessmen, big and small, are both cynical and philosophical about the 'Ali-Baba' system. The majority of their professionally qualified people are Chinese and Indians and they are content, provided that these people are left free to run the business without interference. The salary of the dormant *Bumiputra* partners is an accepted form of 'tax' which is small in relation to other taxes and to the profit which they hope to make. They would rather pay this 'tax' than be denied the chance to operate in a country where they see good profits to be made, or to see those profits destroyed by another explosion of violence by frustrated Malays.

BN politicians claim that, by gaining managerial experience, Malays will in the long run acquire the skills to run such businesses themselves. The proportion of Malay managers has increased considerably since 1971. Though there is an encouraging trend, it may give a false impression as companies, both foreign and Chinese, have been obliged to take on more than they would choose. Many Chinese businessmen have little confidence in Malay managers (higher, middle or lower) and prefer to keep them out of the way to let the Chinese get on with the business, content to pay the 'tax' of the Malay managers' salaries. Nevertheless there are now Malays to be found at every level, managerial, administrative and technical, in most businesses, sometimes developing high degrees of skill. Their performance has improved markedly over the last few years. They can generally earn more, often for a lot less work, in these roles in commerce and industry than they could in the Civil Service. Article 153 of the 1957 Constitution specified a quota of 4 Malays to each non-Malay in government service recruiting and this still stands, but, though Malays still predominate in the lower ranks, their proportion in the public service appointments requiring professional qualifications is well below their 50 per cent proportion of the population as a whole.[16]

Dr. Mahathir

In July 1981 Dato Hussein Onn resigned and Dr. Mahathir bin Mohamad became Prime Minister with Musa Hitam as his Deputy. Their accession marked a major change of direction.

Dr. Mahathir was always a controversial figure. He was one of those who lost his seat in 1969 to the PAS and he accused the MCA of treachery to the Alliance by encouraging Chinese voters to vote

PAS in order to exclude him, as a leading 'ultra', from the Government. Later, he publicly condemned the Tunku's leadership, accusing him of constant capitulation to the Chinese, upon which Mahathir was disowned by Razak and expelled from UMNO.[17] He was, however, readmitted in 1972, made a Minister in Razak's Government in 1974, became Hussein Onn's Deputy in 1976 and Prime Minister in 1981.

This is all the more surprising as he had written a highly controversial book, *The Malay Dilemma*, first published in 1970, which set out to show that the Malays were inferior in worldly terms to the Chinese and Indians for historical, environmental, social and genetic reasons and must always lose in open competition against them. The book was immediately banned and remained banned until shortly after he became Prime Minister in 1981.

His thesis was that the Malay race had become soft as a result of living for many centuries with unlimited access to fertile, well watered land, protected from invasion and mass migration by the jungles, swamps and mountains, with excellent (river) communications, free from famine, pestilence and extremes of climate, able to provide all the food, timber etc. they needed with an average of two months work per year. By contrast the Chinese and Indians, bred and refined by centuries of hardship ensuring survival of the fittest, were hard, industrious and ambitious, with strong clan and family cohesion.

He also (as a qualified medical doctor) drew attention to the Islamic Malay customs of marriage, whereby mating with close cousins was positively encouraged. Since it was regarded as shameful not to marry, the weaklings or idiots of the family were mated with those of another family, to produce idiots, who survived in the soft environment to breed more idiots. This put the Malays at a further disadvantage against the Chinese and Indians who had traditionally powerful safeguards against interbreeding.[18]

He further drew attention to the Malay character as influenced by Islamic philosophies. Malays were not money conscious, were inclined to spend rather than save and were forbidden by Muslim tradition to lend on usury but not forbidden to borrow, so many became heavily in debt to non Muslim Chinese and Indians.[19]

He condemned the British for importing the Chinese and Indian immigrants, and later, in the breakneck haste of Malayanization, for allowing British investments to be taken over by Malaysians as of right so that the Chinese, with their business acumen, their banks, their family ties and their personal wealth, 'in the mad scramble which followed ...... won hands down'. The Chinese therefore 'almost completely replaced the British business circles which used to control Government contracts'.[20]

He said that there never was true racial harmony, only accommodation, tolerance and lack of inter-racial strife; and that Independence was achieved in the honeymoon of inter-racial cooperation brought about by the Tunku's Sino-Malay coalitions in the elections of 1952 and 1955.[21]

His conclusion from this analysis was that the Malays' inferiority and the inequities following from it could only be fairly compensated by artificially handicapping the Indians and Chinese. He condemned many of the effects of the special rights but still considered them justified.

> 'Everyone knows that more often than not these Malay directors have neither a single cent invested, nor probably have they the personal capacity to contribute to the all-important job of making profits for the company. Everyone knows that some of these Malays are merely selling their names .... But everyone also knows that there is no alternative if the Malays are to get acquainted with the nerve centres of big business rapidly, as they must, if the gap between them and the non-Malays is not to be permanent'.[22]

He gave a similar justification for the Ali-Baba business but said that, despite it all, 'for every step forward that the Malays make in the economic field other races make ten'.[23] So, both as regards the Malays congenital weaknesses and the remedies, he appeared to make an analysis verging on despair. It is therefore no surprise that the book was banned.

As a Minister, and as Prime Minister, Dr. Mahathir has shown great administrative ability and shrewd political judgement. Within 9 months of assuming office he called a General Election (22 April 1982) and secured 132 of the seats for the BN, one more than in the previous election, leaving the opposition in disarray with only 22 seats. He cut some of the ground from under the feet of PAS by recruiting into his Government Anwar Ibrahim, the leader of the Muslim Youth Movement, (ABIM), whose advocacy of applying an Islamic style of moral code to the whole Malaysian population had gathered an enthusiastic response from the younger 'ultras'.

Like Dr. Mahathir, Anwar Ibrahim has been highly critical of the failure of the NEP to improve the lot of the poor Malays, arguing that it benefits only a few, 'who are probably not even competent to run a business'. He has also deplored the racial aspects of the NEP, believing that the poor Chinese and Indians have as much right to improvement as poor Malays.[24]

Dr. Mahathir is the first Malaysian Prime Minister who did not receive a British education. His desire to shake complacent and paternalistic British attitudes was reinforced by the Malaysian Government's embarrassment and distress at the British discontinuance in 1980 of subsidized University places for foreign students.[25] He was unimpressed by the poor input of British investment in comparison with that of Japan, Singapore, Australia and other countries; he was particularly annoyed at the accusation by some people in the City of London, and in the British press, that the take-over of Guthries (for whose shares they paid what some regarded as higher than market price in a long-expected take-over bid) had been a form of nationalization. He ordered that British goods should not be bought unless they were at least 10 per cent cheaper than others, and advised Malaysians to look to Japan, South Korea and Singapore as models rather than to Britain.[26] This 'Look East' policy was aimed to inspire a stronger work ethic than that in modern Britain and to correct the automatic assumption amongst many Malaysians that 'Britain is best'.

Early in 1983 relations with Britain began to improve and Dr. Mahathir paid a successful visit to London. Perhaps most encouraging of all is that Lee Kuan Yew, who has always preferred dealing with strong 'ultras' who can carry Malay opinion with them rather than weak compromisers, gets on extremely well with Dr. Mahathir.

Economic and Political Prospects for Malaysia

Throughout the 1960s and 1970s Malaysia's Gross Domestic Product (GDP) grew impressively, even though not quite matching that of Singapore. This was accompanied by a high level of investment and personal saving (compulsory, as in Singapore) and by a steady expansion of exports (see Figure 32).

Figure 32. Economic Performance: Malaysia and Neighbours[27]

	GDP per head ($ US) 1981	Average Annual Growth of GDP % 1960-70	GDP % 1970-81	Exports % 1960-70	Exports % 1970-81	Savings as % GDP 1960	Savings as % GDP 1980	Investments as % GDP 1960	Investments as % GDP 1980
Singapore	5123	8.8	8.6	4.2	12.0	-3	30	11	43
Malaysia	1637	6.5	7.7	5.8	7.4	27	32	14	29
Philippines	781	5.1	6.1	2.2	7.0	16	25	16	30
Thailand	750	8.4	7.3	5.2	11.8	14	22	16	27
Indonesia	520	3.9	7.6	4.0	8.7	8	30	8	22
Hong Kong	4673	10.0	9.4	12.7	9.4	6	24	18	29
Japan	9700	10.9	4.7	17.2	8.9	34	31	34	32

In comparison with Singapore, Malaysia has the great advantage of rich natural resources (e.g. tin, timber, palm oil and, more recently, petroleum) and exports accounted for more than half the GNP in 1980.[28] Though the economy is vulnerable to any severe fall in the prices of tin and rubber, it is now sufficiently diversified to survive these. Since rubber is a labour-intensive industry, however, a fall in rubber prices or demand can cause considerable domestic hardships; this can cause tension and was a contributory factor in creating the climate for the 1969 riots.[29]

The easy flow of Chinese capital and know-how from Singapore also helps Malaysia, which is an attractive field for investment and trade for Chinese businessmen. The general prognosis of the banking community is that East Asia will still outperform the rest of the world in the 1980s, as it did in the 1960s and 1970s.[30]

Both Malaysia and Singapore felt the effects of the recession slightly later than the industrialized world. Malaysia's export earnings fell by 9 per cent in 1981,[31] and, though they recovered slightly in 1982, the growth of GDP in that year fell to 4.6 per cent. In 1983 it was expected to rise again to about 5 per cent.[32] The underlying strength of their economy should enable them to maintain a growth rate well above their rate of population growth, even if not as high as in the 1960s and 1970s.

The greatest threat to Malaysia's economy and to her internal security will probably arise from the education system and problems of language. The fact that the main medium of instruction in most primary schools and in all secondary and tertiary education has been Malay for all races means that English is taught as a second or (in the case of Chinese and Indians) a third language. This policy puts Malaysia at a disadvantage in competition with Singapore, where the great majority of the rising generation can speak – and trade – in English. Malay is of little use for international business except with Indonesia. The academic standards at Universities are also prejudiced by the fact that most of the teaching is in Malay whereas a large proportion of the books (an overwhelming proportion in technical subjects and Law) are in English. The Government has taken a number of significant measures to improve the standard of English at school and university level over the last few years but the overall effect of a diffusion of effort between two or three languages cannot fail to handicap Malaysian students in comparison with Singaporeans and Japanese.

More damaging still is the distortion of University admissions as part of the attempt to redress the inferior academic levels of the Malays. There is a calculated 'weighting' in the assessment of grades and in the admissions quotas and procedures which result in the anomaly that virtually every qualified Malay will get to University whereas only 1 in 9 qualified non-Malays will get a place. The proportion of Malay undergraduates rose rapidly, as was intended, and by 1982 had reached 50 per cent at the University of Malaya and 82 per cent at the National University. The Chinese are realists and they know that, unless the proportion of Malays receiving higher education does start to fill the backlog there will be an explosion of Malay resentment. Nevertheless, the effect has been that large numbers of far more able Chinese and Indian boys and girls, well qualified for University education, were denied it. The children of rich Chinese and Indians could go overseas to University but many others could not. This wastage of some of the best talent will not only have a cumulative effect on Malaysia's economic and administrative efficiency but will also cause increasing frustration amongst the *non-Bumiputras* which could make the racial mixture more explosive.[33] This frustration, along with exasperation over the preference which companies are obliged to give to Malays in allocating the better paid managerial posts, is causing a significant flow of talent, as well as of capital, out of Malaysia.

Politically, Malaysia is likely to remain calm unless some unexpected strain is thrown on the community such as a serious rise in unemployment or the emergence of a fanatical sect intent upon crippling or driving out one of the other races. The Communist threat is no more than a nuisance though this, too, could develop if resentment were to become more intense amongst the Chinese rural communities.[34] The CPM threat in urban areas is less likely to materialize so long as the standard of living continues to rise. After the 1969 riots a number of disgruntled urban Chinese got out of Kuala Lumpur and joined the CPM in the jungles in East Selangor and South Pahang but could not accommodate to the hardship and soon defected, some bringing in valuable information to the police as SEPs. During the 1970s, the police effectively separated the jungle guerrillas from their CPM supporters in the towns.

The strong domination of the BN Government by UMNO produces a political stability which the other BN parties accept, having seen the danger of a challenge to this domination in May 1969.

Political realism, perhaps combined with the fear of Malays running amok and the monopoly of guns in the hands of Malay policemen and soldiers means that the Chinese generally accept the wisdom of bowing to the reality of Government power, as their forbears had to do for centuries in Imperial China.[35]

Unemployment must remain a source of instability, as it is in any country in which the population is growing as fast as it is in Malaysia. The population has grown from 11 million in 1970 to about 14 million in 1983. Put another way, there are 120,000 extra people coming of age to seek jobs each year, in addition to those already unemployed. The majority of the unemployed are between 15 and 25[36] – the peak age at which frustration customarily explodes into violence on the streets. With 45 per cent of the population under 15,[37] this problem is likely to get worse rather than better. Ever since 1970, overtime has been restricted and the compulsory age for retirement (as in Japan) lowered to 55, but the most urgent need is to restore a high rate of economic growth to keep well ahead of population growth, as thus far it has. In a multiracial society recession is more dangerous than in other societies because of the cycle of recession – unemployment – discrimination – explosion.[38]

There was a sharp reminder in the second half of 1983 of the inherent delicacy of the social and political balance in Malaysia. In August the National Front Government, with its overwhelming majority in Parliament, passed 23 amendments to the Constitution. These included three which were highly controversial: one restricted the power of the King, as Constitutional Monarch, to withholding the Royal Assent for a Bill passed by Parliament for a maximum of 15 days, after which it would automatically become law; the second placed a similar restriction on the Sultans of the states in relation to their State Assemblies; and the third transferred the authority to impose a State of Emergency from the King to the Prime Minister. The King, after consulting his fellow-rulers[39] refused to sign the controversial bill, making it clear that these three provisions were unacceptable. This caused a Constitutional crisis.

Under the existing Constitution, any law 'directly affecting the privileges, position, honours or dignities of rulers' required the consent of the Conference of Rulers. The Conference met in October (in the absence of the King, who was suffering from a 'serious heart ailment') and rejected the proposed amendments.

In December the crisis was resolved in what was seen as a compromise by Dr. Mahathir. The King signed the Bill on the understanding that there would be changes in it and these changes were duly passed by Parliament in January. The power of the King to delay a Bill was increased from 15 to 60 days, and the restriction on the power of delay of State rulers was removed altogether – though both the King and the rulers gave a verbal assurance that their powers would not be used unreasonably. Regarding the third contested provision, the King retained his power to declare a State of Emergency but verbally undertook to do so only on the advice of the Prime Minister.[40]

The crisis had been a very real one, and the Malay community was split from top to bottom. Dr. Mahathir, backed by the Islamic fundamentalist Anwar Ibrahim, had summoned mass rallies to demonstrate support but attendance and enthusiasm were patchy. Some other ministers were seen to be lukewarm and many of the traditional Malays were positively alarmed, since they regarded the protection of Malay special rights as ultimately dependent on the power of the Sultans to restrain hasty action in the sometimes volatile political arena and above all to preserve the Constitution. Some of them voiced their fears of Malaysia becoming an Islamic Republic with a Khomeini at its head, while the supporters of the Bill spoke of their anxiety lest a future king might attempt to act as an absolute monarch.

As one senior cabinet minister put it early on in the crisis, the opposition to the government came no longer from the Communists but from a section of the Malay community who did not realize that if Malay unity broke down UMNO, the backbone of the National Front, would be broken and chaos would ensue, playing into the hands of the radicals who were trying to imitate the revolutionary example of Iran.[41]

With this crisis resolved, the risk of political collapse or of racial violence declined but it recalled the Tunku's reminder after the 1969 riots (quoted on page 303) of 'how dangerous it can be to disregard the Constitution and to play about with the sensitiveness, traditions and customs of the various races'. As the memory of 1969 recedes, the frightening image of Malays on the rampage will pass from the minds of a new generation of young people. Yet it could not be called a healthy form of equilibrium, based as it is upon an artificially weighted political dominance by the 50 per cent

Malay community, if that dominance were tolerated by the other community only out of fear of communal violence or of the guns of the police and the army.

The encouraging factor is that Malaysia's economic success and rising standard of living is building up a national spirit, encouraged by the national philosophy of *Rukunegara* launched to restore racial harmony and unity after the 1969 riots. So long as all the communities retain a realistic attitude towards the risk of racial violence and the horror that results from it, it will not occur.

Most Malaysians agree that the main threat of communal violence will come, not from the Communists or from radical Chinese or Indian politicians, but from the Malays.[42] After 12 years, the NEP has made less difference than was intended to the great majority of the poorer Malays. Malay ownership is thus far largely ownership by government institutions in the name of the Malays. The Government has felt obliged to maintain this as its primary method because some Malays, having received shares under the NEP, have sold them at a profit, usually to Chinese, thereby defeating the object. Meanwhile, the gap between rich Malays and poor Malays seems wider than ever and the appearance of a growing class of idle rich Malays, holding directorships or sinecures requiring little or no work, makes a bitter impression on poor Malays and some of them question whether the bad effects of the NEP may be outweighing the good.[43] If this proved to be so, the poorer Malays, exasperated by disappointed expectations, might search for a scapegoat and either turn again to extreme Islamic or radical politics, thereby upsetting the stability of BN dominance or, worse still, reach for their *parangs* as they did on 13 May 1969. This seems unlikely at present – but it seemed unlikely then.

Chapter 19 Singapore – The Social and Economic Miracle

The Race Riots of 1964

Singapore's success story has aroused great controversy. Its admirers point to the highest standard of living in Asia outside Japan, coupled with parliamentary government and social tranquility in a multiracial society. Its detractors say that these have been achieved by unacceptable erosion of civil liberties, by negation of parliamentary and trade union opposition, by detention without trial and by surreptitious denial of freedom of speech and freedom of the press.

Singapore's social and economic achievements since 1963 have been reminiscent of those of two larger island states which built their success on commerce, import of materials and export of manufactures – England in an earlier epoch and Japan since 1868 and especially since 1945. It is a tiny island, 22 miles by 12 miles, with no natural resources other than a harbour, and land on which to build several airfields. Its only major assets are its location, and its 2½ million able and industrious people (76 per cent Chinese) and for such a small country its growth rate has been phenomenal.

So have its housing and education programmes, its public order, health and sanitation and, in fact, almost any of the criteria by which good government is normally judged. Whether this justified the price paid in personal freedom, measured by liberal democratic standards, will be the subject of the next and final chapter of this book.

Singapore's beginnings as an independent state were not auspicious, as was described in Part I of this book. Though in material and educational terms it was ready for self-government and started down the road to it before Malaya, internal political strains and the strength of clandestine Communist activity set back the process. In 1963, on the eve of merger with Malaysia, it was touch and go whether Lee Kuan Yew or the Communist faction of the PAP would gain control. In the event, Lee Kuan Yew survived that challenge and has held unbroken power as Prime Minister, first of a self-governing dependency, then of a State in the Federation and finally as an independent nation. In the whole of his quarter of a century of power there was only one significant outbreak of public disorder – in 1964.

Singapore has never faced a racial problem remotely as difficult as that in Malaya because there was a natural and inevitable domination, both politically and economically, by one race, the Chinese. The small Malay minority (15 per cent) worked mainly in rather menial jobs, or in poor agricultural and fishing villages, many of them in the 55 small islands possessed by Singapore. When Singapore merged with the Federation of Malaysia many of them expected that the special rights for Malays enshrined in the Federation's 1957 Constitution would apply also to them. This, however, never was part of the agreement for merger and would never have been accepted by any Singapore government. When this became clear to the Malays there was considerable resentment, and this was further aroused in Malay language newspapers from the mainland, where the 'ultras' were still incensed by the attempt by the PAP to get candidates elected in the Federal Elections in April 1964 (see pages 282–283).

To clarify the position, Singapore's Minister for Social Affairs, Othman Wok, sent out an invitation on 22 June 1964 to 114 Malay organizations to meet him with the Prime Minister on 19 July. Over 1,000 Malays attended (from 101 of the 114 organizations) and Lee Kuan Yew spelled out his policy: that all Singaporean citizens had equal rights, regardless of race; and that there were to be no special rights for Malays, no job quotas, no special licences and no land reservation.[1]

On 21 July there was a demonstration by Malays protesting that, since Singapore was now part of the Federation, their same Constitutional privileges should apply. Exchanges of taunts and insults with Chinese bystanders on the streets developed into fighting in which two people were killed and over 100 injured. A curfew was imposed from 9.30 p.m. to 6 a.m. but rioting continued next day and the curfew was reimposed.[2]

Next day the curfew was extended all day except for two periods, 5.30–10 a.m. and 3.30–6 p.m. to enable people to get to and from work. There was, however, another major Malay procession to celebrate the Prophet's Birthday. In pursuance of their Confrontation with Malaysia, a number of Indonesians had clandestinely entered Singapore in small boats or by parachute and some of these had attempted to arouse the religious zeal of the more fanatical Malays.[3] At the same time the violence of the two previous days had brought out the Chinese Secret Society gangs. There were widespread riots in 12 separate districts and police fired tear gas.[4] The riots continued for 5 days during which 22 people were killed and 454 injured, 256 arrested for unlawful assembly and rioting and another 1,579 for curfew-breaking.[5] The curfew was gradually relaxed but kept in force at night (8 p.m. to 5 a.m.) until Sunday, 2 August.[6]

Tension gradually subsided but exploded again a month later when a Malay trishaw-rider was stabbed to death in Geylang on the night of 2/3 September. Rioting again exploded and spread for another 5 days and nights during which there were 212 separate incidents in which 12 people were killed, over 109 injured (of whom 24 were admitted to hospital), 240 arrested for rioting and over 1,000 for curfew-breaking.[7] The curfew was lifted on 11 September and there were no further incidents.

These riots were the worst and most prolonged in Singapore's post-war history with a total of 34 killed in the two five day periods of rioting, compared with 18 in the 1950 Hertogh riots (p. 73) and 13 in the 1956 SCMSSU and Middle Road Union riots (p. 132). They were, however, nothing like as bad as the 1969 riots in Kuala Lumpur (see Chapter 17). The initial explosions arising from marches and demonstrations caused relatively few casualties. In Kuala Lumpur there had thereafter been large crowds of Malays running wild through the Chinese areas, burning and slashing, and giving rise to some equally wild shooting. The rioting in all other cases, however, including that after the first few hours of terror in Kuala Lumpur, consisted primarily of widespread incidents, and it was small ranging gangs of rioters out for blood who caused most of the deaths. This appears to be characteristic of the racial rioting in the mixed urban communities of Malaysia and Singapore, on the rare occasions on which it has occurred.

One lesson particularly noted from the 1964 Singapore riots was the influence of the vernacular press, both Malay and Chinese. Some of the Malay newspapers, especially those published in the Federation, and some of the more chauvinistic Singapore Chinese papers, were highly inflammatory and the price of this in loss of life had a great influence in the much criticised Government measures to control the press, as will be discussed in the next chapter.

The Foundation of PAP Dominance

The political stability of Singapore since 1963 has been a product of the almost total dominance of the political system by the PAP since that date. The foundation for that dominance has been a grass-roots community organization which has probably never been equalled by any other political party in the world and should be widely studied as a model by political scientists.[8]

The burgeoning of this organization dates from the PAP split in July 1961 (see page 154) when the left wing faction broke away to form the Barisan Sosialis (BS). The majority of the PAP Constituency Party Branch Committees (35 out of 51) opted to join the BS.[9] This is no surprise, for it is in the nature of such committees to be manned by political activists on the fringes – the right extreme of right wing parties and the left extreme of left wing parties, because those are people with the most powerful motivation to give up their spare time to political work.[10]

The 35 defecting branches quite legally retained the premises, furniture, bank deposits etc for Barisan.[11] Many of the surviving 16 PAP branches lost some of their most active cadres. As well as rebuilding or creating new branches from scratch, the PAP launched a concerted drive to use the existing People's Association, with its network of community centres, to maintain contact with the public and gather their support. Though they were not unreasonably accused of using the Government structure of community centres for party political purposes, this crisis proved a blessing in disguise for the PAP.

This organization had been set up by the legislative Assembly in 1960 under the *People's Association Ordinance* as a statutory body with the Prime Minister as Chairman for the stated purpose of 'organization and promotion of group participation in social, cultural, educational and athletic activities for the people of Singapore to encourage a sense of national identification and multi-racial solidarity'.[12] For these purposes, community centres were set up in every one of the 51 constituencies. This organization was spurred by the 1961 split, and 103 community centres had been built by September 1963 rising to 188 by 1970.[13] This expansion was especially lavish in areas of recent resettlement under urban renewal plans, where grievances were high and where, in the September 1962 merger referendum, the number of blank ballot papers, indicating support for BS, was highest. In two constituencies of this kind, 14 and 15 community centres, respectively, were constructed by the Government, and only one or two in some 'safe' PAP constituencies.[14] Because they provided services and facilities which the people wanted (e.g. sport, radio servicing, flower arranging and dancing classes, newspapers, television and Kindergartens) these community centres, with two or three full time professional staff in each, drew people away from the similar activities offered by the BS.

Despite these activities, however, the BS still managed to win 13 of the 51 seats, with 37 per cent of the vote, in the 1963 General Election, so the PAP decided to extend its activities in 1964 by forming People's Management Committees to manage the community centre activities, made up of local citizens appointed by the constituency MP. The next year (1965) it formed Citizens' Consultative Committees (CCCs) in every constituency, whose members were again selected by the MP, taking advice from local community leaders. The role of the CCCs was 'to transmit information, make recommendations on the needs of the people to the Government, and keep the people informed of Government actions and policy in these matters.'[15] It was initially Government (and PAP) policy that members of the CCCs should not also be PAP members but this policy was gradually eroded as party membership increased, and as many of the more active CCC members decided to join the party. CCCs met their MPs at regular intervals to articulate demands for local facilities such as bus stations, drains and roads and also dealt directly with local officials of departments responsible for these services. It was a cardinal feature of PAP policy that the MP should ensure not only that grass roots grievances were transmitted upwards, but also that the CCC's were publicly seen to achieve a response wherever possible. If it transpired that the local MP had failed to get redress for a grievance which should have been redressed, he could expect short shrift from Lee Kuan Yew.[16]

At the same time the CCC, again led by its MP, was expected to be the vehicle for furtherance of Government campaigns such as the 'Keep Singapore Clean and Pollution Free' campaign. Another role was to resolve local disputes, especially those which might lead to racial conflict. In June 1969, for example, some of the Malay/Chinese tension spread across the causeway after the 1969 riots in Kuala Lumpur, leading to an incident in which Chinese from a neighbouring constituency had raided a Malay district; twenty people were slashed in the fighting and the Malays were planning retaliation. The CCC was swiftly mobilized to make house visits to calm fears and soothe tempers and managed to organize a friendly meeting of representatives of both sides on neutral ground to avert further violence.[17]

Since these constituency organizations were devised, the PAP have won every seat in every General Election (1968, 1972, 1976 and 1980) though they lost one by-election in 1981. Voting is compulsory and the positive PAP vote has averaged more than 75 per cent (see Figure 33). There are, of course, other reasons for their popularity as will be discussed later. The BS by contrast have been plagued by internal dissension and boycotted the 1968 election. They returned to the hustings in 1972, when they put up 9 candidates and attracted 4.6 per cent of the votes but won no seats – and have, in fact, won no seats since 1963.

The PAP did, however, lose one seat to the Workers' Party in a by-election in October 1981 by a narrow margin (653 votes) which was largely due to complacency. The seat (Anson) had been vacated by Devan Nair on his becoming President of the Republic. He had

Figure 33. Voting in Singapore General Elections[18]

Election Year	Total Seats	Won by PAP	Won by Opposition	% Valid Votes Cast PAP	% Valid Votes Cast Opposition	Remarks
1959	51	43	8	54.1	45.9	
1963	51	37	14	46.9	53.1*	* 37% for BS
1968	58	58	Nil	86.7	13.3	51 PAP returned unopposed
1972	65	65	Nil	70.4	29.6	8 PAP returned unopposed
1976	69	69	Nil	73.4	26.6	16 PAP returned unopposed
1980	75	75	Nil	76	24	

Note: Voting is compulsory. Spoiled votes (amounting to about 2 per cent) are not included.

won the Constituency in a by-election in 1979 with a majority of 86 per cent and it had been held by his predecessor also with a large majority (74 per cent). The PAP organization regarded it as a safe seat and overlooked the facts that many of the residents were threatened with compulsory eviction due to port development and that inflation had hit a temporary peak of 9.8 per cent.[19]

The winner was an Indian lawyer, J.B. Jeyaratnam, leader of the Workers' Party, for whom he had frequently turned in good election performances (e.g. 40 per cent of the vote against a senior PAP cadre, Fong Sip Chee, in 1976). He has, since his election, vigorously represented all opposition parties in Parliament, (who have, and have on average since 1968, obtained the votes of 24 per cent of the electorate). His interventions have been articulate even if, at times, ill-informed and irritating. Soon after his election, for example, he accused the PAP of corruption but was unble to substantiate the charge and Lee Kuan Yew made him look a complete fool in the subsequent debate. Jeyaratnam has been relentlessly harried by PAP members anxious to acquire merit, but he alone performs what is Parliament's primary function in a democracy – the public cross-examination of Ministers. His outspoken attacks go some way towards negating the common accusation that Singapore is really a one-party state. The defeat has also shaken the PAP so that they will be jerked into more conscientious attention to the grass roots, as they were by their narrow squeak in 1961–63, but for which they would never have succeeded as they did.

Housing, Health and Population Growth

Another crucial factor in holding popular support has been the PAP's housing programme. Singapore's population growth has

Table 34. Population Growth in Singapore[20]

Year	Population
1819	150
1824	10,683
1850	50,000
1870	100,000
1900	210,000
1921	418,358
1950	1,500,000
1970	2,075,000
1980	2,413,945

been phenomenal. When Stamford Raffles raised the British flag in 1819 the population was 150. Within 5 years it was 10,000. Thereafter it doubled every 20 years until 1921 and continued to rise to about 1½ million in 1950 and 2½ million in 1983.

In 1953-54 Dr. Goh Keng Swee, later to be Lee Kuan Yew's Finance Minister and Deputy Prime Minister, conducted a social survey on urban incomes and housing. Over 80 per cent of households, with an average of nearly 4 per household, occupied only 1 room, and 25 per cent of all households shared a room with another family. A further study in 1955 of Upper Nankin Street in Chinatown found that, of 1,814 inhabitants, only 3 households did *not* have to share kitchen, washing and lavatory facilities - the latter generally being open buckets, each shared by 20 to 40 adults.[21] As late as 1966, population densities of more than 110,000 per square mile were recorded in Chinatown.[22]

As soon as Lee Kuan Yew became Prime Minister in 1959 he abolished the Singapore City Council and its functions were taken over by the Central Government. In 1960 he formed a Housing and Development Board (HDB) and launched two five year plans for urban renewal, building 50,000 units in high-rise blocks by 1965 and a further 60,000 by 1970.[23] By 1972, 42 per cent of the population lived in HDB housing and 70 per cent by 1981, with a forecast of 75 per cent by 1986.[24] Water supply had been doubled by 1970 and electrical and other services developed in parallel. Rents were subsidized. A flat with two bedrooms, living room, bathroom and kitchen had a rent of about S $250 (US $125) in 1982 and its purchase price was S $30,000 (US $15,000).[25] In 1980, 55 per cent of all homes and 58.4 per cent of public flats were owned by their occupants and the proportion was rising fast.[26]

The HDB housing areas, though they have a high population density (65,000 per square mile in those built in the 1960s),[27] do not seem to have the adverse social effects which they seem to have elsewhere. This may be partly because Singaporeans can see for themselves that on such a crowded island there is no other way of having open space; also because great care and expense have been devoted to making best use of the space between the blocks, which are arranged in 'New Towns' each of 600-1,000 units (say 2,500-5,000 inhabitants), each with its own shops, community centres, playing fields, swimming pools, parking space, etc.

Another factor is that almost all those over 20 (and many others) will themselves have had first hand experience of the alternatives. They also observe the Chinese custom of extended families living together. Most flats have five rooms including kitchen and bathroom. They are small by West European standards but seem to suit Chinese family lifestyles. In one flat visited by the author in 1982 there were eight people of three generations aged from 74 to 8. They seemed to be enjoying a high standard of living in terms of food, household appliances, colour television, video films etc. They had three substantial wage packets coming in, with low costs for food and rent, and gave the impression of being a happy and lively family, finding enough room to do their own things at all ages; and they were well on the way to owning the flat.[28]

Future generations 20 years on, with the old shop houses of Chinatown no more than grandfathers' tales, wanting more cars and more living space, may well become exasperated with high-rise living. There is already some provision for this in a calculated range of quality of apartments for richer and poorer people mixed in the same new towns, with some building of detached suburban homes.

Meanwhile, Singapore has achieved one of the world's most successful family planning programmes. A population growth of 4.4 per cent per annum in 1957 had fallen to 1.3 per cent by 1975. Ironically, however, this is partly countered by the great improvement in public health so that the target of zero population growth rate is unlikely to be achieved until about 2025 by which time the population is expected to have reached 4 million.[29]

There can be no doubt that problems will arise before the end of the century, with the population above 3 million, working in high-technology industries producing a largely middle class society doing brain rather than manual work, with middle-class incomes and middle-class expectations in housing and consumer goods. A pragmatic people, however, and a pragmatic government which has brought about the revolution in the patterns of work and living in the 1960, 70s, and 80s, are more likely to solve their problems than most of the rest of the world.

Education

To meet the challenge of a growing population with rising expectations, Lee Kuan Yew has always given very high priority to education. This has certainly been a major factor in their success to date. In 1963, the Government spent nearly one third of its budget on education.[30] During the brief merger with Malaysia, Malay was a compulsory language but, since then, all communities have been required to study one second language and this is usually English. English is also increasingly becoming the medium of instruction, 90 per cent choosing the English stream at primary school.[31] For those entering University in 1982, 100 per cent of the teaching was in the English medium, other languages and literature being studied in the same way as for any other foreign language. Chauvinistic pressure for Chinese as the medium is now minimal since everyone knows that the English-educated earn twice as much as the Chinese educated and Chinese pragmatism prevails.[32]

Streaming begins at the age of nine and Lee Kuan Yew has said that ability to rise high can be detected in the first three years at school;[33] thereafter, every effort is made to extend and develop the brightest to their maximum potential. The top 6 per cent of students are screened for 'superschools' where students take a heavy curriculum in two languages.[34]

As in Malaysia, the Malays' performance in Singapore is far below that of the Chinese and Indians – only more so – while the Indians do as well as the Chinese. Figures for highest level attained for the whole population show clearly the Chinese/Malay pattern of achievement which are picked out from the population figures in Figure 35. The proportion of those with only lower secondary education or less is roughly in proportion to the population. Most of these are older people, whose schooling was finished (or non-existent) before Independence. The Chinese/Malay achievement ratio, however, rises to 2.64 to 1 in Upper Secondary schools (A level or equivalent) and to 8.68 to 1 in tertiary education (degree or equivalent). The Chinese/Indian ratio can be computed from the figures in the chart and are remarkably similar at every stage. The Indians, especially the older ones, have a marginally higher percentage at tertiary level, probably because more of the Indian immigrants were clerks rather than labourers. Another interesting ratio which can be computed from the figures is that the 'others' have a nearly 10 to 1 better rate of attainment of tertiary qualifications in proportion than the Chinese. This is because a high proportion of the 'others', amounting to 2.75 per cent of the population, are Europeans or Eurasians, most of them in managerial or white

EDUCATION

Figure 35. Highest Qualification Achieved Age 5 and Over (Singapore)[35]

Highest Qualification Attained	Population				Ratio Chinese/Malay	
	Chinese	Malay	Indian	Other	Actual	In proportion to population
Ethnic Populations	1,707,826	321,079	155,001	47,004	5.31	—
Highest Qualification:-						
Nil	464,612	85,210	32,534	4,300	5.46	1.03
Primary	552,123	118,850	50,696	8,493	4.65	0.88
Lower Secondary (O level etc)	155,837	25,890	16,424	7,385	6.01	1.13
Upper Secondary (A level etc)	75,440	5,371	6,708	7,069	14.04	2.64
Tertiary (University etc)	31,286	679	3,515	8,519	46.08	8.68

collar jobs. A survey of those under the age of 30, however, or a nationwide survey conducted in 30 years time, would show a very different picture.

The Chinese/Malay ratios of attainment shows depressingly little prospect of change. Figure 36 shows that, while 9 per cent of young Chinese who enter the English stream primary schools go on to get University degrees only 1 per cent of Malays do so and this does not take any account of the relatively higher proportion of Malays who attend vernacular primary schools, so this suggests that the Chinese/Malay ratio of tertiary achievement in the population in a whole (8.68 to one, see Figure 35) will increase rather than decrease. The same seems likely to apply to a lesser extent to secondary levels.

Education in Singapore is neither compulsory nor wholly free (though it is heavily subsidized). This is in keeping with the Government's policy of developing a self reliant meritocracy rather than a welfare state. The charge for primary school is very small (S $3 or US $1.50 per month) and even this can be made up for families in real need. Parents subscribe S $9 per month (US $4.50) for secondary education. The overwhelming majority of children do, of course, go to school but the Government philosophy is that it will be valued more if it is paid for.[37]

Savings and Incomes

As pointed out earlier (page 313), savings in Singapore in 1980 amounted to 30 per cent of GDP. Of this a large proportion was through the Central Provident Fund (CPF). In 1955, the CPF was launched as a form of National Insurance with a compulsory deduction of 5 per cent of earnings, to provide a reserve for bad times and old age. It is now a great deal more than that, the compulsory deduction being 25 per cent. As an alternative to saving it can be used by instalments for purchase of the occupants' home, whether this is private or public housing.

The pattern of incomes reflects the characteristics of a meritocracy with an average standard of living fast overtaking that of some European countries and likely to be amongst the highest in the world by the end of the century.

Figure 37 shows some *examples*, which may indicate the pattern of relative pay scales for those in full time employment, from top management to unskilled labourers.

SAVINGS AND INCOMES

Figure 36. Performance in English Stream Education 1973–81 (Singapore)[36]

Exams passed by those who started in English stream primary schools	Annual Average 1973–81 (%)			1981 (%)		
	Chinese	Malay	Indian	Chinese	Malay	Indian
Primary: PSLE*	80	60	70	95	70	95
Secondary: 3 O Levels	50	16	25	55	16	31
5 O Levels	30	6	12	34	7	16
2 A Levels (or equiv.)	12	1½	6	16	1½	5
University degree or equivalent	7	0.5	2.5	9	1	3

*Primary School Leaving Examination

331

Figure 37. Examples of Incomes, Singapore 1983[38]

Gross Salary including extras	S$ per month	US$ per year
Graduates (govt & private)	(a)	(b)
1. Investment Corpn Chairman	40,000	240,000 (b)
2. Bank Managing Director, age 35	20,000	120,000 (b)
3. Top Government Official	16,000	96,000 (c)
4. Senior Government Minister	14,000	84,000
5. Civil Servant, fast stream, late 30s	6,000	36,000 (c)
6. Middle manager, govt or private	2,500	15,000 (b)
7. Junior manager, govt or private	2,000	12,000 (c)
8. Graduate entry, engineer or civil servant	1,700	10,200
Non graduates (construction industry)		
9. Quantity Surveyor	3,500	21,000
10. Building foreman (age 30)	2,000	12,000
11. Secretary (A levels, age 30)	1,400	8,400
12. Clerk (O levels, age 30)	1,200	7,200
13. Semi-skilled manual worker	1,000	6,000 (b)
14. Truck driver	900	5,400
15. Unskilled labourer, male	600	3,600 (b) (d)
16. Unskilled labourer, female	450	2,700 (e)

The following comments refer to the letters in the table:

(a) Monthly figures are given in Singapore dollars, because Singapore scales are always shown thus. Annual salaries are converted to US dollars (at 2 to 1) to facilitate international comparisons.

(b) The ratios top management/middle management/semi-skilled/unskilled are fairly normal for an industrial country. Senior managers may also have perks such as company cars.

(c) Apart from the very top posts in commerce and industry (e.g. 1 and 2), higher civil servants (e.g. 3), are generally better paid than those of equivalent responsibilities in industry. There is, however, a constant drain to industry from the middle levels of government service, particularly the most promising ones (e.g. 5). At junior levels (e.g. 7)

government service once again generally pays better than industry.
(d) For a worker on a low salary scale living in a public (HDB) flat the basic expenses might be S $250 to S $300 rent per month plus S $150 per month for food. Those living with large families earning several incomes are not badly off by Asian or by average world standards.
(e) Unskilled female construction workers are a breed peculiar to Southeast Asia. Many of them are migrant labour (especially Hakka Chinese from Malaysia) and they do very heavy work for low pay.

Unskilled labourers keeping, say, a wife with young babies and who therefore cannot work would have difficulty in finding an HDB rent from a single labourer's income, so such families will probably have to live in traditional Asian attap (palm leaf) or zinc roofed houses (10.8 per cent of the total houses in Singapore in 1980) or in rooms in shop houses (2.9 per cent).

Not shown in Table 37 are the semi-employed fringe (to be found in most 3rd world countries), doing casual labour in the fields or urban areas, or scratching subsistence living as hawkers, smallholders or fishermen. They may earn as little as S $100 per month, or may handle very little money at all. These are amongst the 5 per cent without any formal education. Some are probably content with this life or at least resigned to it as inevitable. Many of them are Malays living a traditional life on some of the inlets or the small islands off Singapore.

Another important factor in Singapore is the number of guest workers who fill many of the unskilled jobs. In 1982 there were over 100,000 of these[39] who were not citizens of Singapore but had annual work permits. Unemployment in 1982 was only 4.5 per cent which the Prime Minister stated was the minimum possible unemployment in practice because it covered people between jobs or those who had made an application for new jobs before leaving existing jobs and there were in fact more unfilled vacancies than there were people registered as unemployed.[40] Apart from a number of those with skills which the Government knows it will need for many years to come, guest workers will not be permitted to naturalize. Others will not have their work permits renewed as and when Singaporeans become available to fill their jobs, so there need be no appreciable unemployment for the next 10 years. The aim is to have a homogeneous Singaporean work force by 1991.

'We can see what has happened in Britain, France and even West Germany, because they used immigrants – whether West Indians, or Africans, or Turks, or Yugoslavs – to do those heavy and tough jobs. They have inherited grave social problems. The Japanese, on the other hand, do all their own heavy and dirty jobs. They have no social problems or riots. Instead they have high productivity from their homogeneous work force'.[41]

With an overall shortage of labour and this guest worker hedge against unemployment, the Government has been able to take forceful measures to compel employers to modernize and automate their plants in order to keep competitive against Japan, Taiwan and South Korea. With this in mind, at risk of increasing inflation, the National Wages Council (NWC) gave three successive high wage increases in 1978, 1979 and 1980 – the increase in 1980 being 14 per cent to 18 per cent – about double the inflation rate of 8½ per cent in that year. From 1981 onwards, Lee Kuan Yew announced that, to cope with the recession, NWC wage increases would be based on increases in productivity.[42]

Singapore's Economic Performance

To sum up, the foundations of Singapore's economic miracle have been: political stability founded mainly on an outstanding constituency organization for local public information and feed back; a phenomenal programme of rehousing and public health; high expenditure on education with streaming from 9 years old to select and bring on the best to their maximum potential; shifting the medium of instruction to English as a world trading language; high capital formation fuelled by compulsory saving and the attraction of foreign investment; incomes high by Asian standards and rising fast in real terms, with differentials high enough to provide incentives; and the manipulation of wage rates, tax incentives and government investment to encourage industry to modernize and automate to keep ahead of competitors.

A good example of Singapore's economic management arose when the British announced in January 1968 that they would run down and withdraw their large army, naval and airforce bases by

1971. At this time British spending accounted for 25 per cent of Singapore's GNP and the bases employed 25,000 local people. The withdrawal also meant that Singapore would have to divert more of its resources to its own defence. The PAP's reaction was to inform the people of the crisis and arouse their patriotic support for the plans for dealing with it. These plans were the platform on which they called the April 1968 General Election and won every seat. They used this political mandate in August 1968 to restrict industrial disputes by passing an Employment Act and Industrial Relations (Amendment) Act, but compensated the workers by substantial increases in benefits and by increasing the employers' contribution to the Central Provident Fund.[43] The effect was to make a virtue of necessity; the industries and commercial activities which were rapidly developed to replace the work on the British bases proved far more profitable. This created a momentum of growth which has carried the economy through the 1974 oil price rises and the recession of the early 1980s.

By 1972, foreign or joint venture firms accounted for nearly 70 per cent of the value of Singapore's industrial production and 83 per cent of her direct exports, employing more than half her labour force, 12 per cent of whom were guest workers. Singapore in 1973 became the world's third largest oil refining centre (after Houston and Rotterdam) and by 1975 became the world's third busiest port (after Rotterdam and New York).[44]

Annual investment had risen to 43 per cent of GDP by 1980,[45] the highest in the world and, as recorded in Figure 32 on page 313, her GDP per head was the highest in Asia outside Japan, with whom Singapore was fast catching up.

Perhaps the most impressive of all the accolades for Singapore came from a survey of 45 countries published in 1981 by an American firm, Business Environment Risk Information (BERI). This survey had assessed, each year, the operational, financial and political risks for foreign investors, the 'free market environment' (i.e. propensity towards nationalist interference with foreign investments), and the labour force evaluation, adding up to an overall ranking order for 'Future Profit Opportunity Recommendations'. Out of the 45 countries (11 Asian, 14 West European, 10 North Central and South American, and 10 for the Middle East and Africa) Singapore was in the first four in each of the eight categories and top or equal top in five of them.

Singapore ranked equal top with West Germany, Japan, Switzerland and the USA in the overall recommendation for 'Future Profit Opportunity', defined as having the lowest risk on the level of capital committed; on remittable profits; on payments; and on operational procedures etc.

Singapore emerged top of the 45 in all the three forecasts of 'Political Risks' (1981) and 'Future Political Risks' (1986 and 1991). This was defined as the least propensity to risks to multinational corporations from external or internal causes leading to political unrest: xenophobia, nepotism, nationalism, corruption, wealth distribution and social conflicts etc.

Perhaps most significant of all was the 'Labour Force Evaluation' in which Singapore was again a clear first, her nearest competitors being Taiwan, Switzerland and the Netherlands. This was an amalgam of four separate gradings: the labour laws and their application; relative productivity (wages/output per day measured in SDRs); worker attitude (measured by lost working days and absenteeism); and technical skills (measured by skilled manpower compared to job market requirements). Singapore was below Switzerland, the Netherlands and Japan in technical skills though well above Taiwan, South Korea and (surprisingly) France. She was, however, a clear first in productivity and comfortably top of the aggregate of the four labour evaluations.[46]

BERI's gradings are made three times annually by a panel of 105 executives in companies, banks, governments and institutions worldwide, and are both qualitative and quantitative. Their principal clients, who pay very heavily for their reports, are some 250 multinational companies in the USA, West Europe and Japan. The 1981 report was a convincing endorsement of Singapore's social and economic achievements which have been the primary aims of Lee Kuan Yew's policies.

But have these aims been achieved at too high a cost in civil liberties and quality of life for the people of Singapore? Will the strain begin to tell in years to come? And are the seeds being sown for future social conflict? These are the questions to be tackled in the next chapter.

Chapter 20 The Price of Success

Is The Price Too High?

In 1976, Devan Nair, founder member of the PAP and subsequently President of the Republic, edited a remarkable collection of essays[1] which included a blistering indictment of the PAP by the Dutch Labour Party (DLP) tabled before the Socialist International (of which Singapore was then a member) in May of that year. The DLP began by quoting a summary of the indictment by the former Chief Minister of Singapore, David Marshall.[2]

1. We have a one-party parliament; every member of parliament belongs to the same party.
2. We have a law by which a person expelled by his political party automatically ceases to be a member of parliament; a provision unique and unparalleled.
3. The Prime Minister may appoint whomsoever he pleases to be a judge of the High Court.
4. Radio and Television are owned and run exclusively by Government; and are consistently used for political brainwashing. No opposing views are ever permitted.
5. No newspaper may publish without a licence from the Government; every newspaper can be closed forthwith by the Government without any explanation.
6. The Government can put its political opponents in prison for ever (on a two-year current basis) without trial.
7. The Government can deprive citizens of their citizenship.
8. Our children are prevented from entering institutions of higher learning in Singapore unless they get 'official suitability certificates'.

This was a formidable case to answer, coming as it did from a distinguished Singapore lawyer with a long record of public service. The DLP expanded on Marshall's accusations in a 10,000 word document, adding a number of others such as 'Suppression of the

Trade Union Movement'. Devan Nair submitted a detailed reply to these accusations in a statement to the Meeting of the Bureau of The Socialist International in London on 28–29 May 1976, documented with 26 Annexes, including answers to specific points and public statements and letters from Lee Kuan Yew and others. The full DLP indictment, with these replies, plus essays by Dr. Goh Keng Swee and others, were published in Devan Nair's book and provide the best available record of the arguments for and against the criticisms of the price which Singapore has paid for her social tranquility and economic success, enabling the reader to make his own judgement.

Detention and Dissent

The spearhead of the DLP attack was targeted on the Government's powers of detention under the Internal Security Act (ISA) of 1963 which it accuses the PAP of using to intimidate or lock up political opponents, trade unionists, journalists, intellectuals and other dissenters.

The ISA in Singapore was a transfer to the elected Government of the power already vested in the Government since 1948 under the Emergency Regulations; renewed (as the Preservation of Public Security Ordinance – PPSO) in 1955; passed on to a joint British-Malaysian-Singaporean Internal Security Council (ISC) in 1957; then to the Federal Government (incorporated in its own existing ISA) on merger in 1963; and finally to the new independent Singapore Government on the collapse of the merger in 1965. It is therefore not new. The point at issue is whether the power of detention without trial is still necessary in the 1980s or whether its existence and its use have become counter productive.

Under the ISA (as under its predecessors) the Government has the power to detain any individual without trial for a period not exceeding two years if it is satisfied that the individual is acting in a manner prejudicial to the Security of the State and the maintenance of public order.[3]

This power was undoubtedly necessary during the Emergency because of the widespread use of terror and intimidation of people who resisted the activities of the Communist Party, and especially of informants and witnesses, with the intention of making liberal forms of law and public trial by jury unworkable (e.g. see page 107).

DETENTION AND DISSENT

There was still a need for it during 1962-66 while Confrontation with Indonesia was in progress because of the links between infiltrators acting for the Indonesians and members of the Clandestine Communist Organization in Sarawak (see pages 278-282). It was perhaps coincidental that Confrontation coincided with the battle for merger – and with it the powerful Communist challenge to take over the PAP and the Government of Singapore in 1961-63. This was described in Chapter 8. These powers were used to detain Lim Chin Siong and other left wing leaders in 1956 (see page 130) and again in February 1963 (see page 159).

The opposition party (BS) claimed that between 1963 and 1966, 72 of its leaders and party cadres spent periods in detention under this Act.[4] The DLP Paper further accused the Government of arresting political activists under the criminal law and holding them on remand before General Elections,[5] so that they could be classed as 'criminal' rather than 'political' detainees. They quoted the example of the 1963 election (see pages 159-160). The Paper suggested that there were 40 or 50 political detainees still held in 1976 and, in his answer, Devan Nair gave details of 64 held on 22 May 1976, of whom 53 were held after a discovery of arms and ammunition in the possession of two CPM front organizations in June 1974. Only 11 of the 64 had been in detention for more than two years[5].

The DLP's evidence for its accusation that the Government used the ISA to neutralize free trade unions and to muzzle the freedom of the press will be discussed later in these two contexts.

The Government's argument is that the abuse of democratic freedoms by the Communists or their front organizations to subvert and dislocate the life and prosperity of the people continues all the time and must be kept in check. The Kuala Lumpur riots in 1969 and the resurgence of Guerrilla Communism had, certainly until 1976, provided evidence for this. The arguments for the powers to be retained are similar to those used for the retention of the power to detain terrorists or their supporters in Northern Ireland during the period 1971-76. Since 1976, however, the British Government has released all detainees and detained no more, though it has kept the power in existence for reactivation in the event of terrorism or intimidation getting out of hand, and this could perhaps be the answer for Singapore.

One further indictment in the DLP Paper is that, 'as a condition for release, the Lee Kuan Yew regime demands from detainees a public confession to some activity against the state and renunciation of their political beliefs'.[7] The PAP's answer is that the only requirement is 'to renounce and disavow the CPMs use of armed force, terror and assassination as means of securing political change'.[8] Lim Chin Siong did give such a renunciation on Television and was released in 1969. He is now a successful businessman.

In Western eyes these abject renunciations on television strike a distasteful note, but they are in keeping with a characteristic of the Chinese described on pages 181-83 under 'SEP', i.e. when they do decide to break with a movement or a philosophy, they reject it vehemently and completely.

The Trade Unions

During the period of self-government before independence (1959-63) the left wing faction of the PAP (later becoming the BS) made a concerted attempt to take over and use the trade union movement as a political organization and Lee Kuan Yew took equally determined action to prevent this. In 1961 the existing Singapore TUC was dissolved and two separate organizations emerged – a PAP-sponsored National Trades Union Congress (NTUC) and a BS-sponsored Singapore Association of Trade Unions (SATU). In 1963 SATU was deregistered and its leaders detained on the orders of the joint Malaya/Singapore Internal Security Council, under the ISA, as part of 'Operation Cold Store'. In this operation, 111 people were detained, including Lim Chin Siong (for the second time) and his Barisan colleagues, on the grounds that they were supporting the Brunei revolt and the Indonesian Confrontation to prevent the formation of Malaysia.

The eventual result is that now almost all trade unions are consolidated under the NTUC whose Secretary-General is a member of Lee Kuan Yew's Cabinet. Strikes are virtually unknown.[9] This has undoubtedly been a factor in Singapore's rapid economic growth and the flow of foreign capital to finance it. The question, as with every balance to be struck between 'total order' and 'total freedom', is whether these benefits for the many will build up such frustration amongst the few that dissent will explode into violence. There is little doubt that, at the moment, the great majority of Singaporeans would not wish to see their prosperity disrupted by British-style stoppage of production by strikes or by the exploitation of industrial disputes for political purposes.

Lee Kuan Yew's declared intention is now to move towards the Japanese system of 'house unions' whereby the management and union leaders in a corporation work together to increase earnings by increasing productivity and profits. 'The Japanese' he said to a National Day Rally in August 1981, 'have got it right'.[10]

Freedom of Speech and Freedom of the Press

Another power inherited from the 1948 Emergency Regulations was the Printing Presses Ordinance whereby it was unlawful to operate a printing press without a licence. The licence has to be renewed each year and can be revoked at any time. The DLP Paper accused the PAP Government of abusing this power in May 1971 to revoke the licences of two English language newspapers, the *Singapore Herald* and the *Eastern Sun*. At the same time, the ISA was used to detain four directors and journalists of one of the Chinese language papers, *Nanyang Siang Pau*.[11]

The Government's case was that both the *Eastern Sun* and the *Singapore Herald* had been receiving foreign funds which were provided for subversive purposes; and furthermore that the *Singapore Herald* had been inciting resistance to National Service and advocating permissiveness in matters of sex and the use of drugs. *Nanyang Siang Pau* was accused of stirring up Chinese racialism – and it was pointed out that the Jawi newspaper *Utusan Melayu* had been banned in 1970 for stirring up Malay racialism after the 1969 riots in Kuala Lumpur.[12]

All 3 of these issues are sensitive ones in Singapore: racialism for obvious reasons in a multiracial society; permissiveness especially over hard drugs which are far more of a scourge in Asia than in Europe or the USA; and foreign influence on the press. Foreign subversion is of particular concern to the Government because Singapore is a very small country with disproportionate influence in the world and is therefore a tempting target for any of its larger neighbours.[13]

Three years later the Government replaced the Printing Presses Ordinance with the Newspaper and Printing Presses Act of 1974 which, in addition to retaining Government licensing of printing presses, divorced editorial control from financial ownership, by the issue of Management Shares. Each management share carries a voting power of 200 Ordinary Shares on editorial matters including hiring and firing of staff, though on financial and administrative matters all the shares carry equal weight. The management shares may be issued only to people approved by the Government and the newspaper is obliged by the law to issue management shares to any person whom the Government may nominate. Printing licences still have to be renewed annually, and both they and the authority for an individual to hold management shares can be revoked at any time. Management shares may only be held by citizens of Singapore.

Newspapers may not receive foreign funds without the approval of the Minister of Culture who would only give such approval if satisfied that the funds were for bona fide commercial purposes.[14]

In practice, most of the management shares are held by owners and senior executives of the newspapers and the only Government nominees are the executive Chairman of the Straits Times Press (1975) Ltd and a director on the Executive Committee of Singapore News and Publications Ltd which incorporates previous Chinese language newspapers. Nevertheless the powers are there and all the directors know that their management shares could be revoked if they stepped out of line, so they have to impose a degree of self censorship. The effect of this is apparent to anyone reading the Singapore papers.

Singapore's radio and television are owned by the Government but people can without difficulty tune in to foreign broadcasts. The Government has for a long time provided the BBC with a booster transmitter, encouraging people to listen to the BBC as the best source of world news. Singapore radio and television are, however, used to promulgate and explain Government policies to a far greater extent than in most European countries or in the USA.

Another power which is held by the Government and can be abused is the power of compulsory requisition of land for development under the Land Acquisition Act of 1966 with Amendments up to 1974. Under this Act the Government can requisition any land it wants by compulsory purchase at a price not greater than its market value as at 30th November 1973. The purposes of the Act were to ensure that the rapid acquisition and reallocation of land for factories and new public housing (as described in the previous chapter) should not be blocked by prolonged litigation by individual landowners; and to avert the rabid land speculation which would have occurred if the price had not been fixed. Nevertheless, the market value of a piece of land for *private* development is very much higher than it was in 1973 and it was represented to the author that this enabled government officials to apply pressure on individuals to conform over some quite different matter by hinting that their property might be requisitioned under the Act at 1973 prices.[15]

Such abuse by officials would be unlikely if there were a reasonably strong opposition in the Singapore Parliament. This, clearly, is one of the primary reasons for having a Parliament and was very well expressed by Tun Razak when he recalled Parliament in Kuala Lumpur in 1971 after its 20-month suspension:

> 'If you want to serve the people, too much power is no good because even if you don't intend to misuse it you may do so inadvertently ... especially through delegation. You can't check everything yourself. You may be sincere, but can you be sure that all the officers who act in your name are sincere? Now with a democratic system you've first of all got Parliament and the State Assemblies to put a brake on you; then you've got the opposition parties, who will make a public outcry if things start to go wrong; but most important of all you know that every few years you've got to face the electorate who will hold you accountable for all that has been done.'[16]

The Law in an Orderly Society

No one could live in Singapore, or even visit it, without being impressed by the manifestations of an orderly, clean and law abiding Society. In contrast to Communist countries (such as the Soviet Union) where the atmosphere is one of dull acquiescence or disciplined displays of fervour, Singapore people are lively, enthusiastic and enterprising. Once again, however, Singapore's detractors consider that the orderliness is achieved only at the price of oppression.

The law, by West European standards, is very tough in matters great and small. The fine for dropping litter is S $500 (US $250). The death penalty is imposed for murder, kidnapping, and for unlawful possession of weapons, and is mandatory for trafficking in hard drugs. Corporal punishment is administered for violent crime and is greatly feared. The result is that the rate of robberies and thefts in Singapore is 10 per day compared with 1,800 per day in New York City – a ratio of 1 to 60 in proportion to the population.[17] Singapore society is largely rid of the scourge of the secret societies.

Trial by jury was abolished in 1969 – allegedly because Lee Kuan Yew, who was a highly successful defence lawyer before he entered politics, knew how easy it was to play on the emotions of a jury to secure a wrong verdict. The judiciary ranges from the magistrates and district courts to a Supreme Court and there is a final right of appeal to the judicial committee of the Privy Council in London. There is also an independent Commission to ensure the status and independence of the judiciary.[18]

A major part of Lee Kuan Yew's philosophy is to develop a self-disciplining society and to encourage a steady drift of responsibility away from the state to individuals, families and private companies. He hopes that eventually the best companies will adopt a 'cradle to grave' care for the welfare of their workers and their families as the big Japanese companies do. He is now considering putting corporations rather than families at the head of the waiting lists for public housing. The corporations would then buy flats and resell them, by deductions from pay over a period, to those workers willing to make a long term commitment to the company.[19]

There is no unemployment benefit or old age pension as such in Singapore and the high level of compulsory saving under the CPF (as described in the previous chapter) is intended to enable the citizen to rely on his own savings in sickness and old age. There are special welfare arrangements available in cases of real need and no family available to meet it. Normally, however, those in work are expected to take care of those out of work or too old to work. Lee believes that the problem for old people is not so much one of money as of loneliness, and in 1982 he introduced legislation to compel children to look after their aged parents:

'I know that not all parents are easy to live with, but I am saddened that Confucian morality and custom will now require legislation before filial obligations are honoured. The old cannot be discarded because they are no longer useful. If sons and daughters treat their parents in this way, they are encouraging their own children to treat them likewise in their turn.'[20]

A Parliamentary Democracy or a One-Party State?

If the majority of the voters in Singapore tire of the PAP Government, dislike its discipline and want to get rid of it could they in fact do so? In other words, is Singapore really a parliamentary democracy? The DLP paper described the electoral system as 'a farce' and the conduct of the secret ballot as 'dubious'.[21] Is there truth in their accusation that Singapore's one party dominance makes it in effect a one party state, because of the PAP's power to control or influence the media or to use their administrative powers under the law to harrass, muzzle or imprison political opponents in order to prevent them from being elected? Furthermore, if the PAP did *not* have these powers, would the majority of the electorate have wished, or would they wish now, to elect some other Government to replace the PAP?

First, there is no reason to doubt the fairness of the electoral process itself or the secrecy of the ballot. It is conducted precisely as it has been in Britain since 1872, with the same safeguards against fraudulent voting (by numbering ballot papers) and for ensuring that the ballot is secret. If a vote is challenged by a defeated candidate it is then possible for a High Court Judge to conduct a check that all ballot papers are genuine and that no one has voted twice, but to link any individual voter with his ballot paper would require the connivance of the Judge, the Returning Officers *and* the counting agents appointed by all the candidates taking part, and would involve a conspiracy so wide as to be inconceivable. There is therefore nothing dubious about Singapore's secret ballot.

Except in the 1968 elections, which the opposition boycotted and allowed 51 out of 58 candidates to be returned unopposed, the opposition vote has never been less than 24 per cent. It has, however, always been split and the highest vote received by any individual party was 12.2 per cent for the Workers' Party in 1972. Under the Westminster 'first-past-the-post' system it is very unlikely that any party anywhere (other than, say, a regional party putting up a few candidates only in its own region) would ever win a seat with only 12.2 per cent of the vote.[22]

Would this 12.2 per cent – or the total opposition vote of 25–30 per cent – have been higher but for the harrasment or detention of opposition politicians? The answer is probably 'yes, but not very much higher'. In some cases those politicians, knowing that they were bound to lose, deliberately provoked their own arrest to gain sympathy for others of their party by martyrdom. Overall the threat of arrest or administrative harrassment will have hampered political campaigning more than martyrdom will have gained for it, but to suggest that more than a handful of the 70-75 per cent who voted positively for the PAP would otherwise have voted for the opposition in the secret ballot underestimates the common sense and independence of the Singapore people. Nevertheless, the harrassment which has been recorded in the DLP paper and, much more convincingly, in the books of Professors Chan Heng Chee and Mary Turnbull,[23] has undoubtedly been interpreted by many Singaporeans as having a blatantly political motive even if it did not materially affect the verdict of the electorate. In the long run it has therefore probably been counterproductive as well as superfluous.

Another unhealthy aspect of Singapore's democracy is that there is no Second Chamber. Following a report by a constitutional commission in 1966, a presidential council of senior political leaders was formed, on the lines of the British Privy Council. David Marshall was included but he resigned after seven months in protest against its limited functions and the obligation of secrecy. This council has now restricted its own activities to the safeguarding of communal minority rights (as distinct from the rights of individuals), and its recommendations can be overturned by a two thirds majority vote in Parliament.[24] Again it would appear that the PAP has nothing to lose and, in the long run, much to gain, from introducing some kind of effective second chamber or review body.

The PAP's argument is that this is taken care of by the extensive CCC and party organizations at constituency level, but in a state where political advancement is synonymous with advancement in approval from the PAP, party officials and MPs may be inclined to stifle inconvenient or irritating complaints. Nevertheless, the grass roots organization is probably the best in any elected political party in the world and does provide a better channel to the top than most citizens have elsewhere.

The furious internal reaction in the PAP to the loss of the seat in the Anson by-election in 1981 does suggest that, after 15 years (i.e. since the Barisan MPs walked out in 1966), the Government had got accustomed to having no opposition in Parliament, and Ministers are no doubt irritated by having to 'waste time' debating in the House with the lone opposition member. They can be expected to mobilize sufficient effort to ensure that they regain the Anson seat at the next election but it will be best for the health of Singapore democracy if at least some opposition members are elected. The comment by Tun Razak on page 343 explained why.

The 25 per cent who vote against the PAP probably come mainly from two categories of the population: liberal intellectuals and people who have failed to get in on the mainstream of prosperity; plus a small number of others who are more temporarily disappointed or disturbed by the way the political system is working.

The first category consists of a proportion of intellectuals who have a distaste for the materialistic, populist, elitist and authoritarian aspects of the PAP style of government. Cynics will say that this is because they do not find that they have scope for their talents in a modern meritocracy, and sense that they are unlikely to reach positions of power. This, however, maligns and underestimates many of them, whose objections are honestly liberal.

The second – and much larger – category consists of those who have failed (or do not wish) to get even an unskilled job in modern industry or business which would get them into the income bracket of those who can afford the rent of an HDB or other modern flat, and are therefore still down at the standard of living of the Singapore of 30 years ago. There is a huge gulf between the attap hut or shop house and the mainstream of Singaporeans living in HDB flats with washing machine, refrigerator and colour TV and they are on the wrong side of that gulf. They amount to less than 20 per cent of the total population and will vote, with some bitterness, for any party but the PAP.

These two categories, however, have very little in common and the dissenting intellectual liberal leadership is most unlikely to strike a chord with the 'born losers' under the attap roof. Their likeliest response will be from disappointed or disgruntled members of the mainstream, like those who turned to Jeyaratnam in the Anson by-election in 1981 (pages 324–325).

The only other anti-PAP vote comes from a small number but wider range of people who feel strongly that the PAP would govern better if it faced a stronger opposition in Parliament. These people are, by definition, only likely to vote for an opposition candidate if they are confident that the PAP will retain its overall majority. There is at present no other political party which they would like to see ruling the country.

The fact remains that Singapore is *not* a one party state; it *is* a parliamentary democracy. These 25 per cent can and do vote against the PAP but the great majority have consistently voted, freely and fairly, to have a PAP Government rather than any of the available alternatives, even though some of them might have preferred a more effective opposition;[25] and the people *do* retain the power and opportunity, every five years at least, to dismiss the Government by secret ballot if they so wish.

Does It Work?

Apart from its self-evident economic and social success, the most impressive aspect of Singapore society is the remarkable candour of its leaders. They do not conceal their problems from the people; nor do they conceal the criticisms of their detractors.

Lee Kuan Yew's series of broadcasts in 1961, published as *The Battle for Merger*, were quoted freely in Chapters 3 to 8 of this book; they must be amongst the frankest of all political communications from a Prime Minister direct to his people. Nothing was concealed or glossed over and this can be confirmed with hindsight. The struggle for control of the PAP was at the time far from over and Lee's courage in laying it bare played a big part in his winning the referendum for merger and the subsequent general election in 1963.

Since then he has regularly explained his plans and his philosophy on television and radio. Unlike the BBC, Singapore radio and TV do not give a 'right of reply' for the opposition view. The PAP would argue that communication of problems and policies direct from the elected Prime Minister to the electorate is a proper part of the democratic process and it certainly ensures that those who are asked to put his plans into effect do understand their purpose. President Roosevelt did the same.

Lee's National Day Message in 1981 was a good example of this. He made it clear that the high wage increases awarded by the National Wages Council in 1978–80 were specifically aimed to force employers to cut manpower and automate (see page 334). Many democratic leaders might have tried to conceal or fudge the true purpose. He then gave an example of a company in Singapore which failed: Rollei had decided in 1970 to transfer its camera manufacture from Germany to Singapore because German workers' wages were at that time twelves times higher than those in Singapore. Rollei did not, however, keep up with new technology. The

DOES IT WORK?

Japanese kept ahead with research and development so, although Japanese workers were paid three times Singapore wages, Rollei could not sell their cameras and had to close down their operation. Lee spelt out the implications of this and other experiences for Singapore:

> 'In the 1980s we must move our products and services up-market ... We must aim to become, by the 1990s, an information and a brain services centre ... We have got to keep moving upwards in technology. Other developing countries have seen how South Korea, Taiwan, Hong Kong and Singapore have done it and are catching up ... We have to use our national strong points against other countries ...
>
> If we want to increase our per capita productive output we must have higher per capita investment in more automated and computerised machines which in turn require better educated and more highly trained workers to operate. These machines and workers will become most productive when they are working under enlightened and efficient management, a management that knows how to motivate its workers, how to get them loyal to and identified with the company ... The company must care for the welfare, employment and future of its workers to win their loyalty.
>
> Goods and services are not going to get cheaper ... So HDB homes will not get cheaper. The answer is to increase our earning capacity by increasing productivity. ... Then, despite higher prices, you can still afford to buy HDB homes (and) the latest and most energy-saving of refrigerators, washing machines and colour televisions. All this depends on higher levels of education.'[26]

Critics will detect something of the 'big brother' in this kind of exhortation by the leader, but Lee Kuan Yew struck a chord with people enjoying a rising standard of living. He used a very different style when talking 20 years earlier to people when most of them had a very different lifestyle and expectations in 1961, in his *Battle for Merger* broadcasts, but again he struck the right note. The 1981 lifestyle was even more different from that of the people living in shop houses in 1955 (see page 326), the year he was first elected to the Assembly. From the viewpoint of the 70 per cent now living in the HDB flats, the system has worked, and this is where the PAP vote seems unassailable.

Lee was equally explicit two years later when he tackled the problems of recession in 1983:

'Unlike our ASEAN neighbours we have no agricultural base to fall back on. However bad a depression, we have still to have the foreign exchange to pay for food imports, although our exports of manufactured products will fall.'

He urged people to use the time to improve their education in readiness for the inevitable end of the recession:

'So those people who are well-educated, well organized and highly productive will recover quicker than those who are inadequately educated and unprepared to meet the new challenges of the computerized-robotized society of the 1990s.'[27]

The start of 1984 saw encouraging signs that Singapore was climbing out of the recession. The economic growth rate for 1983 was 7.2 per cent, more than double that of Japan or the USA, and productivity increased by 4.6 per cent, with inflation at 1.1 per cent. More encouraging still for the future was the steady growth in tertiary education, the number of science and engineering students on course for graduation in 1985 being more than double that for 1980.[28] So prospects for Singapore, though still vulnerable either to a world debt crisis or a major outbreak of protectionism, looked very good.

Has this all been achieved at an unnecessary price in suppression of dissent? Though some may question the validity of the reasons given for detention of certain opponents of the regime, dissent is by no means stifled or concealed. The Dutch DLP accused the PAP of being 'totalitarian' but no totalitarian government would have published the DLP's indictment in full, with its supporting data, as Devan Nair did in 1976. And Professor Chan Heng Chee's *Dynamics of One-Party Dominance* was published by the Singapore University Press, coupling its balanced analysis of the grass-roots strength of the party with outspoken criticism of its more authoritarian features, as quoted earlier in this book. These criticisms have not prejudiced her continuance as a highly respected Professor in the National University of Singapore in a department headed by a PAP MP. There is plenty of criticism to be read and heard in Singapore.

The PAP can fairly claim, however, that if they had allowed the proponents of the alternative marxist society to gain control of their party (as they almost did in 1961) and of the Singapore government, the regime would certainly have been a totalitarian one and would have used much more ruthless methods to hold onto power, as such regimes do elsewhere; and that the right to challenge the government by secret ballot every five years would certainly have been removed. The PAP would also claim that, if the politicized leadership of the trade unions had been left with the power to disrupt the economy for political purposes, Singaporeans would not now enjoy their present standard of living; nor if the cutting edge of the communication from the Prime Minister to the people had been blunted and blurred by 'equal time' on television for dissenting voices.

These, it may be said, are the traditional arguments of the dictator. There remains, however, the decisive difference that dictators do not submit themselves to general elections. For the mainstream of Singaporeans, their lives have seen a dramatic improvement and they would rather keep the man who led them to this, even if he is sometimes seen as a rather imperious team captain. Unlike some of the older democracies, Singapore is intolerant of people who kick through their own goal. A firmly led disciplined society has probably been right for Singapore in the past quarter-century of growth and most of her people clearly think so.

There are, however, some questions for the future: has the control of dissent kept the safety valve closed for too long and sown the seeds of conflict to come? Are all the measures by which it has been controlled (such as the Internal Security Act, the Newspaper and Printing Presses Act and the Government control of radio and television) still justified? Do the threats they aimed to counter still exist?

Prospects for Singapore

Lee Kuan Yew has expressed his intention to step down when he becomes 65 in September 1988. Until then, Singapore is likely to continue on its present road to a disciplined prosperity, under one-party dominance. The only feasible interruption would be an invasion by one of its larger neighbours such as Malaysia or Indonesia, and this would only occur if there had been a revolution in one of those countries. Their leaders would still know very well, however, that Singapore's economy is the mainspring of Southeast Asia's prosperity and that its disruption would lead to a massive withdrawal of the foreign investment on which it depends, so even the wildest of revolutionary or military governments, whatever their rhetoric, would be unlikely to cut the ground from under their own feet.

After 1988, the continuance of the success story will depend on the emergence of a successor who has Lee's rare combination of a brilliant brain with stamina and the ability both to manage and to communicate; also a successor who has the political skill to command the loyalty of a vibrant political party, including the loyalty of those he has defeated in the contest for the succession. It is therefore likely that Lee Kuan Yew will guide the PAP towards a firm selection of that successor well before 1988 so that he may become established as Deputy Prime Minister in plenty of time. Unless he is satisfied that the succession will be stable, Lee may well defer his own retirement. He might also bow to the probable popular demand that he should move across the Istana and succeed Devan Nair as President of the Republic.

The process of selection is well under way. Its foundation lies in the selection of PAP candidates for election. The process begins with a scientific screening, supplemented since 1980 by IQ and psychological tests.[29] One of the primary tasks at that stage is to eliminate any who are motivated by self-interest. Candidates then have an interview with the Party Chairman, Dr. Toh Chin Chye, followed by a more detailed second review of shortlisted candidates by Lee Kuan Yew and other senior Cabinet Ministers. The quality of PAP MPs does appear to visitors to be amongst the highest in any democratic Parliament, and the absence of any taint of corruption is quite remarkable, the more so as it is in a part of the world notorious for that disease.

The final selection of Lee Kuan Yew's successor is being facilitated by a frequent shuffling of young talent between responsible jobs to test their range of capacities. In 1983 there were 4 or 5 front runners, mostly in their early 40s, i.e. averaging 15 years younger than Lee Kuan Yew. Few of these were long standing politicians. The oldest, Ong Teng Cheong (born 1936) first entered Parliament in 1972 and Goh Chok Tong (born 1941) in 1976. Lim Chee Onn (born in 1944) entered Parliament from the Civil Service in 1977 and Tony Tan Keng Kam (born 1940), now Minister for Finance and Trade and Industry, came from the business world in 1979. The latter two won by-elections for seats vacated by older men as part of the declared PAP policy of self-renewal. Other rising stars may enter the field before 1988.

The selection of Lee Kuan Yew's successor, and of a strong PAP Central Executive Committee to whom he is accountable, are the most crucial factors governing the continued success and stability of Singapore and the realization of her full potential in the world boom which is widely expected in the 1990s. The authoritarian powers which the PAP has used its dominance to enact have been important in the achievement and continuance thus far of its economic success and social order. These same powers could, however, be an Achilles heel if they were to fall into the hands of a leader who was stupid, evil, arrogant or feckless. There is therefore a very strong case for putting some of these powers at least into abeyance, even if they are kept on the statute book in reserve in case there is a period of instability and disruption during the first years of power for Lee Kuan Yew's successor. Many of them are superfluous so long as Lee Kuan Yew remains as Prime Minister and there would be every advantage in politicians and – more important – officials becoming accustomed to doing without them while he is still in control. With or without these powers Singapore (unlike Malaysia) faces virtually no risk whatever of racial disturbance, politically motivated street violence or terrorism. As the BERI report suggested, it is probably the best bet for investment anywhere in the world.

In the long term, Singapore's prospects of continuance of this stability would benefit from the repeal or suspension of some of the provisions of the ISA or of the Newspaper and Printing Presses Act before they become too deeply ingrained. Lee Kuan Yew in one of his earliest parliamentary speeches, on 4 October 1956, explained why there had been no violent revolutions in Britain for over 300 years – because Britain had allowed political parties of all colours to compete freely for power, including the communists (see pages 118-9). These same arguments could now well be applied to the case for a relaxation of some of the restraints which were necessary in the 1960s, but no longer needed in the 1980s in one of the most stable and best governed democracies in the world.

Notes

CHAPTER 1   INTRODUCTION

1. Robert S. McNamara, *The Essence of Security*, London October 1968
2. J. K. Zawodny, *Organisational Problems and Dynamics of Violent Political Movements*, presented to the Eighth World Congress of the International Political Science Association, Munich September 1970, p. 1
3. Leonard Schapiro 'Changing Patterns in the Theory of Revolution and Insurgency' *Royal United Services Institution Journal*, September 1970
4. For example:
    Richard Clutterbuck, *The Long Long War*, London 1967
    G. Z. Hanrahan, *The Communist Struggle in Malaya*, New York 1954
    M. C. A. Henniker, *Red Shadow over Malaya*, London 1955
    Harry Miller, *Menace in Malaya*, London 1954
    Edgar O'Ballance, *Malaya – The Communist Insurgent War 1948-60*, London 1966
    J. B. Perry Robinson, *Transformation in Malaya*, London 1956
    V. Purcell, *Malaya Communist or Free?*, London 1954
    Kernial Singh Sandhu, 'Emergency Resettlement in Malaya' in *The Journal of Tropical Geography* Vol 18 August 1964, University of Malaya in Singapore 1964
5. In the rural areas of Malaya a large proportion of the civil population concerned did not grow food but earned their living from cash crops (such as rubber) and minerals (such as tin). This was perhaps one of the reasons why Mao's techniques did not succeed in Malaya. The question of whether these people should be treated as peasants or as an industrial proletariat was the subject of bitter controversy in the MCP in 1949 – see Chapter 9
6. Edmund Wilson in *To The Finland Station*, New York 1940, gives a masterly account of the evolution of revolutionary philosophy, tracing some of it back to writers who lived long before the French Revolution, but these were theorists, not practitioners
7. New York (Vintage) 1957
8. Captain C. E. S. Dudley, 'Insurrection: from the Jacobins to Mao Tse Tung' in *The Royal United Service Institution Journal*, May 1966
9. Schapiro *op. cit.*
10. Edmund Wilson, *To the Finland Station*, New York 1940, pp. 388-9, cited by R. N. Carew Hunt, *The Theory and Practice of Communism*, London (Pelican) 1963, p. 171
11. Schapiro *op. cit.*
12. Alan Moorehead, *The Russian Revolution*, New York (Bantam Books) 1959, p. 231
13. The Bolsheviks were never more than a minority. Even in the Constituent Assembly election which was held immediately after the revolution they

polled less than 25 per cent of the votes cast, compared with 58 per cent by the Social Revolutionary Party. Moorehead p. 267
14. Moorehead pp. 236–60
15. Andrew C. Janos, *The Seizure of Power: A Study of Force and Popular Consent*, Princeton University 1964, pp. 46–51
16. *ibid* pp. 62–9
17. Malaparte, *Coup d'État*, cited by Janos, *op. cit.* pp. 52–7
18. N. N. Sukhanov, *The Russian Revolution of 1917* London 1955, p. 621, cited by Janos, *op. cit.* p. 55
19. See for example Lin Piao's foreword to the second edition of *Quotations from Chairman Mao Tse Tung*, Peking, Foreign Language Press 1966 ('The Little Red Book') and, on pp. 40–1 of the same book, Mao's 1963 statement 'On Krushchev's Phoney Communism and its Historical Lessons for the World'
20. e.g. Regis Debray, *Revolution in the Revolution?* London (Pelican) 1968. Debray applies his theories specifically to Latin America, but some others, such as Leo Huberman and Paul M. Sweezy think that they may be applicable elsewhere (see their foreword to the book)
21. See also Frantz Fanon, *The Wretched of the Earth* London (Penguin) 1967, Chapter 1, and the foreword to the book by Jean-Paul Sartre
22. Schapiro *op. cit.* Also Debray pp. 115–27 and Che Guevara, *Guerrilla Warfare*, London 1962, p. 111
23. Patrick Seale and Maureen McConville, *French Revolution: 1968*, London (Penguin) 1968, pp. 210–18
24. Georges Sorel, *Reflections on Violence*, (English translation by T. E. Hulme) London 1925, p. 137
Hannah Arendt, in *On Violence*, London 1970 (p. 89) points out that Nechaev and Bukanin had commended the unifying effect of violence half a century earlier, and a century ahead of Sartre and Fanon
25. Sorel p. 123
26. *ibid.* p. 211. Under Sorel's definitions, the State uses 'force' while the revolutionaries use 'violence' against it
27. *ibid.* p. 22
28. *ibid.* pp. 297–8. In his praise of violence, Sorel even commended lynch law in America as preferable to the incompetence and corruption of European judicial systems, pp. 206–7
29. *ibid.* pp. 298–9
30. *The Economist*, 20 June 1970, pp. 11–12, in a comment on the practice of kidnapping foreign diplomats as hostages to bring about the release of imprisoned revolutionaries
31. Lt. Col. Marc Geneste, in an Interview 1963. See also Otto Heilbrunn, 'The Algerian Emergency' in *The Royal United Service Institution Journal*, August 1966. Also Frantz Fanon (p. 32), quotes M. Meyer as saying in the French National Assembly that the French Republic must not be prostituted by allowing the Algerian people to become part of it
32. Semantically speaking it is wrong to refer to a fighting man as a '*guerrilla*'. The Spanish word 'guerrilla' means 'small war' and the man who fights it is a *guerrillero* – the word used throughout by Debray, *op. cit.*, and by his translator. Nevertheless, in Anglo-American usage the word 'guerrilla' has come to mean the fighting man himself and the war is usually known as 'guerrilla warfare'. I have used this wording throughout
33. In an article on the Tupamaros (the most successful of the 'urban guerrillas') in Uruguay in the *Observer* on 9 August 1970 the writer commented:

NOTES

'Unlike Che Guevara, they have learned what every Latin American General has always known – that power in these parts lies in the city, not in the countryside. The Tupamaros use the city as the Vietcong uses the jungle.'

34. For example, apart from Mao's own work, see:
    J. L. S. Girling, *Peoples' War*, London 1969
    Sir Robert Thompson, *Defeating Communist Insurgency*, London 1966
    George K. Tanham, *Communist Revolutionary Warfare: The Vietminh in Indochina*, New York 1961
    Michael Elliott-Bateman, *Defeat in the East – The Mark of Mao Tse Tung on War*, London 1967
35. Mao Tse Tung, *On Protracted War* (May 1938) cited in his *Quotations from Chairman Mao Tse Tung*, Peking 1966, p. 153
36. Mao Tse Tung and Che Guevara, *Guerrilla Warfare*, London 1962, p. 113
37. Cited in Richard Clutterbuck *The Long Long War*, London 1967, p. 3
38. Cited in Clutterbuck, *op. cit.* p. 3
39. Debray pp. 41–2
40. *ibid.* pp. 46–7. Debray also cites the 'agitprop' patrols used in South Vietnam, which are well described by Malcolm Browne in *The New Face of War*, London 1966, pp. 121–35
41. Debray pp. 44–6 and 115–25
42. Clutterbuck, *op. cit.* p. 5
43. T. A. Critchley, in *The Conquest of Violence*, London 1970, gives an impressive historical account of the containment of revolutionary violence in Britain with an astonishingly small loss of life. No one was killed in any political riot or demonstration in England, Scotland or Wales between 1920 and 1973 and only three in the subsequent 10 years. The total for the 140 years 1843–1983 was eleven.
44. Sir Robert Thompson, in Foreword to Clutterbuck's *The Long Long War*, p. viii
45. Clutterbuck *op. cit.* p. 70
46. For example:
    J. Kennedy, *A History of Malaya*, London 1932
    Lennox A. Mills, *Malaya – A Political and Economic Appraisal*, Minneapolis 1958
    Ooi Jin Bee, *Land, People and Economy in Malaya*, London 1963
    T. H. Silcock and E. H. Fisk, *The Political Economy of Independent Malaya*, Singapore 1963
    K.J. Ratnam, *Communalism and the Political Process in Malaya*, Singapore 1965
    V. Purcell, *Malaya – Communist or Free?*, London 1954
47. Miller p. 15
48. F. S. V. Donnison, *British Military Administration in the Far East 1943–46*, London 1956
49. Sir Robert Thompson, *Defeating Communist Insurgency*, London 1966, p. 18
50. Silcock and Fisk, Appendix
51. Purcell, *Malaya*, p. 273
52. Thompson, *Defeating Communist Insurgency*, p. 19
53. Including Miller, pp. 19–34 and Clutterbuck, *The Long Long War*, pp. 13–24
54. See Clutterbuck, *op. cit.* p. 14. Confirmed by Alan Blades in a letter to the author, 1969

NOTES

55. Clutterbuck *op. cit.* pp. 15–16. Also O'Ballance, p. 50
56. F. Spencer Chapman, *The Jungle is Neutral*, London 1949, pp. 161–75
57. Chapman, p. 317–18
58. John Davis, *Interview*, 1966
59. V. Purcell, *The Chinese in South East Asia*, London 1965, pp. 306–11
60. Chapman pp. 231–40, and Donnison 380–1
61. Davis, *Interview*, 1966
62. Chapman pp. 411–13
63. Davis, *Interview*, 1966
64. Chapman p. 371
65. Chapman pp. 404–12
66. Donnison pp. 384–5
67. Chapman p. 419
68. Donnison pp. 158 and 385–8
69. *ibid.* p. 385
70. *ibid.* p. 386
71. Chapman p. 419
72. *ibid.* p. 419

CHAPTER 2   THE FIRST ATTEMPT AT AN URBAN REVOLUTION

1. Lucien W. Pye, *Guerrilla Communism in Malaya*, Princeton 1956, p. 66n.
2. Alan Blades, comments and letter to the author, 25 July 1969
3. G. G. Thomson, in comments on the author's first draft, June 1969. In a covering letter to these comments he adds that it was the Communists' own failings rather than clever policy on the part of the government which brought them to defeat
4. Pye p. 70
5. G. G. Thomson, comments
6. SORO (Special Operations Research Office of the American University), *Casebook on Insurgency and Revolutionary Warfare*, Washington 1962, p. 597
7. SORO p. 593
8. Harry Miller, *Menace in Malaya*, London 1954, p. 94
9. Pye p. 194
10. V. Purcell, *Malayan Politics* in *Politics in Southern Asia* (Ed. Saul Rose), London 1963. Mr. Purcell was a member of the Malayan Planning Unit
11. G. G. Thomson, comments
12. For a description of this, see F. S. V. Donnison, *British Military Administration in the Far East, 1943–46*, London 1956, Chapters IX and XX
13. Donnison p. 389
14. Donnison p. 390. Very few of these 3,500, however, were Party members – see Chapter 4
15. Miller p. 62
16. *Straits Times*, 5 February 1946
17. Blades, comments
18. Donnison p. 392
19. Donnison pp. 392–3
20. A fortuitous and particularly dangerous situation arose over one of these, Lim Ah Liang, who was shot and slightly wounded before his arrest. He was named for deportation, and inoculated to comply with Hong Kong transit regulations. Unfortunately, between inoculation and his sailing

NOTES

dates he fell ill from some quite unrelated cause and died. The MCP at once accused the government of poisoning him, and they marshalled a funeral procession several miles long which became a demonstration to whip up feeling against the police. Blades, comments

21. Donnison pp. 394-5
22. There was an exact parallel in Northern Ireland in August 1971, when internment without trial was instituted on the grounds that the intimidation of witnesses by the IRA made fair trial under the normal safeguards of British Law impossible
23. Blades, comments
24. S. S. Awberry and F. W. Dalley, *Labour and Trade Union Organisation in the Federation of Malaya and Singapore*, Government Press, Kuala Lumpur 1948, p. 26
25. The following are compiled from 1947 Census figures quoted by Awberry and Dalley (pp. 3 and 4):

	Federation	Singapore	Total
Chinese	1882874 (39%)	728523 (77%)	2611397 (45%)
Malays	2400441 (49%)	116583 (12%)	2517024 (43%)
Others	591923 (12%)	86638 (11%)	678561 (12%)

26. Pye p. 74
27. Pye p. 76
28. See Chapter 1 for the background of Lai Tek's recruitment as a British agent. It may appear that he was allowed to go too far, but it is worth remembering that the two most notorious police agents in pre-revolutionary Russia, Azev and Malinovsky, were both allowed to go a great deal further than this. In 1904 Azev, as head of the Fighting Section of the Social Revolutionary Party, planned and connived in the assassination of his own employer, Plehve, the Minister of the Interior. Nevertheless, he continued thereafter as a trusted and highly paid police agent. Even the Revolutionaries themselves may have been aware of his police activities and content to accept the risk of betrayal in the belief that they were getting greater dividends from their access through him to police secrets. Both sides probably regarded him confidently as 'their man', and Azev no doubt released to each side only such details of his real activities as would encourage this view. It is significant that, when the Bolsheviks attained access to police files in 1917, they showed little determination in tracking down agents, presumably because their disclosures might have embarrassed many leading Bolsheviks. Malinovsky returned voluntarily to Russia in 1918, and seems to have been surprised to find himself tried and condemned to death. Lenin's behaviour during his trial suggests that he himself must have been aware of Malinovsky's double game all the time, and he seems to have had a grave struggle with his conscience over approving his execution. See Alan Moorehead, *The Russian Revolution*, New York (Bantam Books) 1959, p. 88 and Bertram Wolfe, *Three Who Made a Revolution*, Boston (Beacon Press) 1955, pp. 266, 479 and 535-57.
29. 'Police Socialism' dates back to 1901, in Russia. Its psychology was well expressed by the Chief of the Moscow police at the time: 'In order to disarm the agitators, it is necessary to open and point out to the worker a legal solution to his difficulty, for we must bear in mind that the agitator will be followed by the youngest and boldest of the crowd, while the average worker will prefer the less spectacular and quiet legal way. Thus split up, the crowd will lose its power.' See Moorehead p. 53.

NOTES

30. Miller p. 64
31. Pye p. 80. It is interesting that precisely the same comments arose in Hong Kong in 1967. When there is no need for them to operate underground, Communist Party leaders seem to betray normal bourgeois frailties, claiming that a position of social respectability for them is an asset to the Party
32. Blades, comments
33. Miller p. 64
34. Miller p. 74
35. *Trade Union Registry: Annual Report, 1948* Government Press, Kuala Lumpur 1949, p. 2. Also Charles Gamba, *The Origins of Trade Unionism in Malaya*, Eastern Universities Press 1962, p. 155
36. Blades, comments
37. Awberry and Dalley pp. 65–6
38. *Straits Times*, 28 April 1948
39. *Straits Times*, 24 April 1948
40. G. G. Thomson, Interview, 1968
41. *Straits Times*, 29 April 1948
42. *Straits Times*, 30 April 1948
43. G. G. Thomson, Interview 1968. Thomson considers that the SFTU blundered in failing to accept the ban on the procession and to go ahead with the rally only. In the event a procession would inevitably have formed as the people left the rally. If it had been peaceful, it would have been the demonstration of strength that they wished. If, on the other hand, the police had intervened and violence had ensued it would have given the MCP a propaganda victory in their policy of a crescendo of opposition and confrontation. The MCP would therefore have gained either way. Thomson thinks that the failure of the 1948 May Day demonstration provoked the MCP to trigger off the violence in the rural areas prematurely, thereby launching into guerrilla warfare before they were ready. G. G. Thomson, comments
44. John Davis, Interview, 1966
45. Miller p. 77
46. Awberry and Dalley p. 26. This had recently been restricted by the government to 10 per cent
47. *Trade Union Registry: Annual Report, 1948*, Government Press, Kuala Lumpur 1949, quoting the *Trade Union (Amendments) Ordinance 1948* published on 12 June 1948, and the *Trade Union (Amendments No. 2) Ordinance, 1948*, published on 19 July 1948, p. 1
48. *ibid.* p. 2
49. Pye pp. 83–4
50. Douglas Hyde, in *The Roots of Guerrilla Warfare*, London 1968, pp. 23–4, suggests that 'the delegates from the South-East Asian countries returned home knowing that they had been given the go-ahead to get on with the job of making revolutions' and that, encouraged by Communist successes in China, they were influenced by Chinese experience, but that they still knew the Moscow line on revolution better than Mao Tse Tung's theories of guerrilla warfare. Ruth McVey, in *The Calcutta Conference and the South East Asian Uprisings*, Cornell University, New York 1958, suggests that the influence of the Calcutta conference may have been exaggerated, but both authors note that within a few months an armed struggle had broken out in Burma, Indochina, Malaya, Indonesia and the Philippines

NOTES

CHAPTER 3   THE COMMUNIST PARTY STRUCTURE IN SINGAPORE

1. Pye p. 173
2. See also Lee Kuan Yew in *The Battle for Merger*, Singapore 1961, p. 18 whose views on this are discussed in Chapter 6
3. Pye p. 77
4. Lee Kuan Yew *op. cit.* p. 16
5. Pye p. 77
6. Pye p. 78
7. Blades, comments
8. In *The Battle for Merger*, pp. 19, 21 and 85
9. This also became one of the main planks in the platform of Lee Kuan Yew's own People's Action Party, and contributed greatly to its success. Blades, comments
10. Pye p. 219
11. Douglas Hyde, *I Believed*, London 1951, pp. 64–6
12. *ibid.* pp. 239–40
13. Blades, comments. See also Chapters 7 and 8
14. This was in 1948. Later, military operations in the Federation made this too dangerous, and people living 'outside' seldom knew the location of camps 'inside' the jungle. They would instead be contacted by jungle-based couriers at their known places of work in the fields or estates, or sometimes at pre-arranged rendezvous near the jungle fringe. This system was part of a rural insurgency and is described in Chapter 10
15. Their arrest was part of a police operation following an unsuccessful attempt to assassinate the Governor of Singapore. G. G. Thomson, comments
16. Blades, comments
17. *Report of the Singapore Riots Commission in 1951*, Singapore 1951
18. Blades, comments

CHAPTER 4   THE SURVIVAL OF THE STUDENT ORGANIZATION

1. There is an unavoidable overlap in the terms 'High School' and 'Middle School'. In the Chinese education system the Middle School is the equivalent of the British Secondary School, which takes boys from the end of primary education (age about twelve) up to entry standard for University (i.e. 'higher' education). Many of these, however, bear the title 'High School', though they are collectively known as Middle Schools
2. G. G. Thomson, comments
3. Dr. Goh Keng Swee, then Singapore's Defence Minister, reported in the Singapore *Sunday Times*, 29 January 1967
4. Lee Kuan Yew, in a broadcast over Radio Singapore on 15 September 1961, published in *The Battle for Merger*, Singapore 1961, pp. 8–9
5. On the other hand Alan Blades, in his comment, considered that the students were generally better at keeping secrets than adults, and were often more fanatical and more difficult to talk round
6. 'Yung', a student at the Chinese High School for whom the ABL made a strong bid. See Chapter 5
7. Another boy who got involved with the MCP whilst at school, and whose identity is safeguarded by a pseudonym
8. See Chapter 9 for more details of this change of policy

NOTES

9. Extract from MCP Directive of October 1951, quoted in G. Z. Hanrahan, *The Communist Struggle in Malaya*, New York 1954
10. See Chapter 5 for an account of the function of the 'Hsueh Hsih' cells for the study of Party affairs and techniques
11. Douglas Hyde, Interview, 1969
12. *ibid.* Douglas Hyde estimates that open front members sometimes had no contact with the secret organization for five or ten years and acted on their own initiative, guided only by their general knowledge and study of Party policy. In some cases they went their own way, using the Party to further their own ideals
13. *ibid*
14. *Straits Times*, 24 May 1954
15. *Straits Times*, 14 May 1954
16. *Straits Times*, 15 May 1954
17. Legislative Assembly, Singapore, Sessional Paper, No. CMD 53 of 1956, *Singapore Chinese Middle School Students' Union*, Singapore October 1956. (Hereafter known as 'White Paper, SCMSSU, 1956')
18. Chinese High School and the Catholic High School (boys); Chung Cheng (Main and Branch) and Yong Eng High Schools (mixed); Nanyang, Chung Hwa (two branches), Nan Hwa and Nan Chiau Girls' High Schools
19. *Straits Times*, 22 May 1954
20. The psychology of the boys and girls locking themselves into the Chinese Schools lay in the retreat to a congenial environment away from the environment of a society which seemed to them to be alien and anti-Chinese. This group psychology was fully and ably exploited by the Communists. G. G. Thomson, comments
21. *Straits Times*, 24 May 1954
22. G. G. Thomson, comments

CHAPTER 5   SUBVERSION IN THE CHINESE MIDDLE SCHOOLS 1954-6

1. White Paper, SCMSSU, 1956
2. For further details of these powers see Chapter 6
3. Restrictions were also placed on police practices which made it very difficult for them to prevent demonstrations from getting out of hand. For example, the police were debarred from stopping the display of inflammatory posters and the use of loudspeakers to whip up the crowds to take the law into their own hands. The fact that the police were forced to stand by while this happened brought them into contempt and encouraged the crowd to go further. Blades, comments
4. *Straits Times*, 29 April 1954
5. *The Times*, London 13 May 1954
6. Michael Gorrie, interview, 1967
7. *The Times*, London 14 May 1954
8. The senior British official in the Singapore Legislative Assembly
9. *The Times*, London 17 May 1954
10. Blades, comments
11. *The Times*, London 23 May 1954
12. *The Times*, London 17 May 1954. It must be noted, however, that the British Governor still retained much of the control over Internal Security measures. See Chapter 6
13. White Paper, SCMSSU, 1956, p. 1
14. *ibid.* p. 3

NOTES

15. *ibid.* p. 4
16. *ibid.* p. 18
17. *ibid.* p. 20
18. White Paper, SCMSSU, 1956, p. 14
19. These were also sometimes known as Senior Middle (SM 3, 2 and 1) and Junior Middle (JM 3, 2 and 1)
20. White Paper, SCMSSU, 1956, p. 15. These are, of course, standard Communist techniques all over the world. In *The New Face of War*, London 1966, pp. 230–3, Malcolm Browne describes the Vietcong organization amongst South Vietnamese students in Paris. The HQ was in a garage, which provided the front for their organization. Here the students would gather in a happy atmosphere, with guitars, games, food and drink. Senior students acted as waiters, and were 'addressed neither as "boy" nor "sir" but as "comrade".' There were discussion groups and cultural evenings. There was no direct political pressure (which would have involved a security risk) but promising students found themselves invited to become waiters or group leaders. They were persuaded that on graduation it would be better not to return to South Vietnam but instead to work in North Vietnam for the liberation of the South. The Vietcong claimed that 91 per cent of the South Vietnamese in Paris were on their side.
21. White Paper, SCMSSU, 1956, p. 15
22. See later in this chapter for discussion of the position of the teachers
23. White Paper, SCMSSU, 1956, p. 15
24. SCMSSU Study Outing June 1956, quoted in White Paper, SCMSSU, 1956 p. 14. This is in accordance with a standard technique outlined by Mao Tse Tung and quoted in the same document.
25. Lee Kuan Yew, in *The Battle for Merger*, Singapore 1961, published some notes which he ascribes to Lim Chin Siong, who, he says, used them for '. . . a talk he gave in commemoration of the death of Stalin, to his immediate supporters in the Anti-British League cell, whose instruction in Marxism-Leninism was his personal responsibility. This talk was given by him in June 1953 . . .' (p. 99). There is no doubt about the Communist nature of these notes. For example, 'Dear Comrades! We must not forget that we have taken an oath before the Red Flag and Comrade Stalin. We have already become combatants for national liberation! Today, when our most respected and loving leader has left us for ever, and at a time when the enemy has become all the more fanatical in his attacks against us, our duty has clearly become all the greater . . .' and '. . . Comrades should take a further step in striving to become glorious Party Members in their work' (p. 121)
26. 'Yung', interview, 1967
27. The Chinese Middle School Students Arts Society, banned in 1956
28. 'Yung', interview, 1967. Also *Straits Times* 18 and 19 April 1955
29. Douglas Hyde, comments on first draft, June 1969
30. White Paper, SCMSSU, 1956, p. 8
31. White Paper, SCMSSU, 1956, p. 16
32. *ibid.* p. 14. Presumably these particular executives (i.e. monitors) were ones whose posts had not been captured by the Standard Committee's nominees
33. 'Ching', interview, 1967
34. 'Yung', interview, 1967. For example, the tale of Liew Fu Lan, aged sixteen, who was arrested and killed by the Kuomintang, or one of Mao Tse Tung's poems

NOTES

35. Goh Keng Swee, reported in the Singapore *Sunday Times*, 29 January 1967
36. Central Committee of the Malayan Communist Party, *Record of Decisions*, 13 June 1940 (quoted in Hanrahan p. 98)
37. In this and the next two quotations, the italics are the author's
38. Liu Shao Shi (then Vice-Chairman of the Chinese Communist Party) in a message to the Second National Congress Youth Corps, quoted in White Paper, SCMSSU, 1956, p. 12
39. Basic Knowledge Textbook of the China New Democratic Youth Corps, quoted in White Paper, SCMSSU, 1956, p. 12
40. White Paper, SCMSSU, 1956, p. 12
41. White Paper, SCMSSU, 1956, p. 12
42. White Paper, SCMSSU, 1956, pp. 8 and 11
43. 'Yung', interview, 1966
44. White Paper, SCMSSU, 1956, p. 7
45. 'Yung', interview, 1967
46. 'Ching', interview, 1967
47. White Paper, SCMSSU, 1956, p. 17
48. 'Yung', interview, 1967
49. White Paper, SCMSSU, 1956, p. 17
50. 'Yung', interview, 1967
51. MCP Directive of 11 June 1956, quoted in White Paper, SCMSSU, 1956, p. 1

CHAPTER 6   SELF-GOVERNMENT

1. Douglas Hyde, interview, 1969
2. *ibid.* See also Chapter 8 for Lee Kuan Yew's account of the relationship between Lim Chin Siong and the MCP Underground organization
3. Lee Kuan Yew, *Battle*, p. 1
4. Lee Kuan Yew, *Battle*, p. 27
5. *Singapore Legislative Assembly Debates, Official Report*, 21 September 1955, Column 749
6. *Constitutional Commission, Singapore*, Report by Sir George Rendel, 22 February 1954, Government Printing Office, Singapore 1954, pp. 3, 9, 10, 17 and 18
7. Blades, comments
8. David Marshall, in a talk on 'The Struggle for Nationhood' at St. Andrew's Cathedral, Singapore on 12 July 1969
9. *Straits Times*, 23 April 1955
10. *Report on the Singapore All Party Mission to London April/May 1956* (Singapore Sessional Paper No. Cmd 31 of 1956), p. 20
11. *SLA Debates*, 27 April 1955, Column 141
12. David Marshall, interview, 1968
13. *Rendel Report*, p. 19
14. Lee Kuan Yew, *Battle*, p. 19
15. Lee Kuan Yew, *Battle*, pp. 17 and 18
16. *Straits Times*, 5 May 1955
17. *ibid.*, 6 May 1955
18. G. G. Thomson, comments
19. Lee Kuan Yew, *Battle*, pp. 66 and 67
20. David Marshall, interview, 1968

21. *SLA Debates*, 27 April 1955, Column 141
22. *SLA Debates*, 27 April 1955, Column 148
23. *Straits Times*, 23 April 1955. The sections revoked were Nos. 3, 6, 17, 18, 19, 22, 25, and 32. In addition to the relaxations mentioned in the text, the police also lost the power to seize transport, arms, foodstuffs, defence materials and printing premises if they judged this to be in the interests of public safety
24. *SLA Debates*, 27 April 1955, Column 155. Lee Kuan Yew was willing to accept the Emergency Regulations as such so long as they were necessary during the Emergency in Malaya. G. G. Thomson, comments
25. Lee Kuan Yew, in *SLA Debates*, 16 May 1955, Column 204
26. *Straits Times*, 25 April 1955
27. *SLA Debates*, 16 May 1955, Columns 176–86
28. *Straits Times*, 29–30 April 1955
29. *SLA Debates*, 16 May 1955, Columns 188–90
30. *ibid*. Column 191
31. *ibid*. Columns 176–86
32. *The Times*, London, 13 May 1955
33. G. G. Thomson, comments
34. *SLA Debates*, 16 May 1955, Columns 176–86
35. *Straits Times*, 13 May 1955
36. *Straits Times*, 16 May 1955
37. G. G. Thomson, comments
38. *SLA Debates*, 16 May 1955, Column 175
39. *ibid*. Columns 201–2
40. *ibid*. Column 225
41. *SLA Debates*, 21 September 1955, Column 751
42. *SLA Debates*, 12 October 1955, Column 856
43. *Report on the Singapore All-Party Mission to London April/May 1956* (Singapore Sessional Paper No. Cmd 31 of 1956) p. 18
44. *ibid*. p. 52
45. *ibid*. p. 68
46. *ibid*. p. 20
47. *ibid*. p. 15
48. *ibid*. p. 7
49. *ibid*. p. 6
50. David Marshall, interview, 1968
51. Sing. Cmd No. 31 of 1956, p. 8
52. *ibid*. p. 7
53. *ibid*. p. 8
54. *ibid*. p. 14
55. *ibid*. p. 15
56. David Marshall, interview, 1968
57. Lee Kuan Yew, *Battle*, p. 25. He names these as Lim Chin Siong, Devan Nair, Chia Ek Tian and Goh Boon Toh
58. Lee Kuan Yew, *Battle*, p. 25
59. Lim Yew Hock, interview, 1965
60. Blades, comments
61. *White Paper*, SCMSSU, 1956
62. *Straits Times*, 20 October 1956
63. *SLA Debates*, 4 October 1956, Columns 322–3
64. In the debate following the riots, Lee Kuan Yew, though he accused the government of deliberately provoking the riots at a time of their own

NOTES

choosing, admitted that 'once mobs were on the streets, the only answer was force'. *SLA Debates*, 6 November 1956, Column 584
65. *ibid.* Column 328
66. *ibid.* Column 400
67. *ibid.* Column 402. In a later debate after the riots and after the detention of Lim Chin Siong, Lee Kuan Yew said 'To fight the Communists, one must understand . . . what they are after. Is it evil? I am not convinced myself that Communism is an evil force. In fact, I agree with about 75 per cent of what they want to do. But it is that 25 per cent of how they do it that I object to and oppose.' *SLA Debates*, 6 November 1956, Column 581
68. *SLA Debates*, 4 October 1956, Column 333
69. *ibid.* Columns 331–2
70. *Straits Times*, 11 October 1956
71. *Straits Times*, 11 October 1956
72. *Straits Times*, 13 October 1956

CHAPTER 7   THE RIOTS OF OCTOBER 1956

1. Lee Kuan Yew, *Battle for Merger*, pp. 69–70 and Blades, comments
2. *SLA Debates*, 5 November 1956, Column 417 and 6 November 1956, Column 501. In the debate, the Minister for Education (Chew Swee Kee) said that Lim Chin Siong urged the crowd at Bukit Timah that instead of shouting '*Merdeka*' (Freedom) they should now shout 'Pah Mata' (Bash the Police)
3. Blades, comments
4. Lee Kuan Yew subsequently accused the Government of deliberately provoking the riots in order to carry out a purge, at a time to suit themselves, initially by their acting against the SCMSSU and other front organizations, and finally by the calculated action of the police in allowing the crowd to build up and get out of hand outside the Chinese High School on 25 October, *SLA Debates*, 5 November 1956, Column 479. Also 6 November 1956, Column 576
5. Blades, comments
6. Mr. Samuel Dhoraisingham, interview, 1968
7. G. G. Thomson, comments. Thomson considers that the Communists made a blunder here. Had they persuaded the students to go home they would have scored a propaganda victory, and could then have put the Government on the defensive by peaceful agitation in the Chinese press, which they controlled. The Government would eventually have had to give way or initiate the use of force. As it was, by encouraging the students to use violence they provoked a test of arms which the Government was bound to win, and bound to emerge with a favourable image as restorers of the peace. This, of course, is just what did happen. Dominic Puthucheary, the younger brother of one of the Middle Road leaders, stated (in an interview in 1969) that both his brother (James) and Lim Chin Siong realized this and did their best to discourage violence, but all other sources consulted confirmed Thomson's view
8. In the subsequent debate in the Assembly the Chief Minister commented 'The member for Tanjong Pagar [Mr. Lee Kuan Yew] described the use of British troops as having a poisonous effect on the population. I wonder how many of the ordinary people of Singapore would have accepted that description when they first saw British troops manning road blocks on the morning of the 26th after a night of constant mob violence or during

NOTES

the days and nights that followed?' *SLA Debates*, 6 November 1956, Column 573

9. Alan Blades commented as follows: 'I think that it was recognized later that so long as the Police Force was still a going concern, this was the way it must be – joint control, each service under its own officers, the Police in the front line and doing the ferreting, the military backing up; supplying Cordons and Control Points and filling in wherever the Police might be otherwise engaged. . . . the request for aid was never, even remotely, in the nature of a cry of distress when almost all was lost. It was part of a well practised plan of prudence – to present an overwhelming deterrent at the earliest tactical juncture . . . the civil authority . . . would have hesitated to ask for aid if it meant the immediate handover of control to a military command.'
10. Blades, comments
11. There is no doubt that various gangsters, other than those who were Communist led, did take the opportunity to use violence during the riots, though not on any significant scale
12. Blades, comments
13. G. G. Thomson, comments
14. Alan Blades, who by 1958 had become Commissioner of Police, commented 'I held this view strongly and, in preparation for the next stage of constitutional development in 1958 in Singapore, ordered the cessation of the use of the rifle as a police weapon, except in the Gurkha and Reserve units, and had them stored in armouries for emergencies only. But Lee Kuan Yew and his Ministers held quite the opposite view. . . .' Unarmed police, however, are very rare outside Britain itself and one or two other countries in the Commonwealth
15. G. G. Thomson was at that time in charge of the Singapore Government Information Service. World cover was scanty, as world news was dominated by the Russian action in Hungary. The British intervention in the Suez war, fortuitously, did not occur until a few days after the riots. Had this been the other way round, the revolutionaries would have had a magnificent propaganda point, and the appearance of British troops in Singapore might have been greeted very differently. The British action in Suez was certainly the subject of some pointed comment in the debate after the riots. See, for example, *SLA Debates*, 5 November 1956, Column 480
16. G. G. Thomson, comments
17. In *The Battle for Merger*, p. 21
18. G. G. Thomson, comments
19. Blades, comments
20. Douglas Hyde, interview, 1969. See also his article 'The Star that Fell', published in the *Far Eastern Economic Review* just after Lim's release from detention in July 1969
21. Hong Kong provides about 50 per cent of Communist China's foreign exchange
22. *The Economist*, 27 May 1967
23. A. J. Shephard, 'The Communist Failure in Hong Kong' in the *Commonwealth Journal*, April 1968, p. 98
24. $HK 500 was a reasonably high monthly wage in Hong Kong
25. Denis Bloodworth, in the Singapore *Sunday Times*, 30 September 1967
26. Denis Bloodworth, in the Singapore *Sunday Times*, 15 October 1967
27. *The Economist*, 27 May 1967
28. *The Economist*, 27 May 1967

NOTES

29. Denis Bloodworth in the *Singapore Sunday Times*, 15 October 1967
30. A. J. Shephard, pp. 85–6

CHAPTER 8   THE STRUGGLE FOR POLITICAL CONTROL

1. Milton E. Osborne, *Singapore and Malaysia*, Cornell University New York, U.S.A. 1964, p. 4
2. *Report of the Singapore Constitutional Conference*, London H.M.S.O. April 1957, (Cmnd 147) p. 16. In the event the Constitution did not come into force until 1959
3. Lee Kuan Yew disowned the 'moderate' label in the *Singapore Legislative Assembly Debate* on 8 October 1958 (Column 808)
4. *Singapore Cmd* 33 of 23 August 1957
5. *SLA Debates*, 12 September 1957, Column 2629–30
6. The inclusion of the Borneo territories in the merger was not at this time part of the plan
7. The writer was based in Kuala Lumpur from 1956–8 and recalls a widespread feeling amongst British and Malayan officials that Singapore was a cesspit of Communism and must be kept out of the Federation at all costs
8. G. G. Thomson, comments
9. *Cmd 147* p. 5
10. *ibid.* p. 6
11. *ibid.* p. 7
12. *ibid.* pp. 14–15
13. *ibid.* p. 10
14. Compare discussion between the Governor and David Marshall in 1955 – see Chapter 6
15. *Cmd 147* p. 9
16. *SLA Debates* 26 April 1957, Columns 1707–8
17. Lee Kuan Yew, *Battle* p. 51 and pp. 58–64
18. *Cmd 147*, p. 9. Before the 1959 elections, Lee Kuan Yew successfully insisted that the existing Public Service Commission be dissolved and the members of its successor selected by the incoming Prime Minister (Blades, comments)
19. *Cmd 147*, p. 10
20. *SLA Debates*, 12 September 1957, Column 2634. Lee also quoted (Column 2629) from his election manifesto: 'The by-election is to find out if you who elected me as PAP candidate in April 1955 approve of the stand that I, as a member of the PAP and of the recent Constitutional Mission to London took on two issues, which are the constitutional proposals and the anti-subversion clause.'
21. In *The Battle for Merger*, p. 26
22. *Sing Cmd 33* of 1957 and *SLA Debates* 12 September 1957, Columns 2597–600. Three of those arrested were later deported to China as proven Communists. It was the Communist 'second team' which was arrested, the first team having already been detained since the 1956 riots.
23. Lee Kuan Yew, *Battle*, p. 26
24. Legislative Assembly Singapore Sessional Paper No. Cmd 33 of 1957, *The Communist Threat in Singapore*, Singapore 23 August 1957
25. *ibid.* pp. 1–2
26. *ibid.* p. 3
27. *ibid.* p. 3
28. *ibid.* pp. 4–6

NOTES

29. *ibid.* p. 4
30. *ibid.* pp. 6–7
31. *SLA Debates* 12 September 1957, Columns 2601–2. It is interesting that he still referred to the PAP leadership as 'non-Communist' and not 'anti-Communist'
32. Lee Kuan Yew, *Battle*, p. 34
33. Lee Kuan Yew, *Battle*, p. 37
34. Osborne, *Singapore*, p. 6n.
35. Blades, comments
36. See Lee Kuan Yew, *Battle*, p. 37
37. Lee Kuan Yew, *Battle*, p. 39. Also quoted in the *Straits Times*
38. Osborne, *Singapore*, p. 93
39. Fong Swee Suan, James Puthucheary, S. Woodhull, Chan Chiaw Thor and Devan Nair
40. Alan Blades comments: 'To Lee Kuan Yew, these activists were the "Dynamos" of society. His attitude was "put them somewhere where they will have to show which way they want to bounce; if our way well and good; if not we shall know where we stand and can deal with them accordingly!" A conversion rate of even only 1 in 10 would be worthwhile. Devan Nair was a case in point. He was one of the most virulent Communist sympathizers when first detained with the rest of the University of Malaya group in January 1951.' See also Lee, *Battle*, pp. 33 and 75
41. Lee Kuan Yew, *Battle*, p. 31
42. *ibid.* p. 41 and p. 30
43. *ibid.* pp. 41–44
44. Osborne, *Singapore* pp. 10–11
45. *ibid.* p. 12
46. Lee Kuan Yew, *Battle*, p. 59
47. *Straits Times*, 31 March 1961
48. The PLEN, in fact, headed the MCP Town Committee in Singapore until 1962, when he left for Indonesia
49. Lee Kuan Yew, *Battle*, p. 46. Dominic Puthucheary, in an interview in 1969, identified this relative as being one of the PLEN's sisters, who had been helped by Lee when she suffered injury from burns. Lee also sponsored her for membership of the Assembly, but she later joined his opponents
50. *ibid.* p. 47
51. *ibid.* p. 73 and Osborne, *Singapore*, p. 17
52. Osborne, *Singapore*, p. 18
53. *ibid.* pp. 18 and 96, and Lee Kuan Yew, *Battle*, p. 74. The fact that the defeated PAP candidate was a Malay drew strong Malay reaction and frustrated the Communists' hope that the breakaway party (The Barisan Sosialis) would be multi-racial. G. G. Thomson, comments
54. Osborne, *Singapore*, pp. 18 and 93
55. Lee Kuan Yew, *Battle*, pp. 48–55
56. *ibid.* pp. 53, 76
57. *ibid.* pp. 78–9
58. *ibid.* p. 47
59. Osborne, *Singapore*, p. 13
60. *Nangyang Siang Pau* (a Singapore Chinese newspaper) 8 May 1961, quoted in Osborne, *Singapore*, p. 14
61. Lee Kuan Yew, *Battle*, pp. 47 and 55
62. Osborne, *Singapore*, p. 15. Also *SLA Debates* 30 July 1963, Column 301
63. Osborne, *Singapore*, p. 19

NOTES

64. Lee Kuan Yew, *Battle*, p. 80
65. In assessing their value as a source, it must be remembered that these broadcasts were made during a crisis in which Lee Kuan Yew was fighting for his political life
66. Osborne, *Singapore*, p. vi n.
67. *Singapore Command Paper No. 53* of 1961
68. *SLA Debates*, 20 November 1962, Column 281–328
69. *SLA Debates*, 16 March 1962, Columns 293–99
70. G. G. Thomson, comments
71. Osborne, *Singapore*, p. 25
72. *SLA Debates*, 6 July 1962, Column 1022
73. Osborne, *Singapore*, p. 28
74. G. G. Thomson, comments
75. *Straits Times*, 1 January 1963
76. As in 1956 (see Chapter 7) Lim Chin Siong 'took no evasive action when detention was imminent, ignoring a tacit warning from Lee Kuan Yew who would rather have had him out of the way.' Blades, comments
77. G. G. Thomson, comments. Confirmed by Dominic Puthucheary (interview 1969). See also Osborne, *Singapore*, p. 32
78. *Straits Times*, 1 January 1963
79. During the next year, the Barisan Sosialis gained control of most of the Nanyang University Students' Societies, and of the Committee of the Students' Union, which was dissolved by the government in 1964. See Federation Government White Paper, *Nanyang University Communist Activities*, Kuala Lumpur 1964. Also 'Yung' (interview) 1967
80. 'The Brunei revolt also had the effect of persuading the U.K. Government, almost overnight, that it must abandon a position which it had taken up over a Kuala Lumpur condition for Merger – that Lim Chin Siong and the rest of his associates should again be put in detention before Merger became effective in August 1963 – a condition which suited Lee Kuan Yew so long as he could lay it clearly at the door of the Federation.' Blades, comments
81. Osborne, *Singapore*, p. 33
82. Osborne, *Singapore*, p. 34
83. Blades, comments
84. Osborne, *Singapore*, pp. 35 and 93–111
85. *Straits Times*, 27 September and 8–9 October 1963
86. G. G. Thomson, comments
87. Osborne, *Singapore*, p. 84
88. Blades, comments
89. G. G. Thomson, comments

CHAPTER 9 THE FIRST YEARS OF THE EMERGENCY

1. This conference was followed by similar outbreaks of violence in other South East Asian countries, but it is an exaggeration to say that 'orders' were given for these uprisings at the conference, as part of some co-ordinated plan conceived for South East Asia in Moscow, as is sometimes suggested. See Ruth McVey, *The Calcutta Conference and the South East Asian Uprisings*, Cornell University, Ithaca, New York 1958
2. Charles Gamba, *The Origins of Trade Unionism in Malaya*, Eastern Universities Press, Singapore 1962, p. 335
3. Alex Josey, *Trade Unionism in Malaya*, Singapore, Donald Moore 1954,

NOTES

p. 17. In June 1948 there were 302 unions in the Federation of Malaya, with a membership of 150,000. Of these, 129 unions with a membership of roughly 82,000 were controlled by the Communist-led PMFTU

4. This was probably planned at the PMFTU meeting in Singapore in April, and endorsed by a meeting next day of the MCP Supreme Executive, which was in the next building. During this Open Front period, PMFTU leaders made no effort to conceal their membership of the MCP. See Gamba p. 334
5. Victor Purcell, *The Chinese in South East Asia*, London, Oxford University Press 1965, p. 330. See also Edgar O'Ballance *Malaya – The Communis Insurgency 1948-60*, London 1966, pp. 77-9
6. Gamba p. 333
7. *Straits Times*, 9 June 1948
8. Miller p. 83. He in fact described it as the 8th Regiment, but this regiment was in Kedah, so presumably this is a slip or a misprint. The Perak Regiment was the 5th
9. John Davis, interview, 1966
10. Gamba pp. 342-3
11. *The Emergency Regulations Ordinance 1948* (amended up to 31 March 1953) Kuala Lumpur, Government Press 1953
12. P. B. G. Waller, *A Study of the Emergency Regulations in Malaya 1948-1960* (Draft) Stanford Research Institute, Bangkok 1967, and R. D. Rhenick Jnr., *The Emergency Regulations in Malaya*, Master's Thesis, Tulane University, U.S.A. 1964
13. Sir Robert Thomson, *Defeating Communist Insurgency*, London 1966, pp. 53-4
14. Blades, comments. This is further discussed in Part III.
15. Gamba p. 350
16. Gamba p. 363
17. Sir Robert Thompson, interview 1965; also his *Defeating Communist Insurgency*, London 1966, p. 52
18. *Emergency Regulations Ordinance*
19. Miller p. 91
20. P. B. G. Waller, *Notes on the Malayan Emergency Strategies and Organisation of the Opposing Forces*, Stanford Research Institute, California, U.S.A. 1967, p. 21. Also Miller p. 93
21. Based on Waller, *Notes*, p. 17
22. Purcell, *Chinese*, p. 332
23. Malayan Communist Party, *Strategic Problems on the Malayan Revolutionary War*, December 1948, published in G.Z. Hanrahan, *The Communist Struggle in Malaya*, New York 1954, pp. 102-15
24. This was later recognized by the government in their resettlement policy. Waller, interview, 1970
25. Miller, pp. 154-9
26. This is probably correct. See also Clutterbuck, *The Long Long War*, Chapter 18. Casualties inflicted by bombing were negligible until 1956, when the RAF began precision bombing on targets fixed accurately by intelligence agents
27. *Supplementary Views of the Central Politburo of the Malaya Communist Party on 'Strategic Problems of the Malaya Revolutionary War'*, 12 November 1949, cited by Hanrahan pp. 117-29
28. Miller, p. 119. See also Chapters 11 and 12
29. Kernial Singh Sandhu, 'Emergency Resettlement in Malaya', *Journal of Tropical Geography*, University of Malaya in Singapore August 1964,

which provides a comprehensive study of resettlement, so the subject is therefore only outlined briefly in this book
30. Sandhu, *passim*. A summary of the categories and sizes of villages is in Figure 13. The majority were in a village of between 1,000 and 5,000 people, since this was found to give the best balance between economy, control and defence
31. Thompson, *Defeating Communist Insurgency*, pp. 103 and 210
32. Waller, interview, 1970
33. The price of rubber rose from 38 cents per lb. in 1949 to 108 cents in 1950, and averaged 169 cents per lb. in 1951, during which it once reached a peak of 237 cents per lb. Ooi Jin Bee, *Land, People and Economy in Malaya*, London 1963, p. 206 and Dunlop Malaya Estates Ltd., *The Story of a Rubber Tree* (mimeograph), Malacca 1965
34. Davis, interview, 1966. The limitations on the ability of an insurgent movement to absorb recruits are described by Sir Robert Thompson in *Defeating Communist Insurgency*, p. 66 and in his foreword to Clutterbuck, *The Long Long War*, London edition, Cassell 1967
35. *Emergency (Tenants Registration) Regulations*, Kuala Lumpur 1951
36. Thompson, p. 85. Malcolm Browne, in *The New Face of War*, London 1966, pp. 265-6 lists 9 separate U.S. agencies alone, not to mention 5 or 6 Vietnamese agencies. Michael Clark, in *Algeria in Turmoil*, London 1960, p. 9, listed 6 in Algeria
37. The Police Circle was a group of districts, an intermediate level to ease the span of command of the State Chief Police Officer (CPO). Major operations (see Chapter 11) normally straddled the boundaries of two or more districts, and were therefore handled on the police side by one Officer Superintending the Police Circle (OSPC) and the Circle Special Branch Officer (CSBO), serving whichever DWEC was nominated to run the operation. There were sometimes MIOs in the large independent districts (such as the city of Ipoh) whose police officers had the same ranks as those in the Police Circles in rural areas
38. Waller, interview, 1970
39. Miller, p. 101
40. Waller, interview, 1970
41. See Lucian Pye, *Guerrilla Communism in Malaya*, Princeton 1956, p. 339. This book consists of an analysis of interviews with 60 SEPs in 1952-3
42. Chapman p. 156
43. Blades, comments
44. See also Clutterbuck, *The Long Long War*, pp. 168-9. This book contains a fuller account of the SEP phenomenon on pp. 101-11. See also Pye *passim*
45. Malayan Communist Party *Directive* of 1 October 1951; English translation published in *The Times*, London, on 1 December 1952
46. Miller p. 225
47. His escort had been left behind due to a breakdown. The MRLA platoon diary, captured later, gives no indication that they were awaiting him, or that they knew who he was afterwards. They were on a mountainous road used by many VIP cars, and they seized the chance when one approached unescorted. Miller p. 225
48. Waller, interview, 1968
49. Sir Robert Thompson, *Defeating Communist Insurgency*, pp. 52-5
50. For an account of the Federation's advance to independence see Lennox A. Mills, *Malaya – A Political and Economic Appraisal*, Minneapolis, The

NOTES

    University of Minnesota Press 1958; see also Clutterbuck, *The Long Long War*, pp. 135–49
51. MCP Directive of December 1948
52. Sir Robert Thompson, in a talk to the Royal Commonwealth Society in London on 8 November 1966 reported in the *Commonwealth Journal*, February 1967, p. 14
53. Sandhu p. 168
54. See Browne pp. 103–4
55. O'Ballance pp. 119 and 129
56. Thompson, *Defeating Communist Insurgency*, p. 135
57. Miller p. 218
58. *ibid.*
59. 'Security is development; without development there can be no security', Robert S. McNamara, *The Essence of Security*, London 1967
60. Ooi Jin Bee p. 206
61. Thompson, *Defeating Communist Insurgency*, pp. 60–8
62. O'Ballance p. 119
63. Sandhu p. 180
64. Waller, interview, 1967
65. An attempt was made in August 1950 to counter Malay resentment against the spending of money on the Chinese, by setting up the Rural and Industrial Development Authority (RIDA), designed to develop rural areas, particularly for the Malay farmers. In his Report on RIDA (Kuala Lumpur, Government Printing Office 1957) D. E. M. Fiennes criticized the three watertight compartments into which the rural community was divided: plantations, Chinese smallholders and Malay farmers. He said that almost every educated Malay went into government service, and virtually none into organizing the development of the productive economy of the Malay people. For this reason, RIDA achieved little success.
66. Waller, *Notes*, p. 52
67. Clutterbuck, *The Long Long War*, pp. 59–60
68. Thompson, *Defeating Communist Insurgency*, pp. 94–7
69. See also Thompson, *Defeating Communist Insurgency*, p. 100
70. Thompson, *Defeating Communist Insurgency*, p. 93
71. O'Ballance p. 105
72. Miller p. 223
73. Clutterbuck, *The Long Long War*, p. 131

CHAPTER 10   ORGANIZATION FOR SURVIVAL

1. See Clutterbuck, *The Long Long War*, pp. 170–3
2. Based on Waller, *Notes*, p. 17
3. Waller, *Notes*, p. 19
4. Based on Clutterbuck, *The Long Long War*, p. 88
5. See also Emergency Regulation No. 4C
6. See Clutterbuck, *The Long Long War*, pp. 89–90
7. *Straits Times*, 28 August 1958
8. K. S. Sandhu, *Working Papers* made available to the author at Singapore University in 1966

CHAPTER 11   THE DEVELOPMENT OF A SUCCESSFUL TECHNIQUE

1. See Arthur Campbell, *Jungle Green*, London 1953

NOTES

2. Clutterbuck, *The Long Long War*, pp. 51–4
3. Brigadier M. C. A. Henniker, *Red Shadow over Malaya*, London 1955, pp. 131–2
4. This predilection for major operations persisted amongst some commanders for several more years, see Clutterbuck, *The Long Long War*, pp. 51–2. It was also the bane of the life of many regimental soldiers in Vietnam, who longed to be left to get on uninterrupted with the war around the villages without repeatedly being picked up by the higher staffs and borne away in helicopters to join the throng in some alien area of jungle. (Interviews with Lt. Col. G. C. Troy, 1967, and interviews and correspondence from Vietnam with Lt. Cols. Charles K. Nulsen and Robert B. Osborn, 1962 to 1968)
5. At this period (1950) the strength of the guerrillas in Malaya (10,000) was double that in South Vietnam in 1959–60 (5,000) – that is, four times higher in proportion to the population. Had the South Vietnamese Army applied such tactics in its own jungle areas in those early days, the Vietcong main force units might have been cut back, as they were in Malaya, rather than allowed to grow into hundreds of thousands. The fact that the guerrillas in Malaya never progressed beyond these early stages was not for lack of trying on their part – Chin Peng's plan was the same as Giap's – but because they were prevented from doing so. See Sir Robert Thompson in his foreword to Clutterbuck, *The Long Long War*, London 1967, p. viii
6. John Davis, interview, 1966
7. Henniker p. 132
8. *ibid.* p. 138
9. *ibid.* pp. 134–5
10. *ibid.* p. 135–6
11. The SAS was a regiment of hand-picked British soldiers, each man selected after a parachute course and intensive tests of physical and mental endurance in the Welsh mountains, and trained to operate independently in enemy territory. They were particularly successful in operating in small patrols in the remote parts of the jungle
12. Henniker pp. 142–3
13. *ibid.* p. 146
14. *ibid.* pp. 147–54
15. *ibid.* p. 137
16. *ibid.* p. 187
17. *ibid.* p. 140
18. It was later found necessary to extend this period to four or six months
19. Waller, interview, 1968

CHAPTER 12 THE FINAL PATTERN

1. A number of detailed examples of the recruitment of agents are given in Clutterbuck's *The Long Long War*, pp. 95–100
2. An example of such a deception plan was given in the account of Operation HIVE in Chapter 11
3. Waller, interview, 1970
4. Waller, interview, 1970
5. Clutterbuck, *The Long Long War*, p. 122
6. Clutterbuck, *The Long Long War*, p. 114

NOTES

CHAPTER 13   OPERATION COBBLE 1956-7

1. Richard Miers, *Shoot to Kill*, London 1959, p. 142. This was in fact an overestimate – Miers, p. 211
2. *ibid.* pp. 140-1
3. *ibid.* p. 142
4. *ibid.* p. 143
5. 1956 Census
6. Miers p. 145
7. *ibid.* p. 150
8. *ibid.* p. 158
9. Now Lord Chalfont
10. Miers pp. 177-9
11. Many of those charted for the Selumpur Branch had, unknown to Special Branch, already been eliminated in various ways – see Miers p. 211
12. These included some not predominately Chinese, and therefore not listed in Figure 23
13. Miers p. 185
14. This lack of 'policemen on the beat' was one of the biggest single weaknesses of the Vietnam war. There was no real equivalent to a police force in the hamlets. Security was in the hands of the Popular Force (an equivalent of the Home Guard) which generally lived with its families in a separate wired compound well outside the hamlet. Even the hamlet and village chiefs seldom dared sleep in the hamlets, but came in by the day. Any ordinary villager who had failed to obey Vietcong orders, or, even more daringly, had given information to the government, had no protection at night from 'the man with the knife', of whom the villagers were far more frightened than of the Vietcong units in the jungles outside. (Interviews with three Vietnamese colonels visiting Singapore, 1966, confirmed on a visit to Vietnam by the author, 1967)
15. This description is based upon a four-day visit by the author to 1 SWB in Segamat in January 1957, in which he went through a complete cycle of gate checks, street patrols and perimeter patrols in Pekan Jabi; also the initial cordon and search of Buloh Kasap, a rubber patrol and an ambush
16. pp. 167-213
17. Miers p. 213
18. Tunku Abdul Rahman, at a Press Conference in Kuala Lumpur on 26 August 1958, reported in the *Malay Mail*, 27 August 1946

CHAPTER 14   THE CRUMBLE AND THE HARD CORE

1. Frank Kitson, *Gangs and Counter-gangs*, London 1966. For a fuller exposition of Frank Kitson's philosophy, see his *Low Intensity Operations*, London, 1971
2. Kitson, interview, 1969. See also *Malay Mail*, 27 August 1958
3. Clutterbuck, *The Long Long War*, p. 166
4. Tunku Abdul Rahman, Press Conference, 26 August 1958
5. *Straits Times*, 27 August 1958
6. Hor Lung, Statement published in the *Malay Mail*, 27 August 1958
7. *ibid.*
8. Tunku Abdul Rahman, Press Conference, 26 August 1958
9. Free passages to China had been offered as early as January 1952 to those refusing resettlement, and 700 had applied for them. Detained persons

NOTES

(including SEPs) could be deported at their own consent or request which came to the same thing. The offer of repatriation without interrogation was part of the Merdeka surrender terms published on 1 September 1957

10. *Straits Times*, 27 August 1958
11. The ambush of one of these is described in Clutterbuck's *The Long Long War*, p. 171
12. *Straits Times*, 27 August 1958
13. *Malay Mail*, 27 August 1958
14. Interviews, Colonel Napoleon Valeriano 1963 and Colonel Charles K. Nulsen 1968
15. Clutterbuck, 'Military Engineering as a Weapon in the Cold War' in the *Military Engineer*, Washington July–August 1963, pp. 231–2 and Clutterbuck, *The Long Long War*, pp. 153–5
16. Clutterbuck, 'Military Engineering', pp. 229–31 and *The Long Long War* pp. 150–2. Also Waller, interview, 1970
17. *The Resurgence of Armed Communism in West Malaysia*, Kuala Lumpur 1971
18. *ibid.* p. 5
19. *ibid.* p. 8

CHAPTER 15   THE BALANCE SHEET IN 1963

1. See also *The Danger and Where It Lies*, Information Services, Federation of Malaya, Kuala Lumpur 1957, pp. 57–63 for an account of Communist Trade Union tactics in the Federation of Malaya
2. Robert Moss, in *Urban Guerrillas* (London 1972) analyses a series of urban guerrilla and terrorist campaigns from that of the *Narodnaya Volya* in Russia in 1881 to the Black Panthers and the IRA in the 1970s. He concludes that urban terrorism without a mass base is a 'faulty weapon' with a poor record of success
3. G. G. Thomson, comments
4. Clutterbuck, *The Long Long War*, p. 74

CHAPTER 16   MALAYSIA AND HER NEIGHBOURS

1. Arnold C. Brackman, *Southeast Asia's Second Front*, London, Pall Mall Press 1966, pp. 140–41.
2. Douglas Hyde, "Sarawak: an Insurgency in Retreat" in *Spectrum*, Vol. 2 No. 4, July 1974.
3. E.D. Smith, "The Undeclared War" in *War in Peace*, Vol. 4 Issue 41, November 1983, pp. 813–5. Smith commanded a Gurkha battalion in Borneo and later became a Brigadier.
4. P.J. Banyard, "With Silence and Stealth" in *War in Peace*, Vol. 4 Issue 41, November 1983, pp. 818–9.
5. General Sir Walter Walker, "How Borneo Was Won" *Round Table* Vol. LIX, 1969.
6. J. Clementson, "Malaysia in the Seventies: Communist Resurgence and Government Response". *Royal United Service Institute Journal*, December 1979, p. 54.
7. Douglas Hyde, *op. cit.*
8. Richard Sim, "Malaysia: Continuing The Communist Insurgency", *Conflict Studies* No. 110, London, Institute for the Study of Conflict, 1979, p. 17.

NOTES

9. William Shaw, *Tun Razak: His Life and Times*, Kuala Lumpur, Longman 1976, p. 164-9 and C.M. Turnbull, *A History of Singapore, 1819-1975*, Kuala Lumpur, Oxford University Press, 1977, p. 288.
10. See pages 72-3. The 1956 riots, though they occurred later, were not primarily communal.
11. Shaw *op. cit.* p. 176 and Turnbull *op. cit.* p. 292.
12. Turnbull, *op. cit.* p. 293.
13. A British diplomat in Singapore in conversation with the author in September 1965.
14. Shaw, *op. cit.* p. 180.
15. Richard Sim, *op. cit.* p. 8.
16. Abdul Rahman, Director of Special Branch, Kuala Lumpur, in an interview with the author, 1971.
17. "*The Resurgence of Armed Communism in West Malaysia*", Kuala Lumpur, Ministry of Home Affairs, 1971, p. 8.
18. Malaysian Government Press Statements, 1975.
19. J. Clementson, *op. cit.* p. 53.

CHAPTER 17　　　　　　　　　　　　　　　THE 1969 RIOTS IN KUALA LUMPUR

1. The precise figure will never be known as most of the bodies, many burned beyond recognition, were buried by the authorities without reference to the relatives in order "not to inflame an already ugly racial situation" according to the National Operations Council, *The 13 May Tragedy: A Report*, Kuala Lumpur 1969 p. 68 (hereafter referred to as NOC *Report*). This *Report* also gave the official figure of deaths as 196 (*ibid* p. 88). John Slimming in *Malaysia: Death of a Democracy* (London, John Murray, 1969) estimated 800. A senior politician, who was closely involved, told the author in an interview in Kuala Lumpur in 1982 that he estimated "about 1,000". This is the estimate which the author found most convincing.
2. 1963 figures. C. Mary Turnbull, *A Short History of Malaysia, Singapore and Brunei*, Singapore, Graham Brash, 1980, p. 252. Though the total population had risen from 5.3 million to 7.2 million during the 15 years from 1948 to 1963, the balance between races had not greatly changed (see p. 33).
3. R.S. Milne and Diane K. Mauzy, *Politics and Government in Malaysia*, Singapore, Times Books, 1978, p. 38-41.
4. Karl von Vorys, *Democracy without Consensus*, Kuala Lumpur. Oxford University Press, 1976, p. 206. In practice the Law Courts have continued to use English, because of the enormity of the task of translating every law, regulation and precedent into a language which does not in any case provide for the many shades of meaning involved in legal argument.
5. Turnbull, *op. cit.* pp. 262-3 and Milne *op. cit.* p. 371.
6. This is in marked contrast to Northern Ireland where, despite efforts to avert it, voters have consistently voted on communal lines. On one side are the Roman Catholic descendants of the original Irish native population and, on the other side, the Protestant descendants of the settlers who came from England and Scotland in large numbers from the 17th century.
7. This, again, has been an ugly feature of Protestant/Catholic strife in the poorer housing areas of Northern Ireland.
8. NOC, *Report* pp. 15-16.
9. Shaw, *op. cit.* pp. 194-5.
10. For an analysis of the development of the PPP and PAS in the 1950s see Vorys, *op. cit.* p. 147-9. The PAS was at that time known under its English

NOTES

initials as PMIP but has since 1969 been more generally referred to under its Malay title, PAS, and this version will therefore be used in this book.

11. Goh Cheng Teik, *The May Thirteenth Incident and Democracy in Malaysia*, Kuala Lumpur, Oxford University Press, 1971, p. 16.
12. Based on Goh, *op. cit.* pp. 12-13.
13. *ibid.* pp. 14-15.
14. *Straits Times* 13 May 1969, cited in Goh, *op. cit.* p. 19.
15. For an analysis of this decision see Vorys, *op. cit.* pp. 317-8 and 324-5.
16. Shaw, *op. cit.* pp. 205-6.
17. There are full descriptions of the provocation and the rioting in Vorys, *op. cit;* also, less detailed, in Shaw *op. cit.* and NOC, *Report*.
18. Shaw, *op. cit.* p. 206 and interview with Dato Harun, January, 1982.
19. NOC, *Report* p. 38.
20. The *parang* is a machette used for reaping or slashing undergrowth, and is also used as a weapon.
21. Vorys, *op. cit.* p. 334.
22. This was reported by Peter Simms in *Life* Magazine on 21 July 1969. This report is cited by Vorys, p. 360, who also gives the Tunku's explanation about the difficulty of imposing a house curfew in Kampong Bharu, p. 366. The author, in interviews in Kuala Lumpur in 1982, found much residual indignation about the shooting of Chinese fleeing from burning houses.
23. *ibid.* p. 338.
24. *ibid.* p. 345.
25. Shaw, *op. cit.* p. 212.
26. Vorys, *op. cit.* p. 346.
27. Shaw, *op. cit.* pp. 212-3.

CHAPTER 18   MALAYSIA'S NEP AND FUTURE PROSPECTS

1. Shaw, *op. cit.* p. 219 and Turnbull, *op. cit.* p. 264.
2. Tunku Abdul Rahman, *May 13: Before and After* (Kuala Lumpur, Utusan Melayu Press, 1969).
3. Shaw, *op. cit.* p. 240.
4. Milne, *op. cit.* p. 158.
5. Shaw, *op. cit.* p. 244.
6. Harold Crouch, Lee Kam Hing and Michael Ong (eds) *Malaysian Politics and the 1978 Elections*, Kuala Lumpur, Oxford University Press, 1980 p. 297.
7. *ibid.* pp. 232-3 (one US dollar was very roughly two Malaysian dollars)
8. Turnbull, *op. cit.* p. 262.
9. Sir Anthony Heywood, interview, Singapore, January 1983. *Bumiputra* means, roughly, "sons of the soil" and is deemed to cover Malays, aborigines, Dyaks and other indigenous races in East and West Malaysia. It specifically excludes "immigrant races" (Chinese and Indians) and foreigners.
10. Shaw, *op. cit.* p. 236.
11. Milne, *op. cit.* p. 347.
12. *The Economist* 12 September 1981 and 5 June 1982.
13. *The Economist* 11 June 1983.
14. Shaw, *op. cit.* p. 239.
15. *ibid.* p. 235.
16. Milne, *op. cit.* p. 267.
17. Goh Cheng Teik, *op. cit.* pp. 29-32.
18. Mahathir bin Mohamad, *The Malay Dilemma*, Petaling Jaya, Federal Publications, 1981. pp. 17, 21 and 29.

NOTES

19. *ibid.* pp. 157, 168.
20. *ibid.* p. 50.
21. *ibid.* 7.
22. *ibid.* p. 43.
23. *ibid.* pp. 7-8.
24. Anwar Ibrahim, interview with the author in Kuala Lumpur, January 1982. See also *Asia week* 24 August 1979.
25. Roughly 20% of all Malaysian University students were at British universities, numbering between 15,000 and 20,000. When the British required payment of full fees, only the rich could send their children and these were mainly Chinese. The British have now relaxed these rules for Malaysians, to come more in line with the USA, Canada and Australia.
26. *The Economist* 10 April 1982
27. Compiled from *The Economist* 13 November 1982
28. *Handbook of World Development*, Harlow, Longman, 1981 pp. 125-6
29. C.C. Too, Interview, Kuala Lumpur, January 1982
30. *The Economist* 17 April 1982
31. *The Economist* 11 June 1983
32. *The Economist* 20 November 1982
33. Resentment is by no means confined to families with children denied University places. There are still "National Type Primary Schools (Chinese) and (Tamil)" where the vernacular may be used but there are continual complaints of "insidious" encroachment of Malay through providing only Malay textbooks for certain subjects, Malay lyrics for songs etc (*Straits Times* 9 January 1982). A leading Chinese businessman, in an interview in Kuala Lumpur in 1982, told the author that there were very few Chinese families which did not have a grievance about the educational opportunities of at least one of the family.
34. The same threat has existed for the past 25 years – see page 260.
35. Mahathir, *op. cit.* p. 24
36. Shaw, *op. cit.* p. 235-6
37. *The Economist* 13 November 1982
38. C.V. Devan Nair, President of Singapore, in an interview with the author in Singapore, January 1983.
39. Under the Malaysian Constitution, the Sultans elect one of their number in turn to hold office as King (or Yang di-Pertuan Agung) for a period of five years, during which the King also remains Sultan of his own State. At the time of this crisis the King was the Sultan of Pahang.
40. *Straits Times*, 9 January 1984
41. *Far East Economic Review*, 20 October 1983
42. This view was strongly expressed to the author by a senior Malay newspaperman in Kuala Lumpur in 1982
43. Milne, *op. cit.* p. 344

CHAPTER 19   SINGAPORE: THE SOCIAL AND ECONOMIC MIRACLE

1. *Straits Times* 20 July 1964
2. Shaw, *op. cit.* p. 174 and *Straits Times* 22 and 23 July 1964
3. Shaw, *op. cit.* p. 174
4. *Straits Times* 24 July 1964
5. Police figures quoted in *Straits Times* 28 July 1964
6. *Straits Times* 3 August 1964

NOTES

7. Fong Sip Chee, *The PAP Story*, Singapore, Times Periodicals Pte Ltd., 1980 pp. 151-3. Also *Straits Times* 10 September 1964.
8. Chan Heng Chee, *The Dynamics of One Party Dominance*, Singapore University Press, 1976, gives a superbly researched and detailed account of this organization at constituency level. The fact that she is generally critical of the PAPs other methods of achieving its dominance (e.g. of the detention of opposition politicians and trade unionists and curbing of press freedom, as discussed in the next chapter) makes her objective study of the constituency organization all the more convincing.
9. Fong Sip Chee, *op. cit.* p. 105
10. This is a phenomenon common in parliamentary democracies worldwide. In Great Britain, for example, the Labour Party has always had to contend with a disproportionate number of Trotskyists in its Constituency Party Management Committees, politically far away from the mainstream of party voters but elected because they volunteer to do the hard work, if necessary working 12 hours a day. The Constituency Workers in the Conservative Party similarly tend to be on the right wing of that Party.
11. Fong Sip Chee, *op. cit.* p. 105
12. Chan Heng Chee, *op. cit.* p. 154
13. Seah Chee Meow, *Community Centres in Singapore. Their Political Involvement*, Singapore University Press, 1973. p. 31. cited in Chan Heng Chee, *op. cit.* p. 155.
14. Chan Heng Chee, *op. cit.* p. 155
15. *Reprint of Citizens' Consultative Committee Rules with Amendments* 1967, cited in Chan Heng Chee, *op. cit.* p. 136.
16. An MP in an interview with the author, Singapore 1982.
17. Chan Heng Chee, *op. cit.* pp. 141-2
18. Compiled from
    Chan Heng Chee *op. cit.* p. 190 (1959-72 Elections)
    Fong Sip Chee *op. cit.* p. 214 (1968-76 Elections)
    Time 25 January 1982 (1980 Elections)
19. *Time*, 25 January 1982
20. Sources: 1819-1921: *Peoples Action Party 1954-1979*, Singapore, PAP, 1979 p. 95
    1950 Interpolated
    1970 *Encyclopaedia Britannica* 1981 Vol. 16 p. 786
    1980 *Census of Population 1980, Singapore*, Singapore Department of Statistics 1981
21. John Drysdale, "How Singapore became No. 1" *Straits Times* 2 January 1982
22. *Encyclopaedia Britannica*, 1981, Vol. 16 p. 787
23. Chan Heng Chee, *op. cit.* p. 29
24. K.G. Tregonning, *Singapore: Its Successes and Its Future*, Singapore, Sassoon, 1980, p. 23
25. Han Fong Aik, Accounts Clerk, interview, Singapore 1982
26. *Census of Population 1980, Singapore*, Release No. 6 p. 8. See also *Singapore = Success*, Singapore Government Publication, 1979.
27. *Encyclopaedia Britannica* 1981 Vol. 16 p. 787
28. Lim Lee Im, then aged 22 and one of the third generation, spent three evenings with the author in her family's flat and in those of her friends in other blocks; also, along with other friends and cousins, in some of the oldest parts of Chinatown. The contrast, especially in space and hygiene, was staggering.
29. C. Mary Turnbull, *A History of Singapore*, 1819-1975, Kuala Lumpur, Oxford University Press, 1977 p. 311

NOTES

30. *ibid*. p. 312
31. In the HDB flat of Lim Lee Im's family (see pages 15 and 327) and in other Chinese households visited in 1982, the author noticed that the teenage and younger children spoke to each other entirely in English. Only grandfather (74) did not speak it.
32. Dr Goh Keng Swee, First Deputy Prime Minister (Education) in an interview with the author, January 1982.
33. *Economist* 3 September 1983
34. *Time* 25 January 1982
35. Extracted from *Census of Population, 1980, Singapore*
36. Compiled from Singapore Government Publications
37. Professor S Jayakumar, Minister of State for Home Affairs and Law, interview, January 1982.
38. Compiled by extrapolation from *Census of Population 1980, Singapore* Release No. 7 (July 1981) and from interviews with Dr Goh Keng Swee (Deputy PM) and Han Fong Aik (Accounts Clerk, construction industry) in January 1982.
39. Dr Goh Keng Swee, interview January 1982
40. Prime Minister's New Year Message, 1982, printed in the *Straits Times*, 1 January 1982
41. *ibid*.
42. Prime Minister's Eve of National Day Message, 1981. Transcript received from Prime Minister's Office.
43. Turnbull, *op. cit.* pp. 306-7
44. *ibid*. pp. 308-9
45. *Economist* 13 September 1983
46. John Drysdale, "How Singapore became No. 1" in the *Straits Times* 2 January 1982

CHAPTER 20   THE PRICE OF SUCCESS

1. C.V. Devan Nair, *Socialism that Works: The Singapore Way*, Singapore, Federal Publications, 1976.
2. Originally published in *The Law Gazette*, London, Vol. 4 March-June 1969
3. Chan Heng Chee, *op. cit.* pp. 202-3
4. *The Plebian* No. 76, 16 February 1969, cited in *ibid*. p. 203
5. DLP Paper in Devan Nair, *op. cit.* p. 255
6. Devan Nair, *op. cit.* p. 207
7. DLP Paper in Devan Nair, *op. cit.* p. 256
8. Devan Nair, *op. cit.* p. 135
9. Turnbull, *op. cit.* p. 307
10. *Time*, 25 January 1982, p. 17
11. DLP Paper in Devan Nair, *op. cit.* p. 261
12. Chan Heng Chee, *op. cit.* pp. 205-6 and Turnbull, *op. cit.* p. 322
13. Devan Nair, *op. cit.*, has published the full DLP indictment of the PAP Government's handling of the media (pp. 261-2), his own answers (pp. 131-5) and an illuminating series of public statements and press conferences on the subject by Lee Kuan Yew (pp. 170-186). The cross-examination of the Prime Minister by world journalists about the actions against the *Eastern Sun*, the *Singapore Herald* and *Nanyang Siang Pau* in 1971 is particularly valuable to any reader wanting to understand these issues.

NOTES

14. A summary of the Act is in Devan Nair, *op. cit.*, pp. 199–201, setting out the reasons for it, and giving details of the holders of all the management shares of Singapore newspaper companies in 1976.
15. Interviews in Singapore, January 1982, with a number of senior Chinese businessmen who were in other respects supporters of the Government.
16. Shaw, *op. cit.* p. 216
17. *Time* 25 January 1982
18. *Encyclopaedia Britannica*, 1981, Vol. 16 p. 788
19. *Time*, 25 January 1982
20. Lee Kuan Yew in a statement quoted in *The Economist*, 30 January 1982
21. Devan Nair, *op. cit.* p. 138
22. Chan Heng Chee, *op. cit.* p. 190
23. *op. cit.*
24. Turnbull, *op. cit.* pp. 319–20
25. The pros and cons of Proportional Representation (PR) are outside the scope of this book. Some argue that PR would have denied Singapore the strong decisive government which has led it to success; others that the 25% who oppose it, whether for intellectual reasons or because they feel deprived, should have a proportionate voice in Parliament. For what it is worth, the author's view is that both Britain and Singapore would benefit from a Single Transferable Vote instead of the "first-past-the-post" system or, better still, from the German-style list system. See Richard Clutterbuck, *Britain in Agony*, London, Penguin, 1980 p. 287–9.
26. Prime Minister's Eve of National Day Message, 1981.
27. Prime Minister's New Year Message for 1983, *Straits Times*, 1 January 1983
28. The Singapore *Straits Times*, 1 January 1984.
29. It is interesting that Sir Michael Edwardes, who transformed British Leyland from heavy loss to potential profit in 1977–82, began by introducing psychological tests for all his managers, including those already in post and as a result 150 out of 240 were fired or shifted to different jobs. Michael Edwardes, *Back from the Brink*, London, Collins, 1983.

Bibliography – Parts I and II

A – PRIMARY SOURCES

1 Interviews

BLADES, Alan. Singapore Police Officer from 1945–64, Director of Special Branch up to and during the 1954–6 riots, and then Commissioner of Police. Gave interviews and also commented in detail on first draft of Singapore section of this book.

'CHING'. Born 1941, son of a small contractor in Johore. Was involved with the Communist Movement at High School in Johore Bahru, 1956–9. Arrested 1959 and released. Later at Nanyang University (1963–8).

DAVIS, John. Commanded Force 136, the British mission with the Communists in the jungle (1943–5). Then served in the Malayan Civil Service till 1960. A Chinese speaker, he frequently talked to surrendered guerrillas and Chinese villagers during the Emergency.

DHORAISINGHAM, Samuel. Citizen during Singapore Riots 1946.

GENESTE, Marc. French army officer who fought in Indochina and Algeria.

GOH KENG SWEE. Leading member of Singapore Peoples Action Party (PAP) and later Finance Minister and Defence Minister.

GORRIE, Michael. District officer in Selangor during resettlement. Worked in Malaya and Singapore for more than twenty years.

HYDE, Douglas. Ex-member of the British Communist Party and News Editor of the *Daily Worker*. Author of *I Believed* and other books on Communism. Has interviewed many Communists in detention, including Lim Chin Siong in Singapore. He also commented on parts of the first draft for this book.

KITSON, F. E. A British army officer with experience in counter-insurgency operations in Kenya and Malaya.

MARSHALL, David. Singapore's first Chief Minister in 1955.

NULSEN, Lt. Col. Charles K. Served with U.S. Army in Vietnam, 1961–2 and 1966–7.

OSBORN, Lt. Col. Robert B. Served with U.S. Army in Vietnam, 1964–5 and 1970–1.

PUTHUCHEARY, Dominic. Brother of James Puthucheary, one of the leaders of the Peoples Action Party in Singapore in 1956. Dominic was a supporter and was later arrested and detained in 1962.

THOMPSON, Sir Robert. Secretary for Defence, Malaya 1957–60 and Head of British Mission, Vietnam 1960–4. Author of several books on revolutionary war.

THOMPSON, G. G. Director, Political Study Centre, Singapore. Was on Lord Mountbatten's Intelligence Staff in 1945 and was in charge of Information Services in Singapore in 1956. He lived in Singapore for over twenty years and became Singapore citizen. Gave interviews and also commented in detail on first draft of Singapore section of this book.

TROY, Lt. Col. Guy C. Served with U.S. Army in Vietnam in 1967–8.

VALERIANO, Colonel Napoleon. In Army of the Philippines.

WALLER, P. B. G. A British officer who served with the Malaysian Police from 1950 to 1966. He was Personal Staff Officer to Colonel Gray, Commissioner of Police in 1950–1. Later he commanded Police Field Force units in Pahang, and was OC District Police, Ipoh for the planning and launching of Operation GINGER.

'YUNG'. Born 1942 of poor Hokkien parents (father unemployed, mother a street hawker). Was on the fringe of the Communist movement at the Chinese High School, but later took part in the attempt to defeat its control of the Students Union at Nanyang University, 1960–5.

2 Documents

Documents	Abbreviation in Notes
Chief Statistician, *Monthly Digest of Statistics*, Singapore	Stats, Singapore
Commonwealth Relations Office Cmnd 620 of 1958 *Exchange of letters with Federa-*	CRO Cmnd 620 of 1956

BIBLIOGRAPHY

Documents	Abbreviation in in Notes
tion of Malaya on Internal Security Council in Singapore	
Constitutional Commission, Singapore. Report by Sir George Rendel, 22 Feb 1954	Rendel Report
Department of Statistics, *1957 Population Census of the Federation of Malaya, Report No. 14*, Kuala Lumpur	Census 1957
Emergency Regulations Ordinance 1948 (amended up to 31 March 1953), Kuala Lumpur, Government Press 1953	Emergency Regulations Ordinance, or ERs
Emergency (Tenants Registration) Regulations, Kuala Lumpur 1951	ERs (Tenants Reg)
Household Budget Survey 1957–58, Kuala Lumpur	Household Survey
*Malayan Communist Party (MCP) *Constitution*, March 1934	MCP, Const 1934
*MCP *Directive*, 11 June 1956, quoted in White Paper SCMSSU, 1956	
*MCP Political Bureau, *Party Directive* of 1 October 1951	MCP, 1951
*MCP *Record of Decisions*, 13 June 1940	MCP, 1940
*MCP *Strategic Problem of the Malayan Revolutionary War*, December 1948	MCP, Directive of December 1948
*MCP *Supplementary Views of the Central Politburo of the Malayan Communist Party on Strategic Problems of the Malayan Revolutionary War*, 12 November 1949	MCP, 1949
Malayan Union and Singapore, Summary of Proposed Constitutional Arrangements, Colonial Office, Cmd 6749 of March 1946	Colonial Office Cmd 6749 of 1946
Minutes and Council Papers of the Legislative Council, Federation of Malaya (First Session) August 1955–Sept 1956. Paper No. 21 of 1956, Wednesday 16	Razak Report 1956

* These MCP documents were published as Appendices in Hanrahan, G Z., *The Communist Struggle in Malaya*, New York 1954

BIBLIOGRAPHY

Documents	*Abbreviation in Notes*
May 1956, *Report of the Education Committee 1956*	
Monthly Statistical Bulletin of West Malaysia, Kuala Lumpur	Stats, KL
Report of Rural and Industrial Development Authority (RIDA) 1950–5, Kuala Lumpur 1956	RIDA 1956
Report of Singapore Constitutional Conference London. (S of S for Colonies – Cmnd 147) HMSO, London 1957	Cmnd 147
Report of the Singapore Riots Commission 1951, London 1951	
Resurgence of Armed Communism in West Malaysia, Kuala Lumpur 1971	Resurgence
Singapore Legislative Assembly Debates (*Official Report*), Government Printing Office, Singapore	

Bound Volumes:
Vol I, 22 Apr 1955–7 June 1956
Vol 2, 29 Aug 1956–6 Dec 1956
Vol 3, 9 Jan 1957–30 Jul 1957
Vol 4, 21 Aug 1957–8 Jan 1958
Vol 7, 13 Aug 1958–5 Nov 1958
Vol 11 (Nos 1 to 19), 1 Jul 1959–20 Dec 1959
Vol 12 (Nos 1 to 13), 13 Jan 1960–1 Jun 1960
Vol 13 (Nos 1 to 11), 20 Jul 1960–16 Nov 1960
Vol 14 (Nos 1 to 14), 29 Nov 1960–14 Jun 1961

Unbound and Unnumbered – Individual Days
16 March 1962
6 July 1962
20 November 1962
30 July 1963

SLA Debates (with date)

Singapore Legislative Assembly, Sessional Papers No Misc 2 of 1956. *Correspondence between the Chief Minister and the* — Sing Misc 2 of 1956

BIBLIOGRAPHY

Documents	Abbreviation in Notes
Secretary of State for the Colonies on the subject of Re-opening the Constitutional Conference	
No Cmd 15 of 1956 – White Paper on Educational Policy	Sing Cmd 15 of 1956
No Cmd 31 of 1956 – *Report on Singapore All-Party Mission to London Apr/May* 1956	Sing Cmd 31 of 1956
No Cmd 53 of 1956 – *Singapore Chinese Middle School Students' Union Singapore 1956*	White Paper SCMSSU 1956
No Cmd 33 of 1957 – *The Communist Threat in Singapore*	Sing Cmd 33 of 1957
Cmd 33 of 1961 – *Memorandum Setting out Heads of Agreement for a Merger between the Federation of Malaya and Singapore*	Sing Cmd 33 of 1961
Singapore Paper No. 34 of 1954 Constitutional Commission, text of Governor's Despatch 11 March 1954	Sing Paper 34 of 1954
S of S for Colonies Reply 23 Apr 1954	
Stateman's Yearbook 1947–57	Stateman's Yearbook
Trade Union (Amendments) Ordinance 1948 Kuala Lumpur 12 June 1948	T.U. Ord 12 June 1948
Trade Union (Amendments No. 2) Ordinance 1948, Kuala Lumpur 19 July 1948	T.U. Ord 19 July 1948
Trade Union Registry: Annual Report 1948, Government Press, Kuala Lumpur 1949	T.U.R. *Annual Report* 1948
United Nations *Statistical Year Book*, 1948–57	UN Stats
White Paper, *Nanyang University Communist Activities*, Kuala Lumpur	White Paper, Nanyang, 1964

B – SECONDARY SOURCES

3 - Books

Author and Title	Abbreviation in Notes
Arendt, Hannah, *On Violence*, London 1970	Arendt
Awberry, S. S. and Dalley F. W. *Labour and Trade Union Organisation in the Federation of Malaya and Singapore*, Government Press; Kuala Lumpur 1948	Awberry & Dalley
Barraclough, Geoffrey. *An Introduction to Contemporary History*, London (Pelican) 1967	Barraclough
Brimmel, J. H., *Communism in South East Asia*, London 1959	Brimmel
Brinton, Crane, *The Anatomy of Revolution*, New York (Vintage Edition) 1957	Brinton
Browne, Malcolm, *The New Face of War*, London 1966	Browne
Campbell, A., *Jungle Green*, London 1953	Campbell
Carew Hunt, R.N., *The Theory and Practice of Communism*, London (Pelican) 1963	Carew Hunt
Carr, E. H., *What is History?* London (Pelican) 1964	Carr
Chapman, F. Spencer, *The Jungle is Neutral*, London 1949	Chapman
Clark, Michael, *Algeria in Turmoil*, London 1960	Clark
Clutterbuck, Richard, *The Long Long War*, London 1967	Clutterbuck, *The Long Long War*
Clutterbuck, Richard, *Protest and the Urban Guerrilla*, London 1973	Clutterbuck, *Protest*
Crawford, Oliver, *The Door Marked Malaya*, London 1958	Crawford
Critchley, T. A., *The Conquest of Violence*, London 1970	Critchley
Dalley, F. W. and Awberry, S. S., *Labour and Trade Union Organization in the*	Awberry & Dalley

BIBLIOGRAPHY

Author and Title	Abbreviation in Notes
Federation of Malaya and Singapore, Government Press, Kuala Lumpur 1948	
Debray, Regis, *Revolution in the Revolution?* London (Pelican) 1967	Debray
Donnison, F. S. V., *British Military Administration in the Far East 1943–46*, London 1956	Donnison
Elliott-Bateman, Michael, *Defeat in the East – The Mark of Mao Tse Tung on War*, London 1967	Elliott-Bateman
Engels, Marx, Lenin. *The Essential Left*, New York 1962	*The Essential Left*
Fall, Bernard B., *Street without Joy*, London 1964	Fall, *Street*
Fall, Bernard B., *The Two Vietnams*, London 1963	Fall, *The Two Vietnams*
Fanon, Frantz, *The Wretched of the Earth*, London (Penguin) 1967	Fanon
Fisk, E. K., and Silcock, T. H., *The Political Economy of Independent Malaya*	Silcock and Fisk
Gamba, Charles, *The Origins of Trade Unionism in Malaya*, Eastern Universities Press, Singapore 1962	Gamba
Giap, Vo Nguyen, *Peoples' Army, Peoples' War*, New York 1962	Giap
Girling, J. L. S., *People's War*, London 1969	Girling
Guevara, Che, *Guerrilla Warfare*, London 1962	Che Guevara
Hanrahan, G. Z., *The Communist Struggle in Malaya*, New York 1954	Hanrahan
Han Suyin, *And the Rain my Drink*, London 1956	Han Suyin
Henniker, M. C. A., *Red Shadow Over Malaya*, London 1955	Henniker
Hosman, S. T., *Counterinsurgency: A Symposium*, Rand Corporation, Santa Monica, California 1963	Hosman (Rand)
Hyde, Douglas, *Confrontation in the East*, Singapore 1965	Hyde, *Confrontation*
Hyde, Douglas, *I Believed*, London 1951	Hyde, *I Believed*

BIBLIOGRAPHY

Author and Title	*Abbreviation in Notes*
Hyde, Douglas, *The Roots of Guerrilla Warfare*, London 1968	Hyde, *Roots*
Information Services, Federation of Malaya, *The Danger and Where it Lies*, Kuala Lumpur 1957	*The Danger and Where It Lies*
Josey, Alex, *Trade Unionism in Malaya*, Singapore 1954	Josey
Kennedy, J., *A History of Malaya*, London 1962	Kennedy
Kitson, Frank, *Gangs and Counter-gangs*, London 1966	Kitson, *Gangs*
Kitson, Frank, *Low Intensity Operations*, London 1971	Kitson, *Low Intensity*
Lee Kuan Yew, *The Battle for Merger*, Singapore 1961	Lee Kuan Yew, *Battle*
Lenin, Engels, Marx, *The Essential Left*, New York 1962	*The Essential Left*
Malaparte, *Coup d'Etat*, Bernard Grasset, Paris 1931	Malaparte
Mao Tse Tung, *Guerrilla Warfare*, London 1962	Mao Tse Tung, *Guerrilla Warfare*
Mao Tse Tung, *Quotations from Chairman Mao Tse Tung*, Peking 1966	Mao Tse Tung *Quotations*
Mao Tse Tung, *Selected Works*, New York 1954–8, Vols I to IV	Mao Tse Tung *Selected Works*
Marx, Engels, Lenin, *The Essential Left*, New York 1962	*The Essential Left*
McConville, Maureen and Seale, Patrick, *French Revolution 1968*, London (Penguin) 1968	Seale and McConville
McCuen, John L., *The Art of Counter-Revolutionary Warfare*, London 1966	McCuen
McNamara, Robert S., *The Essence of Security*, London 1968	McNamara
Miers, R. C. H., *Shoot to Kill*, London 1959	Miers
Miller, Harry, *Menace in Malaya*, London 1954	Miller

BIBLIOGRAPHY

Author and Title	Abbreviation in Notes
Mills, Lennox A., *Malaya – A Political and Economic Appraisal*, Minneapolis 1958	Mills
Moorehead, Alan, *The Russian Revolution*, New York (Bantam) 1959	Moorehead
Moss, Robert, *Urban Guerrillas*, London 1972	Moss
O'Ballance, Edgar, *Malaya – Communist Insurgent War 1948–60*, London 1966	O'Ballance
Oldfield, J. B., *The Green Howards in Malaya*, Aldershot 1953	Oldfield
Ooi Jin Bee, *Land, People and Economy in Malaya*, London 1963	Ooi Jin Bee
Purcell, V., *Malaya, Communist or Free?* London 1954	Purcell
Purcell, V., 'Malayan Politics', in *Politics in Southern Asia*, (Ed Saul Rose) London 1963	Purcell, *Malayan Politics*
Purcell, Victor, *The Chinese in South East Asia*, London 1965	Purcell, *Chinese*
Pye, Lucian W., *Guerrilla Communism in Malaya*, Princeton U.S.A. 1956	Pye
Ratnam, K. J., *Communalism and the Political Process in Malaya*, Singapore 1965	Ratnam
Robinson, J. B. Perry, *Transformation in Malaya*, London 1956	Robinson
Rose, Saul (Ed), *Politics in Southern Asia*, London 1963	Saul Rose
Scalapino, Robert A. (Ed), *The Communist Revolution in Asia*, Prentice Hall, New Jersey, U.S.A. 1965	Scalapino
Seale, Patrick and McConville, Maureen, *French Revolution 1968*, London (Penguin) 1968	Seal and McConville
Seton Watson, Hugh, *The Pattern of Communist Revolution*, London 1960	Seton Watson

BIBLIOGRAPHY

Author and Title	Abbreviation in Notes
Silcock, T. H. and Fisk, E. K., *The Political Economy of Independent Malaya*, Singapore 1963	Silcock and Fisk
Sorel, Georges, *Reflection on Violence*, London 1925	Sorel
Special Operations Research Office, The American University, *Casebook on Insurgency and Revolutionary Warfare*, Washington 1962	Soro
Sukhanov, N. N., *The Russian Revolution 1917*, London 1955	Sukhanov
Tanham, G. K., *Communist Revolutionary Warfare: The Vietminh in Indochina*, New York 1961	Tanham
Thompson, Sir Robert, *Defeating Communist Insurgency*, London 1966	Thompson, *Defeating Communist Insurgency* (or *DCI*)
Trotsky, L., *The Russian Revolution*, New York (Doubleday Edition) 1959	Trotsky
Wilson, Edmund, *To the Finland Station*, New York 1940	Wilson
Wint, Guy, *Communist China's Crusade*, London 1965	Wint
Wolfe, B. D., *Three Who Made a Revolution*, Boston (Beacon Press) 1955	Wolfe

4 - Articles and Monographs

Author and Title	Abbreviation in Notes
Bloodworth, Denis, Article in the Singapore *Sunday Times*, 30 September 1967	Bloodworth, 30 Sep 67
Bloodworth, Denis, Article in the Singapore *Sunday Times*, 15 October 1967	Bloodworth, 15 Oct 67

BIBLIOGRAPHY

Author and Title	*Abbreviation in Notes*
Clutterbuck, Richard, 'Military Engineering as a Weapon in the Cold War' in the *Military Engineer*, Washington July–August 1963	Clutterbuck, *Military Engineering*
Dobby, E. G. H., 'Resettlement Transforms Malaya' in *Economic Development and Cultural Change*, 1953 pp. 163–81	Dobby
Dudley, C. E. S., 'Insurrection from the Jacobins to Mao Tse-Tung' in the *Royal United Service Institution* Journal, May 1966	Dudley
Dunlop Malaya Estates Ltd., *The Story of a Rubber Tree*, (mimeograph) Malacca 1965	Dunlop
Goh Keng Swee, reported in the *Straits Times*, Singapore 17 April 1967	Goh Keng Swee, Apr 1961
Goh Kweng Swee, reported in the *Sunday Times*, Singapore 29 Jun 1967	Goh Keng Swee, Jun 1961
Heilbrunn, O., 'The Algerian Emergency' in the *Royal United Service Institution Journal*, London August 1966	Heilbrunn, *Algerian Emergency*
Heilbrunn, O., 'Terrorist Warfare' in *British Army Review*, August 1966	Heilbrunn, *Terrorist Warfare*
Hyde, Douglas, 'The Star that Fell' in the *Far Eastern Economic Review*, July 1969	Hyde, *Star*
Janos, Andrew C., *The Seizure of Power – A Study of Force and Popular Consent*, Princeton University U.S.A. 1964	Janos
Lin Piao, in *Peking Review*, 3 September 1965 quoted in *Current Scene*, Hong Kong 26 September 1966	Lin Piao
Marshall, David, *The Struggle for Nationhood*. Talk at St. Andrew's Cathedral Singapore 12 July 1969	Marshall, *Struggle*
McVey, Ruth T., *The Calcutta Conference*	McVey

Author and Title	Abbreviations in Notes
and *The South East Asia Uprising*, Cornell University, New York 1958	
Osborne, Milton E., *Singapore and Malaysia*, Cornell University, New York 1964	Osborne, *Singapore*
Osborne, Milton, *Strategic Hamlets in South Vietnam – A Survey and a Comparison* [with Malaya], Cornell University, New York 1965	Osborne, *Hamlets*
Rhenick, R. D., *The Emergency Regulations of Malaya*, Master's Thesis, Tulane University, U.S.A. 1967	Rhenick
Sandhu, Kernial Singh, 'Emergency Resettlement in Malaya' in *The Journal of Tropical Geography*, Vol 18, August 1964, University of Malaya in Singapore 1964, pp. 157–83	Sandhu, *Resettlement*
Schapiro, Leonard, 'Changing Patterns in the Theory of Revolution and Insurgency' in the *Royal United Service Institute Journal*, September 1970	Schapiro
Shephard, A. J., 'The Communist Failure in Hong Kong' in *The Commonwealth Journal*, April 1968	
Spitzen, Alan B., *The Revolutionary Theories of Louis Auguste Blanqui*, New York 1957	Spitzen
Stewart, Neil, *Blanqui*, London 1939	Stewart
Thompson, Sir Robert, 'The Other War' in the *Straits Times*, Singapore, 28 January 1967	Thompson
Thompson, Sir Robert, 'Vietnam', lecture to the Royal Commonwealth Society, London on 8 November 1966 reported in the *Commonwealth Journal*, February 1967 p. 14	*Vietnam*
U.S. Military Assistance Command, Vietnam, *Revolutionary Development* in	*Revolutionary Development*

Author and Title *Abbreviation in Notes*

Command Information Pamphlet No. 4–67, Saigon, February 1967

Waller, P. B. G., *A Study of the Emergency Regulations of Malaya 1948–1960*. (Draft) Stanford Research Institute, Bangkok 1967 — Waller ER's

Waller, P. B. G., *Notes on The Malayan Emergency: Strategies and Organization of the Opposing Forces*, Stanford Research Institute, California, U.S.A. 1967 — Waller, *Notes*

Zawodny, J. K., *Organisational Problems and Dynamics of Violent Political Movements*. Paper presented to the Eighth World Congress of the International Political Science Association, Munich September 1970 — Zawodny, *Organisational Problems*

Zawodny, J. K., 'Soviet Partisans' in *Soviet Studies*, Oxford 1966 — Zawodny, *Soviet*

5 - Newspapers and Periodicals

Commonwealth Journal
Current Scene (Hong Kong)
The Economist
Far Eastern Economic Review
Journal of Tropical Geography (University of Malaya in Singapore)
Malay Mail (Kuala Lumpur)
Military Engineer (Washington)
Nanyang Siang Pau (Singapore)
Observer
Royal United Service Institution Journal
Straits Times
Sunday Times (London)
Sunday Times (Singapore)
The Times

Bibliography – Part III

---

1 Interviews

Singapore: Government

DEVAN NAIR, C.V.	President of the Republic
LEE KUAN YEW	Prime Minister
GOH KENG SWEE	1st Deputy Prime Minister
RAJARATNAM, S.	2nd Deputy Prime Minister
JAYAKUMAR, S.	Minister of Law and Home Affairs
LIM CHYE HENG	Director, Internal Security Department, 1982
TAN, Miss Lily	Oral History Unit
TAN KAY CHEE	Oral History Unit

Singapore: non-Government

BOGAARS, George	Chairman, Keppel Shipyard
CHAN HENG CHEE, Dr.	National University of Singapore (Political Science)
DRYSDALE, John	Journalist and Author
GALLAGHER, Susan	Public Relations Consultant
HAN FONG AIK	Accounts Clerk
HENNINGS, J.D.	British High Commissioner
HEYWOOD, Sir Anthony	Businessman
LAU TEIK SOON, Professor	MP (PAP) and National University of Singapore (Political Science)
LIM LEE IM	Woman Police Constable
WALKER, Ralph	Hogg Robinson (Far East) Pte. Ltd.
WONG LING KEN, Professor	National University of Singapore (History)

Malaysia: Government

GOH CHENG TEIK, Dr.	Minister, Prime Minister's Office
TOO, C.C.	Head, Psychological Warfare Section
Officers of the Police Special Branch	

Malaysia: Others

ANWAR IBRAHIM	Then ABIM, Later Minister
AZMI KHALED, Dr.	University of Malaysia
BENTLEY, William	British High Commissioner
BLUMER, Anthony	International Chamber of Commerce
CHOW, David	*Business Times*
FORD, Laurence	Zeta Hogg Robinson, Sdn. Bhd.
HARUN BIN IDRIS, Datuk,	Former Chief Minister, Selangor
HUSSEIN HAMID	Zeta Hogg Robinson Sdn. Bhd.
KHOO KAY KIM, Professor	University of Malaya (History)
LEE KAM HING, Dr.	University of Malaya (History)
MOHAMED FOUZI, Dr.	University of Malaya (Anthropology and Sociology)
NORDIN SOFEE	Managing Editor, *New Straits Times* Group
STEWART, Brian	Rubber Growers' Association
TAN KOON SWAN	Chairman, Multipurpose Holdings Bhd.
UNGKU AZIZ, Professor	Vice-Chancellor, University of Malaya
WHITE, Alan	British High Commission

2 Documents

Census of Population, 1980, Singapore
Lee Kuan Yew, *Eve of National Day Message*, 1981

National Operations, Council, *The 13 May Tragedy: A Report*, Kuala Lumpur 1969
Reprint of Citizens' Consultative Committee Rules, with Amendments, Singapore, 1967
Resurgence of Armed Communism in West Malaysia, Kuala Lumpur, 1971
Singapore = Success Singapore, Government Publication, 1979

3 Books

Brackman, Arnold C., *Southeast Asia's Second Front*, London, Pall Mall, 1966
Chan Heng Chee, *The Dynamics of One Party Dominance*, Singapore University Press, 1976
Crouch, H. Lee Kam Hing and Michael Ong (Eds.) *Malaysian Politics and the 1978 Elections*, Kuala Lumpur, Oxford University Press, 1980
Devan Nair, C.V., *Socialism that Works: The Singapore Way*, Singapore, Federal Publications, 1976
Encyclopaedia Britannica, 1981, Vol. 16
Fong Sip Chee, *The PAP Story*, Singapore, Times Periodicals Pte. Ltd. 1980
Goh Cheng Teik, *The May 13th Incident and Democracy in Malaya*, Kuala Lumpur, Oxford University Press, 1971
Mahathir bin Mohamad, *The Malay Dilemma*, Petaling Jaya, Federal Publications, 1981
Milne, R.S. and Mauzy, D.K., *Politics and Government in Malaysia*, Singapore, Times Books, 1978
People's Action Party 1954-1979, Singapore, PAP, 1979.
Rahman, Tunku Abdul, *May 13: Before and After*, Kuala Lumpur, Utusan Melayu Press, 1969
Seah Chee Meow, *Community Centres in Singapore: Their Political Involvement*, Singapore University Press, 1973
Shaw, William, *Tun Razak: His Life and Times*, Kuala Lumpur, Longman, 1976
Sim, Richard, *Malaysia: Containing The Communist Insurgency*, Conflict Studies No. 110, London, Institute for the Study of Conflict, 1979

Vorys, Karl von, *Democracy without Consensus*, Kuala Lumpur, Oxford University Press.

Articles

Banyard, P.J., "With Silence and Stealth", *War In Peace*, Vol. 4 Issue 41, November 1983

Clementson, J., "Malaysia in the Seventies: Communist Resurgence and Government Response". *Royal United Service Institute Journal*, December 1979

Drysdale, John, "How Singapore Became No. 1" *Straits Times*, 2 January 1982

Hyde, Douglas, "Sarawak: An Insurgency in Retreat" *Spectrum*, Vol. 2, No. 4, July 1974

Lee Kuan Yew, "New Year Message 1982", *Straits Times*, 1 January 1982

Lee Kuan Yew, "New Year Message 1983", *Straits Times*, 1 January 1983

Lee Kuan Yew, "New Year Message 1984", *Sunday Times*, 1 January 1984.

Smith, E.D., "The Undeclared War", *War In Peace*, Vol. 4, Issue 41, November 1963

Walker, General Sir Walter, "How Borneo was Won" *Round Table*, Vol. LIX 1969

Newspapers and Periodicals

Asia Week
The Economist
New Straits Times
Straits Times
Sunday Times (Singapore)
Time Magazine

Index

Ah Chiau, 80, 255
Ah Kwang, 182
Algeria, 25, 28, 32, 371
Algeria in Turmoil (Clark), 371,
'Ali-Baba' system, 308-9, 311
Alliance Party, 102, 160, 263, 282-3, 290-8, 304-5, 309
Ampang, 293, 297
Anatomy of Revolution, The (Brinton), 21
Anson, by elections, 154-5, 160-1, 163, 324-5, 346-7
Anti British League (ABL), 59-62, 64, 65, 69, 78, 91-3, 97, 99, 266
Anwar Ibrahim, 311-12, 317, 378
Arendt, Hannah, 355
Arrests, in Malaysia, 50-1, 169, 211-19, 222-5, 240-4, 269
  in Singapore, 48-51, 55, 66-71, 75, 81-2, 118-19, 135-6, 159-60, 269-70, 321
Asia Youth Conference, Calcutta, 56, 167
Asri, Mohammed, Dato, 304
Associated Press, 157,
Association of Southeast Asian Nations (ASEAN), 284, 350
Awberry, S. S., 357, 359
Ayer Baloi, 79-80, 82, 255
Azev (Russian police agent), 358
Azahari, A. M., 159, 179

Back from the Brink (Edwardes), 381
Bahau, 215
Baling, 103, 112, 227, 257
Bank Bumiputra, 306
Banyard, P. J., 375

Barisan Nasional (BN) (Malaysia), 304-5, 309, 311, 315-16, 318
Barisan Socialis (BS) in Singapore, 153-7, 159-62, 322-4, 339, 340, 346, 368, 369
Battle for Merger, The (Lee Kuan Yew), 104, 157, 348-9, 360
Batu Anam NV, 235
Batu Pahat, 40, 206-10
Benes, President, 47-8
Blades, Alan, 51-2, 130, 161-2, 182, 360, 365-6
Blanqui, Louis Auguste, 21-4
Bloodworth, Denis, 366-7
Bombing, negligible results from, 172, 370
Bong Kee Chok, 282
Borneo, 158, 278-82
Bourne, General, 227
Brackman, Arnold C., 375
Briggs, Sir Harold, 175, 178, 186, 214, 274
Brinton, Crane, 21
Britain in Agony (Clutterbuck), 381
British Military Administration in the Far East 1943-46 (Donnison), 356-8
Browne, Malcolm, 181, 362
Brunei, 278-9, 340
Bukit Siput, 231, 237-8, 240-4, 250
Bukit Timah, 66, 121-4, 128, 130
Buloh Kasap, 235, 240, 374
Bumiputras, privileges for, 306-9, 315, 317-18, 377
Burma, 28, 49, 56
Business Environment Risk Information (BERI), 335-6, 353

Calcutta, 39, 56, 167
Calcutta Conference and the South East Asia Uprisings, The (McVey), 359, 369
Campbell, Arthur, 372
Casebook on Insurgency and Revolutionary Warfare (Special Operations Research Office, American University), 357
Castro, Fidel, 25, 142, 277
Casualty figures,
  in Borneo, 281-2
  in Malayan Emergency, 167-8, 170, 175, 184-9, 195-6, 216-9, 264, 272-3, 289
  in Malaysia (after 1966), 286, 289, 292, 301-2, 316-17, 321, 376
  in Singapore riots, 72-3, 132-3, 270, 321
Census of Population, 1980, Singapore, 379, 380
Central Provident Fund (CPF), 330, 335, 344
Chaah, 208
Chang Yuen Tong, 148-9
Changi gaol, 99, 137
Chan Heng Chee, 346, 350, 379, 380, 381
Chapman, F. Spencer, 37-41, 182, 357
Cheng Yew Leng, 92
Chia Chu Kang, 207-10
Chia Ek Tian, 364
Chin Peng, 39, 54, 98, 103, 112, 168, 195, 227, 259-60, 272-3, 284, 286
China, 28, 33, 80, 271-2
  deportation to, 51, 81, 367
  repatriation to, 255, 374-5
  revolutionary philosophy of, 17, 19, 24-5, 28-9, 45, 93-4, 170, 271-2
Chinese, the, in Malaysia and Singapore
  citizenship, 49, 157-8, 160, 303
  education, 47, 52, 63-4, 75, 79, 83, 96-8, 104-5, 136, 266, 314-15, 327-31, 334, 337
  discrimination against, 283, 288, 289-90, 309, 315-16, 378
  employment, pattern of, 35, 202-10, 231-8, 256, 289-90, 349-50

  -language newspapers, 51, 341-2, 368, 380
  Musical Gong Society, 118
  population, proportion of, 33, 52, 207-10, 231-8, 275, 278, 281, 319-20, 376
  rivalry between Communist and Kuomintang supporters, 55, 109
  secret societies, 51, 63, 131, 161, 163, 298, 321
  support for Communists, 18, 45-6, 64, 75, 96, 119-20, 161, 170-81 184, 191, 194, Ch. 10, Ch. 11, Ch. 12, Ch. 13, 251-2, 256, 259-60, 263-9, 271-3, 277, 285-8, 339
  taste for secret activities, 63, 90, 182
  treatment by Japanese, 38-41
  wealth of, relative, 35, 289, 305-6, 311
Chinese in South East Asia, The (Purcell), 356, 370
'Ching', 92, 362, 363
Circle Special Branch Officer, 178-9
Citizens Consultative Committees (CCC), 323-4, 346
Civil liberties, 163, 319, 336, 337, 340, 343-4, 346, 350, 353
Civil Rights Convention, 121, 136
Clark, Michael, 371
Clementson, J., 375, 376
Clutterbuck, Richard, 354, 356, 357, 370, 373, 374, 375, 381
'Cold Store', Operation, 159, 340
Commonwealth Journal, 366, 372
Communalism and The Political Process in Malaya (Ratnam), 356
Communist Organization, Clandestine (CCO), in Sarawak, 297-82, 339
Communist Party, Malayan (MCP) (before 1963)
  ABL — *see* Anti-British League
  attempt to control PAP, 103-6, 110-11, 115-16, 145-63, 264, 268 322, 325, 339-40, 348, 351
  Calcutta Conference, 56, 167
  communication problems, 67-71, 179-80, 198, 202-5

400

INDEX

controversy amongst leaders, 53–6, 172–4
death penalty for reading leaflets, 194
declared illegal, 66, 169
dedication, 63–4, 206, 271, 277
directives, 85, 170–1, 173–4, 184, 187, 195
disruption of organization in Singapore, 37, 45, 66, 71, 81, 130–1
formation, 37
front organizations, 41, 46–9, 58–62, 65–6, 79–81, 84–91, 118, 121–2 148–9
fulltime party workers, 52
National Service, reaction to, 82–4, 86, 90
organization and structure, 18, 37–9, 41, 46, 58–66, 68, 71, 75–9, Ch. 5, 99–100, 137, 167–74, 183–6, 194–6, Ch. 10, 214, 220–9, 231–9, 252–7, 259–60, 266–9, 271–3, 277, 281
resettlement, reaction to, 176
Second World War, in, 37–44
security, 59, 66–71, 77–9, 148–9, 179, 202–6, 212, 267
Singapore Town Committee, 58–62, 66–71, 76–7, 266, 270
strategy, aims and achievements, 45–7, 51, 54, 56, 66, 71–2, 75, 79, 81, 85, 136–8, 148–50, 167–75, 183–6, 195, 259–60, 266–9, 271–3
strength of, 37, 41, 52–3, 56–7, 59
student organization, *see* Students
subscriptions and extortion, 50–1, 56, 203–6, 235, 237–8
suggests truce talks, 98, 227
support, *see* Chinese
surrenders, *see* Intelligence and Surrendered Enemy Personnel (SEPs)
terror and intimidation, 51–2, 77, 95–7, 169, 184, 198, 205–6
trade union activity, 46, 50–5, 58–60, 62, 84–6, 100, 104, 108–11, 115, 118, 121–4, 130, 134–5, 137–9, 146–8, 167–8, 173, 266, 269–70
Communist Party of Malaya (CPM) (after 1963), 259–60, 264, 284–8, 303, 315, 318, 339–40
Communist Revolutionary Warfare: The Vietminh in Indochina (Tanham), 356
Communist Struggle in Malaya, The (Hanrahan), 354, 361, 370
Communist Threat in Singapore, The (Legislative Assembly Singapore Paper), 367–8
Community centres, 322–3, 326
Community Centres in Singapore: Their Political Involvement (Seah), 379
Confrontation with Indonesia, 158–62, 264, 279–82, 284, 320–1, 339, 340
Conquest of Violence, The, (Critchley), 356
Constitution
    Malaysian, 290, 301, 303, 308, 316–18, 320, 378
    Singaporean, 101, 113–15, 142–4, 150, 346
Corruption, 181, 187
Coup d'Etat (Malaparte), 355
Couriers, 67–71, 179–80, 202–5
Critchley, T. A., 356
Criticism and self criticism, 94–6
Crouch, Harold, 377
Cuba, 25, 28, 143, 272, 277
Czechoslovakia, 47, 49

Dalley, F. W. 357, 359
Danger and Where It Lies, The (Information Services, Kuala Lumpur), 375
Davis, John, 39, 357, 359
Debray, Regis, 17, 25, 27, 30–1, 272, 276–7, 286
Defeat in the East — The Mark of Mao Tse Tung on War (Elliott-Bateman), 356
Defeating Communist Insurgency (Thompson), 356, 370–1
De Gaulle, General, 26

INDEX

Democracy without Consensus (Vorys), 376, 377
Democratic Action Party (DAP), 292-8, 303-5
Detention without trial, 52, 66, 107, 111, 118-19, 158-60, 189, 222-4, 240, 303, 337-9, 341, 345, 379
Devan Nair, 66, 111, 259, 324, 337-9, 350, 352, 368, 378, 380, 381
Dhoraisingham, Samuel, 365
Dissent, in Singapore, 271, 324-5, 336 337-40, 344-8, 350-1
District War Executive Committee (DWEC), 175, 192, 199, 217, 302
Donnison, FSV, 35, 356-8
Drugs, 341, 343
Drysdale, John, 379, 380
Dudley, CES, 354
Dutch Labour Party (DLP), 337-40, 345-6, 350, 380
Dynamics of One Party Dominance (Chan Heng Chee), 350, 379, 380, 381

Economic growth
  in Malaysia, 284, 312-14, 316, 318
  in Singapore, 162-3, 263, 277, 284, 312-14, 319, 334-6, 340, 350-3
Economist, The, 355, 366, 378, 380
Education,
  in Malaysia, 52, 290, 314-5, 378
  in Singapore, 52, 63-4, 75, 79, 83, 96-8, 104-5, 119-21, 136, 266, 314, 327-31, 334, 337, 349-50
  language of instruction in, 290, 314, 328, 330, 378, 380
  payment for, 330
  streaming, 328, 334
  see also Schools, Students
Edwardes, Sir Michael, 381
Election ballot, secrecy of, 345, 348, 351
Elections
  in Malaysia
    (1955), 102, 291
    (1963), 162
    (1964), 292, 294
    (1969), 291-7, 304-5
    (1974), 304-5
    (1978), 305
    (1982), 311
  in Singapore,
    (1955), 102
    (1959), 149-51, 324
    (1961), 152-6, 160
    (1963), 160-1, 323, 324
    (1968), 324, 335, 345
    (1972), 324
    (1976), 324
    (1980), 324
    (1981), 163, 324-5
Elliott Bateman, Michael, 356
Emergency Regulations, 106-7, 111, 168-9, 194, 240, 264, 274, 278, 338, 341
Emergency Regulations in Malaysia, The (Rhenick), 370
Emergency Regulations Ordinance, 1948, The (Kuala Lumpur Government Press), 370
Emergency, State of, 56, 168-9, 261, 270, 289, 301, 316-7
Emergency (Tenants Registration) Regulations (Kuala Lumpur), 371
Encyclopaedia Britannica, 1981, Vol. 16, 379, 381
Engineers, Military, 258
Essence of Security, The (McNamara), 354, 372
Exports, 312-14, 350

Far Eastern Economic Review, 366, 378
Federal Priority Operations, Ch. 12, Ch. 13
Fang Chuan Pi, 153
'Fang Ping An', 153
Fanon, Frantz, 27, 355
Federation of Trade Unions, 138-9
Fiennes, D. E. M., 372
Fisk, E. H., 356
Foco Theory, 30-1, 276-7
Fong Feng, 53
Fong Sip Chee, 325, 379
Fong Swee Suan, 105, 109, 111, 124, 151-4, 368

402

INDEX

Food denial operations, 212-18, 221 224-6, Ch. 13
Forts, jungle, 258-9
French Revolution 1968 (Seale, McConville), 266, 355
Front Organizations, 118

Gamba, Charles, 359, 369-70
Gangs and Counter-Gangs (Kitson), 374
Gavin, Lt.-Col. J. M. L., 37.
General Labour Union (GLU), 46, 50, 52-3, 269
Geneste, Lt.-Col. Marc, 355
Gent, Sir Edward, 49, 168, 169
Gerakan Party, 293-8, 303-5
Giap, Vo Nguyen, 373
Girling, J. L. S., 356
Goh Cheng Teik, 377
Goh Chok Tong, 353
Goh Keng Swee, Dr., 132, 157, 284, 326, 338, 360, 363, 380
Gombak, 298-300
Goode, Chief Secretary, 85, 107
Gorrie, Michael, 361
Greene, Hugh Carleton, 191, 193
Grisek Branch, 252
Guerrilla Communism in Malaya (Pye), 357
Guerrilla Warfare (Mao, Guevara), 355, 356
Guevara, Che, 30, 355-6
Gurkhas, 72, 213-6, 250, 280-1
Gurney, Sir Henry, 169, 184, 186, 371

Haji Ghafar, Kampong, 210
Handbook of World Development, 378
Han Fong Aik, 379, 380
Hanrahan, G. Z., 354, 361, 363, 370
Harun bin Idris, Datuk, 295, 298
Heilbrunn, Otto, 355
Helicopters, 116, 133, 270
Henniker, Brigadier M. C. A., 213, 215, 354, 373
Hertogh, Maria, riots over, 72-3, 117, 270, 283, 321
Heywood, Sir Anthony, 377

History of Malaya, A (Kennedy), 356
History of Singapore, A (Turnbull), 376, 379, 380, 381
Hitler, Adolf, 23, 27
Ho Chi Minh, 29
Hock Lee Bus Strike, 84, 108, 120
Hoe Puay Choo, Mrs., 158
Hokkien Association, 124-5, 134
'Hong', 79-81, 267
Hong Kong, 53, 138-41, 313, 357
Hong Lim, by-election, 152-3, 156, 160
Hor Lung, 198, 206, 229, 235, 250, 253-6
Housing in Singapore, 153, 162, 323, 326-7, 333-4, 344, 347, 349-51, 379
How Borneo Was Won (Walker), 375
'Hsueh Hsih' cells, 93-6, 98, 138, 267, 361
Huberman, Leo, 355
Hungary, 366
Hunt, R. N. Carew, 354
Hyde, Douglas, 65, 99, 137, 360, 375

Immigrant workers, 333-5
Incomes, in Singapore, 330-5, 334-6, 348-51
Independence, Brunei, 279, 282
Independence, Malaysia (Merdeka), 32, 142, 159, 229, 268, 291-2, 311, 375
Independence, Singapore, 151, 162, 284, 319-20, 328, 338
Indians in Malaysia and Singapore, 35, 72, 282, 289, 291-6, 302, 304-6, 309-11, 314, 328-9, 378
Indochina, 32, 56
Indonesia, 32, 56, 158-62, 264, 279-82, 284, 313-14, 321, 339, 352
Industrial Coordination Act (1975), 308
Industrial relations, 335-6, *see also*, Strikes, Trade Unions
Infiltration, White Paper on Communist, 146-8
Inflation, 325, 334
Information Services, 190-4, 224-5

403

INDEX

Intelligence,
  advance, precise information, 213–19
  agents and informers, 37–8, 53, 178–83, 193–4, Ch. 11, Ch. 12, Ch. 13, 269, 275, 282–3, 298
  background, 217, 221–3, 251
  contact, 251
  coordination, need for, 178
  cutouts, 59, 67–71, 179, 204
  in Borneo, 280–1
  Surrendered Enemy Personnel (SEPs) as source of, 175, 181–3, 193, 211, 218, Ch. 12, Ch. 13, 251–7, 315
  techniques, 18, Ch. 11, Ch. 12, Ch. 13, 251–9, 275, 286
  see also Police Special Branch
Internal Security Act (ISA), 338–40, 351, 353
Internal Security Council (ISC), 144–5, 154, 156, 338, 340
Internal Security Organization, 113–14, 116–17, 141, 143–5
Investment, 313–14, 334–6, 349
Investment, foreign, 35, 153, 284, 306, 314, 335–6, 340, 352
Ipoh, 38, 46, 256, 285–7
Ireland, Northern, 31, 107, 204, 339, 358, 375

Janos, Andrew, C., 355
Japan, 37–41, 161, 176, 312–14, 334–6, 341, 344, 349–50
Jayakumar, S., 380
Jeyaratnam, J. B., 325
Johore, 79, 199, 227, 229, 253, 255, 260
Jones, Major Gwynne (later Lord Chalfont), 243–4, 249
Josey, Alex, 173, 369
Jungle Green (Campbell), 372
Jungle is Neutral, The (Chapman), 357
Jury, trial by, 107, 338, 344

Kallang, 123
Kampong Bharu, 300, 377
Kangkar Bahru, 209, 220
Katong, 127–8
Kebun Bahru, 252

Kedah, 257–8, 260, 285–7, 295
Kelantan, 35, 286–7, 295, 304–5
Kennedy, J., 356
Kenya, 32, 251
'Kim Cheng', 254
Kin Fai, 231
Kitson, Frank, 251–2, 374
Kluang, 67, 69
Korea, 312, 334, 336
Korean war, effect of, 176, 371
Kowloon, 138–9
Kuala Lumpur, 32, 47, 50–1, 111, 142–3, 159, 167, 174, 186, 219, 264, 277, 286–8, 298–302, 315, 321, 324, 339, 343, 377
Kulai, 180, 210

Labour and Trade Union Organization in the Federation of Malaya and Singapore (Awberry, Dalley), 357
Labour Front, 102
Lai Tek, 37, 39, 45, 47, 53–4, 269, 358
Lam Lee, 209
Lam Swee, 173, 192
Land Acquisition Act (1966), 341–2
Land, People and Economy in Malaya (Ooi), 356, 371
Language laws, 290, 303, 314, 376
Latimer, Capt., H. S., 217, 220
Lau Ing Sien, Madame, 97
Lau Yew, 47–9
Lee Hoi Fatt, 80
Lee Kuan Yew
  administrative skill and leadership, 162–3, 263, 271, 319–20, 322–4, 336, 340, 352
  British, and, 112, 118–19, 142, 353, 364
  Communists, and, 77, 99, 104–6, 110, 115, 118–19, 137, 142, 147–53, 162–3, 264, 267, 271, 353, 363, 365
  double first at Cambridge, 104
  education, attitude towards, 162, 327–30, 350–2
  law and order, attitude towards, 118–19, 132, 271, 338, 340, 343–4, 351, 364

INDEX

lawyer, skill as, 104, 111, 344
Malays, attitude towards, 312, 320
media, skill in use of, 104, 157, 160, 348-51, 380
merger with Malaysia, part in, 156-8, 160-1, 278, 282-4
moderate label, disowns, 367
People's Action Party (PAP) and, 83, 115, 135-6, 141, 146, 151, 154-5, 163, 271, 283, 319, 323, 338
political skill, 136, 141, 149-51, 154-5, 160-3, 271, 319-20, 322-5, 335, 352
security and, 107, 118-19, 132, 163, 271, 340, 364, 367
successor to, 163, 351-3
Trade Unions, and, 104, 111, 334-5, 340-2
welfare and, 344, 381
Lee Siew Choh, Dr., 155, 159, 162
Lee Ta Lim, 92, 96
Lee Yek Han, 153
Lenin, V. I., 17, 20-6, 94, 358
Lennox-Boyd, Alan, 112
Licenses to operate business or newspaper, 290, 308-9, 337, 341-2
Liew Yit Fan, 47-9
Lim Chee Onn, 353
Lim Chin Siong, 99-100, 104-6, 109-12, 115, 119, 121-2, 124, 130, 135-7, 145-6, 149, 151, 154-6, 159, 339, 340, 362, 365
Lim Chong Eu, Dr., 293
Lim Lee Im, 15, 379, 380
Lim Yew Hock, 103, 116, 119, 142-3, 145, 146, 150
Lin Piao, 355
Liu Shao Shi, 363
Long Long War, The (Clutterbuck), 354, 356, 370, 373, 374, 375
Lo Wu, 139

Mahathir bin Mohamad, Dr., 305, 309-11, 317, 377, 378
Malacca, 33, 158, 301
Malaparte, Curzio, 24, 355
Malay Dilemma, The (Mahathir), 310-11, 377, 378
Malay Mail, 374, 375
Malay, Malayan, Malaysian definitions, 33
Malaya - A Political and Economic Appraisal (Mills), 356, 371
Malaya Communist or Free? (Purcell), 354, 356
Malaya - The Communist Insurgency (O'Ballance), 354, 370
Malaya, University of, 66, 75, 368
Malayan Communist Party (MCP), see Communist Party
Malayan Democratic Union, 47
Malayan People's Anti-British Army, 56, 167-70
Malayan People's Anti-Japanese Army (MPAJA), 37-41, 45, 46, 48, 50, 56, 58, 80, 167-70
Malayan People's Anti-Japanese Union, 38, 50
Malayan Races Liberation Army (MRLA), 172, 180, 181, 194-5, 198, 202, 206, 219, 230, 256, 266
Malayan Union, 49
Malays,
  incomes, relatively low, 35, 289, 305-6, 308, 311, 320
  Islamic militants, 72-3, 283-4, 292, 298, 305, 310, 312, 318, 321
  population, proportion of, 33, 52, 231-8, 278, 281, 289, 376
  predominance in army and police, 72, 136, 292, 301, 316, 318
  racial feelings, 72-3, 129, 247, 260, 271, 277, 311, 372
  sophistication, relative lack of, 310-12, 328-30
  special rights for, 283, 289-90, 303, 309, 311, 317, 320
  traditional way of life, 206-9, 275, 310-11, 333, 372
  violence by, nature of, 291, 298, 300-2, 309, 315-18, 321
  see also 'Ali-Baba' system, Bumiputras
Malaysia: Continuing the Communist Insurgency (Sim), 375

INDEX

Malaysia: Death of a Democracy (Slimming), 376
Malaysia in the Seventies: Communist Resurgence and Government Response (Clementson), 375, 376
Malaysian Chinese Association (MCA), 282-3, 291-7, 302, 304-6, 309
Malaysian Indian Congress (MIC), 282, 291-6, 302, 304-5
Malaysian Politics and the 1978 Elections (Crouch et. al.), 377
Malinovsky, 357
Malta, 113
Management shares, 307, 342, 381
Man Kam To, 139
Mao Tse Tung, 17, 19, 24-5, 28-9, 45, 93, 138, 170, 195, 272
Marcuse, 17, 25
Marshall, David, 84, 98, 102, 103, 106, 107, 110-15, 145, 149, 154, 160, 227, 337, 346
Marx, Karl, 21, 94
Masses Executives (MEs), 199-205, 208-10, 216, 220-9, Ch. 13, 254, *see also Min Yuen*
Mauzy, Diane K., 376, 377, 378
May 13: Before and After (Tunku Abdul Rahman), 377
May Thirteenth Incident and Democracy in Malaysia (Goh), 377
McConville, Maureen, 266, 355
McGillivray, Sir Donald, 277
McNamara, Robert S., 17, 354, 372
McVey, Ruth, 359, 369
Media, 104, 157, 160, 321, 342, 351
  foreign influence on, 341-2
  government influence on, 256, 322, 337, 339, 341, 348, 351, 353, 379, 380
Melanesia, 33
Menace in Malaya (Miller), 354, 357
Merdeka, *see* Independence
Merger of Malaysia and Singapore, 142-3, 149-51, 155-63, 278-84, 319-20, 323, 328, 338
Meyer, M., 355
Middle Road Group, 99-100, 104, 108, 110-11, 122, 130, 134-5

Miers, Lt.-Col. Richard, 241-2, 249, 374
Miller, Harry, 192, 354, 356-8
Mills, Lennox A., 356, 371
Milne, R. S., 376, 377, 378
Ming Lee, 235, 243, 249
Min Yuen (People's Organization), 170, 174, 179-80, 184, 193-6, 214, 220-9, Ch. 13, 251-8, 260, 286-8
Modernization of industry, 334, 336, 348-50
Moorehead, Alan, 354-5, 358
Moss, Robert, 375
Mountbatten, Adml. Lord, 50-1
Mouvement Socialiste, 26
Muar, 40
Multipurpose Holdings Berhad (MHB), 306-7
Musa Hitam, 309
Mussolini, Benito, 23, 27
My Accusation (Lam Swee), 173

Nanyang Siang Pau, 341, 368, 380
Nanyang University, 78, 92, 96, 159, 161, 369
Nanyang University Communist Activities (Federation Government White Paper), 369
Narodnaya Volya, 375
National Operations Council (NOC), 280, 302, 376
National Service Ordinance, 82, 84, 86, 90
Negri Sembilan, 213, 229, 252-3
New Democratic Youth League (NDYL), 46, 58, 95
New Economic Policy (NEP), 305-9, 312, 318
New Face of War, The (Browne), 356, 362, 371
Newspaper and Printing Presses Act (1974), 341-2, 351, 353
Ng Heng, 227
Nicaragua, 28
Notes on the Malayan Emergency: Strategies and Organization of the Opposing Forces (Waller), 370
Nulsen, Lt.-Col. C. K., 373, 375

INDEX

O'Ballance, Edgar, 354, 357, 370
Observer, The, 355
Ong Eng Guan, 149, 152-3, 156, 160
Ong Teng Cheong, 352
Onn, Dato Hussein, 305, 309-10
On Protracted War (Mao Tse Tung), 356
On Violence (Arendt), 355
Ooi Jin Bee, 356, 371
Organizational Problems and Dynamics of Violent Political Movements (Zawodny), 354
Origins of Trade Unionism in Malaya, The (Gamba), 359, 369-70
Osborn, Lt.-Col. Robert B., 373
Osborne, Milton, E., 367-8

Pahang, 195, 219, 260, 305, 315
Palestine, 31, 269
Paloh, 220-1
Pan-Malayan Federation of Trade Unions (PMFTU), 53-4, 58, 168
Pan-Malayan Islamic Party (PMIP or PAS), 292-7, 303-5, 309-11, 376-7
PAP Story, The (Fong), 379
Paris, 1968 revolution, 25-6
Parliament, suspension of, in Malaysia, 301-3
Pearl Harbour, 37
Pekan Jabi, 235, 240-1, 374
Penang, 33, 46, 158, 292, 295-6, 301, 304
People's Action Party (PAP)
  cadres in, 146-8, 152, 322, 325
  communication with public, 322-4, 326, 335, 346, 348
  dominance of, 135-6, 322-4, 334-8, 350-1, 379
  foundation of, 83, 376
  in Malaysia, 161-2, 292-3, 320
  in opposition, 102, 107
  indictment of, at Socialist International, 337-40, 350, 380
  internal power struggle in, 17, 18, 103-7, 110-12, 115-16, 135-6, 145-9, 152-61, 264, 268, 322, 325, 339-40, 348, 351
  labour disputes, participation in, 100, 108
  left wing leaders, arrest and release of, 130, 135, 151, 159, 339, 365
  organization of, 146-8, 152, 322-5, 346, 379
  performance in elections, 149-50, 160, 163, 282-4, 323-5, 345-8
  selection of Parliamentary candidates, 352-3
  see also Elections
People's Association, 322
People's Awakening News, 217
People's Progressive Party (PPP), 292, 304-5
People's War, The (Girling), 356
Perak, 39, 199, 229, 255-6, 260, 285-8, 292, 295-6, 301, 304
Perbadanan Nasional (PERNAS), 306
Permodalan Nasional Berhad, 306-7
Petir, 149
Petrograd, 19, 23-4
PETRONAS, 307
Philippines, 28, 56, 256, 264, 279, 284, 313
Plehve (Russian Interior Minister), 358
Plenipotentiary of the Malayan Communist Party, 148-9, 151, 153
Police,
  cooperation with army, 365
  expansion of (1949), 172
  intimidation of, 198
  plan for 1956 riots, 116-17
  reorganization after Hertogh riots, 73-4
  riots, performance in, 72-3, 121-41, 269-70, 297, 300-1, 321
  Special Branch, 37, 48, 71, 77-8, 80-1, 102-3, 111, 118, 130-2, 135, 153, 159, 178-83, 191-4, 202-5, 211, Ch. 11, Ch. 12, Ch. 13, 251-7, 265, 269-70, 282, 286, 315
  unarmed, 291
  village posts, 176-9, 198-200, 224, 232-3, 245-8, 274-5, 291
Political Economy of Independent Malaya, The (Silcock, Fisk), 356

Politics and Government in Malaysia (Milne, Manzy), 376, 377, 378
Politics in Southern Asia (ed. Rose), 357
Pontian, 80
Population growth, 314, 316, 325-7
Press, *see* Media
Productivity, 334, 336
Progressive Party, 102
Psychological Warfare Service, 190-4
Public Security, Ordinance for Preserving, 111, 123, 338
Public Service Commission, 145
Purcell, Victor, 354, 356-7, 369
Puthucheary, Dominic, 159, 365, 368, 369
Puthucheary, James, 66, 159, 365, 368
Pye, Lucian W., 357-9

Quotations from Chairman Mao Tse Tung, 355-6
Racial Conflict, 260, 283, 290-1, 311, 316, 319, 324, 341, 353, *see also* Riots
Radio cars, police, 73-4, 116, Ch. 7
Rahman, Tunku Abdul, 98, 112, 155-7, 162, 186, 190, 227, 261, 263, 264, 282-4, 291, 300, 302, 303, 317, 377
Ratnam, K. J., 356
Razak, Tun Abdul, 98, 206, 261, 283-4, 297, 300, 302, 303-8, 343, 347
Recession, 264, 288, 314, 316, 335, 350
Red Shadow Over Malaya (Henniker), 354, 373
Reflections sur la Violence (Sorel), 26, 355
Rendel Commission, 101, 103
Rendel Constitution, 84, 119
Rendel Report, 82, 363
"Repatriation" of foreign owned estates, 307
Repatriation to China, free, 255, 374-5
Resettlement, 170-7, 207-10, 257-9
Resurgence of Armed Communism in West Malaysia, 375, 376
Resurgence of guerrilla warfare 260, 264, 284-8, 339
Revolution in the Revolution? (Debray), 355
Revolution(s)
  unsuccessful, 23-4
  urban, cf. rural, 18-19, 264-7
  urban: French origin, 20-1
Rewards for information, 180-3, 243, 249, 254
Rhenick Jr., R. D., 370
Rhios Islands, 148, 151
Rhodesian African Rifles, 241
Rifle Brigade, 251
Riots,
  in Hong Kong (1967), 138-41
  in Malaysia (1967), 292
  in Malaysia (1969), 264, 285, 289-302, 303, 314-15, 318, 324, 339, 341
  in Singapore (1951), 72-3, 117, 270, 283, 321
  in Singapore (1955), 108
  in Singapore (1956), 121-38, 140-42, 268-70, 321
  in Singapore (1964), 264, 283, 319-22
Road building reduces guerrilla activity, 258, 375
Robinson, J. B. Perry, 354
Roots of Guerilla Warfare, The (Hyde), 359
Royal United Services Institution Journal, 354-5
Rukunegara, 318
Rural and Industrial Development Authority (later MARA), 306, 372
Russian Revolution, The (Moorehead), 354-5, 358
Russian Revolution, The (Sukharnov), 355

Sabah, 278-82
Sambanthan, Tun, 302
Sam Kongsi, 209
Sam-Sams, 257-8
Sandhu, Kernial Singh, 177, 354, 370-1
Sarawak, 278-82, 339
Sarawak: an Insurgency in Retreat

(Hyde), 375
Sartre, Jean-Paul, 17, 25, 355
Savings, personal, 312-13, 330, 335, 344
Schapiro, Leonard, 354-5
Schools, 52, 60, 65, 75-9, Ch. 5, 121-6, 266
  as training grounds for Party workers, 79-81, Ch. 5
  Chinese High School, 76, 88, 90, 92, 97, 99, 109, 120-2, 124, 131, 136, 266-7, 270, 361
  Chinese Middle Schools, Ch. 5
  Chung Cheng High School, 76, 88-9, 92-3, 96-7, 109, 120, 122-6
  Chung Hwa Girls High School, 76, 88, 90, 109, 361
  Foon Yew High School, 92
  Nan Chiau Girls High School, 76, 109, 361
  Nan Hwa High School, 76, 361
  Nanyang Girls High School, 76, 90, 97, 109, 361
  Pontian High School, 80
  Yong Eng High School, 361
  see also, Education, Students
Seah Chee Meow, 379
Seale, Patrick, 266, 355
Sedition Act (1948), 303
Seenivasagam brothers, 292
Segamat, 231, 235, 245-8
Seizure of Power: A Study of Force and Popular Consent, The (Janos), 355
Selangor, 50, 198, 218, 229, 260, 295-7, 300-1, 315
Self-Protection Corps, 170, 199, 201
Selkirk, Lord, 154
Selumpur, 231, 235, 240-2, 244-5, 249-50
Seremban District, 213
Setapak, 298-300
Sha Tau Kok, 139
Shaw, William, 376, 377, 378, 381
Sheng, Dr., 155
Shephard, A. J., 366-7
Shoot to Kill (Miers), 374
Short History of Malaysia, Singapore and Brunei (Turnbull), 376, 377
Siew Lau, 172-3, 184
Silcock, T. H., 356
Sim, Richard, 375
Simms, Peter, 377
Singapore All Party Mission to London April/May, 1956, Report on the, 363-4
Singapore and Malaysia (Osborne), 367-8
Singapore Association of Trade Unions (SATU), 161, 340
Singapore Chinese Middle Schools Students' Union (SCMSSU), 84-6, 88, 95, 97-8, 111, 118, 121, 135, 266-7, 270
Singapore Chinese Middle School Students' Union ('White Paper SCMSSU 1956'), 361-3
Singapore Constitutional Conference, Report of the (London HMSO), 367
Singapore Factory and Shop Workers' Union (SFSWU), 100, 111, 124, 130, 269
Singapore Federation of Trade Unions (SFTU), 53-8, 100, 266, 269
Singapore: Its Success and Its Future (Tregonning), 379
Singapore People's Alliance (SPA), 150, 154-5, 158, 282-3
Singapore Riots Commission in 1951, Report of the, 360
Singapore Women's Association (SWA), 46, 118
Slimming, John, 376
Smith, E. D., 375
Socialist Front (SF) (Malaysia), 283, 292, 294
Socialist International, 337-8
Song Choh Eng, 97
Soon Loh Boon, 86, 118
Soong Kwong, 50
Sorel, George, 26-7, 355
Southeast Asia's Second Front (Brackman), 375
South Wales Borderers (SWB), 241, 243, 374
Special Branch, *see* Police

INDEX

Squatters, 38, 170-5, 264
Sri Medan, 208
Stalin, Josef, 94, 362
Standard of living, in Singapore, 326-7, 330-4, 347, 349-51
State War Executive Committee (SWEC), 175, 192, 199, 215, 302
Story of a Rubber Tree, The (Dunlop Malaya Estates Ltd.), 371
Straits Times, 105, 192, 206, 354-381 *passim*
Strategic Problems of the Malayan Revolutionary War (Malayan Communist Party), 370
Strikes, 50-6, 62, 84-6, 100, 108-11, 121-4, 137-8, 167, 266, 340
Students,
  ability to keep secrets, 78, 360
  Anti-British League (ABL), 60, 65, 76, 78, 90-3, 97-9, 266
  communist organization amongst, 77-82, 86-93, 96, 98-9, 122, 137, 266-7
  cooperation with strikers, 84-6, 108-9, 120-1, 123-6, 128
  criticism and self-criticism, 94-6
  education, 47, 52, 63, 64, 75, 79, 83, 96-8, 104-5, 119-21, 136, 266
  High Schools, *see* Schools
  indoctrination of, 65, 83, 89, Ch. 5
  intimidation of and by, 77, 95-7
  M.C.P. membership, 64, 75-8, 81, 83, 87, 92, 98, 111-12, 266-7
  Mutual Assistance Association, 88-92
  Nanyang University, 78, 92, 96, 159, 161, 369
  National Service, reaction to, 82-4, 86, 90
  organization of, 66, 75-83, 98, 266
  SCMSSU, *see* Singapore Chinese Middle School Students' Union
  sit-ins, 84, 85, 128
  student committees, 66, 76-7, 90-1
  Student Parent Association, 122
  University of Malaya (ESI), 66, 75, 76, 368
  Youth Committee (Singapore Communist Party Organization), 60
  see also, Education, Schools
Study of the Emergency Regulations in Malaya, A (Waller), 370
Suez, 269, 366
Suffolk Regiment, 213
Suharto, 281
Sukarno, 159, 161-2, 264, 281-2
Sukhanov, N. N., 24, 355
Sunday Times, Singapore, 360, 363, 366, 367
Sungei Siput, 168, 180, 210, 255
Supplementary Views of the Central Politbureau of the Malaya Communist Party on 'Strategic Problems of the Malaya Revolutionary War', 370
Surrendered Enemy Personnel (SEPs), 175, 181-3, 193, 211, 218, Ch. 12, Ch. 13, 251-7, 282, 285, 315, 340
Sweezy, Paul M., 355
Symonds, Gene, 109

Tambang 7th Mile, 235, 240, 244
Tan Chee Khoon, Dr., 293, 295, 298, 302, 305
Tanham George, K., 356
Tanjong Pagar (constituency), 365
Tan Keng Kam, Tony, 353
Tan Siew Sin, 295, 302
Television, *see* Media
Templer, General Sir Gerald, 30, 186, 190-1, 206, 274
Tenang, 231, 238, 240, 244, 250
Tengah, Kampong, 235, 240-1, 253
Teo, Andrew, 109
Thailand, 28, 35, 37, 259-60, 264, 277, 284-8, 313
Theory and Practice of Communism (Hunt), 354
Thermidorean Reaction, 20, 23
The Times, 361, 364
Thirteen May Tragedy: A Report (NOC), 376
Thompson, Sir Robert, 32, 168, 187, 191, 193, 356

410

INDEX

Thomson, G. G., 137, 162, 357, 359-60, 365
Three Who Made a Revolution (Wolfe), 358
Tkachev, 21-2
Toh Chin Chye, Dr., 352
Tongkang Pechah, 209
Too, C. C., 193, 378
To the Finland Station (Wilson), 354
Trade Unions, 56, 59, 63, 65, 100, 138, 167, 173, 268, 337-8, 340-1, 351, 379
   General Labour Union (GLU), 46, 50, 52, 53, 269
   Hong Kong (FTU), 139
   Middle Road Group, 100, 104, 108, 110-11, 122, 130, 134-5, 147
   National Trade Union Congress (NTUC), 340
   Ordinances, 53, 82, 168, 270
   Pan-Malayan Federation of Trade Unions (PMFTU), 53-4, 58, 167-8, 173
   Singapore Association of Trade Unions (SATU), 161, 340
   Singapore Bus Workers' Union (SBWU), 59, 108-11, 130
   Singapore Federation of Trade Unions (SFTU), 53-5, 58, 100, 266, 269
   Singapore Factory and Shopworkers' Union (SFSWU), 100, 111, 130, 147, 266, 269-70
   Singapore General Employees Union (SGEU), 147
   Singapore Harbour Board Employees Union (SHBEU), 54-5, 60
   Singapore Trade Union Working Committee (STUWC), 147
   Singapore Women's Association (SWA), 46, 58, 118
   Trishaw Riders' Union, 52, 59, 62
   Trade Union Congress (TUC), 100, 115, 135, 139, 146-8
   see also Industrial Relations, Strikes
Trade Union Registry: Annual Report, 158, 359

Trade Unionism in Malaya (Josey), 173, 369
Transformation in Malaya (Robinson), 354
Tregonning, K. G., 379
Trengganu, 35, 295
Trishaw Riders' Union, 52, 59, 62
Tropical Geography, Journal of, 370-1
Trotsky, L. D., 22-3
Troy, Lt.-Col. G. C., 373
Truce Talks, 98
Tunku Abdul Rahman, *see* Rahman
Tun Razak, His Life and Times (Shaw), 376, 377, 378, 381
Tupamaros, 27, 355-6
Turnbull, C. Mary, 346, 376, 377, 379, 380, 381

Undeclared War, The (Smith), 375
Unemployment, 316, 333-4, 344
United Malay National Organization (UMNO), 150, 154-5, 160, 282-3, 291-8, 304-5, 310, 315, 317
United People's Party, 152, 154, 160
University of Malaya, *see* Students
Urban Guerrillas (Moss), 375
Uruguay, 27

Valeriano, Col. Napoleon, 375
Vietcong, 187, 272, 356, 362-4
Vietnam, 28, 32, 168-9, 176, 178, 187, 256-7, 264, 272, 280, 362, 373
Village government, 186-90
Vorys, Karl von, 376, 377
Voting compulsory in Singapore, 163, 324

Walker, General Sir Walter, 280, 375
Waller, P. B. G., 370
Wilson, Edmund, 354
With Silence and Stealth (Banyard), 375
Witnesses, intimidation of, 107, 338
Wolfe, Bertram, 358
Woodhull, S., 66, 154, 159, 368
Workers' Party, 149, 154, 324-5
Working Papers (Sandhu), 372

Wretched of the Earth, The (Fanon), 27, 355

Yenan, 271
Yeong Kwo, 198
Yong Eng High School, 361
Yong Peng, 180, 199, 206, 208-10, 220, 255-6, 271
Young, Col. A. E., 186
'Yung', 92, 97, 362-3

Zawodny, Professor J. K., 17, 354